The Edisons
of Fort Myers

Drawing of Seminole Lodge by Claudia Maggard

The Edisons of Fort Myers

Discoveries of the Heart

Tom Smoot

Pineapple Press
Sarasota, Florida

To Ann

Inquiries should be addressed to:

Pineapple Press, Inc.
P.O. Box 3889
Sarasota, Florida 34230

www.pineapplepress.com

Library of Congress Cataloging-in-Publication Data

Smoot, Tom, 1934-
  The Edisons of Fort Myers : discoveries of the heart / Tom Smoot.
     p. cm.
  Includes bibliographical references.
  ISBN 1-56164-312-2 (hb : alk. paper)
  1. Edison, Thomas A. (Thomas Alva), 1847-1931. 2.
Inventors—Florida—Fort Myers—Biography. 3. Electric
engineering—Florida—Fort Myers—History. 4. Edison, Mina Miller,
1865-1947. I. Title.

  TK140.E3S58 2004
  621.3'092'2—dc22

                                                              2004018348

First Edition
10 9 8 7 6 5 4 3 2

Design by Shé Heaton
Printed in the United States of America

Contents

Foreword

In *The Edisons of Fort Myers, Discoveries of the Heart*, author Tom Smoot retraces the last forty-five years of Edison's life as reflected by his two great loves: his second wife, Mina, and his winter estate in Fort Myers, Florida. There is, of course, no doubt of his feelings for Mina. After reading this history, there also will be no doubt of his feelings for this unique place.

"There is only one Fort Myers," Edison said, "[and eventually] ninety million people are going to find out."

After honeymooning with Mina in Fort Myers in 1886, Edison spent most winters there until his death in 1931, enjoying the growing adoration of the nation and the world, reveling in his passion for fishing, while, even there, never ceasing his efforts to discover and to invent.

Meticulously researched, this book offers a fascinating look at these years from a unique perspective. It chronicles the great inventor's life at times of relative leisure—which nevertheless included considerable and constant effort at discovering new things—and provides insights into his relationships with business associates, friends, and especially his wife and family.

In the process, the book also indelibly captures the sights and sounds of the birth and evolution of an American town. Its First Citizen in life, Edison and his family would play a great role in Fort Myers' growth, contributing financially and otherwise to its betterment and to the welfare of their neighbors from their very first days there. The town and its people, in turn, would leave their mark on the Edison family forever.

The author depicts well fishing in the Caloosahatchee River, Fort Myers as a "dry" community, the pool, roses, wildlife, Ford's Home known as The Mangoes, a camping trip with Burroughs and Ford, Alligator Alley, Chautauqua celebrities,

Lucy Bogue, Charles' wedding, Mina known as "Mud," new lab, old lab, Jim Newton and Edison Park, a Texas Leaguer against the Philadelphia Athletics, a 1,500-foot dock protruding into the Caloosahatchee River, Charles, wife Carolyn, known as "Pony," nationwide radio address to celebrate the 50th anniversary of the light bulb, Mina as Fort Myers' "Most Influential Citizen," Mina known as "Billie," Thomas known as "Dearie," Mina as "pioneer in race relations," social justice, "Roundtable," Garden Club, Dunbar Community, Bible Class, Berne and Sidney Davis, Jubilee Singers, Plant Guild, bird life, Edward Hughes, Edison Pageant of Light and purchase of Ford home to complete shrine.

Beyond the pages of this fine book, of course, this story continues to impress and to inspire countless admirers today.

Donated to the City of Fort Myers by Edison's widow, Mina, and opened to the public in 1947, the Edison Winter Estate is today authentically maintained and attracts tens of thousands of visitors annually. It includes the family's winter home, Seminole Lodge, built in 1886, extensive botanical gardens and Edison's laboratory. Among other quests, Edison spent much time here experimenting with thousands of specimens, searching for a domestic plant source for rubber.

The Estate features vintage automobiles, some 200 Edison phonographs and hundreds of other artifacts preserved in its museum, one of the best Edisonia artifact collections in existence. The gardens include much rare and exotic tropical vegetation.

Next door is the winter home of industrialist Henry Ford, who purchased the three-acre estate in 1916 to be closer to his good friend Edison. Ford features prominently in *The Edisons of Fort Myers*. Many other luminaries of the time, venturing to Fort Myers to spend time with Edison, also appear, including then President-elect Herbert Hoover and another great industrialist of the time, Edison's friend Harvey Firestone.

Also prominent in the book is Charles Edison, Thomas and Mina's second child, who would eventually take charge of his father's business empire. Charles would go on to become Secretary of the Navy and Governor of New Jersey.

Foreword

Much of the impressive collection on exhibit at the Edison Winter Estate is owned by the Charles Edison Fund, which carries on charitable works in Governor Edison's name. Among other priorities, the Fund is committed to historic preservation, especially of this and other Edison historic sites.

In Fort Myers, the Edison Winter Estate's collections are in danger and the buildings need extensive restoration. Unfortunately, the same is true for other important Edison sites across the country, especially for the Edison National Historic Site in West Orange, New Jersey.

Like the estate in Fort Myers, the West Orange site includes Edison's family home and his place of work, in this case an extensive laboratory and manufacturing complex: his Invention Factory. Edison earned half of his 1,093 patents here and pioneered the concept of team-based research and development. This is where he systematically tackled countless technological quests, sometimes failing, often brilliantly succeeding. This is where Edison created the invention industry.

Like Edison's Winter Estate in Fort Myers, the Invention Factory is in grave danger. The National Trust for Historic Preservation has listed the site as one of our most endangered national treasures. The buildings need repair and the collections are quickly deteriorating.

Today we are working to stem the decline and to ensure that the legacy of the man *Life* magazine named "Man of the Millennium" for his contributions to humanity will continue to inspire genius.

Together with the National Parks Service and in collaboration with leading corporations and countless individual benefactors and friends, the Edison Preservation Foundation, a sister organization of the Charles Edison Fund, has embarked on an international campaign to raise $90 million to preserve the Edison legacy, including the Invention Factory and other Edison sites, like Fort Myers. As of this writing, the Edison Preservation Foundation has raised $25 million.

That campaign has far to go but is certain to get there. Edison showed us the way. "Opportunity is missed by most people," he once said, "because it is dressed in overalls and looks like

ix

work." With patience, perseverance and hard work, Edison's legacy will be preserved so that his ideas, vision and passion for innovation will continue to be celebrated and publicized. Beyond the need to save this invaluable piece of our national heritage, the Edison legacy must be preserved for its importance in inspiring the young and the not-so-young to explore, to tinker, to invent and to transcend perceived limits.

As Edison recognized, there is always another frontier to tackle, another quest on the horizon. In providing a fascinating glimpse into this great American's life, this book chronicles the nature of his tireless quest and once again identifies the great need to preserve and remember his contributions and his legacy.

The author has done a great service for all the Edisons, the Edison Legacy and the Fort Myers community. He has produced a rich, meaningful and historical experience. And for me, it was as if I were part of the assembled Fort Myers crowds to which Edison often waved from the back of his train platforms. All aboard.

John P. Keegan, President
Charles Edison Fund
Edison Preservation Foundation

Preface

There has long been a need for a book about the "Great American Wizard," Thomas Alva Edison, and his love affair with "Myers," the name he used to refer to his favorite Florida town. Coinciding with that affair was another, an affair of the heart— his remarkable introduction and forty-five-year marriage to Mina Miller, his second wife. The two had pet names for each other. She was "Billie" and he was "Dearie." The home in Fort Myers was Seminole Lodge to Billie and his "jungle" to Dearie.

There has been a tendency to look principally toward the information coming from the experiences and recollections of Bob Halgrim, C. A. Prince and Jim Newton, who knew Edison first hand, and from Chet and Janett Perry and Sidney and Berne Davis, who knew Mrs. Edison. These individuals have contributed greatly to the present body of knowledge of the Edisons in Fort Myers. Unfortunately, their involvement with Edison occurred in the last half of the 1920s and thereafter. Edison first arrived in Fort Myers in 1885 when thirty-eight years of age, almost forty years before the earliest experiences of these privileged people. This narrative will not only take into account the valuable information made available by these individuals but also report on the years before their association.

I decided early in 1998 to undertake the research and writing for this project. Had I come upon the plan earlier, I would have made better use of my leisure time while attending trustee meetings of the Charles Edison Fund in West Orange, New Jersey. The Charles Edison Fund is a private foundation to which the late Charles Edison left his estate. Charles was the second child of the second marriage. Those meetings occurred in the town where the Edison National Historic Site and its archives are located. I also would have carried a handheld tape recorder during visits with my friend, Jim Newton, one of the legendary individuals who had a personal relationship with Edison and who wrote the much acclaimed book, *Uncommon Friends*. Those meetings with Jim were spellbinding, though it never occurred to me to log any of his stories. A partial retirement caused by an uncooperative vocal chord inhibited my ability to perform as an attorney and thus gave me an unforeseen opportunity to undertake this project. Since then, I have delved into the hefty files of correspondence, vendor invoices, and other documents accumulated by the late Edison-Ford Winter Home historian, Les Marietta, Ph.D. To this I have added additional documents from the Edison National Historic Site, the Edison Papers Project, the Charles Edison Fund, the Edison Winter Home Archives, the Henry Ford Museum and Greenfield Village Archives, and clippings obtained from microfilm copies of early Florida newspapers.

What follows is not a biography of the incredible life of Thomas Edison, but an account of his rather considerable forty-six-year experience in Florida. It will show his brief first encounter with Fort Myers as well as his introduction, courtship and marriage to Mina Miller, all occurring at the same time in his life. By this time, Edison had already made his major discoveries of the phonograph, the carbon transmitter telephone, and the first practical incandescent light bulb and central electric system. Fort Myers was where he came to relax his frenetic body and mind.

No story of Edison's Fort Myers connection would be complete without considerable space devoted to Henry Ford, his Fort Myers neighbor of fourteen years. Ford is introduced in Chapter Thirteen and remains prominent thereafter.

This account is not meant to be the final word on Edison's life in Fort Myers. As new information is uncovered on the life of the great inventor, this work and subsequent similar works will be subject to revision. Yet, I have sought to do my best here to accurately and faithfully reflect the current book of knowledge of Thomas Alva Edison in Fort Myers.

1

A New Beginning

To dry one's eyes and laugh at a fall,
And baffled, get up and begin again.
—Robert Browning

1885

In late February 1885, the most celebrated man in the country boarded a train in the North destined for New Orleans. He was without his overcoat despite a bitter cold winter and would be in New Orleans before grappling with his coatless plight. There the matter would be remedied by a distress wire to his private secretary in New York to send the coat south. There was first a side trip to Adrian, Michigan, the home town of traveling companion and longtime friend Ezra Gilliland, whose face bore a distinguishing handlebar mustache. In Adrian they visited Gilliland's family before proceeding on to Cincinnati, arriving there on February 24.[1] There the two visited old acquaintances from their vagabond days as telegraphers. Gilliland and Edison had met as fledgling telegraphers in Adrian and later became roommates in Cincinnati. A large segment of Edison's youth had been as an itinerant telegraph operator, which took him to many towns in the Midwest and the South. Gilliland had been a part of that youthful chapter in his life. On the train also were Gilliland's wife Lillian and the inventor's daughter Dot, eleven years old.

Dot had become the constant companion of her father fol-

Thomas Edison in
1884.

Courtesy of Edison-Ford
Winter Estates.

lowing her mother's death in August 1884. The marriage to Mary
Stillwell had produced three children, Marion "Dot," Thomas Jr.
and William. The inventor's feelings about his daughter can be
gleaned from one of his many notebook annotations, which frequently were no more than marginal doodles. In one such entry,
he wrote, "Dot Edison angel Miss Marion Edison Sweetest of
all."[2] Marion ("Dot") recalled that, "Father and I were inseparable. . . . I accompanied Father on all his trips. . . ."[3] Only a month
after her mother's death she accompanied her father to the
International Electrical Exhibition in Philadelphia where her
father renewed his acquaintance with Gilliland after a lapse of
several years. Mary Edison's death had caught father and daughter by surprise causing intense grief for both. Dot recalled arising
that morning to find her father shaking with such grief and sob-
bing he could hardly relate to her that her mother had died.
Although Edison was consumed by his work in science, many
times at the expense of time with Mary and the children, he
deeply loved her and her death had a profound impact.

The protagonist, thirty-eight-year-old Thomas Alva Edison,

had only six years earlier invented the phonograph and recorded sound and five years before had invented the first practical incandescent light bulb. It was not just a light bulb he had achieved but a whole system, including a generator, distribution lines, switches, fuses, meters and fixtures. Two months after the advent of the light bulb, the system was completed and put on public display at the laboratory at Menlo Park, New Jersey. Extra trains were run so that hundreds of persons could come to the rural village to view the twenty-five lighted bulbs in the laboratory with twenty-eight more in the office and along the street leading to the depot. It was there in Menlo Park that Edison earned the popular title, "Wizard of Menlo Park."

Three years before this trip began, the first "central system" came on line in New York City. Although "isolated systems" employing a single generator or dynamo were beginning to light factories and homes around the country and the world, lighting for multiple users had not been possible until the central system was introduced. The New York City central system was designed by Edison and constructed by Edison companies.

The excursion continued on to New Orleans, where the World Industrial and Cotton Centennial Exposition was in progress, having commenced on December 1, 1884, and running until May 31, 1885.[4] Giant expositions of modern industrial technology had become a popular means of promoting geographical areas of the world as well as the indigenous products of the locale, and the industrial and technological products of major producers from in and out of the area.

The timing of the trip to New Orleans occurred in a transition period in the life of the inventor. There was the death of his wife and mother of his three children. There was the completion of the electric light and central system. In fact Edison was looking for new challenges. While at another exposition in Philadelphia in September of the previous year, Gilliland had suggested several possible subjects for inquiry including the telephone transmitter. Among the exhibitors at the New Orleans Exposition was Bell Telephone which included some of Edison's telephone inventions.[5] It was Edison who finally made the Bell telephone practical by producing a carbon lampblack transmitter which operated separately from the receiver and was continued in use through the 1970s.

New Orleans became a defining moment in the inventor's life. While there, he first laid eyes on Mina Miller. The comely twenty-year-old had accompanied her father Lewis Miller, a major agricultural implement manufacturer and exposition exhibitor from Akron, Ohio.[6] While the search for a new domestic partner was not apparent when he arrived in New Orleans, meeting Lewis Miller's beautiful daughter may have awakened his latent quixotic qualities. A more formal meeting between the two would occur later in Boston at the home of the Gillilands.

One thing was sure, there was a desperate need for the emotionally and physically exhausted young inventor to regenerate himself. For this reason it was the plan to continue the journey by train to Florida for rest and relaxation. The lure of a warm tropical climate where the inventor might restore his spirit and revitalize his body was a given. Although the 1885 search for a warm winter retreat may have initially been for the season only, fate ended the search in his very own "jungle" in a town the inventor called "Myers." There his "Floridian Bower" would be an object of his affection for the remaining forty-six years of his lifetime and a serious competitor for Mina Miller, the love of his life. Fortunately, Mina too, would share the fondness for both her husband and Fort Myers.

This is not the story of Edison's youth, his life in New Jersey, nor his many inventions before and after 1885, but the story of his love for his "jungle" in "Myers" and the affection that the people of Fort Myers had for him. The Fort Myers years began simultaneously with his introduction to Mina Miller. He was smitten by both.

2

In Search of Eden

And the Lord God planted a garden eastward in Eden.
—Genesis II, 8

1885

While in New Orleans, Edison telegraphed his British-born private secretary Samuel Insull in New York to express his forgotten overcoat to his next stop in St. Augustine, Florida, at the San Marco Hotel.[1] There in St. Augustine he arrived on March 5.[2]

Edison and Gilliland had clearly intended for the trip to Florida to be not only for relaxation with Edison's daughter and Gilliland's wife, but also a time to hunt and fish. Prior to his departure for the trip south, Edison had sent a memo to Insull inquiring about his gun and asking him to send it on to St. Augustine.

The great inventor had been to St. Augustine on the upper Atlantic coast with Mary in 1882, 1883, 1884, and perhaps in earlier years. The Florida East Coast Railroad built by Henry Morrison Flagler, a Rockefeller partner and railroad and hotel tycoon, would soon extend its tracks along the east coast of Florida from St. Augustine South and eventually to Key West, but in 1885 that southbound east coast corridor did not exist. St. Augustine and the neighboring town of Palatka became major tourist destinations, St. Augustine because it was connected to major locales in the north by railroad, and Palatka because of its

The Barracks, later called Tarpon House at Punta Rassa.
Cattle ramp is next to hotel dock.
Courtesy of Southwest Florida Historical Society.

scenic location on the St. Johns River. During the winter of 1884, Edison sent frequent telegrams to Insull from Palatka, a distance of approximately 25 miles from St. Augustine.[3] The trip would have been by scheduled horse-drawn trolleys on rails from St. Augustine to Tocoi, and then from Tocoi across the river to Palatka by boat.[4]

The vacation trip to Florida in 1884 had found Edison in poor health and he regarded the stay in St. Augustine to have a very positive effect upon it.[5] That mild and warm winter climate was no doubt the factor that influenced Edison to come again the following year and ultimately to become a regular winter visitor in his beloved Fort Myers.

Legend has it that while the still youthful inventor relaxed in St. Augustine in 1885, the weather was not good, and someone told him that farther south on the west coast of Florida there would be perfect weather. Edison, Gilliland, and another friend, L. A. Smith of New York headed to Cedar Key on the west coast of Florida and from there down the coast of Florida.[6] Dot Edison and Lillian Gilliland did not make the trip down the west coast but remained in St. Augustine.[7] There were two ways to go to Cedar Key from St. Augustine, one to backtrack to Fernandina, about 50 miles north of St. Augustine on the east coast near the Georgia line, and from there to catch the pre-Civil War Florida Railway southwest through Gainesville to Cedar Key. The other was by horse trolley and boat to Palatka, and from there on the newly constructed leg of the Florida Southern Railway to Gainesville. There, connections could be made with the Florida Railroad on its way from Fernandina to Cedar Key. The latter was a more direct route, but making connections in Gainesville may have posed a scheduling problem.

The Florida Railroad was one of the state's original lines, a rickety, narrow gauge railroad completed in 1861. In later years, Edison told a reporter:

> This railroad was in a deplorable condition. The ties were rotten and the rails in some places were scrap iron. It was said that the Western Union had moved its poles to a considerable distance from the track to prevent their being knocked down. We ran off the track three times. At one place we were detained a day and a half. At another place we ran off the track where there was no operator at the station. I happened to have with me a pocket telegraph instrument. I cut into this station wire and got connection with Jacksonville. They sent on another little train to help us on our way. We finally got to Cedar Keys and went to the only hotel.[8]

The guns Edison had inquired of Tom Whitney in St. Augustine turned up at the old Menlo Park facility in New Jersey and consequently ordered sent on to St. Augustine.[9] Apparently they had not arrived as Edison was leaving St. Augustine for Cedar Key; hence instructions were given by Edison to a railroad agent to forward the guns to Cedar Key on their arrival. The agent was busy with other matters and the guns were delayed until the next day.[10] Edison, finding the guns were not there when he arrived at Cedar Key, was infuriated. He wrote to Whitney, from The Suwanee Hotel, "There is no mortal excuse why they could not have been sent. . . . I'm going to have some explanation from the head office of the Co."[11] The guns finally arrived in Cedar Key on March 14. A letter from Whitney to Edison later lay the blame squarely with the agent.[12]

In the previous year as part of the inventor's continuing quest for the best filament for the electric light bulb, Edison had engaged Whitney to make a fiber search in a small boat along Florida's east coast.[13] Whitney traveled from St. Augustine as far south as Lake Worth collecting fibers along the route and sending them by mail to Edison.

On March 15 the party left Cedar Key and journeyed to Punta Rassa, located near the mouth of the Caloosahatchee River about a hundred miles south of Tampa. The cruise from Cedar Key south to Punta Rassa was on board Captain Dan Paul's yacht, *Jeannette*.[14] Working on that yacht was sixteen-year-old Nick Armeda, who told Edison about George Shultz, the telegrapher and office manager at the Punta Rassa cable station of the International Ocean Telegraph Company.[15] Ever the

Punta Rassa Community with the Tarpon House in center.
Courtesy of Southwest Florida Historical Society.

telegrapher at heart, Edison immediately became acquainted with Shultz, who was also the proprietor of the Tarpon House at Punta Rassa, where the inventor and his party stayed.[16] The Tarpon House, formerly known as the "Barracks," had been a cattleman's rest stop and restaurant serving the cowboys who ended their long cattle drives at Punta Rassa.[17] The character of the Tarpon House changed drastically as the sport fishermen from the North discovered Southwest Florida in the 1880s. It took on the appearance of a rustic sportsman's resort rather than a gathering place for Florida cowboys.

Punta Rassa had been the site of Fort Dulaney, which was established in 1837 for United States Army operations against the Seminole Indians.[18] The fort was washed away in a hurricane in 1841, but then reopened in 1856 as a military post. After two years it was closed again when the remnant of Seminoles under Chief Billy Bowlegs departed Fort Myers for the reservation in Arkansas and the Seminole hostilities ground to a close.[19] But in 1864 during the Civil War, a building generally referred to as the "barracks" was constructed at Punta Rassa by the Federals to house those persons involved in loading cattle for shipment to the Federal garrison in Key West.[20] The barracks was a large building, one hundred feet long by fifty feet wide, constructed on fourteen-foot pilings to protect against the storm surge that had devastated the earlier structure.[21]

Punta Rassa, twelve miles west of Fort Myers at the mouth of the Caloosahatchee, had been a loading dock for cattle en route to markets in Key West and Cuba since the late 1850s.[22] It remained so until about 1914. They came in great cattle drives from Kissimmee, Bartow, Fort Meade, and Arcadia to Olga, where the cattle would swim across the Caloosahatchee River and then were driven to Punta Rassa. There they were loaded on four-masted schooners with decks partitioned with cow pens.[23] The tiny settlement was an important part of the Southwest Florida scene, for it was not only a military fort and cattle shipping point but also the location of the cable to Key West and Cuba. In 1866 the International Ocean Telegraph Company obtained an exclusive right for twenty years to link Florida with Cuba by telegraph line and to build telegraph lines throughout the state.[24] The telegraph line reached Punta Rassa on May 29, 1867. A submarine cable was then installed from Punta Rassa to Key West and from there to Cuba. It was through Punta Rassa that news of the sinking of the *Maine* in Havana Harbor on February 15, 1898, was cabled to the mainland of the United States.

George R. Shultz arrived in Punta Rassa shortly after the Civil War.[25] Shultz, who came from Newark, New Jersey, was employed by the International Ocean Telegraph Company and a part of the team responsible for constructing the telegraph lines from Jacksonville to Punta Rassa. Shultz became the cable office manager and retained that position for fifty years. His office was located in a part of the old barracks. The telegraph company also controlled the shipping rights, the cow pens, and the dock.[26] Cattlemen, arriving with their herds, needed a place to hide from mosquitoes and sand fleas during the night, and George and Josephine Shultz allowed them to bed down on the floor in the barracks.[27]

After the war, more and more ships called at Punta Rassa and it became the largest cattle embarkation point in the state.[28] Cattle shipments to Cuba resumed and millions of dollars of gold doubloons found their way into the economy of Southwest Florida.[29] In 1871, over one hundred schooner loads, with a total of 12,896 head, were shipped from Punta Rassa to Key West and Cuba.[30] Punta Rassa was an excellent location for taking on cattle because vessels drawing eleven feet could dock within one hundred feet of the mainland.[31] The telegraph company charged fifteen cents per head for loading at its docks so Captain F. A. Hendry put in his own competing cow pens and wharf and charged ten cents per head. In 1878, Hendry's cattle facility was sold to Jake Summerlin, who with his son Sam was a major participant in the cattle market at Punta Rassa.[32] Summerlin had lived in the barracks at Punta Rassa for several years before he acquired the Hendry pens and wharf. To accommodate the cattlemen, Jacob Summerlin built the Summerlin House there in 1874.[33] It became a familiar and picturesque landmark for the next one hundred years and the subject of many artists' works and can be seen on canvases hanging on the walls of many

Southwest Florida homes and buildings.[34] Jacob Summerlin also had homes in Fort Ogden, Bartow, Fort Meade and Orlando where he was a local politician and a town benefactor.

Eventually, sports fishermen arrived and in the 1880s the building known simply as the barracks was transformed into the Tarpon House.[35] Three meals were provided each day to guests. About the same time travelers to and from Fort Myers came to need both lodging and meals as they awaited steamers bound for Key West and Tampa; hence, the hotel became a hostel for travelers and sportsmen. The Tarpon House had eleven upscale rooms (because they opened on to a gallery overlooking the water) and those were reserved for favored guests. These were jestfully referred to as "Murderer's Row." No doubt Edison and his party occupied the preferred accommodations.

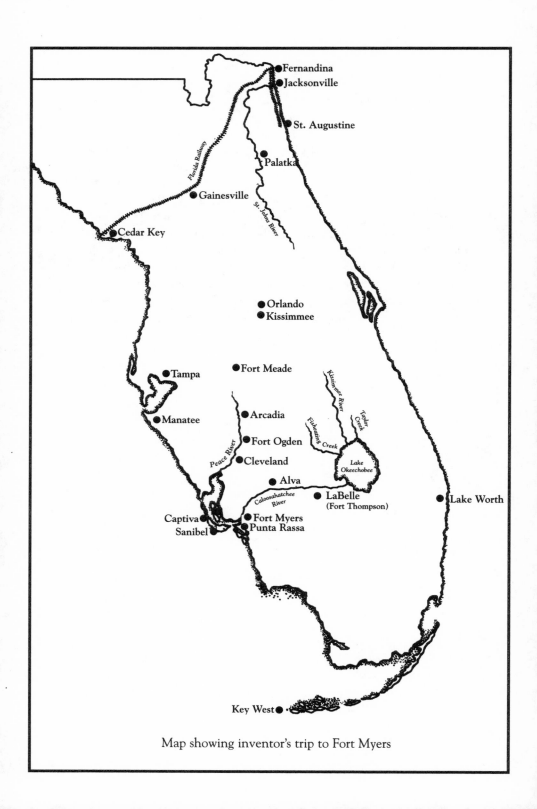

Map showing inventor's trip to Fort Myers

3

Bamboo

In . . . Lee County . . . are some remarkable Bamboos, grown near Fort Myers, which are high enough for fence rails.
—Garden and Forest, 1889

1885

It is not clear how long Edison remained on "Murderer's Row" at the Tarpon House in Punta Rassa, but a couple of days is a reasonable guess.[1] One can only speculate whether the party hunted and fished at Punta Rassa as they had planned, but it is likely they did. One day while smoking cigars on the veranda of the Tarpon House, Shultz told Edison of a quaint little town a few miles upriver. Shultz may also have told him of bamboo stands along the riverfront. Bamboo was a continuing interest for Edison because of its fiber content and use in an improved incandescent light filament. For whatever reason, Edison became intrigued and continued the excursion upriver to Fort Myers.[2] Located on the south bank of the Caloosahatchee (river of the Caloosas) twelve miles from the river's mouth at Punta Rassa, the town was surrounded by palmettos, pines, an occasional oak hammock and sabal palms everywhere. Reports also indicated stands of bamboo here and there.[3] East a few miles, the river narrowed to several hundred feet and commenced its serpentine journey to Alva, sixteen miles upriver, and beyond.

The site now recognized as downtown Fort Myers was originally established in 1841 not as Fort Myers, but as Fort Harvie during the deadly, long and expensive Indian war of 1835–1842. Before the establishment of Fort Myers, a terrible massacre of whites by Indians occurred in 1839 at a trading post on the banks of what is now Cape Coral, downriver from where Fort Harvie would be established two years later. At the hands of Billy Bowlegs and other Seminoles, sixteen soldiers were killed during the attack at Harney Point.[4] The violence occurred at the trading post established by Lieutenant Colonel William S. Harney, under an agreement reached between the highest-ranking general in the American Army and the principal chief of the Seminoles.[5] The agreement purported to give the Seminoles a tract of land embracing much of Southwest Florida, including all of what is now Lee County and much of what is now Charlotte, Glades, Hendry and Collier counties.[6] The agreement also provided for the trading post to be established in the area for the convenience of the Indians. James B. Dallam was appointed trader and Colonel Harney, together with twenty-eight dismounted dragoons, were sent to give Dallam protection while the trading post was being established.[7] Word reached the Indians that the treaty had not been entered in good faith and would not be honored by the white man. The Indians were furious and reacted with the night massacre. The attack came from bands of Indians led by Chief Hospetarke, Chief Chakaika, and Billy Bowlegs. Trader Dallam was one of the victims. A burial party arrived two weeks after the slaughter and found two of Harney's men who were still alive and in hiding. They also found a dog which had belonged to Dallam. Dallam's corpse was the only one untouched by wolves or vultures leading to the conclusion that the dog had stood as sentinel over his master's body.[8] Colonel Harney and thirteen others had escaped.

Fort Harvie was named for Lieutenant John M. Harvie, who died on September 7, 1841, of malaria.[9] The fort was abandoned a few months after its opening when the Indian war appeared to have ended. By 1842, most of the Indians had been deported to the West and many more had been killed in battle or from disease. Among those who remained was Billy Bowlegs, one of the principal leaders of the Seminoles of South Florida. [10] During the next several years, conflict and skirmishes with these tribal remnants continued and sentiment grew for the remainder of the Indians to be removed from Florida.

In 1850, on orders from Major General David E. Twiggs, Brevet Major Ridgeley took command of two companies of artillery and proceeded south to the Caloosahatchee River to select a "suitable place for the establishment of a post" and to "immediately throw up such light works as may secure his stores and remove from the Indians any temptation to which his isolated position might give rise."[11] The order also called for the post to be called Fort Myers in honor of Lieutenant Colonel Abraham Charles Myers, a West Point graduate who was chief quartermaster of the Department of Florida. Colonel Myers, who hailed from Georgetown, South Carolina, was a direct descendant of Moses Cohen, the first rabbi of Charleston, South Carolina. The occasion of the honor to Colonel Myers was his courtship of Marion Twiggs, the daughter of General Twiggs. [12] Major Ridgeley sailed up the Caloosahatchee and determined that the ruins of Fort Harvie was the best location for the new post.

Fort Myers endured as well the Indian skirmish of 1855–1858. The latter was sometimes called the Billy Bowlegs War.[13] That war erupted following an attack by Billy Bowlegs and a war party of about thirty Seminoles against an exploring party of eleven men led by Lieutenant George L. Hartsuff.[14] Lieutenant Hartsuff and his men left Fort Myers on December 7, 1855, en route to the Big Cypress. Since the Hartsuff party embarked on their ill-fated journey from Fort Myers, it is curious to note that the war also ended in Fort Myers at Billy's Creek, with the surrender of Chief Billy Bowlegs.[15] Following surrender, the once-proud, but also pragmatic Billy Bowlegs left Fort Myers with his remaining tribesmen aboard the steamer *Grey Cloud*, bound for Arkansas and the reservation.[16] As the steamer cruised downriver past Harney Point in what is today Cape Coral, Billy Bowlegs' thoughts were no doubt on that terrible pre-dawn massacre that occurred nineteen years before his removal to Arkansas. Following the end of the Indian war, the fort was closed again in 1858.

In 1861, Colonel Myers resigned his position in the United

States Army and was appointed lieutenant colonel in the Confederate States Army where he became the acting Quartermaster General and later the permanent Quartermaster General.[17] In 1863 Myers fell out of favor with President Jefferson Davis of the Confederacy when it was said that Mrs. Myers had remarked that the President's wife looked like a squaw and Myers was replaced.[18]

In January 1864 as the Civil War raged on, Fort Myers was again reopened as a Union outpost with five companies of U. S. Regulars and Union Rangers. When it did, it became the only Union base on the mainland of south Florida.[19] It served two purposes: It provided a sanctuary for deserters and northern sympathizers, and a staging area for raids on cattle being driven north to the Rebel armies in Georgia.[20] To counter the deserter problem and remove the threat posed by the Union against the northbound drives of Florida cattle, the Confederate cow cavalry was formed.[21] Cow cavalry operations extended to the cattle ranges from the Caloosahatchee River to the Kissimmee River. In the face of mounting evidence of the futility of their cause, the cow cavalry in February 1865 was mobilized from Tampa and Fort Meade under Major William Footman and proceeded with several companies of horsemen toward Fort Myers.[22]

The troops made their way to Fort Thompson, then a deserted Seminole War outpost on the Caloosahatchee near the present town of LaBelle, arriving there on February 19, 1865.[23] Lieutenant F. C. M. Boggess, a member of the expedition, said that "on the night that their anticipated attack was to be made it rained until the water was knee deep over the entire county."[24] A skiff that had been launched to carry the ammunition across the river capsized, ruining most of the powder.[25] The next day, in very wet conditions, the Cattle Guard arrived at the outskirts of Fort Myers and following a few skirmishes with pickets at Billy's Creek, arrived outside the garrison about mid-day. The Union forces in Fort Myers were from the Second Florida Cavalry and three companies of the Second Regiment, U.S. Colored Troops.[26] Instead of rushing the fort, Major Footman sent Lieutenant Allen and Corporal Pasteur under a flag of truce demanding the Union take down the Stars and Stripes from the fort.[27] The fort's commander, Captain James Doyle, sent back a note exclaiming "if you've got more men than I have, crack your whip."[28]

At 1:10 P.M., Major Footman "cracked his whip" and opened fire. The battle continued on through the afternoon but with no substantial advantage to either side. Captain F. A. Hendry, a leader of one of the Cattle Guard Companies, wrote that the day was spent in "one of those bloodless battles, one man killed, a lot of pickets, horses and cattle captured. . . ."[29] One member of the Confederate expedition reported few casualties.[30] Many years later, John Pasteur, one of the couriers who had carried the flag of truce to the fort, told *The Fort Myers Press* that although the rebels had been ordered not to shoot any men, one of the captured Union pickets had been killed when he tried to escape.[31] A *New York Times* reporter who was present during the fight stated a much different outcome with a Confederate loss estimated at 20 to 40 men.[32] Whatever the facts of that battle might have been, Major Footman fell back to the Fort Thompson road as night fell and the siege was abandoned. More rain may have been a factor.[33] Lieutenant Boggess gave the severe weather credit for "saving the lives of many. . . ."[34] A shortage of food and horsefeed may also have contributed.[35] Two months later the war would be over and the fort again closed.

After the war settlers began to arrive with the first coming from Key West on February 21, 1866. By 1885, the year Edison first came, Fort Myers was a remote part of Monroe County, with the well-settled port of Key West as its county seat. With a population of 349 in 1885, there was a favorable vote for incorporation and the pineapple was adopted as the symbol of the city. Several general stores competed with one another. Among them, E. L. Evans, who advertised he paid the highest price for syrup, eggs, butter, potatoes, hides and country produce.[36] W. H. Towles and James E. Hendry, Sr. opened a general store at the corner of First and Jackson.[37] Transients and visitors had a choice of lodging at the Keystone Hotel, the Frierson House or the Braman House.[38] In the waning months of 1884, just five months before the arrival of Thomas Edison, the community got its first newspaper, *The Fort Myers Press*.[39] The weekly paper campaigned for a scheduled steamship to and from Fort Myers and the campaign was met with the arrival of the scheduled steamship *Manatee* in May 1885— two months after the arrival of Edison.[40]

Before the *Manatee*, public transportation from Fort Myers involved first a trip by schooner to Punta Rassa and then by scheduled steamship to either Key West or Cedar Key. Before the Disston dredges completed the canal cut from the Caloosahatchee into Lake Okeechobee in 1883, travel upriver had been to a dead end short of the lake.[41] A railroad into Fort Myers would not arrive until 1904; however, Henry B. Plant took the Plant system to Arcadia in 1886 and on to Punta Gorda in 1887.[42] When the railroad arrived in Punta Gorda, travel by way of Cedar Key was no longer necessary and a passenger could travel by train to Punta Gorda and then by steamer to Fort Myers.

The local press was also critical of rising sentiment in Key West to eliminate the mail boat stops at Punta Rassa, because those stops delayed the business mail deliveries between Key West and Tampa. Such action would have left Punta Rassa and Fort Myers without mail service. The article showed the inferior status of Fort Myers in the eyes of Key Westers due to its location at the northern extreme of Monroe County. The *Press* suggested a separation of the Fort Myers area from Monroe County, whose county seat was in Key West and whose political concerns were only as broad as its island geography. A little tongue in cheek in the same issue was evidenced by the following: "The spongers of Key West are spending their money in a jolly manner. The sellers of bad whiskey are in clover."[43]

Second-rate status was not limited to relations with the county seat. The postal officials at one time insisted that "Fort" be dropped from the name of the town. The people in the town objected and eventually the full name was restored. But others continued to refer to the city as "Myers," including its exalted winter resident, Thomas A. Edison.

4

Myers Discovered

❦

The Only True Sanitarium of the Occidental Hemisphere.
—Huelsenkamp & Cranford

1885

Early view of Fort Myers waterfront.
Courtesy of Southwest Florida Historical Society.

The Fort Myers Press reported:

> About noon of Friday last week, March 20, the
> elegant yacht Jeannette, of Cedar Key, Capt.
> Dan Paul, came up the river, passed Fort Myers
> a few miles, returned and anchored. Her party
> consisted of Thomas A. Edison, Ph. D., the dis-
> tinguished electrician, Mr. L. A. Smith, of New
> York, and Mr. E. T. Gilliland, of Boston.[1]

Lodging in Fort Myers was at the twenty-room Keystone
Hotel, which had its own river wharf. That Friday afternoon and
evening very likely found the three men walking around the
town. Edison liked what he saw. While strolling on the docks,
Edison may have seen the yacht *Canary*, which ran regular trips
between Fort Myers and Punta Rassa, making the connection
with scheduled steamers for Key West and Tampa.[2] Scheduled
steamer service to Fort Myers would not arrive until May. Edison
stopped at E. L. Evans' General Store. While speaking to Evans,
the subject of bamboo came up and Evans offered to take the
inventor—no doubt by horse-drawn cart—down First Street
toward Billy's Creek to show him some bamboo.[3]

Evans then brought Edison back to town and introduced
him to C. L. Huelsenkamp, a local real estate agent whose adver-
tisment appeared regularly in *The Fort Myers Press*.[4]

Huelsenkamp & Cranford newspaper ad appearing
in March 24, 1885, edition, *Fort Myers Press*.

The meeting with Evans proved providential, for out of it came a friendship that would span the inventor's forty-six-year Fort Myers experience.

On the following day, the relaxed and rejuvenated inventor paid a visit to the real estate office and C. J. Huelsenkamp showed Edison the thirteen-acre riverfront Summerlin place, which was about a mile downriver from town.[5] It was owned by Samuel Summerlin, son of wealthy cattle baron Jake Summerlin, and included a small house.[6] There were reportedly bamboo stands on the property, which may have been a factor tipping the scales and piquing Edison's interest. Summerlin had acquired the property a few years earlier for $500. Before leaving Fort Myers on Saturday, March 21, 1885, a deposit receipt contract had been presented to Edison by Huelsenkamp & Cranford and he had signed it. It called for a purchase price of $3,000 with $100 paid as a deposit and the balance due at closing 90 days hence.[7] Thus began a forty-six-year love affair with what would be his "jungle" and for him as advertised a "True Sanitarium of the Occidental Hemisphere." On Saturday, the day after his arrival, Edison left en route to Tampa and points north.[8]

The *Press* reported:

> They remained here until Saturday evening, when they set off on their return to Tampa, whence they proceeded northward. They were much pleased with the Caloosahatchee and with Fort Myers; and Mr. Edison is negotiating for the purchase of a good location here. If he buys a place, he says he will fit it up handsomely and make it a pleasant abode, if such a thing is possible. He will also bring along a 40-horsepower steam engine and set up his workshop and laboratory, for a portion of the year. The people of Fort Myers are highly pleased at the prospect of such a distinguished addition to their community.[9]

In reporting that they are "off on their return to Tampa," the *Press* could have simply meant a stop in Tampa on the return journey to Cedar Key, 150 miles by water north of Tampa, and from there to Fernandina on the primitive train. If, however, the return were indeed to Tampa, the Edison party would have caught the new narrow-gauge Plant Investment Company train from Tampa to Kissimmee, Orlando and Sanford—a mere six-and-one-half hour trip. Train service from Tampa to Kissimmee had been completed in the previous year. From Sanford the party would have gone by steamboat on the Saint Johns River to Palatka, a distance of approximately sixty miles on the Peoples Line of Steamers owned by the Plant System.[10] From there they would have traveled by horse-drawn trolley to St. Augustine to rejoin Dot and Mrs. Gilliland.

The Fort Myers Press also carried this item:

> Thomas A. Edison is to have the Summerlin Place, just at the bend of the river about one mile from the business center of Fort Myers. It embraces thirteen acres of land and is a location of decided natural beauty. When Mr. Edison fits it up as he proposes it will no doubt be magnificent. He does not, as we understand, propose to wait long before making a commencement.[11]

Thomas Edison's love affair with Fort Myers faced some stiff competition in the months following his initial trip. The fair maiden from Ohio, whom he met for the first time at the Industrial and Cotton Exposition in New Orleans, was about to come center stage in his life. Her presence in his mind would obscure the ongoing matters of science, and his attention to the business obligations of acquiring a winter home in paradise. In the end, he would make his paradise in Florida his honeymoon destination and would lovingly share it with his bride for the rest of his life.

Huelsenkamp & Cranford, the real estate agency procuring the sale, requested an abstract of title from Peter T. Knight, the clerk of the Circuit Court for Monroe County in Key West, showing the brief title history of the thirteen acres. The abstract of title certified by the clerk was mailed to Edison in July.[12] The abstract revealed that the land had been patented by the United States of America to William Allen in 1879, that Allen and his wife, Nancy, had deeded the property to Francisco Abriel of Havana, Cuba in 1877 (prior to the patent), and that Abriel

22

deeded the property to Samuel Summerlin in 1879.[13]

In mid-July, Edison visited his friend Gilliland (called "Damon" by Edison, who was called "Pythias" by Gilliland) at Woodside Villa outside Boston.[14] The two intended to share the Fort Myers property and build adjacent homes. Edison's mood was evident in a diary entry:

> Damon and I went into a minute expense account of our proposed early paradise in the land of flowers, also a duplicate north and we concluded to take short views of life and go ahead with the scheme. It will make a savage onslaught on our bank account. Damon remarked that now all the wind work is done there only remains some little details to attend to, such as "raising the money," etc.[15]

A few days later, Edison playfully noted:

> Damon and I, after his return, study plans for our Floridian bower in the lowlands of the peninsular Eden, within the charmed zone of beauty, where wafted from the table lands of the Oronoco and the dark Carib Sea, perfumed zephyers forever kiss the gorgeous flora. Rats! Damon took the plans to Boston to place them into the hands of an architect to be reduced to a paper reality. Damon promised to ascertain probable cost chartering schooner to plow the Spanish main loaded with our hen coops.[16]

Excerpts from Edison's short-lived diary give a glimpse of a seldom observed romantic. It also reveals his rich intellect and humor, which blossomed during the brief period of his life when he fell in love with both his "Floridian bower" and a young lady named Mina.

In August, *The Fort Myers Press* reported that Edison, through his agent, Huelsenkamp, had hired Colonel J. P. Perkins to survey the land and forward the plat to Edison so that he could determine where to locate the proposed buildings.[17] Colonel Perkins was a jack of all trades, advertising in *The Fort Myers Press* his surveying skills, his legal skills and his services as a real estate agent. An architect was also engaged to render plans for their project. Alden Frank of Boston billed Edison $200 for plans for a dwelling and a machine shop. [18] Since the house would be duplicated, one for Edison and the other for Gilliland, the architect prepared plans for just one dwelling. Meanwhile Gilliland, who was about to leave American Bell to become associated with Edison, notified his new associate of his intention to put the drawings in the hands of the lumber company and to seek bids at once.[19] The business partnership between Edison and Gilliland was announced in *The Fort Myers Press* in December. After explaining that business disagreements between Gilliland and the directors of American Bell had caused him to withdraw from that association, he was in the process of forming a new partnership with Thomas A. Edison. The news report concluded:

> This makes the strongest combination of genius and talent the country can produce, for Gilliland is but a little way behind Mr. Edison in the number of patents to his credit, standing second in that respect on the records of the patent office.[20]

At some point Gilliland learned through a Chicago newspaper that things in Florida were not all they were thought to be. In fact, for "Myers," it was pretty "rough."[21] Whether the article referred to the weather or to other conditions is not known. He forwarded the clipping to Edison with the suggestion that it be sent to Huelsenkamp for his thoughts. Whatever Huelsenkamp responded, it may have further slowed the purchase transaction, but it did not end it.

Telegrams and correspondence suggest that the time for closing or perhaps other due dates prescribed by the contract had been missed. The contract called for a ninety-day closing which would have occurred on or before June 21. In September Huelsenkamp & Cranford telegraphed Edison suggesting that if he wanted the property, he would have to give "prompt action."[22] It is clear from his inaction that Edison's mind was focused on Miss Miller and that business be damned. Later in the month Huelsenkamp & Cranford wrote Edison that Summerlin wished to withdraw from the trade because Edison had not been timely in meeting his contractual obligations, but acting as agents for Edison, they "held that as he [Summerlin] had made no protest we had a right to claim the deed...."[23] The real estate agents then reported that they had obtained the property for $2,750 instead of $3,000 as originally agreed upon, with no explanation why the price was reduced. The transaction was closed.

Following the closing, the deed was mailed north as instructed. In October, Edison sent a handwritten memo to his secretary, Samuel Insull, "Sammy," requesting the deed and all papers relating to the Florida property be delivered to him at the laboratory in New York City.[24] The deed and papers ultimately found their way to Edison's lawyer, John Tomlinson, who forwarded them on to Key West, the county seat for Monroe County, for recording.[25]

In mid-October, Edison telegraphed his Fort Myers agents to ascertain the depth of the water in the Caloosahatchee River.[26] Speculation was that he planned to bring the lumber for his home and the equipment for his laboratory by river vessel. The response assured Edison there was "entire safety . . . in relying on from six to six-and-one-half feet of water in the river channel, and seven-and-a-half feet at high tide."[27] Later in October, the local press reported that Edison was loading a vessel for the construction of his buildings.[28] This news turned out to be premature, since the vessel did not sail for another seven weeks.

In November, *The Fort Myers Press* ran the contents of a letter dated October 23, 1885, from Edison to Huelsenkamp and Cranford, which read as follows:

> Gents: Please have prepared at once a map drawn to scale, of my lots, showing everything that it will be necessary to know in order to locate our buildings; also show the position of the old house and the avenue or street that passes through the property. We will erect two dwelling houses on the river front, and will place the laboratory building and dwelling for workmen on the other side of the avenue. If practicable will move the old house and make it over or repair it and use it for employees. Our steam

launch draws about three feet and a half and we will build a pier out far enough to reach that depth, and would like to know about how far that will be, in order to provide necessary material.

Our buildings are being made in Maine and will be loaded on board a ship at Boston. The ship will touch at New York and take on board the engine, boilers, machinery and apparatus for laboratory and furniture, & etc., for dwelling houses. The ship will also bring a steam launch and a small lighter. We propose to unload everything at Punta Rassa and tow it up the river in the lighter. We were unable to procure vessels sufficiently light in draught to go up the river. We would like to have ascertain [sic] what arrangements can be made for unloading the ship on the docks at Punta Rassa and necessary storage room for furniture and such material as cannot be exposed to the weather during the time the buildings are being erected. We will send three or four employees to superintend the work. They will probably require assistance in hauling the material as well as in construction of the buildings. Will probably need four carpenters and four laborers, can they be obtained at Fort Myers?

The ship will leave here in three weeks. We hope to have the buildings completed and ready for occupation in January. An agent will leave here in about a week, who will come direct to Fort Myers and do what he can to prepare the grounds, build the pier, etc. Having explained to you fully what we propose to do and how we propose to do it, I would ask that you furnish us with all the information you can to aid us in carrying out our plans, and greatly oblige.

Yours very respectfully,
Thos. A. Edison per Gilliland[29]

Edison sent Eli Thompson to Fort Myers to superintend the operations and, more immediately, to see that the schooner was unloaded properly at Punta Rassa. Thompson arrived in late November bringing plans and specifications for the residences and a laboratory.[30] While awaiting the arrival of the schooner, Thompson saw that the land was cleared and a wharf readied for the steam launch and lighter carrying the structural parts for the homes. The wharf, constructed by Joseph Vivas, extended 357 feet from shore.[31] The Kennebec Framing Company framed the houses before shipment to Florida, at a cost of $6,714.85. Edison and Gilliland split the cost two-fifths each, with the remaining one-fifth charged to the business or "laboratory" account.[32]

1886

Although it appears to have been the intention of both Edison and Gilliland to take title to distinct portions of the original thirteen acres in Fort Myers, Edison initially acquired title to the entire tract in his name. Gilliland did not acquire title to his parcel until Edison deeded it over to him in April 1886. Mina Edison also signed the deed to Gilliland, since the marriage occurred in February 1886 and Florida law required the wife to release her dower right in the property by signing the deed to the land being conveyed.

In early January 1886, J. S. Knowles of Boston, L. G. Perris, and A. K. Keller of New York arrived to assist Thompson in the construction.[33] Keller had been with Bell Telephone and took charge of the steam launch *Lillian*, which had been shipped from New York on December 23 along with the buildings. Gilliland bought the launch in Boston and named it the *Lillian* in honor of his wife.[34] Before departing New York, Keller received five certificates of deposit drawn on the Bank of the Metropolis in New York totaling $1,150, and a letter from Edison instructing him to deliver the certificates, made payable to Jno Gould, captain of the schooner *Julia S. Bailey*, on the safe delivery of the cargo at Punta Rassa.[35] Keller considered going to Key West to meet the schooner so that he could remove about six inches from the steam launch's keel to make it more adaptable to local waters.[36]He proposed to do so while the steam launch rested on the deck of the schooner en route from Key West to Punta Rassa. Whether he carried out this mission is not known.

The charter for the schooner *Julia S. Bailey* and its trip to Punta Rassa cost $1,350, with an extra $250 for delay caused by time in port for loading in both Portland, Maine, and New York City.[37] The schooner finally arrived at Punta Rassa in mid-January and Thompson, Knowles, Perris, Keller and J. F. Highsmith all hurried there to supervise the unloading.[38] Records show that twelve workers were paid for the unloading job.[39] From there the *Lillian* made its way up the Caloosahatchee to Fort Myers. The lighter was towed to carry the freight. The unloading took about two weeks, as reported in *The Fort Myers Press*.[40]

In addition to the *Julia S. Bailey*, the Mallory Line (New York to Key West) and other ships assisted with the move. Edison sent a large shipment of chemicals from New York to Tampa aboard the steamer *Fannie A. Milliken*. The steamer became grounded and all was lost; however Edison collected $10,083.17 from the insurance company, which he distributed among himself, Gilliland, and his laboratory account.[41]

Among the items to be sent to Florida were "old fixtures returned from Menlo Park and refinished etc. as per Robb's memorandum."[42] The contents of the memorandum are unknown, as is the identity of Robb. Edison had been in the process of abandoning the Menlo Park location, hence it is logical that he would have salvaged lighting fixtures from his Menlo Park residence for use in Florida. The invoice on which the memorandum was noted also called for a number of new fixtures identified from the Bergmann & Co. catalogue.[43]

Other orders shipped to Florida in early 1886 included a piano, stool and cover,[44] two French bathtubs,[45] two refrigerators,[46] two Sprague 1/2 horsepower automatic motors,[47] 500 10-candlepower lamps,[48] a four-horsepower Babcock & Wilcox boiler,[49] 2,000 fire bricks for the water tube boiler to run the dynamo,[50] a large assortment of chairs, rockers, feather pillows, a walnut washstand, mattresses, [51] an itemized list of groceries,[52] bed spreads, towels, table mats, pillow shams and sideboard cover,[53] six arc lamps,[54] a cherry bedroom suit, hair mattresses, cane settees, reed couches, rattan table, Nottingham lace curtains, safety pins, opaque shades with spring rollers,[55] slop jars, two dinner sets, tablespoons, egg beaters, cuspidors,[56] a double set of "Orchestrones,"[57] various paintings identified by name,[58] nails,[59] a bundle of brass pipe,[60] extra shafting and prop wheels, presumably for the steam launch and for machines in the laboratory and machine shop.[61] A Stuart lathe destined for the machine shop, a 1,000-volt (10-amp) Municipal Light Dynamo and a No. 6 Dynamo were also included, presumably to run the isolated electric systems in the residences and the machine shop.[62]

By mid-February 1886, the two houses had been erected and the workers were busy with construction of the laboratory.[63] Meanwhile the press reported that Gilliland, with a large party of friends, was expected in Fort Myers on February 15.[64]

A reporter for the local press went downriver on February 20 to see what progress had been made at the Edison-Gilliland site. He was surprised to find the buildings in place, most of the palmettos and other wild growth cleared, and a neat fence around much of the property.[65] A Mr. Bassler, a capable landscape gardener from Philadelphia, was on hand to plant limes, lemons, coconuts and other vegetation on the grounds. At the entrance from Riverside Avenue, now McGregor Boulevard, Spanish bayonets of graded sizes had been planted. The reporter seemed most interested in the two residences, which faced the river and were separated by a "broad avenue or driveway leading up from the entrance" on Riverside Avenue. Bassler had placed two "splendid specimens" of the century plant along the driveway next to the residences. The houses were two-story with a broad piazza running around three sides, while a large kitchen was attached to each. Wires were being installed so that the houses could be lighted by electricity.

5

Enter Mina

Got thinking about Mina and came near being run over by a street car. If Mina interferes much more will have to take out an accident policy.
—Thomas Edison, 1885

1885

By all accounts Mina Miller was a beautiful young woman with rich black hair and great dazzling eyes.[1] She was twenty and her suitor, thirty-eight—nearly twice her age. From Akron, Ohio, she was the daughter of an agricultural implement inventor and manufacturer and had been reared in an environment of society and affluence. She had ten siblings. Her father, Lewis Miller, was a deeply committed Methodist who found time throughout his busy adult life to actively pursue his devotion to God and church.

Mina's father was not only an industrialist, but he also left his mark on Americana with his brainchild, the Chautauqua Association, located in southwest New York state on Lake Chautauqua. Miller, with Rev. John Vincent, later Bishop Vincent of the Methodist Episcopal Church, established that institution, where hopefuls announced their presidential campaigns and where people continue to this day to gather in the summer months for a smorgasbord of contemporary lectures, opera, symphony, drama, recreation, religion and good weather.

Mina Miller in 1885.
Courtesy of Edison-Ford Winter Estates.

The Miller cottage, or Founder's Cottage, remains on the grounds, entailed to a Miller descendent, currently Nancy Arnn, granddaughter of Lewis Miller.

Mina Miller was a product of Akron High School. Following graduation, she attended Mrs. Johnson's Ladies Seminary, a finishing school in Boston. While there, she became an acquaintance of Lillian Gilliland, wife of Edison's long-time friend, Ezra Gilliland.

The newly reconstituted friendship/partnership between Edison and Ezra Gilliland was built not only on their common scientific and business pursuits but also on a social relationship that introduced society, dress and manners to Edison, a man not known for his social graces.[2] Gilliland's station in life had greatly improved since his days as a telegrapher in Cincinnati, for he

31

and the charming Mrs. Gilliland were then a part of Boston middle-class society.[3] During the summer of 1885, after his return from his trip to Fort Myers, Edison became a visitor at the Gilliland home in Boston, coming from his office and laboratory in New York City. During this time Edison seemed very comfortable with the societal ways of the Gillilands.

Twelve-year-old Marion (Dot) remained constantly at her father's side. Tom, Jr., who was nine, and Will, who was seven, were in safekeeping with their maternal grandmother, Mrs. Margaret Stilwell.[4] Dot reminisced many years later that her father had made known to Mrs. Gilliland "that he wanted a home, a wife and a mother for his three children and asked Mrs. Gilliland . . . to introduce him to some suitable girls."[5] Mamma G, as Edison called her, was quick to oblige. Eligible young ladies appeared as guests at the Gilliland home and the young widower found his way to Boston to be a part of the scene. Daughter Dot was on hand, observing some of the contenders, but her selection was at odds with that of her father. Dot selected a blonde for her stepmother; most likely, she recalled because her mother had been a blonde.[6]

At one of the gatherings at the Gilliland home someone asked Mina to play the piano for the assembled group. Later she recalled that though she had never played for an audience, when they asked her to play, she thought she would never see these people again, so she played.[7] If her playing did not win Edison's heart, then her appearance, personality and charm certainly did, for Edison was smitten. When asked how she felt about Mr. Edison at that time, Mina replied, "Just a genial, lovely man."[8] Mina's appearance in the eligibility lineup at the Gillilands' did not last long. Early in the summer she left Boston for Chautauqua to be with her family.

The Boston social season continued for Edison. Among the ladies in attendance were two friends of Lillian Gilliland from Indianapolis. One was Dot's clear choice and although not selected by Edison, he had very kind words to describe her in his diary. "Miss Igoe is a pronounced blonde, blue eyes, with a complexion as clear as the concience of a baby angel, with hair like Andromache. . . ."[9] Miss Igoe later married Mina's older brother,

Robert Miller.[10] Edison spent a week at Woodside Villa, a sea-side vacation cottage rented by the Gillilands in Winthrop, Massachusetts. While there he kept his only diary.[11] Throughout this time, there is more than sufficient evidence he had a good time, but he longed for Mina. So impressed was Edison with the Boston-Gilliland spectacle that he wired his secretary, Samuel Insull, "Come to Boston, at Gill's house there is lots [sic] of pretty girls."[12] The diary contains several references to the absent Mina. One such entry read:

> awakened at 7 a.m. thought of Mina, Daisy, and Mamma G—put all three in my mental kaledescope to obtain a new combination a la Galton took Mina as a basis, tried to improve her beauty by discarding and adding certain features borrowed from Daisy and Mamma G a sort of Raphaelized beauty, got into it too deep, mind flew away and I went to sleep again.[13]

Mina always prevailed in any comparison and was in fact the measuring stick by which all eligible females were judged. Another entry relates:

> Constantly talking about Mina who me an [sic] Damon use as a sort of yardstick for measuring perfection. . . . [14]

Another entry describes the romantic frame of mind of the Wizard, who under ordinary circumstances would be the opposite:

> This is by far the nicest day of the season, nei-ther too hot or too cold—it blooms on the apex of perfection—an Edenday Good day for an angels picnic. They could lunch on the smell of flowers and new mown hay, drink the moisture of the air and dance to the hum of bees. Fancy the soul of Plato astride a butterfly riding around Menlo Park with a lunch basket.[15]

He was next to see Mina at Chautauqua in August, where he and Dot arranged a visit. In 1878 Edison had been invited to Chautauqua for an electrical lecture, but he was forced to decline because of a scheduling conflict with a trip to Rawlins,

Wyoming, to view the solar eclipse with his tasimeter.[16] Of course, the eclipse could not be postponed. Interestingly, Mina had been engaged to George Vincent, son of the Chautauqua co-founder John Vincent, during the time preceding Edison's visit to Chautauqua, but George did not make the final cut.

Lewis Miller was also present with the family at Chautauqua. He and Edison bonded instantly. Both were self-made men—inventors and manufacturers. But there were differences. Lewis Miller was a devout Methodist, proactive in his religion.[17] Edison believed in God but did not try to define who God was. He believed simply that God was responsible for the laws of the universe. Nevertheless, the two men had mutual respect and admiration. Miller found Edison always "ready with some witty remark no matter what was up. And always in such nice language as compared with . . . others. Nothing of low order came from his lips."[18] Edison said of Miller, "He was one of the kindest and most loveable men I ever knew, and spent his life trying to make it possible for all mankind to reach the higher planes of living."[19]

Edison then invited Mina to go for a trip to Alexandria Bay in upstate New York and from there to the White Mountains of New Hampshire, the Gillilands to chaperone and Dot in tow.[20] She agreed. Edison had by this time taught Mina the basics of Morse Code and since there were several persons in their party, this means of communication enabled him to share his thoughts with Mina privately. Dot recalls that she was on to their clever ruse from the beginning. Pet names could be used and no one would be the wiser, with the possible exception of Dot. "Billie" was Edison's pet name for Mina. When Edison proposed to Mina while on this sojourn in the White Mountains, Dot recalled many years later that she observed the question asked in code and the affirmative reply tapped in code.[21]

According to the custom of the day, and certainly for families such as the Millers, a young man desiring a young lady's hand in marriage would first ask for the father's blessing. Mina no doubt insisted on this bit of protocol, and Edison enthusiastically obliged. On September 30, 1885, following his return to New York City from the excursion in the mountains, Edison wrote to Miller:

I trust you will not accuse me of egotism when I
say that my life and history and standing are so
well known as to call for no statement concerning
myself. My reputation is so far made that I recog-
nize I must be judged by it for good or ill. . . .
He then made assurances that:
the step I have taken in asking your daughter to
intrust her happiness into my keeping has been
the result of mature deliberation, and with the
full appreciations of the responsibility and the
duty I have undertaken to fulfill.[22]

A date was set and plans were begun for an Akron wedding
at Oak Place, the Miller mansion located on a knoll overlooking
the city. In mid-December, a wedding trousseau was obtained in
New York City, where Mina's older sister Jennie joined her to aid
in the selection.[23] Edison asked Mina whether she would prefer
a townhouse on Riverside Drive in New York City or a home in
the country. Mina settled for a home in the country and Edison
acquired Glenmont, a large estate in Llewellyn Park, located in
West Orange, New Jersey.[24] The home had been built by Henry
Pedder with funds embezzled from Arnold Constable and
Company; in the wake of those difficulties Edison had an opportunity to acquire the twenty-three-room mansion at a bargain
price. In the meantime, Edison was invited to Akron at
Christmas to spend time getting to know the family.[25]

1886

Before the wedding, a bachelor's party was held at Delmonico's
in New York City.[26] There was also a special wedding car in
which Edison's friends were assembled for the train trip to
Akron.[27]

The wedding took place at 3 P.M. on February 24, 1886, in
the living room at Oak Place. There were approximately eighty
guests, the immediate family and friends of the bride and groom.
The wedding march from Lohengrin announced the entry of
Edison in Prince Albert coat, accompanied by his best man,

Frank Tappan, a naval officer and friend. Following Edison were Mina's mother, her brothers and sisters. Then came Mina and her father. The Reverend Dr. E. K. Young of the Akron Methodist Episcopal Church conducted the ceremony. The wedding party then proceeded to the library to the strains of Mendelssohn's wedding march, and Kinsleys of Chicago catered the dinner.[28]

That night, the newlyweds and Dot boarded a train that would take them ultimately to their Florida honeymoon. There was a brief stop in Cincinnati to see friends of the inventor.[29] Edison conceived an idea for a mechanical cotton picker as the train passed through Georgia and made some sketches which were then described by Edison to reporters in Atlanta. They proceeded to Florida and spent two weeks in Jacksonville, St. Augustine and Palatka before proceeding on to Fort Myers. Leaving Palatka, the honeymooners boarded the Florida Southern Railway for Gainesville and there changed to the Florida Railway bound for Cedar Key. The *Daily News* of Palatka reported the couple bound for Havana, but there is no other evidence of that city as a destination.[30] Perhaps this was a diversionary tactic aimed at the press. A one-horse Studebaker farm wagon was purchased from a carriage and buggy dealer in Jacksonville, perhaps while waiting for connections to St. Augustine.[31] At some point, Dot joined the Gillilands and proceeded to Fort Myers ahead of the honeymooning couple, arriving there on February 27, just three days after the wedding.[32] The paper reported a Miss Johnson with Miss Edison, so young Dot appears to have had a traveling companion.

Edison and his bride arrived in Fort Myers on March 15 on the *Manatee*,[33] the city's first scheduled steamer which had commenced service just a few months after Edison's initial visit to Fort Myers.[34] The steamer, named for the town of Manatee, proceeded south from Manatee to the Peace River and up that river to Fort Ogden from whence it backtracked to Charlotte Harbor and from there south to Punta Rassa and the Caloosahatchee River and finally Fort Myers. To get to Manatee from the rail terminus at Cedar Key, the Edisons likely rode the *Colonel Safford*, a scheduled steamer. Rail service to Arcadia became available for the first time just a week or so after their arrival in Fort Myers. Since the twin residences were still being trimmed out and neither was ready for occupancy when the couple arrived, they remained at the Keystone Hotel until the houses were suitable.[35]

When finally ready for occupancy, the couple moved into a pleasant two-story house with a living room, dining room, sitting room and bath downstairs and four bedrooms upstairs. The home was surrounded by ten-foot-wide porches. A separate structure adjoined the porch on the north side, housing the kitchen and large lattice porch on the first floor and two bedrooms and a bath on the second floor. The Gilliland home was the same plan in reverse.

On March 31, Edison and Gilliland departed for Fort Ogden aboard their launch, the *Lillian*. The paper reported their trip amid bad weather and the reporter's belief that the party stopped for refuge at Punta Rassa.[36] It was believed they were going to Fort Ogden to meet Mina's parents, the Millers, who arrived early in April.

For Mina Edison, life in Fort Myers was an interesting experience but it was devoid of music, a commodity of which she had never been deprived. Gilliland wrote to Insull requesting an organ be sent to Florida for "there is not even a jews harp down here and we need music badly. . . ."[37]

The honeymoon was not all about the happy couple getting to know one another. There was Dot, who continued to keep a watchful eye on her father. The Gillilands were never far away. Even the in-laws were present. To make matters worse, Edison wrote Sammy, his secretary, to have his men in New Jersey keep him apprised of their progress on several ongoing investigations.[38] He wrote an eight-page letter instructing his men about experiments.[39] Perhaps Mina realized the laboratory would be her husband's jealous mistress, and to protect her place in the scheme of things she, by necessity, took an interest in his work. Edison made several technical notebooks in Fort Myers during the honeymoon. Mina witnessed all the entries and recorded some in her own hand.[40] Among the subjects covered were his work in telegraphy and telephony, including the railway telegraph, the balloon telegraph, phonoplex, and quadruplex. He also noted his observations concerning unknown natural forces. He had begun a notebook before his marriage on "ideas as to the discovery of a new mode of motion or energy and also to the conversion of heat directly into electricity." While in Fort Myers, he considered this matter and also the relationship among the forces of gravity, heat, light, electricity and magnetism.[41]

The Edisons spent time designing the gardens for their tropical home. One notebook contains about twenty-five pages of notes Edison wrote to Eli Thompson, detailing the composition and layout of the gardens, including a drawing in which Mrs. Edison undoubtedly had input. The notebook begins:

> Mr. Thompson—It will require 280 lighter loads of muck to cover 8 acres 4 inches deep—each lighter load 30,000 lbs. or 8,000 cart loads 1,000 lbs. each, or about 1,500 5 ton loads on wood truck.
>
> We shall want a Banana Bed about 20 feet square, you can probably buy these, I noticed up by the windmill on the Island up in the narrow channel of the Caloosahatchee, lots of banana bushes.
>
> Shall want about 1,000 pineapple, I believe there are two ways of planting; one of which is longer but sure, plant this kind, in garden across road. I ordered them of Montgomery from Key Largo. [42]

Edison promised to send Thompson several good books on floriculture and horticulture, along with an assortment of seeds and bulbs. Edison added that he intended to clear about four acres across Riverside Avenue and put up a board fence. A drawing of the fence left no doubt as to how he wanted it constructed. The garden truck and propogating beds would be across the road. "We propose to have our grounds the best manured in Florida [sic]." He instructed Thompson to order six tons of oil cake, two tons of phosphates and two tons of guano. He should get the muck from ponds and "you can hire a cart or use the lighter & yacht and get it to lighter by wheelbarrow and a line of boards." He specified some fine decayed spongy matter to hold the manure and prevent it "going clear through to *China*." [43] Finally, he wanted two hives of bees.

It is unclear how much input Mina had in the initial stages of the Florida residence before her arrival, but she undoubtedly had a hand in the extensive garden notes and when back in New Jersey she ordered decorative fresco stencils for the Florida retreat.[44]

The honeymoon ended April 26 when the Edisons boarded a boat, traveling upriver a short distance to a ferry landing and from there by horse and buggy to the nearest railroad point, which would have been Arcadia, given the status of completion of the railroad construction.[45] The buggy trip was about fifty miles.

By June 1886, just eight weeks after the honeymoon, rumblings began about the expense of the Florida place. Gilliland

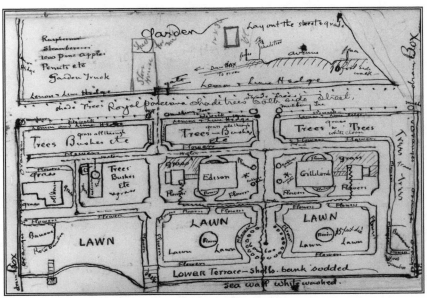

Penciled rendition of landscape design by Edison in 1886.
Courtesy of Edison National Historic Site.

39

wrote to Thompson of his great disappointment that the payroll remained so large. For Edison, the expense of maintaining a large Victorian mansion in West Orange, together with his paradise in the South, became a concern. Perhaps there were other expenses of marriage to which he had not theretofore known with Mary. Gilliland instructed Thompson to pare down the work force in Florida to a small contingent to handle the landscaping plus the engineer and Nick Armeda.[46] The message was clear, however: "wait until the fall and then a force can be hired to finish the laboratory and the houses."[47]

1887

In late 1886, Edison suffered from either pleurisy or pneumonia but he recovered sufficiently to make his third trip to Fort Myers, arriving on February 15, 1887.[48] The visit lasted two and a half months, but toward the end he began to suffer from a painful abcess in the right ear. [49] Surprisingly, there was no mention in the press of Mina despite the abundant media interest during the

1887 picture of Edison with bandaged ear, Charles Batchelor sitting on steps and Ezra Gilliland standing by mule.
Courtesy of Edison National Historic Site.

Florida honeymoon the previous year. Edison arrived in a party of eight unnamed persons and it is open to speculation who was in that exclusive group. [50] There is some evidence that Mina was included as well as daughter, Dot. [51] The sons, Thomas Jr. and William Leslie, were probably not there or if there, for a brief time only.[52] There is also evidence that Edison's assistant, Charles Batchelor, was present sometime during the season.[53] The Gillilands preceded the Edisons, arriving on February 5.[54] Mina's father was in Florida for at least a part of the season and was part of a four-day hunting trip with Edison.[55]

To insure productive use of his time, Edison ordered chemicals for his vacation laboratory, the order consisting of a mere 18 legal pages of detailed description.[56] But all was not to be work for he ordered also a boxed piano, a camera and photographic supplies, two Remington rifles and two boats, tarpon line, Spanish mackerel squids, sheep head hooks, spiral and egg sinkers, dual-forged tarpon hooks, and a cast net. He brought enhancements for the house and grounds including two cisterns, a windmill and a pump.[57] Six medical books were ordered sent to Doctor Kellum in Fort Myers, which leads one to question the Wizard's confidence in early Fort Myers medicine.[58]

Whatever may have been Edison's condition, his minions kept busy installing electricity in the laboratory and it was announced in the *Press* there was electric light in the laboratory.[59] A ten-light machine was also brought from New York resulting in lights coming on in the Edison residence on March 27.[60] Locals were eager to learn when Edison would light the town.[61] It would not be as soon as had been hoped, although one order invoiced on February 7, 1887, called for 25 complete municipal lamps with the curious notation on the invoice, "Lighting the Town."[62] The dynamo to be used for lighting the town arrived in mid-April, but the paper cast doubt on the project being completed in 1887.[63] In fact it was never completed by Edison. Some elusive turn in events caused the abrupt end of the project.

While there is no hard evidence of the presence of the two boys, Thomas Jr., then age twelve, and William, age eight, there is some circumstantial evidence they may have been present for a short time or at least there was an intention for them to be present that may have gone awry. An invoice exists with a notation for one boy's suit, one set of buttons, two naval caps and two sets of "Lillian" embroidery.[64] Sailor suits for the boys were probably intended for outings on the *Lillian*. In April, the steam yacht *Lillian* reportedly passed up the river with flags flying and a merry party abroad.[65] Earlier descriptions of the steam launch had made it out to be a work boat, but perhaps it could also become a yacht with the capacity to entertain.

There were other glimpses of the inventor's life in Fort Myers in 1887. One was the apparent allure of ice, there being no ice available in Fort Myers. Invoices reveal that sacks of ice were delivered to Edison frequently from Crystal Ice Works in Bartow.[66] The ice came from Bartow as far as Cleveland (a few miles east of Punta Gorda on the Peace River) by rail and then by the steamer *Alice Howard* to Fort Myers. Strawberries also seemed to be a favorite item; twenty-two quarts were ordered by Edison at one time and the steamer invoiced him for strawberries regularly during April 1887.[67]

Prior to departing for the season, the Edisons, the Millers, and the Gillilands visited Kissengen Springs about four miles south of Bartow near the Peace River.[68] The waters at the spring drew visitors eager for "a curative for all diseases of the blood, and of indigestion. . . ."[69] Visiting it was no easy task in 1887.[70] The party had to go by steamer from Fort Myers to Punta Gorda, and from there by train to Bartow. According to Ellwood Hendrick's biography of Lewis Miller, the "spring proved to be a lively, bubbling pond, with a spring-house reached by a causeway in the middle."[71] The entire party, except Edison, walked out on the causeway (apparently a wooden dock), which promptly collapsed, sending the party crashing into the shallow water. Unhurt, but thoroughly damp, they went to the nearby hotel while their clothing dried. A day or so later when some of the party arrived in Washington, D.C., they found that the press had run a story entitled "Edison Party Nearly Drowned."[72] Lewis Miller found the newspaper account humorous and had it illustrated with a cartoon showing men engaged in the rescue of the distressed party with the caption, "Women and Children First."[73]

Cartoon drawn for Lewis Miller.
Courtesy of Nancy Arnn.

The Fort Myers Press reported that upon returning to New Jersey, Edison was confined to his room and much of the time to his bed with a painful abscess near his right ear. The paper gave attribution for the story to the *Jacksonville Herald* and cautioned readers to consider the source, since no one in Fort Myers had heard through correspondence of such a malady afflicting the Wizard. The paper also reminded readers that it was the *Jacksonville Herald* that started the dirty lie about an Indian outbreak. The enmity between the two news journals stemmed apparently from the perception of *The Fort Myers Press* that the *Jacksonville Herald* favored the East coast of Florida and either ignored the West coast or maligned it in its reporting. In actuality, Edison did have an abscess which later required an operation.[74] A photograph of the inventor on the porch at Seminole Lodge in 1887 clearly shows the bandage over the ear.

6

Exit Damon

It is more ignominious to mistrust our
friends than to be deceived by them.
—La Rochefoucauld

It was during one of the Boston visits with the Gillilands that
Edison embarked on a once-in-a-lifetime romantic interlude
filled with introspection, the meaning of life, plans for the
"Florida bower," and doting on the lovely Mina. He so regarded
his friendship with Gilliland that during the Boston interlude, he
recorded in his diary many references to his friend, whom he
called Damon—a name inspired by the friendship of Damon and
Pythias of Greek legend.[1]

As a day's activities at the Gilliland's summer seashore retreat
at Woodside Villa drew to a close, Edison recorded in his diary:

11 o clock came and the pattering of many foot-
steps upon the stairs signaled the coming birth
of silence only to be disturbed by the sonorous
snore of the amiable Damon and the demonic
laughter of the amatory family cat.[3]

Damon was also mentioned in the diary in a context inclu-
sive of Fort Myers; "Damon and I . . . study plans for our Floridian
bower. . . ."[3]

The unfortunate end of the friendship impacted Edison's
plans for his "earthly paradise in the land of flowers," for
"Damon" had been part and parcel of the Fort Myers venture.

The Gilliland residence, later called the Guest House.
Courtesy of Edison-Ford Winter Estates.

1885

The Edison-Gilliland friendship had been reestablished at the Philadelphia electrical exhibition in 1884. Edison's work with incandescent light and the central system was diminishing and at the exhibition Gilliland, who was then heading the experimental department for Bell Telephone, suggested that his old friend turn his attention to the telephone transmitter on which Gilliland was then investigating for Bell.[4] Edison devised an improved carbon transmitter for the telephone which resulted in a contract with Bell Telephone. The new carbon transmitter held lasting significance to Bell since its use in telephone transmitters continued until the 1970s. The Bell exhibit at the 1885 World Industrial and Cotton Centenial Exposition in New Orleans included some of Edison's telephone inventions.[5]

Before leaving Bell for Edison in August of 1885, Gilliland was making $5,000 annually.[6] Edison urged Gilliland to come with him and guaranteed him that for a period of five years his annual salary would be larger than it had been with Bell. Gilliland did, in fact, come with Edison and did, in fact, make more during each of the years he worked with him.[7]

John C. Tomlinson, another close associate, played a key role in the breakup of Edison and Gilliland. Tomlinson had come to work for Edison in 1880 at age twenty-four and, according to one New York paper, was a struggling young lawyer with plenty of brains, a good knowledge of electricity and the patent laws, and an extremely modest income.[8] Tomlinson became Edison's personal attorney as well as attorney for his several corporations, and no doubt prospered as a result. It was Tomlinson who reviewed the closing papers for Edison's Florida real estate purchase.

The two friends' dispute grew out of the phonograph which had emerged in late 1877 titillating the rational senses of people everywhere. It was, however, dismissed as a toy with not much practical application. A piece of tinfoil served as the record and could be reused just a few times. The stylus had to be hand regulated, and the instrument was played with a hand crank which, if turned too fast, created an abnormal high pitch, and if too slow, an eerie unintelligible bass. After Edison secured the phonograph patent in 1878, he abandoned further development to concentrate on the incandescent light and central system. In the meantime Charles Tainter and Chichester Bell, a cousin of Alexander Graham Bell, became interested in the phonograph, developing a sound recording machine that they called a "graphophone."[9]

1888

The competition with the graphophone prompted Edison to turn his energies once more to the phonograph, the device he often called his favorite invention. Gilliland persuaded Edison that he needed a practical man to promote and market the phonograph and that he, Gilliland, was that man. Edison, who deemed

Damon his most trusted friend, signed a generous contract prepared by Tomlinson, granting Gilliland a general agency to sell all phonographs in the United States or Canada. The contract provided for a 15 percent markup for the general agent.[10]

Meanwhile, the competing graphophone company entered an exclusive license with Jesse Lippincott to market the graphophone. Lippincott, a wealthy Pennsylvanian who made his fortune in the glass tumbler business, then sought to acquire Edison's phonograph through discussions with Gilliland, not Edison.[11]

Gilliland enlisted Tomlinson to take the offer to Edison. When approached in his New Jersey office Edison was busy conferring on business matters with other men. Because of the importance Tomlinson attached to the subject, the inventor excused himself, and he and Tomlinson walked through the laboratory yard to an apple tree, where they had a lengthy conversation.[12] According to the inventor, Gilliland's name did not come up in the conversation during which Tomlinson asked Edison if he would sell the phonograph. Edison stated his reluctance to sell. "I was not desirous of selling the phonograph. My principal desire was to keep it and exploit it, and therefore . . . I was a reluctant principal in the negotiation, and my counsel, Mr. Tomlinson, found it necessary to bring to bear every consideration that came to his mind to induce me to listen favorably to terms."[13] A short time later, on June 21, Edison recalled that Mark Twain was visiting him when Tomlinson and Gilliland arrived at his laboratory and it was necessary for him to excuse himself from the meeting with his distinguished visitor to meet with them. They presented a letter from Lippincott that outlined a deal to which Edison, after extensive persuasion by Damon and Tomlinson, agreed. The sales price was $500,000. A contract of sale was then prepared by Tomlinson and signed June 28, 1888, by Edison and Lippincott and witnessed by Tomlinson.[14] The Edison Phonograph Works remained in Edison's control and by agreement, the Edison Phonograph Works would manufacture the phonographs to be sold to Lippincott at a price of cost plus 20 percent.

The general agency contract that Edison had signed with Gilliland in the previous year was to be sold by Gilliland to

Lippincott's corporation which had the effect of canceling that agency contract. In return for the cancellation, Gilliland was to receive capital stock in the new corporation, having a par value of $250,000. Par value is a rather meaningless term when discussing actual value, for it is what a willing buyer will pay that determines value. The sale of the general agency contract contained a very unusual proviso that Gilliland would have the option to sell the stock in the new corporation—a "put"—back to Lippincott for a fixed amount equal to its par value, that is, $250,000. Moreover, Gilliland agreed to give 30 percent of the contract to Tomlinson in consideration of his contribution to the deal.

Edison found out about the exchange of stock in return for the exclusive agency agreement at his meeting with Gilliland and Tomlinson on June 21, but did not become aware of the put option on return of the stock for cash until later.[15] At that time he had inquired as to the market value of the stock, and was told by Gilliland and Tomlinson that Gilliland might be able to get $75,000 for it if the whole deal went as planned. Edison stated in an affidavit that he had asked Gilliland if he would receive any cash in the transaction, "and he said no, that as his contract was of prospective value, Lippincott could only pay in kind, that is, in stock having a prospective value."[16] At this point Edison advised Gilliland and Tomlinson to continue the negotiations based on the terms as related to him.

When Lippincott had difficulty meeting one of the cash payments due Edison on the new phonograph contract, he went to Edison and told him the whole story, the side deal, options for cash and all. To say that Edison was angry is an understatement. His most loyal and trusted friend, in concert with his personal attorney, had misled him. His reaction was softened somewhat by the absense of both Gilliland and Tomlinson, who had sailed for Europe a few days earlier. Gilliland had left for Europe to promote the phonograph. Edison cabled him:

> I have this day abrogated your contract. Since you have been so underhanded I shall demand refunding of all money paid you, and I do not desire you to exhibit the phonograph in Europe.[17]

Henceforth, the two great friends were irreparably estranged. Tomlinson too was history.

1889

In January, 1889, *The Fort Myers Press* stated that Gilliland would not be coming to the city that year and that the firm of Edison & Gilliland was dissolved.[18] Toward the end of that month, Edison wrote to William E. Hibble, the caretaker of the Fort Myers properties, directing Hibble to keep separate accounts for the two properties, the boundary line between the two properties to determine to whom charges would be assessed.[19] One exception was noted. Work done on the dock was to be charged one half to each, suggesting that the dock would be available for Gilliland's use. In March, Edison again wrote Hibble asking him to have the tax assessor divide the two properties so that Edison would receive a tax bill for his property and Gilliland a separate assessment for his.[20]

In April, Edison filed a lawsuit in Federal Court against both Gilliland and Tomlinson, alleging fraud, among other things.[21] In the suit he asked for an accounting of the $250,000 they fraudulently received. A year later, a demurrer filed by the defendants, Gilliland and Tomlinson, was sustained in a court order stating that the facts set forth in the bill of complaint filed by Edison were insufficient to support a decree granting the relief requested. The case did not have to end there, for Edison's attorney could have restated the bill of complaint, but for whatever reason that never happened.

In December 1888, Edison's secretary, Alfred O. Tate, who had replaced Insull, corresponded with the Fort Myers caretaker, to say for the first time that Edison and Gilliland were no longer associated.[22] One could certainly infer the division from previous letters directing the separation of their respective expenses. A year later another letter came to the caretaker from Tate, this time requesting that he work exclusively for Edison and not for Gilliland.[23]

1891

In September, upon request, Edison signed a bearer letter for a Mr. Gaston, which introduced Gaston to Major James Evans, Edison's new Fort Myers agent, and advised Evans that Gaston had charge of Gilliland's property.[24] Evans was instructed to deliver to Gaston any property located in the laboratory associated with the steam yacht *Lillian*. It is quite likely that the *Lillian* belonged to Gilliland from the outset and had simply been made available to Edison during the first two years, as all other properties were similarly shared in a happier time.

1892

The Gillilands sold their Fort Myers house and property in 1892 to Ambrose McGregor,[25] a multi-millionaire and major stockholder in Standard Oil. McGregor had become a large property owner in Southwest Florida. Following McGregor's death his widow, Tootie McGregor, became a prominent Fort Myers citizen. Riverside Avenue, which bisected the Edison property, was renamed McGregor Boulevard in 1912 in her husband's memory.[26]

The Damon and Pythius era had passed and there was no further contact between the two. Many years later, in 1929, Ezra Gilliland's widow, Lillian, wrote Edison to congratulate him on his 82nd birthday. She had listened to a radio interview of Edison on his birthday, broadcast from Fort Myers on the day President-elect Hoover visited.[27] The contents of that letter reveal the sentiments of the past. It read:

My very dear Mr. Edison,

> It is with great pleasure I write to congratulate you on your eighty-second birthday.

> My thoughts go back to those old days, when dear old "Gill" met you at the electrical exhibition in Philadelphia and brought you home to our house at Winthrop Beach—and then to the winter in Florida, when you and he went fishing and found the place in Fort Myers "Dot" & I

waiting for you both in St Augustine—and then to the next summer at Winthrop, when you fell so desperately in love with the beautiful (illegible word) girl Mina Miller.

O! such happy days to dwell upon—and last night when I listened in and heard you speak from your house in Fort Myers, after your wonderful day with our great man Hoover the "almost"—President—of the United States—there were tears of joy and sadness come to my eyes—If dearest Gill were only here he too, would enter with all your happiness, for he loved you very dearly, Edison, and regretted all those misunderstandings.

I am very glad that I entered with those days of your courtship, yours has been a happy union. And even though you say you know of no happy people your last forty-five years have certainly been that—

Very sincerely your old time friend
Lillian Gilliland [28]

Perhaps the letter delivered a hopeful plea for reconciliation from a widow, still faithful to her dead husband but trapped by the misdeeds perpetrated by him against his very good friend.

7

The Absence

Absence makes the heart grow fonder:
Isle of Beauty, Fare thee well!
—Thomas Haynes Bayly

A long absence from Fort Myers began with the winter season of 1888 and continued until 1901. It is readily apparent why the Edisons, by then firmly at home in West Orange, New Jersey, did not appear in Fort Myers in 1888. Madeleine, the first of three children of the marriage to Mina Miller, arrived in May 1888. The winter season in Fort Myers would have coincided with the last trimester of Mina's pregnancy. Fort Myers had few doctors and no hospitals and traveling, though possible, was difficult. Train travel came as far south as Punta Gorda resulting in a day-long steamboat ride from Punta Gorda to Fort Myers. A visit to Fort Myers in the following year was no doubt precluded by daughter Madeline's infancy. In 1890 the cycle began again with the birth of Charles.

Although a reprieve from child-bearing occurred pending the birth of Theodore in 1898, the Edisons did not make it to Fort Myers in any of those years. Perhaps it was the danger to young Madeleine and still younger Charles posed by the proximity of the house in Fort Myers to the river, or perhaps there were other reasons. The unpleasantness caused by the breakup of the long-standing relationship with Ezra and Lillian Gilliland no doubt removed the bloom from his "paradise in the land of flowers," if only for a time.[1] In Fort Myers, there would be constant exposure to the identical Gilliland house only a few yards removed from their own Florida bungalow. The McGregors, who acquired the Gilliland home, did not do so until 1892. An additional factor and probably the dominant one was Edison's preoccupation with attempts to mine inferior grade iron ore in competition with superior grade deposits in the Lake Superior region through the use of a magnetic separator. The logistics for transporting the lesser grade were so much better because of its proximity to the furnaces that Edison thought he could be a viable competitor. His obsession with iron ore took him away from home with only occasional weekends at Glenmont throughout much of the nineties. The iron ore project occurred in Ogdensberg, New Jersey, and involved a large expenditure of money and time only to have been ultimately abandoned as commercially unfeasible.

1890

The business of maintaining the Florida estate continued despite Edison's absence. His private secretary, Alfred O. Tate, carried on extensive correspondence with William E. Hibble, the Florida caretaker. Hibble was not a Florida cracker and frequently used disrespectful language in his communications about the locals. "The Crackers are again howling for taxes (that is about all they can do—collect taxes). . . ."[2] In reference to taxes, he said " . . . it is their creed to bleed the Yankees, but leave enough blood to keep them alive for future operations. . . ."[3] An apparent transplant from New York, he spoke of New York as "God's country."

Maintaining the Florida property involved more than just paying taxes. Consider the poor mule who lived on the premises. Hibble wrote to Tate:

> I should like permission to do something with the mule. I have kept the old thing more as a pensioner—let her run out so she has cost very little—but this place has passed an ordinance and she has to be kept up. She is old, crippled

and very little use and every thing in the food line is dear. She will eat her head off and it will pay better to hire what little work needs to be done than to keep her. I have an offer of ten dollars for her but hate to know the old thing will be abused, which she certainly will be if put to hard work.[4]

Accepted protocol during this time was for Edison to communicate with his secretary Tate, and for Tate to correspond directly with the Fort Myers agent or caretaker. Mina Edison followed this procedure as well. She wrote to Tate to request that he communicate with Hibble about paint colors for the house. "Have pretty colors in yellow and white such as they are now painting some of the Orange [New Jersey] homes."[5] Tate promptly communicated the message to Hibble, adding that for the roof, Mrs. Edison wanted a "pretty shade to blend with the yellow and white; say some rich brownish red, but something else if prettier."[6]

Hibble wrote frequent and comprehensive letters as requested by the Edisons, for they were eager to know of progress on the premises, and what expenses to anticipate. In one such letter Hibble reported that some of the chemicals in the laboratory had evaporated forcing him to seal the containers with shellac and asphaultum.[7] He told of a frost that damaged some of the trees he was replacing.[8] He wrote that he had removed the fence in the river in front of the lab, and had another fence built out in the river to make a cleaner beach. He did this, he wrote, because "that place was a malaria factory."[9] The fence built out in the river acted as a barrier, keeping away the hyacinths and river debris. Hyacinths collecting along the shoreline of the river had become a major problem.

Nothing was heard concerning the coming of the Edisons for the 1891 season. However, Hibble reported to Tate that all was in readiness, should they arrive.[10]

1891

The Edisons did not visit Fort Myers that year, but Edison's 87-year-old father, Samuel, did.[11] He brought with him another elderly friend, James Symington. [12] On arrival, Hibble wrote, "Your father and Mr. Symington arrived last evening. They were somewhat exhausted with the trip but this morning Mr. Edison requested me to tell you that he was 'safe and sound and kicking up his heels and feels perfectly at home.'"[13]

Word apparently trickled out that the great inventor was becoming estranged from his Florida winter retreat and that perhaps he would be in the market to sell. Correspondence between Edison and the caretaker occurred over the merits of selling the Fort Myers property. Inquiries were made of shipping rates to send the steam engine and Florida laboratory equipment back to New York.[14] It would cost $600 or $700 if a schooner were chartered to ship the equipment from the bulkhead at the estate to Key West and from there to New York on the Mallory line of steamers. The caretaker suggested that Edison might consider selling the boiler and bricks to the phosphate company at a reasonable price.[15] The bulk of the shipping weight would thereby be avoided. In the midst of correspondence about another potential buyer of the equipment, Edison advised that he might visit Fort Myers in the coming winter and had decided not to sell.[16]

Hibble's duties as caretaker gave way to Ewald Stulpner in 1891.[17] Stulpner was hired by Major James Evans, who had become Edison's local agent at about the same time.[18]

1896

There was a dearth of Fort Myers–related correspondence preserved between the spring of 1893 and the end of 1896, and so there is little evidence of what happened in that period of the absence. Edison seemed ambivalent on the subject of a sale of his Fort Myers property. He would reply to correspondence from a broker as if he were interested in a sale for cash and then correspond with the same broker to say "in fact I do not care whether I sell it or not."[19] Late in 1897, the Edisons leased their Fort Myers "cottage" to a law partner of the general counsel to Edison Electric.[20] Edison sent mixed signals about his intentions in two letters mailed on the same day in January 1898. One answered an inquiry about the price at which Edison would sell the Fort Myers property: $6,000 cash without the machinery and $7,500 cash with the machinery.[21] The other advised that he would not be down that year but hoped to come the next year.[22]

Ambivalence on the part of Edison toward his investment in Florida continued into 1899. An inquiry from Edison to James Evans as to the cost of repairing the house was sent with the further question, "Could the house be rented until I want to use it?"[23] Although there was a practical desire to rid himself of an asset that was not in use and that cost a considerable amount to maintain, there was also a yearning to return to Fort Myers. As to the first question concerning the cost of repairs, Edison wrote again a month later saying that if the cost did not exceed $250, to go ahead with the repairs.[24] As to renting the property, Edison wrote that he wanted $75 per month as rent.[25]

By century's end the Edisons had practically abandoned their Fort Myers home—absent since their post-honeymoon visit in 1887. In 1900, however, they once again traveled to Florida, staying at the landmark Tampa Bay Hotel in Tampa.[26] The hotel had been built by Henry B. Plant and featured classic Moorish architecture, ornate furnishings and world-class service.[27] *The Fort Myers Press* ran an article first reported in the *Tampa Tribune* that told of Edison's visit to Tampa, and the paper speculated, "He will probably start for Fort Myers in a few days." But the Edisons did not make it to Fort Myers.[28] The *Tribune* quoted Edison as saying, "I am not in Florida on business, but merely for the health of myself and family. Mrs. Edison accompanies me as well as our two children. My intention in coming to Florida is merely for pleasure, and to escape the rigors of the winter at home."[29] It is not clear why the Edisons got so close and yet did not proceed from Tampa on to Fort Myers, but there was no direct rail route to Fort Myers from Tampa and transportation was still difficult.

8

Return to Eden

The Great Inventor Arrived At Fort Myers With His Family
Prettiest Spot In Florida Is What He Says Of Fort Myers
—The Fort Myers Press

1901

By 1901 the Gilliland memory had faded, and the iron ore venture into which Edison had invested so much of his personal time
and fortune was no longer an impediment to a trip south.
Moreover, the older children were no longer toddlers, though
the youngest was still an infant. The thought of a return to Fort
Myers became reality on February 27, 1901, when the great
inventor arrived in Fort Myers aboard the steamer *H. B. Plant*.
Captain Gonzalez was flying all the flags on that vessel in honor
of its distinguished passenger.[1] With Edison were Mina, his
cousin Edith, Mina's sister Grace, his daughter Madeleine, son
Charles, baby Theodore, and a maid. Things were not quite in
readiness at the home, which had stood mostly unoccupied for
fourteen years, so the party went directly to the beautiful new
Fort Myers Hotel, which had been opened to much fanfare three
years earlier.[2] Unfortunately, there was no vacancy in the hotel
which hosted a full complement of northern guests each season.
There being no alternative, Thomas and Mina and their
entourage took carriages through town to their winter home on
Riverside Avenue (McGregor Boulevard). The party stayed at

The Edisons in 1901.
Courtesy of Edison National Historic Site.

the Edison home but took their meals downtown.[3] Edison boasted to a local reporter that Fort Myers was "Finer than ever. It is the prettiest place in Florida and sooner or later visitors to the East Coast will find it out."[4]

Charles Edison, then eleven, remembered the trip down:

> We went to St. Augustine first, and then to Belleaire, Florida, on the old Plant System Railroad which had wood-burning locomotives. Every few miles it would have to stop and stock up with wood.[5]

The party remained in Fort Myers for about five weeks.[6]

Edison's business affairs in Fort Myers were not always attended with care. After Edison returned to the North in 1901, Ewald Stulpner, the caretaker hired by James Evans almost a decade earlier, wrote to Edison with a statement attached for his wages for the past twelve months, requesting that he be paid somewhat oftener in the future.[7] Edison annotated the bill with a direction to John Randolph, his private secretary, to pay the twelve-month bill and thereafter to pay it monthly.[8] The direction was not heeded for in the same year Stulpner had to write

Edison three times in order to obtain five months' back wages.[9] Not only did Stulpner's bills include his wages, but he apparently advanced modest sums for the purchase of plants for the grounds, hauling expenses, and repairs to the house. Previous caretakers and agents had obtained deposits from Edison for such expenses. Whether this and other financial oversights were a result of the economic times, Edison's own unwillingness to part with money, or the carelessness of his secretary or others in charge of the purse strings is not altogether clear.

Edison was a strong believer in bringing in rich muck for distribution throughout his gardens. Before the Edisons left Fort Myers, Stulpner had hauled in a good many loads of muck for the gardens and Edison had communicated with Stulpner about hauling even more after he was gone.[10] Stulpner advised that he had hauled sixteen loads of muck, which he had arranged before the rainy season so that the muck would be dry and transportable.[11] He had paid $20 of his own funds to have it hauled. In the following year 196 loads were delivered.[12] Stulpner wrote that he cancelled a contract to haul 200 loads of muck when he discovered that the contractor was taking the muck from someone's private residence.[13]

Having resumed his part-time residence in Fort Myers, Edison began a long and generous role of stewardship in the area. He sent a check for $50 to the Fort Myers Volunteer Fire Department and received a letter of thanks from his old friend, E. L. Evans, writing on behalf of the Fire Department.[14] Evans was no relation to Major James Evans, the former local agent, but had been one of the first to meet Edison on his arrival in 1885. Evans wrote again in 1903 after a fire that swept the city burned the engine house, destroying much of the equipment.[15] Edison again sent $50.[16]

1902

The town was so happy to have their favorite visitor back in regular winter attendance, a new steamer was named for the inventor. The *Thomas A. Edison* went into service in February 1902,

The *Thomas A. Edison* steamer with freight
on first deck and passengers on top deck.
Courtesy of Florida State Archives.

commuting along the upper reaches of the Caloosahatchee. It
was ninety-two feet long and some doubted its ability to negotiate the hairpin turns in the river, which began as the river narrowed about five miles northeast of Fort Myers. Capt. Fred
Menge proved the doubters wrong as he guided the vessel to Fort
Thompson near LaBelle:[17]

> The Thos. A. Edison swang around the sharp
> bends in what appeared a miraculous manner,
> but the men at the wheel and throttle knew
> their business and time and again when it
> seemed that the steamer must crash into the
> rocky banks, and the passengers held their
> breath and a tight grip on some support, she
> went by with just a few feet to spare as graceful-
> ly as if it was a very easy matter. . . . The Steamer
> is well fitted up to accommodate 15 first-class
> passengers, with meals and staterooms, the latter
> being fitted with clean and comfortable beds.[18]

Return to Eden

When the Edisons returned in 1901, Ambrose McGregor, the Rockefeller associate who bought the Gilliland home next to the Edisons, had died. His widow, Tootie McGregor, continued to live in the home. In 1902, Tootie McGregor sold the Gilliland home to Harvie E. Heitman, who exchanged it for a home in town belonging to R. Ingram O. Travers. Travers then lived in the Gilliland house until 1906 when it was sold to the Edisons for $4,850.[19] Undoubtedly Edison had for some time had his eye on the old Gilliland residence, since annexing it would restore the symmetry and character of the estate.

Harper's Weekly announced the return of the Edisons in 1902, quoting Edison as saying, "It's true I haven't been to my place in Florida but once since I bought it fourteen years ago, and then it had grown up so fair and fine I hardly knew it—but I am going this winter!"[20] Mrs. Edison notified the caretaker that they would be leaving for Florida on March 1.[21] On March 3, the steamer *H. B. Plant* proclaimed the arrival of the Edisons, with flags again flying in honor of its distinguished passenger.[22] Invoices record the vacation in detail The livery stable charged for teams and carriages during the month of March, the hardware store for 12 rolls of toilet paper, tea kettle, lamps, shades, mattress, Listerine, and assorted articles. Almost daily entries appeared from the meat market for roasts, steaks, chickens and mutton during March and similarly from the grocery store for ginger ale, chocolate, coffee, sardines, Grape Nuts, L & P sauce, grits, fly paper, prunes, apricots, lard, saltines, and other staples.[23] A bill from Lee County Telephone Co. for telephone service for the season came to $5.[24] The invoice from the livery stable identified several of the entries not only by date but also by the name for whom the carriage or buggy was taken. Mrs. Miller (Mina Edison's mother) and Miss Miller (Mina Edison's sister Grace) were both identified. So was a Mr. Colgate.[25]

In February a new 25-foot naptha launch, the *Mina*, was brought down from New Jersey by Freddy Ott, Edison's longtime assistant.[26] The boat came as far as Punta Gorda by train and from there was launched and brought to Fort Myers by Ott and a guide.[27]

While the Edisons were in residence, Dr. Cyrus Teed, the

61

Horse and Buggy driven by Mina Edison on river bank.

Courtesy of Edison-Ford Winter Estates.

leader of the Koreshan Unity, came into town to lecture on the virtues of Koreshanity.[28] Dr. Teed discovered "cellular cosmogony," which, among other things, assumed the earth a hollow sphere with the sun and moon in the center. Dr. Teed and his followers lived in a commune located in Estero, about fifteen miles south of Fort Myers. The Koreshans of Estero would cross paths with the Edisons throughout their Fort Myers experience.

Another couple from the North, Mr. and Mrs. A. D. Hermance, from Williamsport, Pennsylvania, entertained the Edisons at dinner.[29] Mr. and Mrs. Hermance were regulars at the Fort Myers Hotel, having been the first to arrive that season.[30] The social visit was repaid by the Edisons a week later at a dinner at the Edison place.[31] Social occasions for the Edisons were sparse and confined largely to other winter visitors until years later when they began to mingle with local residents.

While in Fort Myers for the 1902 season, Edison indulged himself in his favorite sport—fishing. His party caught 180 fish weighing a total of 350 pounds at Matlacha while in the *Mina*, his new launch. The local press reported "the Wizard enjoyed his part of the sport with the keen zest of a kid playing hooky from school out-a-fishing."[32]

The family left Fort Myers at 6 A.M. on April 2 on the

steamer *St. Lucie*, bound for Punta Gorda and the northbound train.[33] Traveling by steamer to Punta Gorda, with intermediate stops at Punta Rassa, St. James City, Sanibel and Captiva, took eight hours. The boat arrived at 3:30 P.M., with the train departure just thirty minutes later, at 4 P.M.

Major construction on the Edison dock at Fort Myers occurred during and after the family visit in 1902. A contractor was to extend the dock 500 feet into the river, including the bulkhead. Upon completion he apologized for having built the dock 562 feet rather than the contracted 500 feet.[34] Edison then had a boathouse built alongside the dock.[35] Stulpner reported a slight delay in the construction because the contractor had an attack of "typhoid malarial fever," but later related that he had "done you a good job."[36] The new boat which Freddy Ott brought down remained in the water because the "iron fixtures to raise it have not been put in." A cistern Edison had promised for the caretaker's cottage had not been sent, and Stulpner said he needed it because the artesian well water was not fit for cooking, and surface water such as the windmill water served for drinking when rain water could not be had.[37] The cistern arrived in September.[38]

In July, old-time friend E. L. Evans cut off Edison's credit because of an outstanding bill at the hardware store. An order for a ton and one half of fertilizer would not be delivered until the account had been "balanced."[39] In the following month, Stulpner complained to Edison that he had not been paid since February and that he was "completely without funds." In September, Evans and Company delivered 1,000 pounds of Armour Blood and Bone Potash to Edison's place and promptly wrote to him to say that they had drawn on him that day a three-day sight draft for the amount of $21, which they trusted he would "protect when presented."[40]

1903

Stulpner related to *The Fort Myers Press* that Edison and his family would arrive on Saturday, February 21, and indeed they did.

All but Madeleine, who remained in school in the North, came aboard the steamer *St. Lucie*.[41] Announcing their intended arrival, *The Fort Myers Press* took a professional jab at *The Florida Times-Union*, of Jacksonville, which had reported, "Mr. Edison has not yet announced what point he will visit in Florida." The *Press* states:

> Now if Mr. Edison was going down the East Coast, the Times-Union would have announced the fact in great head lines, but as he is coming to Ft. Myers, the great daily that never discovers anything about the West Coast simply says that Mr. Edison has not yet announced the point in Florida he will visit. Is it not strange that the greatest of inventors should have a winter home in Ft. Myers for seventeen years and Florida's leading newspaper should not have learned of the fact.[42]

In preparation for the arrival, new plumbing was installed in the house and its interior was painted and papered.[43] Five days after Edison arrived he had not yet been in his laboratory but had spent his time fishing instead, mostly in Hancock Creek, where he was said to have caught a fine string of black bass.[44]

With a railroad in sight, and a power and ice company in operation and serving the community, Fort Myers had made remarkable progress since the days of Edison's first arrival. News headlines confirmed, however, that it was still a cattle town, even in 1903, for it was reported that 8,000 head of cattle were sold in one transaction to the Lee County Cattle Company.[45]

As a winter retreat for the well-to-do, Fort Myers provided the tropical backdrop for occasional social gatherings. Mr. and Mrs. A. D. Floweree, winter visitors and friends of the Edisons, often opened their home, Hunter's Rest, to guests. Hunter's Rest was the scene of a lively party on Thursday, March 19, which Mrs. Edison, her daughter and sister attended.[46] Masses of flowers and vines decorated the porch encircling the residence, and the grounds were hung with Japanese lanterns. Dancing occurred on the verandas and the summer dining room. Two violinists, a pianist, a cellist and a guitarist provided dance music. Mr.

Floweree kept the men supplied with good cigars and droll stories, while Mrs. Floweree attended to the ladies.

Professor Thos A. Edison, as the *Fort Myers Press* sometimes referred to him, and his family chartered the *Suwanee* for a few days, fishing at Estero in late March.[47] Heavy rains and a windstorm marred the second day out. Captain Prince declined to take the *Suwanee* on the outside of the barrier islands for the return to the Caloosahatchee River because of the rough water and it could not negotiate the narrow channel along the lee side of the islands so the party was forced to return on the back side in Edison's row boats, which had been towed along. From Punta Rassa at the mouth of the river, a Mr. Surrel took them to Fort Myers in his naptha launch.[48]

Edison had arrived in Fort Myers worn out from his labors in designing a new methodology and manufacturing plant for the production of cement and doing the same for the storage battery. The manufacture of batteries by the Edison Storage Battery Company had just begun before Edison came south.[49] He brought with him a new, improved storage battery for the illumination at night of his naptha launch *Mina*.[50] As usual, fishing was a chief source of relaxation.[51] He landed seventy trout in a couple of hours at Four Mile Island.[52] Robert Thompson, one of the stockholders in the Edison Portland Cement Company, was a guest on the fishing excursion. Thompson and his wife were later entertained on a trip to Sanibel aboard the steamer *Suwanee*.[53]

Tarpon fishing continued to be the rage and though Edison preferred lesser game fish, he and Mrs. Edison engaged in the pursuit of tarpon from time to time. The Fort Myers Hotel was a haven for tarpon seekers and the Caloosahatchee River in front of the Edison home became a favorite hunting ground for the elusive species. The largest tarpon landed during the season was caught by a guest at the Fort Myers Hotel on March 13—171 pounds. Mrs. Edison hooked a "fine fellow" but the fish broke the tackle after she had played it for some time, and it got away.[54]

In mid-March, the Edisons received two more guests associated with the Edison Portland Cement Company. W. S. Mallory was a vice president and Emil Herter had served as chief draftsmen and assistant in the Ogdensberg, New Jersey, iron ore magnetic separator project that had consumed the inventor's time and money in the 1890s. The waste sand resulting from the crushing and separation process in the iron ore project then became the basis for the portland cement business. Mallory worked with Edison using many of the machines and processes used in the failed iron ore project to produce sand for cement at a new plant in Stewartsville, New Jersey.

While in Fort Myers, Edison received word that his new cement plant at Stewartsville, New Jersey, caught fire in the coal grinding operations, resulting in the death of his mechanical engineer and eight workmen.[55] W. S. Mallory, his guest just weeks before, had worked closely in the design of the plant, along with the mechanical engineer killed in the disaster. A pall blanketed the Edison compound and the family returned to New Jersey on April 1, two weeks ahead of schedule.[56]

9

The *Reliance*

The expense is too great when you get the proper yacht.
—Thomas Edison

1904

In January 1904 Edison was suffering from pneumonia and
yearned for Florida and a milder climate. He also hoped for the
solitude needed to work on experiments with sound. He told a
New York Home Journal reporter:

I am working wholly upon sound, trying to
extend the distance at which telegraphing by
sound through water can be successfully accomplished. I have a regular workshop and a laboratory near Fort Myers, on about the same scale as
those here at Llewellyn Park, and every year
about this time I go down there with a half
dozen assistants. I am using steam explosions in
such rapid succession as to form a musical
tone—about two hundred and fifty per second
giving the best results—and by breaking the
tone in long and short pauses, like the dots and
dashes of the Morse alphabet, I can already signal to a distance of three or four miles. It is, of
course, desirable to have the most violent kind
of concussions, and it may be necessary to sub-

Edison's electric launch, *Reliance*.
Courtesy of Edison-Ford Winter Estates.

stitute a chemical explosive for steam. I find the
Florida waters best fitted for my experiments, on
account of their freedom from other sounds. I
hope to be able to hold signal communication at
sea at any distance up to fifteen miles.[1]

In Fort Myers, the property had been readied for the visit.
Stulpner had built a pineapple shed and set out 400 pineapple
plants.[2] He had also set out rose bushes in the place of dead
ones.[3] The Edisons, their three youngest children, Mrs. Edison's
sister and niece arrived on February 25 aboard the steamer *St.
Lucie*.[4] Thereafter they would arrive by train, since the railroad
into Fort Myers became operational that May. In anticipation of
their arrival, the primitive lighting system at the Edison home
was replaced.[5] Outdoor lights illuminated the fountain, the giant
bamboo and other trees and shrubs. A 100-candlepower light
visible for miles was installed at the end of the dock.

The family had a new 36-foot electric launch, ordered from
The Electric Launch Company of Bayonne City, New Jersey.[6]
The company offered several battery choices, some offering more
mileage than others. Edison received a $690 credit for an "A"
battery, probably because he had shipped his own batteries
down.[7] The vessel had a standing wooden roof with canvas storm
curtains, three electric red, green and white sailing lights, three
electric ceiling lights, portable electric light with flexible cord
attachment, flag poles and brass sockets, brass chocks and cleats,

The *Reliance*

Orange N.J. Jan 1 1905

To

THE ELECTRIC LAUNCH COMPANY,
BAYONNE CITY, N. J.

Please enter _Any_ order for a __36__ Foot _Electric_ Launch,

per _Illustration_ pp __50__ with Fittings and Furnishings, as follows:

36 _open_

Ft. Launch, complete with _"A"_ battery equipment { ~~Oak finish~~ / Mahogany finish... } .... $ 2375 00
allowance for "a" Battery 690
Increased mileage can be secured by substituting a larger battery equipment, ... _Net_ 1685 00
as follows:

"B" equipment, additional...
"C" equipment, additional...

FITTINGS AND FURNISHINGS.

Fly Awning, complete with poles, guys, etc. { Over cockpit only.................. / Over entire boat, with brass end poles }		
Standing Roof, light wooden, waterproof, with canvas storm curtains...............	200	00
Set of ...3... Sailing Lights, electric (red, green and white), with screens fitted on roof...........	21	00
Combination Sailing Light, electric..		
Electric Ceiling Lights...3...in number.............@....500	15	00
Portable Electric Light, with flexible cord attachment.........................	4	50
Flag Poles and Brass Sockets..	6	00
Chocks and Cleats, brass..	10	00
Oars, Rowlocks and Sockets........................(2)	12	00
Whistle and Brass Air Pump...	10	00
Name on bows, in brass letters...	2	50
Divan Seat ~~and Back~~ Cushions { Hair and cork filled, denim or canvas covered..... / " " " " cloth covered................. / " " " " leather or linen covered..... }	15	00
Cushions for after deck........sq. ft. { Hair and cork filled, denim or canvas covered. / " " " " cloth covered............. / " " " " leather or linen covered.. }		
Springs for divan seat..		
Slip Covers, linen, for divan seat and back cushions...........................		
Slip Covers, linen, for after deck cushions...................................		
Brussels Carpet, shaped to floor..	45	00
...8...Wicker Chairs, usual size. 3-6.60. A-1-7.5 11.3-6.6.29. 1.—	72	00
One Wicker Table...	7	50
One Wicker Stool, for pilot..	4	50
Pair Cork Fenders and four brass cleats......................................	3	50
Boat Hook, brass tipped..	2	50
Bilge Pump, large..	2	75
Yacht Ensign and Bow Flag..	5	50
Complete Canvas Cover and........Spreaders.................................		
Copper Air Tanks...		
Ice Box, zinc lined...		
Coaming Step...		
Folding Anchor and Rope..	10	00
Brass Deck Rails ~~after rail double height~~ _forw'd. deck_	15	00
.............Life Jackets..		
Life Rings, painted and lettered, per pair....................................		
One mahog boarding Ladder	18	00
One Sande for C with Curtains, frame, roof		
including Seat with cushion tops	78	00
6 Extra 40 V lamps 10 eh. Ceil fixtures		
6 " 40 V " 10 " B. Bulb }	4	80

Total Order............... $ 2250.05

Ship to _Thomas A. Edison_
Fort Myers, Florida (Lee County)

Via _Clyde Line Steamer and Plant System of Railways_

(Signature of Purchaser) _Thos A. Edison_

GUARANTEE.—We guarantee each Launch for one year, and will repair or replace without charge any defect arising from imperfect material or workmanship, providing only that such defective or imperfect part when discovered shall be immediately reported or returned to us. This guarantee cannot of course cover the repairing of damages caused by accident, abuse or neglect.

TERMS.—Net cash, in New York funds, for boats F. O. B. cars or launched and in complete running order at our works; 25 per cent. payable with order and balance when boat is ready for delivery or shipment. Time deliveries are subject to strike, fire, or causes beyond our control.

Copy of invoice for electric launch *Reliance*.
Courtesy of Edison-Ford Winter Estates.

69

oars and rowlocks, whistle and brass air pump. Brass letters spelled out the name *Reliance*. For the interior, Edison ordered divan seat and cushions, brussels carpet shaped to floor, eight wicker chairs, one wicker table, yacht ensign and bow flag, folding anchor and rope, brass deck rails, mahogany boarding ladder and one water closet with privacy curtains from roof (including seat) with cushion top, all for $2,250.05. The launch was trucked to New York for shipment by the Clyde Steamship Line.[8] It was transferred from the steamship to Atlantic Coast Line Railway, probably in Jacksonville, and shipped from there to Punta Gorda, and finally to Fort Myers by steamer.

The new electric launch provided access to the Caloosahatchee's rich and abundant wildlife. While fishing up river one day, Edison and his son Charles hooked two tarpon, Edison's weighing 40 pounds and Charles' weighing 100 pounds.[9] Charles remembered the day in great detail.[10] With only four mullet left, he told his father to let him out in the little boat with the cast net so he could replenish the bait. He set out in the little boat with the cast net and his shotgun. Despite a stiff wind and choppy water, he went to the lee shore and in through the palmettos, shot a rabbit and put its foot in his pocket. Back in the boat, he threw a mullet out on the line and settled down to read a book. When the line began to slowly unwind, Charles assumed he had caught a crab. Suddenly the pace quickened, and as Charles struck the line a large tarpon leapt from the water. After a due struggle, the fish was gaffed and Charles settled down again to read. Then the fish jumped, its head bulged out of the water as it made a final leap, almost upsetting the boat. "The fish with the gaff went off, the pole went overboard, but fortunately I had this line under my arm and the fish was pretty nearly dead, anyway. The boat was swamping so we had to drop everything and bail," Charles remembered later. "Well, we got it in after a good deal of excitement, and then settled down to wait for the launch." When the launch arrived, flags flying, Edison stood on the bow laughing and bragging, We got a tarpon! We got a tarpon! Charles told his father not to laugh but to wait and see what he got. With that he pulled his tarpon up in view of his father. His father turned sheepishly to

Freddie Ott and said, "throw mine overboard." Ott declined to do so and after the Wizard's ego had cooled, they decided to have both tarpon stuffed and hung on the wall at the residence.[11]

Charles remembered that his father spent a great deal of time fishing while in Fort Myers, and that he liked the small fish better than the big ones. They always waged bets on the number and variety of fish caught rather than on size.[12] Edison was happy with his new electric launch and boasted that its range was then about 75 miles, but with the new, improved battery he would bring next year it would go 125 miles without recharging.[13] Edison and his family departed Fort Myers on April 10, just one month before the first train, the Atlantic Coastline Railway, arrived in Fort Myers and one day before the first automobile came to town. The *Press* reported that he left "cross country" by horse and buggy for Punta Gorda, where he caught the Florida Special.[14]

After the family departed for the North, Edison bought an adjacent triangular parcel of ground that squared up the property on the east side of Riverside Avenue, making his Florida estate more like a rectangle and less like a trapezoid.[15]

1905

The Fort Myers Press failed to mention Edison during the 1905 season, nor was there any correspondence indicating a visit. Correspondence confirms that fruit was shipped by Stulpner to Edison every two weeks from mid-December to April 22, affirming his northern presence and his absence from Fort Myers that winter.[16] It was a busy season in Fort Myers, nonetheless. The Fort Myers Hotel underwent a name change to the Royal Palm Hotel; tarpon hunters filled its rooms and vied for prizes for the first tarpon, the largest tarpon and the most tarpon caught in the season. Lavish parties celebrating the sport lasted beyond midnight. Fort Myers was becoming more a tourist destination and less a cattle town. The Bradford Hotel opened for business with a lobby and stores on the ground floor and hotel rooms on the upper two floors. The hotel was named in honor of Bradford

McGregor, the deceased son of Mrs. Tootie McGregor, a part-owner and former next door neighbor of the Edisons. Gilmer M. Heitman became the first citizen in town to own an automobile—an Oldsmobile.[17]

Toward the end of the year and before the 1906 season, Stulpner had a substantial fence built around the Edison property and had minor maintenance done on the houses.[18] Hyacinths continued to clog the riverfront. A river fence was also needed as it was the only means of blocking the hyacinths and controlling the nuisance. Normally during the late fall and early winter months, salt water entered the river as the rains diminished, killing off the exotic water plants and washing them away. But 1905 remained wet and the river swelled with fresh water, creating a backwash of hyacinths that delayed work on the fence in the river.

1906

After a year's absence, the Edisons returned to Fort Myers at the end of February 1906.[19] They brought along Madeleine, Charles and Theodore, Mrs. Edison's sister Grace, and several of Madeleine's schoolmates, all of whom were pupils at a small school run by Grace at Oak Place, the Miller home in Akron. Madeleine planned to enter Bryn Mawr in the fall.

The big event of the season was the chartering of the steamer *Suwanee* for an excursion to Lake Okeechobee which included the family and all their guests.[20] The newspaper reported that the flags of the Morris and Essex Yacht Clubs were hoisted on the *Suwanee*, no doubt because of the party's affiliation with those clubs in New Jersey. Captain J. Fred Menge was at the helm. The group journeyed up the Caloosahatchee through the Disston canals, Lake Flirt, Lake Bonnet, Lake Hicpochee, and finally into Lake Okeechobee. They dropped from sight of land as they headed across the lake en route to the north shore and Taylor Creek. They spent another day on the lake, passing the mouth of the Kissimmee River, then entered Fish Eating Creek. Back in the lake, they experienced a northeaster and realized in what an "ugly mood" that body of water could be. Five days later the steamer returned to the Edison dock, where its passengers disembarked. Edward Miller, Mrs. Edison's brother, arrived in Fort Myers two days after the Okeechobee cruise had begun, which necessitated his sitting out the remainder of their trip at the Royal Palm Hotel while awaiting the return of the *Suwanee* and its passengers.

The trip to the lake was a timely one, as the big political issue of the day was Governor Napoleon Bonaparte Broward's proposed assessment of lands to pay for a massive Everglades drainage project. The issue had been the hallmark of his campaign for governor in 1904.[21] The *Times Union* of Jacksonville opposed the project, but *The Fort Myers Press* favored it. Draining the Everglades and reclaiming the flooded lands within its bounds had provided political fodder in Florida since 1845, when, shortly after its admission into the Union, Florida called upon the federal government to survey the Everglades with a view toward draining it. In 1850 an Act of Congress granted certain swamp and overflowed lands to the State of Florida and authorized their reclamation. Hamilton Disston then began the first massive drainage and reclamation effort by connecting Lake Okeechobee with the Caloosahatchee River in 1883, just two years before Edison arrived in Fort Myers.[22] It was Captain J. Fred Menge, the genial captain of the *Suwanee*, who, as a young man, brought up the first dredge and then stayed on to take charge of dredging operations for Hamilton Disston.

Edison truly enjoyed the trip and was impressed with the change of scenery peculiar to the various creeks and lakes encountered. He chartered the *Suwanee* again a few days later and took the family and their guests for an outing on the beach at the Sanibel lighthouse.[23] He was entranced by the wonders of his Florida home and its surrounding geography. The *Press* reported that his children were to leave on April 1. When Mrs. Edison inquired of her husband whether he would go back on the first with them, rather than a week later as planned, he replied, "Not on your life. What, leave this?"[24] Apparently he was persuasive—Mina and the children stayed another week and they all went back on April 8. [25]

A countywide vote on whether Lee County should remain wet or become a dry county occurred just before the Edisons departed.[26] A bare majority favored the county remaining wet. Edison, a firm believer in the dangers of alcohol, would have been pleased had the vote gone the other way.

Before leaving, the inventor decided to irrigate the nine-acre tract on the opposite side of McGregor Boulevard from his residence. He drafted a contract in his own handwriting in which he and Evans and Company of Fort Myers agreed that Evans would install a complete system of concrete water pipe with a three-inch inside diameter and 2,000 feet more or less.[27] Edison also arranged to have the 2.75-acre rear parcel acquired in 1904 cleared and plowed.[28]

Fred Ott, Edison's long-time assistant, usually preceded the Edisons in Florida to get things in order. He wrote a note to Edison after the return saying his recent trip south had been quite expensive, since he had spoiled a suit of clothes on an automobile. He noted that he had worked "dam [sic] hard down south."[29] Edison replaced his suit.[30]

Edison's commitment to the Fort Myers property surfaced often. For example, he received a rather strange letter in June from a Texas Edison Phonograph dealer. The dealer told Edison that he understood how Edison loved tarpon fishing and that the fishing gounds near Corpus Christi, Texas, were the finest in the world. Would Mr. Edison come as his guest? Edison had his business manager respond that "the finest Tarpon fishing in the world is right in front of my house in Florida."[31]

In October Stulpner reported that the porches on the two homes had been widened to 15 feet and that work had begun to lengthen the dock, which was 919 feet after the extension completed in 1902.[32] The contract for the improvements called for an additional 100 feet plus a pavilion 32 feet by 40 feet at the end. The pavilion was to be identical to the pavilion at the Royal Palm Hotel. The dock would then be 919 feet plus 100 feet plus 32 feet (pavilion) for a total of 1,051 feet from the shore.[33] Later references put the dock at 1,500 feet, leaving the construction of the last 449 feet a mystery.

In addition to the dock extension, the improvements called

for by the contract included a river fence approximately 1,400 feet long to be constructed from the shore into the river as far out as the boathouse. It was to include the newly acquired Gilliland/Travers property.[34] The fence would then keep flotsam from finding its way to the seawall. Hyacinths remained a major problem despite eradication measures.

Stulpner maintained a continuous effort to have the estate in a state of readiness for Edison's next visit. Bamboo was planted around much of the perimeter of the land on the east side of Riverside Avenue and he reported to Edison that the velvet beans and "bamboos" on the new land were doing fine.[35] A cypress wood tank was ordered for the windmill pump.[36] The windmill supplied the water from the shallow well that was used in the homes. An artesian well, which needed no pump and flowed from its own internal pressure, supplied irrigation for the grounds.

1907

Unhappily, Stulpner reported to Edison in January 1907 that a major freeze had enveloped the county with the thermometer dropping to 30 1/2 degrees.[37] The bamboo planted around the clearing on the east side of Riverside Avenue died, as did the vegetables he had planted, but the fruit trees survived unscathed. The worst news relayed by Stulpner was of the great hotel fire at Punta Rassa on December 30 when the Tarpon House, wharf, cable station and a number of pleasure boats burned. Edison's old friend George Shultz, who in 1885 had sent him up river to see Fort Myers, lost everything with very little insurance.

Fred Ott had arrived several days earlier to prepare the house and its equipment for the Wizard's arrival. Presumably, Ott brought with him a new suit of clothes bought with the funds provided by Edison to replace the suit spoiled in the previous season. The 1907 visit commenced with the arrival of the noon train on Wednesday, February 27, 1907.[38] Theodore, the youngest son, came with the Edisons, while Madeleine and Charles remained in school. Madeleine was enrolled at Bryn Mawr in Pennsylvania. A bicycle was rented for use by young

Theodore.[39] Mrs. Edison's brother Ira brought his wife and daughter Margaret. For herself, Mrs. Edison had shipped a volume by L. Rochefoucault and another about Madame de Sevigne, a seventeenth-century French woman, and her letters to contemporaries, including L. Rochefoucault.[40]

Edison spent much of his time during the first week fishing from the *Reliance*, his electric launch.[41] With the extension of his dock and the erection of the pavilion in progress, he would soon have the longest dock on the river.

The year 1907 was eventful for the city as well. During the Edison sojourn the Town Council voted to build sidewalks on both sides of First Street from Hendry to Monroe.[42] Edison bought a $250 membership in the Fort Myers Yacht and Country Club, a new venture for yachting, "golf links" and a club house.[43] *The Fort Myers Press* published a blistering editorial attacking Cyrus Teed, the founder of the Koreshan Unity in Estero, 15 miles south of Fort Myers. The editorial warned the Utopian visionary to stop proselytizing the people of Lee County. It read:

> Let the People of Lee County alone. Quit threat-
> ening them with your power. Set yourself up as a
> little god if you like, make your followers think
> they are living on the inside of the earth, and
> teach them they can populate the earth by your
> peculiar theories. The people of this county will
> not care what you pretend to be, or what you
> believe, so long as you will let them alone. They
> want no Koreshan ideas instilled into the youth of
> this county, and if you will agree to keep on your
> side of the fence we will assure you that our peo-
> ple will not interfere with any of your rites or
> beliefs and the Press will forget that you are living,
> but so long as you endeavor to work your chi-
> canery and humbug and deception on our people,
> and try to curtail their rights in any way the Press
> will be on the side of the people of Lee County,
> and expose your methods.[44]

Teed's lofty theories about electromagnetic fields and their scientific effects echoed contemporary lingo, but failed to prove valid. Ironically, he seemed to want the community's esteem despite his unothodox views.

Other interesting local events and issues surfaced during the Edisons' visit. Town officials and residents met at the courthouse on April 8 to discuss filling and seawalling the waterfront from Hendry Street to Billy's Creek. The excavated land on the river side of the seawall would provide the fill. Hyacinths created a real problem, clogging the shallow waterfront and giving it an unsightly appearance. They trapped sewage dumped into the shallow areas along the shore and harbored typhoid. The plan called for property owners to pay two-thirds of the cost, with the city picking up the other one-third. A sixty to seventy-five foot roadway was to be dedicated to the city by the property owners for a waterfront drive. The property owners would retain title to the land on both sides of the road, including riparian rights, and could maintain docks on the water. The projected path of the improvement was from midway downtown through the large estates lying between the downtown section and Billy's Creek, a distance of about a mile. Opponents protested the $7,000 cost to the city and the proposal was defeated. Some of the property owners dredged and built a seawall but the riverside drive project was not approved.

Also during the 1907 visit, the *Press* ran Governor Broward's State of the State address which urged the legislature to (1) provide for the erection of a suitable State Arsenal at some central point in the state; (2) adopt a uniform system of textbooks for the common schools; (3) adopt a system of compulsory attendance since only 69 percent of school-age children were enrolled in the public schools and only 66 percent of those enrolled attended; (4) adopt a tax levy to support higher education; (5) give the State Board of Health jurisdiction over local health departments so that it could establish regulations designed to prevent typhoid fever and other diseases; (6) address the needs of the State Reform School at Mariana to the end of prevention and reformation of the criminal, rather than his punishment; (7) consider the issue of $10,000,000 in state bonds to cover road building beginning at each county seat and from there branching out east and west, north and south through the

thickly settled areas and connecting with similar systems in adjacent counties, having in mind a general system of roads running
east and west and north and south through the state; (8) pass a
statute prohibiting "Bucket Shops" whereby gambling information is transmitted by telephone or telegraph; and (9) make it a
misdemeanor to circulate through a news bureau or newspaper
any literature bearing false information to the public or to print
any misstatement or falsehood about any candidate or public
official.[45]

The Edisons visited the Fort Myers Woman's Club, the celebrated inventor dutifully signing his name in the minutes and
then promptly leaving, while Mrs. Edison remained to speak of
the labors of her father in establishing the Chautauqua
Institution in western New York.[46] Mrs. Edison, a member of the
Woman's Club, showed her interest with a check for $120 to go
toward the establishment of a permanent city library.[47]
For the first time, the name "Seminole Lodge" seemed to come
into prominence in describing the Edison Winter Estate in Fort
Myers. Clearly Mrs. Edison was responsible for the name for it
appeared on social stationary, in the text of her letters, and the
press picked it up. Edison referred to it as his "jungle."

While the dock, the boat and fishing clearly dominated
Edison's list of vacation playthings, Mrs. Edison saw the house as
hers. The Edisons departed by train for their home in Llewelyn
Park on April 22.[48] The fall found Mina Edison at home at
Glenmont planning for the coming winter and major renovations at Seminole Lodge. She contacted Proctor and Company
of New York for help in making a number of changes in the layout of the rooms in both the original residence and the Gilliland
house, which was to become a guest house, with the first floor
containing a living room and dining room. The separate structure housing the kitchen would become a kitchen for both houses. Proctor's letterhead suggested that its main business consisted
of wall hangings and window treatments, but from the proposal
sent to Mrs. Edison, it appears they also built cabinetry, fancy
doors and windows, and did design work as well.[49] Their correspondence suggested changing the kitchen in the original Edison
residence into a bedroom with closet, clothes press and bath-

room. They suggested combining a sitting and drawing room to create a living room. An interior stairway in the old kitchen would be abandoned and an exterior stairway substituted. An 18-foot bookcase was to be installed on the blank wall in the living room. In the Gilliland house (by then called the Travers House), partitions were to be removed to make way for an enlarged dining room. A covered passageway was to be constructed between the dining room and the kitchen, and major improvements made on the Gilliland kitchen so that it would provide the combined homes with cooking facilities. A pergola was planned by Proctor for a connecting installation between the two houses. Fireplaces were to be reworked with terra cotta tile. French doors were to be installed in the living room, dining room and den. New sash windows were to be installed throughout. Included in the proposal were window and door treatments, new furniture, and wallpaper.

Something caused Mrs. Edison to put a hold on the ambitious project, for Proctor suddenly wrote that the company had stopped all work as far as possible, but that the clothes press with sliding drawers and the large wardrobe were complete, as was the living room bookcase.[50] Correspondence from Proctor strongly suggested the reason for the abrupt change in plans was Mrs. Edison's fear that the work would not be completed in time for their next trip south.[51] Likely the Panic of 1907 and the downturn in the economy had a great deal to do with her decision. J. Proctor suggested she take delivery on the completed items and put the furniture and hangings on hold. Ultimately, the company sent a bill for the completed items and the partially finished window frames.[52] The bookcase yet remains in the living room and the clothes press and wardrobe are in the walk-in closet of Mrs. Edison's bedroom.

The dutiful caretaker Stulpner wrote to Mrs. Edison that he had shipped citrus fruit to specified friends and relatives as instructed, as well as sending his wife's own guava jelly and orange marmalade to both Mrs. Edison and her mother.[53] He wrote also that he had a supply on hand for their next arrival in Florida.

Meanwhile, on the east side of Riverside Avenue, workmen dug another artesian well, such a well being already in existence and used for irrigation on the grounds on the residential side.

Edison, then at his home in New Jersey, took an intense interest in the progress of the drilling of this six-inch well by a company owned in part by W. H. Towles, who also held a contract with Edison for providing and planting royal palms along Riverside Avenue.[54] When the well exceeded 500 feet, Edison told Stulpner to have the pressure taken twice each week. Edison also scrutinized water samples at certain intervals and wrote *The Fort Myers Press* to report his findings that at 140 feet, the water carried 10 percent phosphoric acid and at 160 feet, 25 percent phosphoric acid.[55] Edison deduced the drill had passed through rich phosphate deposits.[56] Stulpner wrote Edison that at 450 feet depth, the well had a flow of 300 gallons per minute, and on the following day he telegraphed that at 600 feet the flow was 1,200 gallons with a 26-inch rise. He asked for advice on how much farther they should drill. Edison telegraphed to keep on drilling since he wanted a higher rise. Finally Edison was notified that the rise was now 35 inches but that the pressure was only 22 pounds, the same as had been the case at 600 feet. Edison wired back, "Guess you better stop. . . ."[57]

10

A Royal Avenue

The Great Inventor Will Plant Riverside Avenue For a
Mile With Royal Palm Trees If Town Will Accept.
—The Fort Myers Press, 1907

1907

A month into the 1907 winter visit, Edison shocked the town
when he told the local press of his intention to offer the town
royal palms from Hendry Street in the midst of downtown, out
Riverside Avenue to the Travers' Place (Gilliland House), which
Edison had just acquired.[1] The route changed somewhat as the
generous offer progressed through the talking stage. It ultimately
became a route commencing at the head of Riverside Avenue
downtown and out Riverside Avenue beyond his own place to
Manuels Branch, a distance of about one mile.[2] The offer included the furnishing and planting of hundreds of trees, constructing
a protective box around each tree, fertilization and care for one
year, and any necessary replacements for two years conditioned
only on the town's willingness to care for the trees thereafter.
The *Press* said the idea would make Riverside the most beautiful
avenue in the state, and the Town Council considered it on
April 4.[3] After the council met it appointed a committee to meet
with Edison and find out more about the offer.[4] The committee
secured a more formal offer in writing from Edison and the council promptly accepted on May 13, with a resolution of thanks
tendered to Edison.[5]

McGregor Boulevard in front of Edison Winter Home.
Courtesy of Southwest Florida Historical Society.

Shortly afterwards, Edison's caretaker, Stulpner, received an offer from a Mr. Barfield of Caxambas, Florida, who proposed to furnish 100 royal palm plants from the Florida Everglades at $1.00 each.[6] Stulpner sent the offer on to Edison with a request for instructions.[7] W. H. Towles, who coincidentally was chairman of the Town Council, and W. T. Hull of LaBelle also submitted a proposal to Stulpner for providing the royal palms. They would obtain trees in Cuba which both men knew well. Towles had shipped thousands of head of cattle to Cuba from Punta Rassa. Their proposition called for plants not less than three feet tall and not more than six feet. The two would bring the trees from Cuba on a large gas-powered schooner. Towles proposed charging $5 each to deliver the palms, plant them, and guarantee them to live through January 1, 1908. Stulpner sent the proposition to Edison and encouraged him to go with the Cuban palms because the plants from the Everglades in Florida were too scarce, grew tall and slender with no body to them, and would vary in size.[8] Edison replied to Stulpner immediately, telling him to accept the offer of Towles and Hull.[9] The contract was made. [10] Hull and his four boys planned to leave immediately for Cuba on the *Doctor Lykes*. The project would require 564 trees planted 20 feet apart. Residents were encouraged to speak to Captain Towles if they wanted royal palms for their own yards.[11]

In late June, *The Fort Myers Press* reported that Hull and his sons had made the trip to Cuba and returned empty-handed due to a quarantine imposed to protect the public against the ravages of yellow fever.[12] One thousand empty sacks had been sent to Cuba to wrap the plants and 989 royal palms were in readiness when the men learned of the quarantine. [13] The contractors then commenced a search for the trees deep in the Florida Everglades, where royal palms occasionally grew in the middle of cypress hammocks. Frank Wilkinson, a veteran woodsman, came into town with 270 royal palms that he had obtained in the Big Cypress, a swampy Everglades area lying east of Naples, Florida. The plants were set out along the avenue in box frames protecting each plant. Hull reported that he would later make arrangements to retrieve the specimens left in Cuba.

Edison attempted to have the quarantine lifted so that the royal palms could be shipped from Cuba but was unsuccessful. He wrote his Fort Myers caretaker, "The quarantine authorities in Washington will not budge an inch for anybody."[14] Towles also had men and teams scouring the South Florida countryside in search of royal palms.[15] Two weeks later, he told Edison they had received no additional plants but that the trees that had been planted looked good. He cautioned that "looking good" should not be interpreted as success for "it takes them a long time to die, if they so choose."[16]

Towles continued to have a difficult time getting the royals out of Cuba. He wrote to Edison, "The trip to Cuba was a failure as . . . Washington has done away with the Musquiter theaery [sic] as to transmission of yellow fever, and now think the only chance to transmit it is by Royal Palms, consequently our efforts there was lost."[17] Towles asked Edison to advance him $1,000 and extend the contract to August 1, since he was sure he would have them all out by mid-July. Edison complied.[18]

Having "them all out" referred to bringing the palms out of the Everglades, not Cuba. This proved to be more difficult than Towles had represented. The men sent into the swamps returned empty-handed because of mosquitoes.[19] The extended deadline of August 1 passed and the contract fell into default. Towles lobbied his congressman in vain for an exemption for the royals in Cuba. Stulpner reported to Edison there was very little yellow fever in Cuba that season and "the danger of bringing it over is very slight."[20] He told the inventor in August that the trees already set out looked very good.

In the meantime, Stulpner proposed going to a nursery in Oneco, Florida, to pick out about 100 seedlings to start in pots as reserves.[21] Edison approved the idea, adding: "I suppose the only thing we can do is to wait and have Mr. Towles perform his contract."[22]

In October Stulpner found 50 royals 24-to-36 inches tall at an establishment in Tampa, and 100 royals 24 inches high at the nursery in Oneco.[23] While at Oneco, he bought 26 other varieties of plants, all of which Edison had requested.[24] He told Edison that the royals Towles brought out of the hammocks in the Everglades, which had looked good in August, were no longer doing well.

In December, the quarantine was still in place. Edison asked Stulpner how many of Towles' royals had survived at that time, and the caretaker replied about 150, some growing a little and others dormant.[25] He added that all of the reserve plants had survived.

1908

Finally, in mid-January, the royals from Cuba arrived. Stulpner told Edison he hoped for a better success with them than with the first lot.[26] Towles brought over 1,100 trees, which he planted and replanted until they were all out.[27] He later sent back to Cuba for 1,300 additional trees.[28]

Ewald Stulpner, who had served as caretaker and local agent, was replaced in early 1908 by Harvie Heitman, who assumed the responsibility of local agent but not as caretaker. Heitman advised Edison in June that Towles' nursery plants had died.[29] Heitman also told Edison that Towles had engaged in careless talk and that he did not believe Towles would generate a stand from his nursery stock within a year. He asked Edison to write a stiff letter insisting that Towles comply with his contract, "else refund your money and state that you want the palms and want them growing without waiting 2 or 3 years. . . ." Three days later Edison responded with a typewritten letter containing the language suggested by Heitman.[30]

Towles wrote Edison in October that he believed the only way to obtain the royals in good shape was to acquire them from nurseries, and that if they had done that from the outset, the trees would be looking good then.[31] Apparently, the Cuban trees that arrived earlier failed to thrive. Towles said "it takes the cuba [sic] palms 5 or 6 months to die."[32] Towles complained he had spent over $3,000 on the project and that only about 300 trees were growing. Edison noted in the margin: "Heitman, you better go ahead and buy the young palms at one dollar [from a nursery] and finish the job—no use fooling with this man."

A year later, Towles drove Heitman down Riverside Avenue past the royals planted for Edison, and said he was hard-pressed for money and anxious to get a settlement.[33] He told Heitman practically all of the palms were alive and would do fine. Some of them, he admitted, were smaller than the contract called for, but others were larger. Heitman wrote Edison that about 90 percent of them were alive and recommended that Doyle, the new replacement caretaker, examine the plants carefully and pass judgment on which ones would live and grow.[34] Towles wanted Edison to pay him $1,200 ($1,500 had already been paid) in settlement of the $3,000 contract price. This represented an adjusted total contract price of $2,700. The letter was typewritten, as were most of Heitman's letters, and a handwritten postscript was appended at the bottom. The postscript stated that the foregoing letter was written at Towles' request and that it appeared to Heitman that there were only 60 to 75 percent of the trees alive, although he had not examined them closely. He asked that Edison let him know whether to take a hard line or not. The postscript and the text of the letter were in conflict as to the percentage thought by Heitman to be alive. Heitman gave Towles a blind copy of the letter without the postscript.

Towles later claimed that a subsequent freeze killed about 200 of the trees.[35] Towles appeared to take no further action on the performance of the contract. Apparently Edison took a hard line when Heitman asked for advice on how to proceed, but then failed to enforce that position. The matter came up again in 1910, when Heitman advised Edison that Towles had taken no action on the palms.[36] Four years after the gift was announced, the dispute was still not settled. Towles finally threatened to reclaim the trees if he was not paid. He proposed to either sell them to the city, to the abutting property owners or to whomsoever he chose.[37] Whether or not Edison paid more than $1,500 on the contract and whether Towles attempted to make good on the threat of reclaiming or sale of the trees is not clear.

With Heitman and Towles, Edison found himself an unwitting pawn lodged between two strong and often conflicting personalities. Town leaders at the time were of two opposing political philosophies. The so-called progressives wanted to borrow against the future to ensure immediate progress, while those opposed to debt tolerated slower growth or life without some of the amenities. Heitman belonged to the latter while Towles was a progressive. Both played active roles in the politics of the community as well as its civic and social life.

Heitman served as a director of the Bank of Fort Myers formed in 1906; Towles was a director of the rival First National Bank of Fort Myers formed in 1908. Both had been on the Town Council. The differences between the men culminated later in 1914, when Towles was chairman of the Board of County Commissioners and the commission voted to build a new brick courthouse, which Heitman thought was excessive. Heitman filed suit for an injunction to stop the project.[38] To get the court order, attorneys had to take the train to Arcadia, where the circuit judge was sitting. As soon as the train left, Towles had a group of men begin to disassemble the wooden courthouse, a project that continued into the night. The next day the lawyers returned with an order enjoining the new courthouse project but the old courthouse had already been razed.[39] The conservatives won the battle though the progressives won the war.

Both Heitman and Towles contributed to the growth of Fort Myers, each in his own way. Towles had been in business with James E. Hendry Sr., operating a general store and as a cattleman shipping thousands of head of cattle to Cuba during the Spanish-American War. He was one of the first county commissioners. Heitman, with the backing of Mrs. Tootie McGregor, built the all-brick Bradford Hotel, followed by the Earnhardt Building across the street. Heitman owned citrus groves and a grocery store, selling many groceries to the Edisons on their winter visits.

Heitman may well have poisoned the well over the royal palm contract. At one point the *Fort Myers Weekly Press* agreed with Towles' position.[40] What could one do when a quarantine prohibited your bringing in the trees? Towles' two trips to Cuba, bringing back 1,100 trees on the first trip and 1,300 trees on the second, certainly showed a good-faith attempt. Obtaining trees from the Everglades could never produce sufficient numbers to line both sides of Riverside Avenue. Perhaps getting the trees from nurseries might have provided a viable option for Towles, if sufficient trees were available from that source. Who was right and who was wrong on this issue may be one of those enduring mysteries.

Harvie Heitman's grocery store in Fort Myers.
Courtesy of Florida State Archives.

Beyond dispute is the legacy of the stately royal palms on McGregor Boulevard, from whence the moniker, The City of Palms, is justly derived, a legacy made possible by the affection for the city had by its foremost winter resident.

11

Rejuvenation

*My darling Charles, We are about to start. Papa's
face is beaming. Wish you were going with us.*
—Mina Edison

1908

From February 23 until March 10, Edison, then sixty-one, was
confined to the Manhattan Eye, Ear and Throat Hospital in New
York while undergoing surgery for an acute abscess on his ear. It
was not the first time he had had trouble with that ear.[1] The
same affliction had occurred while he was in Florida in 1887. Just
days before the surgery, Edison's secretary, John Randolph, committed suicide, adding an emotional burden. The venerable
Wizard needed a time to rejuvenate. Four days after discharge
from the hospital, he left for Florida, a place the inventor rel-
ished for personal relaxation and renewal.

Preparations for a private car, the Pilgrim, had been made
with the Pennsylvania Railroad Company.[2] The Edisons brought
with them their ten-year-old son, Theodore, and a guest,
Margaret Gregory, a friend and contemporary of daughter
Madeleine. Dr. Page, one of the attending physicians in Edison's
recent illness, also accompanied the Edisons. The doctor
planned to remain at Seminole Lodge for ten days.[3] Madeleine
and Mina's brother, John Miller, joined the migration as far as
Philadelphia.

The Pilgrim was stocked with Poland Water, squab, chicken, sirloin steaks, lamb chops, bacon and pancakes. Fresh vegetables were ordered, including spinach, string beans, green peas, potatoes and sweet potatoes. Edison requested no canned vegetables, but wanted an assortment of pies, tarts, bread and rice puddings, green olives, an assortment of cheese, English breakfast tea, moca and java coffees, an assortment of crackers, and two dozen bottles of the best ginger ale.[4]

The train left from Jersey City and pulled into Newark to pick up the Edison party at 9:58 A.M. on March 14, 1908. The Pilgrim arrived in Lakeland, Florida, on the next day at 9:40 P.M., where it was placed on a quiet section of track until the next morning. It was then attached to Atlantic Coast Line Train No. 83, leaving Lakeland at 7:55 A.M. and arriving at Fort Myers at 1:05 P.M.[5]

"Oh how I wish that you were here. Everything is beautiful . . ." began Mina's letter to son Charles, written the day after their arrival. Such a statement afforded little consolation to Charles, who dearly loved Fort Myers but could not be present while he pursued his education at Hotchkiss. Her letters to Charles were very candid and filled with detail. In this one she told of her dislike for the caretaker, the heat in South Florida in March, father's sore throat, which she suspected was the result of taking off his underclothes too suddenly, and finally the wonderful trip down in the private car.[6]

Dr. Page, in Florida to attend to his patient, developed a budding romance with house guest Margaret. Mina observed that he had been pleased with her presence and that Margaret had followed him around like a shadow.[7] "Theodore is as happy as the day is long—working with his swimming, fishing, etc."

There was plenty of excitement for the vacationers in Fort Myers. Mr. Doyle, the new caretaker, almost burned the house down. He underestimated the firewood's capacity to burn while over-stacking the grate in the kitchen stove. "Water was poured upon the flames and saved the day."[9]

About two weeks into the visit, the recovering Edison granted a brief interview to a *Fort Myers Press* reporter. When asked how his recovery was proceeding, he replied, "Young man, this is the finest country on earth in which to regain lost health, and I am as quick to recuperate as soon as I reach Fort Myers. You can say one thing, as a health resort, you have the balance of the world beaten."[10] The reporter said there was nothing unpleasant about the man. He is a "grand earnest man, he makes you feel like the world is a grand place after all."[11]

The much-discussed seawall to run from the heart of downtown Fort Myers to Billy's Creek again became a much debated local issue, with former New York Surgeon General M. O. Terry leading the charge.[12] Edison's property was not in the path but when forced to comment, he replied that he was in favor of the plan.[13] The plan originally involved a scenic riverfront boulevard along the new seawall, but the property owners were not interested in giving up their riverfront. The seawall plan advocated by General Terry involved the property owners footing the bill but not giving up any property for a riverfront boulevard. The project succeeded and work began with a celebration at the Royal Palm Hotel on April 10, 1908.[14]

During his visit, Brentano's New York bookstore expressed to Edison *Bacterial Infection of the Digestive Tract, Anaesthectics and Immunity in Infective Diseases*.[15] The subject matter related to his own ailments and was no doubt a part of the Wizard's self-help medical program. Meanwhile, Mrs. Edison, who was accustomed to patronizing New York salons, purchased several sunbonnets and other items from the local millinery and ladies notions store owned by Miss M. Flossie Hill.[16] Miss Hill subsequently became a close friend of the Edisons.

The Edisons chartered the steamer *Suwanee* for a March party and invited about thirty Royal Palm Hotel guests.[17] Flags and bunting adorned the steamer for the occasion. After fishing the morning at Redfish Point, the party enjoyed a luncheon on board featuring fish chowder and other delicacies. When the party had enough of fishing, "whist," a popular card game, was played.[18]

The launch did not see much use during that season. Papa fished from the dock quite a bit and had the handsome new pavilion at the end of the dock, which made it very comfortable and shady. Mina wrote to Charles that Papa had caught a large sheephead, a spotted trout, a drum, a black bass and a mangrove snapper from the dock.[19] Although Papa had enjoyed success on the dock, Charles' favorite spot, Yellow Fever Creek—"I'm dead in love with that Creek"—was not awash in fish, said Mina. [20] Papa's ear healed well and the abscessed area had almost closed up. She reported he seemed well and happy, though Theodore had become ill during the latter part of the visit.[21]

Mina wrote frequently about the beautiful native birds. She told Charles, "how I wish you might be hearing the little wren warbling over the way."[22] She complained bitterly about Madeleine's latest boyfriend, whom she called one of "the biggest pills that I know."[23] By mid-April she complained of the hot weather, describing everything as sour and "not pleasant."[24] She spoke of her role in society in Fort Myers. There had been a reception and dance at the Fort Myers Yacht and Country Club but Papa did not want to go, so she declined. She told Charles she had probably made the wrong decision because she could have taken Margaret, the house guest, and Edison's new doctor, Dr. Dalton, who had replaced Dr. Page. But, if she had gone, she would have met a lot of people and would have then been obli-

Edison fishes on dock.
Courtesy of David Marshall.

92

An outing on the *Reliance*. Mina is at right with house
guest thought to be Margaret Gregory and one or both
of Edison physicians, Dr. Page or Dr. Dalton.
Courtesy of David Marshall.

The Shultz Hotel at Punta Rassa.
Courtesy of Southwest Florida Historical Society.

gated "to go more or less all the time or people would feel hurt but if I did not go at all, no one would take objections. I suppose there is no use swimming against the tide so I will have to come to society when in Fort Myers."[25] Whether or not to mingle in social circles in Fort Myers became a perennial issue with Mrs. Edison, for it was such activities she wished to escape by traveling south. Mrs. Edison's reluctance to engage in Fort Myers social and civic circles underwent a complete transformation in time.

The next day, Mina wrote to Charles again and told him of having a 180-pound tarpon on her line "and the miserable fish threw my bait."[26] A fisherman in her own right, she wrote that she would be trying again the next morning. On Sunday, she related her plans to go up the Orange River to show off that scenic tributary of the Caloosahatchee to Dr. Dalton.

On April 21 the family returned to New Jersey, again aboard a private car. On the day before the departure Mina wrote, "Papa wanders about in a most dejected manner. He does dislike going, dear man."[27]

Back in New Jersey, Edison received a letter from George Shultz, the hotelier from Punta Rassa, offering to send his stock certificate in the Shultz Hotel Company in return for the $500 agreed to be paid when Edison subscribed to the stock offering. [28] Shultz had lost his famous Punta Rassa hotel to fire in late 1906, and the new hotel corporation was a means of financing the rebuilding of the uninsured structure. The new hotel was completed and opened to the public on January 15, 1908.[29] Actually, Edison had received a similar letter almost a year earlier and had instructed his secretary to send Shultz the check, but apparently it was overlooked.[30]

1909

When it came time to notify Heitman of plans for the 1909 season, Edison wired that Fred Ott would be leaving Orange on January 15 for Fort Myers. Ott, Edison's long-time assistant, was a favorite of Edison's, despite his rough edges, which seemed at times to rankle Mina. If his verbal encounters were anything like his written word, they were indeed salty. After arriving in Fort Myers, he wrote his counterpart in New Jersey, "Please look after this and Rush it down here quicker than hell, first The Cart that I ordered did not come. The flexible cord that I gave you a sample of is among the missing. The portable lamps that I ordered are not what I ordered they look like hell. . . ."[31]

The Edisons arrived in Fort Myers on February 18, 1909, with Theodore, Madeleine, maids and a "party of friends."[32] The mayor greeted the inventor as he stepped off the train, and Edison praised the improvements to the city. "Mr. Mayor, I want to say you have certainly improved your beautiful little city in many ways, which is pleasant to me, but the biggest improvement is in voting whisky out. . . ."[33] This was a reference to a county-wide election held in the previous summer in which the drys had won. [34]

Soon after their arrival, Mina Edison wrote Charles from the "Tea House" at Seminole Lodge bemoaning the depressed state of Papa, who had just lost an appeal in the United States Court of Appeals, preventing his National Phonograph Company from selling its phonographs in New York and subjecting it to heavy cash damages.[35] Mina related to Charles that his father was so worried he took Freddie Ott and went fishing to try to drown his cares. "Worked so hard . . . and now everything, everything against him, it is just too bad. Oh, how I wish that you could jump right in here and help him out."[36] Charles was nineteen and though he did not "jump right in" at that time, he did join his father in business in a few years.

The opposition party in the appeals court case was the New York Phonograph Company, whose attorney was John Tomlinson. Tomlinson was the same lawyer who twenty years earlier had been the inventor's trusted attorney and who in concert with Ezra Gilliland, made a sweet deal for themselves in a bizarre scheme that forever ended their relationship with Edison. [37] In Mina's letter to Charles, written just days after the court's decision, she tells her son that the court decision "means that a lot of money has to be paid to those fellows which takes all the savings and earnings as well as stopping all sales in N. Y. State and then all the other states will come upon him [Edison] too."[38] She cautioned Charles "not to say anything about it to any one for Papa does not want it spread any more than possible."

Mina added that young Theodore was struggling with spelling, reading, geography and arithmetic, though she worked with him each morning while in Florida.[39] She told Charles his brother watched every day for a letter from him, but none came. She reminded him of the great influence he had over his sibling and chided him for not writing to her mother, Charles' maternal grandmother.

Life in Fort Myers in 1909 remained on the primitive side. For example, Edison received a bill from W. C. Bigelow for shoeing a horse on March 15 and for renting a buggy the same day.[40] The mundane chore of paying local vendors was ever present. The Desoto Fish Co. wrote to Edison, enclosing a bill for mullet bought for bait in the previous year.[41] The ice company sent a bill for $13.85, a balance from the previous year, with a cover letter concluding, "We presume he [Edison] failed to notice them [previous bills] at all or if did was at once forgotten owing to the throng of thoughts crowding his brain on very weighty subjects."[42]

Mrs. A. D. Hermance, a regular winter visitor from Pennsylvania, hosted a grand reception honoring Thomas A. Edison at the Royal Palm Hotel on March 18.[43] The event began with a tea in the afternoon, followed by a dinner for sixteen guests in the evening. Menu cards designed by the hostess were preserved as souvenirs of the occasion and contained the following:

Caviar Canapes
Florida Oysters on the Half Shell
Mock Turtle, au Madeira
Salted Almonds New Onions
Fried Fillet of Bass, Tartar Sauce
Julienne Potatoes Sliced Tomatoes
Roasted Larded Young Chicken, Mushrooms
Mashed Potatoes Green Peas in Cream
Fort Myers Salad
Strawberry Shortcake
Angel Cake Almond Macaroons
Vanilla Ice Cream
Brownville Water Crackers
Roquefort Cheese
Cafe Demi Tasse

After "supper" had been served the guests "repaired to the spacious sun parlor and music room, where dancing was indulged in until a reasonably late hour. . . ."[44]

Fishing was a favorite Florida pastime and it wasn't always the large sport fish that piqued the inventor, but the tarpon made the area famous as a fishing resort and was the standard for all local fish tales, including those told by Edison. In June 1909 following the reluctant return to New Jersey, Edison received another letter from Texans bent on enticing him once more to fish for tarpon in their waters, this time at the Oakshore Club near Rockport, Texas.[45] Edison's response, "while the Oakshore Club may have good fishing but if the members want to see real fishing come down to my place near Myers fla [sic]—so many tarpon and other fish come up the shallow river that it raises it 11 inches every season."[46]

As the year progressed, Mrs. Edison again contacted Proctor and Company, the Fifth Avenue wall hanging purveyor, furniture maker and designer, and arranged to continue the ambitious remodeling project that had been abruptly halted during bad economic times two years earlier. The plan was carried out but not without change orders issued from time to time by Mrs. Edison.[47] Some of the changes were cancellations motivated by her "fears that the work will not be completed in time . . . for their coming."[48] The pergola connecting the two houses was to be delayed until everything else was finished. The houses were to be gray with white trim and sashes and the shutters green. The roof was to be painted terra cotta or natural brick.[49]

Proctor wrote Heitman in late November saying that Mrs. Edison was blaming Proctor for the delays, "so we would appreciate it if you would put a large force of men on the work. . . ." [50] Heitman took the request to heart, putting twenty-seven men on the payroll for one week in December and twenty-five the following week.[51]

1910

Concerns over the readiness of the residences prompted Edison to inquire of Heitman in early January whether he could leave New Jersey on February 1 and find the house in order.[52] The answer must have been in the affirmative for the family arrived on February 3.[53]

Although Fort Myers may have had a reputation as a cultural laggard, it was not that on Friday mornings in 1910 when the local Friday Morning Musicale was in session. Mrs. Edison and daughter Madeleine became members and could have attended the meeting on February 18 when Mrs. Matheson read a composition on the life of Richard Wagner and Mrs. Heitman read a story about the opera, *Tannhauser*, by Wagner.[54] Four members offered vocal and instrumental music selections from the opera. At the next meeting, several new records would be played on Captain Gwynne's Victor. Perhaps the Edisons would be inclined to skip that meeting, since Victor was Edison's phonograph nemesis.

On March 9, 1910, the town celebrated its twenty-fifth birthday with speeches by local luminaries.[55] Edison became its guest of honor, taking his place on the platform along with other quarter centenarians. "Three cheers for Thomas A. Edison, the world's greatest scientist," and a hip, hip, hurray rang out among the crowd. There was a parade led by cowboys and an ox team and wagon. A chicken coop in the wagon and an old dog tied behind it symbolized the early days of a quarter century before. There were many attractive and carefully crafted floats and a string of "Honk Honks" (automobiles), still a novelty in Fort Myers.[56]

Mrs. Edison showed off the many improvements made to her home by the army of workmen in November and December. She held an informal reception at Seminole Lodge, receiving guests on the east verandah with her sister Grace Miller, her daughter, Madeleine, and Mrs. M. O. Terry, formerly Mrs. Ambrose McGregor.[57] Musicians played classical and modern piano and violin from the pergola between the two houses.

In late March the launch *Ella J* was chartered for a day's fishing for the Edisons plus Madeleine and Theodore.[58] The *Ella J* was a comfortable launch captained by A. N. Wintle. The launch took them to the mouth of the river at Punta Rassa and then up to Captiva. They did not fish for tarpon but rather for smaller fish. Edison hooked a flying fish, a feat unheard of by locals.

The new Royal Palm Theater was all the rage. It showed silent movies followed by live entertainment. The Edisons entertained with trips to the theater in March, enjoying the featured movies plus live entertainers.[59] Guests included former neighbors Mr. and Mrs. H. O. Travers (former owners of the Gilliland house), Mr. and Mrs. Frank Alderman (prominent local attorney), and Dr. and Mrs. Franklin Miles (originator of Miles Laboratories and local land owner and developer). About this time Mrs. Edison was slowly beginning to socialize with some of the local residents.

Before leaving, the Edisons contemplated the addition of a "bathing pool" between the river and the laboratory, a rarity in Southwest Florida in 1910. The Royal Palm Hotel had opened its sulphur bath pool in 1908 and was probably the only other pool in the area.[60] Edison had drawings prepared for the pool and a water line for fire protection and sent them to Heitman with instructions to proceed with construction.[61] In November, the local press noted the completion of a ferro concrete swimming pool at the Edison place on Riverside Avenue, supplied by the artesian well on the other side of Riverside Avenue.[62]

1911

The Edisons took a family tour of Europe in 1911, which precluded a trip to Florida. Mina, Madeleine and Theodore left ahead of Charles and his father, who came later. Charles later remembered celebrating his twenty-first birthday during the crossing with his father on the *Mauretania*.[63] A member of Parliament met the inventor and his son when they arrived at Liverpool, and a Daimler automobile carried them on a tour of England, France, Switzerland, Austria, Belgium and Holland. Charles recalled that in London, he and his father were invited to the Gallery of the House of Commons to hear the debate to abolish the veto power of the House of Lords. They crossed the channel and met the family; from Paris they "motored" on to Switzerland and Austria. Marion Edison Oeser (Dot), Edison's daughter by his first marriage, accompanied by her husband, Oscar Oeser, a German Army officer, met the party in Austria. Charles described Oscar Oeser as "a very nice fellow."[64] Marion and Oscar separated after the war ended, and Marion returned to the United States.

Meanwhile in Fort Myers, the new Shultz Hotel at Punta Rassa, which opened January 15, 1908, was in trouble, with an outstanding mortgage in default.[65] When the old uninsured hotel burned, loyal friends, including Edison, came to George Shultz's rescue by subscribing to stock in a corporate venture to underwrite the new hotel, at a cost of $23,000.[66] The subscribers came up with about $13,000, and borrowed another $10,000 from Charles B. Hoag, a winter guest at the hotel and a large Standard Oil stockholder.[67] Hoag died soon after and his estate demanded payment. Shultz attempted to call a shareholder meeting so as to engage the other shareholders in the problem, but the shareholders did not take the bait for they considered their initial purchases of stock as a means of helping their friend Shultz—rather than an investment for profit.[68] They did not wish to sink additional capital into the venture. Edison invested in his own ventures and only occasionally became involved in the enterprises of others. Edison confided to local agent Heitman, "What does Shultz want me to do—I bought the stock just to help him without any idea that I would ever get anything from it."[69] Later in 1912 Shultz again wrote Edison, this time to advise of a pending foreclosure on the hotel mortgage.[70] Edison's response: "Shultz—Do as you please I have no kick—I put the money in to help you personally—You should hang on to what you have. TAE"[71]

Heitman wrote Edison during the state legislative session, asking him to lobby a local legislator, opposing proposed legislation that would limit the distance riverfront property owners could either dredge and fill or build wharves to 500 feet from the shore line.[72] Edison instructed his secretary to write his state representative protesting the proposed legislation. Edison had one of the longest docks on the river. Ultimately it reached 1,500 feet. Heitman explained in his correspondence to Edison that the proposed legislation was the action of one man, W. H. Towles, who seemed to come up on the other side of most issues in which Heitman was interested.[73]

Heitman also asked Edison for a small donation of $25 to $50 to support a local campaign to build a recreational pier into the river from the foot of Fowler Street.[74] Heitman thought it would be a benefit to the poorer residents who did not have access to the waterfront. The recreation pier became a local political football, with some residents pointing to the greater need for an emergency hospital. Others pointed out the necessity for a tourist town to have significant amenities to attract visitors, and since the waterfront provided the most alluring feature of Fort Myers, it should be enhanced to the optimum. Both the hospital and the recreation pier passed the Town Council after some vexation aired in the local press.[75]

When caretaker Doyle left, Edison sent down a replacement from New Jersey known only as Zeman. Zeman spoke broken English and was difficult to understand, and although industrious, had little knowledge of plants, particularly those growing in Florida. Heitman thought he lacked common sense, and he became more and more doubtful of Zeman's ability as caretaker. Nevertheless, Edison kept him on for a number of years.

12

Epistles from Mina

❧

It is sweet here Charlsie dear & some day how you will enjoy it.
—Mina Edison

1912

The Edisons were back on schedule in 1912, coming south with
Theodore and Madeleine and three of Madeleine's friends.[1]
Madeleine and her girl friends stayed in the Gilliland house,
which served as the guest house. According to Mina, they
remained independent of the others except for meals.[2] Mina,
Papa and Ted stayed in the "old quarters," the original Edison
home.

Prior to their arrival, William Jennings Bryan, three-time
Democratic presidential candidate, toured the town, including
the Edison winter home and the courthouse, after which he left
by automobile for LaBelle and from there by boat into the
Everglades to assess the progress of the dredging occurring there.[3]

Mrs. M. O. Terry generously offered to assist the county in
building a 50-foot shell boulevard from Whiskey Creek to Punta
Rassa, provided the city carried it from downtown along
Riverside Avenue to the city limits.[4] Mrs. Terry asked that the
boulevard be a memorial to her late husband, Ambrose
McGregor. Thenceforth, Riverside Avenue became McGregor
Boulevard, a lasting tribute to McGregor.[5]

The year 1912 proved a bittersweet one for Mina Edison.

Dearie and Billie in the gardens in 1912.
Courtesy of Edison-Ford Winter Estates.

Letters to Charles at MIT showed first a dread of going south and then a delight once she was there.[6] She wrote of the beauty of their winter place and the wonderful time everyone had, and on the next line that the vacation had been spoiled by leaks and rugs eaten by moths. She raved about the new pool and how much fun the girls had there, and that the birds and the sunshine were heavenly, and "we are happy." Then she wrote of her dislike for the people in Fort Myers. "I feel like putting up a cement wall all about our place and letting those thieves alone. I detest the people down here."[7] Two days later she wrote, "This town is rank . . . it is not much like the early quaint town. It is too bad. Prosperity has turned their heads I fear."[8] A few weeks later, she told of inviting some ladies over to swim in the pool. Her statements reflecting a dislike of the locals were likely precipitated by her husband's difficulty with William H. Towles and her dislike of Captain Fred Menge's flirtations with the girls. Towles continued to demand money on the royal palm project along McGregor Boulevard even though the contract had been in default and half the trees were dead. Menge, as the owner and captain of the

Suwanee, spent too much time on their outings flirting with Madeleine's friends, Mina thought. She did not see how he could run a respectable business while comporting himself in that way. In spite of such criticism, she thought him very well versed in all bird, animal, fauna and fish life.[9] Captain J. Fred Menge and his brother Captain Conrad Menge owned the Caloosahatchee River Steamboat Line, whose fleet included the *Thomas A. Edison*, *Uneeda*, *Suwanee*, *Nyanza*, *May* and *Andros*.

Mina described Papa's nerves as frayed and she worried about being a bore to him.[10] When time to return north, she wrote, "We everyone dread it and wish this bliss could continue a month longer."[11] And in another letter, "Seminole Lodge is the place. . . . It is better to enjoy Papa's free time with him rather than to be home where he is busy."[12]

Some of the ladies from town had called on Mina and left their cards, but she wrote that she was not going to accept any social engagements that year.[13] It made her weary, she wrote, to be forced into the party-giving scheme. The family came to Fort Myers to throw off that stilted way so prevalent in her social cir-

The original Fort Myers laboratory, later removed
to Greenfield Village in Dearborn, Michigan.
Courtesy of Edison-Ford Winter Estates.

cle in New Jersey. Mina did find the time and the inclination to join Madeleine and the girls on a visit to the Koreshan Unity in Estero.[14] Mina thought the place had gone down since Dr. Teed died and after all, in Mina's estimation, it was a "foolish sect."[15]

During the first month of the visit, Mina complained to Charles that Papa had had no rest.[16] She thought his written correspondence left him in constant contact with everything he should be free of. She told her son that Papa had been fishing off the pier, but the electric launch *Reliance* was out of commission.[17]

Communication in writing was not only from mother to son, but also from son to mother. Charles wrote often and in great detail. He frequently used "Mud" as a pet name for her. The following is typical of his wit and personality, though not of his usual detail:

June something or other
Mrs. Thos. A. Edison
Wife of Reknowned Wizzard
Llewellyn Park
Orange, New Jersey
Venerated Madam

>Enclosed please find a bum check for ten dollars the same being reimbursement for monies tendered to undersigned to defray expenses to Boston.

>With kindest personal regards Believe me, dear Madam.

>Your obedient servant and fervent admirer.

>One, Charles Edison[1]

Although the father remained engaged and had not escaped the problems he had intended to leave behind, Seminole Lodge was heaven for Theodore. He had been busy building a cage for the monkeys that had been acquired to complete his father's jungle.[19] As so many Northerners were prone to do, Theodore managed to get a miserable sunburn. As the layers of skin began to peel, he shed a large piece, which he gave to his mother saying it was his pound of flesh without the blood.[20] Mina thought this a brilliant statement from her thirteen-year-old.

The girls entertained themselves in the mornings attending

Theodore, Mina and Thomas Edison in 1912.
Courtesy of Edison National Historic Site.

Madeleine and three house guests on the porch of the Guest House.
Courtesy of Edison National Historic Site.

"picture shows" downtown, probably at the Grand Theater.[21]
Madeleine was twenty-three, but age and maturity didn't seem to
overcome that silly girlish behavior so likely to emerge when girl
friends are together for a time. Madeleine displayed that
demeanor in an unsigned, undated document in her handwriting
entitled Rules for Guests at Seminole Lodge:

- Don't cabbage unto yourself all the fish poles—This has
  been done by guests thereby incurring the grave disapproval
  of the entire family.
- Don't ask Madeleine what she's writing—if its letters, she
  won't want you to know—if its literary plights you won't
  want to know.
- Don't ask her why she writes so many letters. She does it out
  of spite.
- Whatever happens don't ask why—Ten to one none of the
  family could tell you.
- If you perceive that we need someone with a sane understanding to manage us, look the other way. On our account
  try to act as balance wheel. The family all think its great to
  be crazy.
- Don't kill the black snakes under the pool. They are there
  for a purpose.
- Don't make the mistake of thinking you'd like to catch a
  tarpon. You wouldn't. Mother and Father are both after one
  with blood in their eyes—and there are just four tarpon
  poles.
- If you don't think Seminole Lodge is the loveliest spot you
  ever wore your rubbers in, don't let on to Father.
- Don't pick the flowers off the century plants. We might not
  be there to see them bloom again.
- Don't fail to retire to your room during part of each day—so
  that the family may squabble without embarrassment.
- When going on a three days cruise don't discover when you
  are at the far end of the dock that you left your tooth-brush
  in the house. The dock is _____ [left blank] feet long.
  In a case like this, the safe thing to do is to leave your tooth-
  brush behind but if you are obstinate, get Father to take a nap
  in the boat and then run like for the shore. Above all things

107

don't send one of the guides. Father's sleeping powers are fairly good but they wouldn't last that long!

- Don't take any conveyance to the village without making the rounds of the entire family to see if you can't do some errand for them.
- Don't stop Madeleine if you see her start anywhere violently alone, she's only trying to work out her disposition.
- Don't capsize in the sailboat if you can help it. Remember there isn't any man to rescue you in 750 miles—and besides there are the sharks.
- However desperate you become don't flirt with the guides. We once had a guest who did this so that the entire family lost its sleep trying to chaperone her and Mother is very tired this season.
- Don't tell us the perfume of the river hyacinths reminds you of the Jersey meadows by moon light. We're just as sorry about those hyacinths as you are but we don't like to say so.
- Don't hesitate to say you are bored.
- Don't hesitate to say you're enjoying yourself.
- Don't ask us anything about Palm Beach. We don't want to know. [22]

Edison engaged Captain Menge and the *Suwanee* to take a party up the river to Lake Okeechobee to see the changes made by extensive dredging.[23] Mina wrote Charles that the trip could never duplicate the glorious trip to the lake they had taken aboard the *Suwanee* in 1906.[24] Once on the trip, however, she reported to Charles that the *Suwanee* was now palatial since it had been refitted. Mina wrote:

> We just came home yesterday from that wonderful trip into Lake Okeechobee going to the dredges of the new canal thru the Everglades. You would have thoroughly enjoyed the sawgrass experience and the bird life was most interesting and they were the only live thing that we saw through out the canal and they came out of the grass in flocks continually. Birds of the crane family and such life. It was a fascinating, weird experience to see that vast expanse of country

with those silent moving creatures floating in the air and then setting down in the long grasses lost to sight. At one moment the air alive and then was quiet and a strange loneliness over all. They are reclaiming the land and now people are coming in taking land to cultivate . . . an enormous truck garden. Captain Menge will have it that they are all going crazy. It does look pitiful now to see those people come out there taking up a home in that deserted country. Imagine the hardships they are to go thru. After coming out of the Everglades again passing thru Lake Okeechobee and the canals we anchored just below LaBelle in the midst of the palms and Theodore with the help of the crew got out after dark and lighted up the dead trees. There was the same magic spell over all and we sang around the camp fire. You remember the effect of that the time we all went thru. The singing was beautiful in the moonlight. My how Theodore did work and how happy he was in doing it. The Suwanee is very palatial now and we were very comfortable but oh so glad to get off when we reached our little Paradise of a house. It is sweet here Charlsie dear & some day how you will enjoy it. We go in the morning again down the river to Captiva which I am nor the girls at all anxious to do. We would rather stay right here. It is so beautiful and . . . The roses are just coming out and I want to see the bushes in bloom but that pleasure is not for us as they will probably be all over by Saturday when we get back. The swimming pool is great and we are having some fine times in it. . . . Papa is coming to go to bed and as I must be up by five thirty in the morning I must get to bed now. . . . With kisses and love, Devotedly, Mother.[25]

An untitled poem was attached to the Rules for Guests that

109

The *Suwanee*.
Courtesy of Florida State Archives.

related to the trip to the Lake. It is likewise in Madeleine's handwriting, although Madeleine's friends may have contributed.

Captain Menge, Captain Menge
You deserve a laurel wreath
Steered us thro' the saw-grass teeth
Captain Menge, Captain Menge
Captain Bonny
    of the Suwanee
Captain Menge
We have got to say good-bye
See it almost makes us cry[26]

A four-day trip to Captiva Pass aboard the *Suwanee* followed on the heels of the trip to Okeechobee.[27] Mina did not relish this trip but she would go so as not to be objectionable to Papa for she was afraid if she did not, she would "throw cold water over things."[28] Although she preferred to stay at home, Mina later told Charles they had great fun on the Captiva trip, though it was not enjoyed as much as the trip upriver to the Everglades.[29] The fishing was extremely poor and Mina thought that fishing had been spoiled for all time by the dredging "improvements" upriver. "Papa had a tarpon on his line but the miserable fish jumped out of the water once and shook the hook out of his mouth."[30]

Boat trips up and down the river were not the only water

fascination. The pool was a big hit during the season and Edison himself went for a swim.[31]

On Easter Sunday, 1912, Mina wrote Charles the girls had gone to church and Papa was on the pier fishing. "All is happiness and secure on this Easter day."[32] She shipped fruit to Charles as an Easter present. The girls left on the following Tuesday, Papa, Mina and Ted a week later. "Dread this breaking up—have had a glorious time. Girls have been very sweet to me. Even Madeleine has been more gentle."[33] Mina and daughter Madeleine were not immune to mother-daughter conflict. Madeleine's choice of boy friends was not to Mina's liking, and her letters to Charles were seldom silent on that subject. On Tuesday, the girls left for home and Mina wrote, I "feel all the fun is over."[34] The letters written late in the season did not show the disdain Mina's earlier letters showed for the locals nor her general unpleasant perspective. When the Edisons left there was genuine sadness not just for Edison but for Mina as well. Adding to the gloom afflicting the return trip was the terrible news en route that the *Titanic* had sunk with a huge loss of life.[35]

Following their departure, the monkeys for which Theodore had been busy building a cage were evicted from their home.[36] Edison was concerned that the two large males might injure somebody's child. They were relocated in Jacksonville, where they became one of the exhibits at an ostrich farm. Their cage bore the surprising and falacious legend: "These Siamese monkeys were raised on Thomas A. Edison's South Florida Monkey Farm at Fort Myers, Fla."[37]

1913

There is no evidence the Edisons came to Florida in 1913. The newspaper was silent and no correspondence suggests a visit.

13

Camping

Indeed, when I go to the woods or the fields,
or ascend to the hilltop, I do not seem to be gazing upon
beauty at all,but to be breathing it like the air. . . . I
am not a spectator of, but a participator in it.
—John Burroughs

1914

Edison's appearance in 1914 brought more than usual attention because with him were guests including Henry Ford, the automobile industrialist, and John Burroughs, the noted naturalist. Edison was sixty-seven, Ford fifty-one, and Burroughs seventy-seven. Edison had first met Ford in 1896, if only briefly, at the annual convention of the national Association of Edison Illuminating Companies. Ford had been employed at Edison Illuminating in Detroit. Their next meeting was in 1912 when Edison was asked to work on a storage battery suitable for use in the Model T. Burroughs was Ford's friend and was introduced to Edison during the visit.

Ford came with his wife and twenty-year-old son, Edsel, a contemporary of Edison's son, Charles. *The Fort Myers Daily Press* announced their estimated time of arrival a week in

Edison, Burroughs and Ford.
Courtesy of Edison-Ford Winter Estates.

advance.[1] On the following day, a Tuesday, it described a grand reception for the party arriving on the noon train on the following Monday.[2] By Thursday, the paper was admonishing all citizens to be on hand for the event.[3] The Booster Club and the Board of Trade arranged for a parade of Ford automobiles and three bands to escort the celebrites from the train station to the Edison home. On Saturday, the local paper asked all Ford owners to participate in the parade, saying also that motion picture crews would be with the party, presenting a splendid opportunity for valuable promotion of the community in theaters far and wide. [4]

Before reaching the station on Monday, February 23, the train made an unscheduled stop at Tice, an unincorporated community about three miles east of town. There Fort Myers Mayor R. C. Matson, Board of Trade president, Dr. J. B. Porter, Booster Club president F. W. Perry, and W. Stanley Hanson boarded to extend an official welcome and make the last leg of the journey with the famous three.[5] The train was more than thirty minutes late and two thousand people awaited the arrival.[6]

The air was alive with banners and band music. People, straining to see Henry Ford, flooded the courthouse grounds adjoining the station. There were 31 automobiles, mostly "Ford machines," in the procession, organized by David Ireland, a local contractor.[7] Leading were three Model T Touring Cars provided by the local Ford dealer. Burroughs rode with Edison in the first car. In the second car were Mr. and Mrs. Ford, their son, Edsel, and the Edisons' son, Charles. The third car carried the official welcoming party, consisting of the four town leaders who had boarded the train at Tice. The parade route was down Monroe Street to First Street, down First Street to Fowler, down Fowler to Second Street, down Second Street to Hendry, down Hendry to Oak Street (now Main Street), and then out McGregor Boulevard to Seminole Lodge.[8]

In Fort Myers with the Edisons were their children, Madeleine, Charles and Theodore, and their longtime governess and family friend, Lucy Bogue. It was reported that Edison would stay in town four to six weeks, but that Ford would be there just a few days.[9] The paper was wrong about Ford, for he and his wife and son remained until March 10—almost three weeks.

Ford was enjoying widespread popularity in 1914. Just six weeks earlier he had reduced the Ford employee workday to eight hours, had increased the number of shifts from two to three each day and, most important, had raised the daily wage to $5.00, steps unheard of in the industry or in the nation.[10] Only three months before, he had raised the minimum daily wage to $2.34, a pay rate equal to or better than competitors. The success of the Model T and Ford's rise from mechanic to millionaire innovator and manufacturer had already earned him great respect. Giving workers a living wage with which they could purchase the very product they mass-produced was a new and novel idea on which Ford's future success would be based.

Ford also had a gentle side, uncommon in hard-scrabble industrialists who lifted themselves by their own greasy boot straps. From childhood he had carried a love of nature and particularly of birds. He wrote when he was fifty: "The first thing that I remember in my life is my father taking my brother John and myself to see a bird's nest under a large oak log 20 rods East of our home . . . I remember the nest with four eggs and also the bird and hearing it sing. I have always remembered that song, and in later years found that it was a song sparrow. I remember the log layed in the field for a good many years."[11] His home at Fair Lane had 500 birdbaths on the premises.[12] In 1913, he telegraphed Mrs. Edison:

> I AM GREATLY INTERESTED IN THE MCLEAN MIGRA-
> TORY BIRD BILL NOW PENDING IN CONGRESS IT
> EXTENDS FEDERAL PROTECTION TO OUR BIRDS HAS
> ALREADY PASSED THE SENATE BUT MUST HAVE ALL
> THE HELP WE CAN GET TO HAVE THE HOUSE ACT
> AT THIS SESSION IT IS THE ONLY WAY TO SAVE OUR
> MOST USEFUL AND NECESSARY BIRDS FROM
> DESTRUCTION WONT YOU PLEASE GET MR. EDISON
> TO GIVE AN INTERVIEW TO SOME GOOD NEWSPA-
> PER MAN URGING IMMEDIATE PASSING OF THIS
> GREATLY NEEDED MEASURE.[13]

Author, poet, apostle of Emerson and Thoreau, and dean of the nation's naturalists, Burroughs raved when he saw Fort Myers. "I never thought I was coming into such a tropical coun-try as this. Fort Myers reminds me of Honolulu and Jamaica. It is one of the most beautiful spots I have ever seen. I am sure my stay here is going to be one of the most pleasant experiences of my life."[14] An unnamed admirer told the local newspaper that at seventy-seven, Burroughs went around the extensive grounds "just like one of the children." The paper reported that he had made friends with every bird at the place.[15]

Ford and Burroughs had known each other for two years. Burroughs had indirectly criticized Ford, stating that he deplored the desecration of the country by industrialists and by the motor car in particular.[16] In 1912, Ford wrote Burroughs of his admira-tion of his books and offered to present him with a Ford automo-bile. He vowed there would be no publicity in connection with the gift. The car made a convert of the old man, and he was soon chasing over the countryside surrounding his home in West Park, New York, in his Model T.[17] Ford and Burroughs met in mid-1913 and discovered a mutual interest in birds—a common interest that bound the unlikely friendship.[18]

During the Ford-Burroughs visit in Fort Myers, the annual carnival came to town. On opening night, Edison, Ford and Burroughs attended. First, they surveyed the Motordrome, where they witnessed automobile races at top speeds of 60 miles per hour; second, they visited Jennier's Society Circus, where they enjoyed the circus and saw Ed Millette, the greatest head balancer in the world; and finally, they ambled like youngsters through the Midway before departing for Seminole Lodge.[19]

The town had other entertainment as well for its prominent guests. The Louisville Colonels baseball team was in Fort Myers for spring training, with practice between 9 A.M. and 11 A.M. and again between 2 P.M. and 4 P.M. daily. Admission was ten cents.[20]

Chautauqua arrived on February 19, as it had in so many remote areas of the country.[21] The Chautauqua in Fort Myers was inspired by the Chautauqua Institution in Western New York, founded in 1874 by Mina Edison's father and the Reverend John Vincent of the Methodist Church.[22] Countless organizations emulated the concept in rural communities throughout the country, bringing accomplished musicians and speakers to remote villages and hammocks. Programming at the Chatauqua Institution in Western New York consisted of music, lectures and education, and the remote organizations known by the same name strived to do the same.

The first night in Fort Myers, the Chautauqua featured the Chicago Ladies Orchestra, which opened with the Anvil Chorus. The three celebrities arrived a few days later. While there is no evidence of their attendance, Edison and his guests could have seen and heard the Four Bostonians in recital two days after their arrival and could have heard a lecture from Dr. Frederick A. Cook on the same day.[23] Dr. Cook, who claimed to have discovered the North Pole, was not to be confused with James Cook, the famous British navigator of the eighteenth century who mapped much of the South Pacific. Dr. Cook's claims were later discredited, and he was jailed in 1923 for mail fraud.[24]

Following Edison's arrival, a much-anticipated camping trip to the Everglades began. The destination, according to *The Fort Myers Press*, was Rocky Lake, a site about 60 miles into the Everglades (Charles Edison called the site Deep Lake).[25]

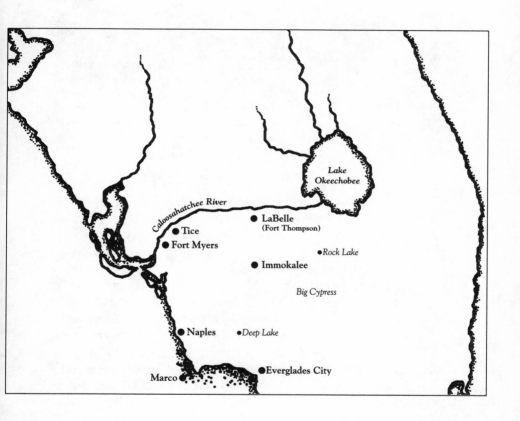

Map showing camping route.

Three Fords on left. Either two Cadillacs (Madeleine's recollection)
or two Buicks (Charles' recollection).
Courtesy of Edison-Ford Winter Estates.

Included on the trip were Mina Edison, Clara Ford, Madeleine, Charles and Theodore Edison, Edsel Ford, Lucy Bogue, and a friend of Madeleine's whose name is revealed only as Bessie. Three guides also accompanied the party, Frank Carson, Len Hibble and Sam Thompson. There is also mention of a cook, who may have been one of the guides.[26]

Ten years after the trip, Madeleine Edison Sloane wrote a splendid account.[27] She fondly remembered that the campers rose bright and early, "with their tooth brushes rolled into neat packages & all their oldest and toughest looking clothes on their backs."[28] They had with them guns, rods, food, tents and matching red blankets. Some, however, did not follow the dress code but showed up in white duck skirts and Panama hats or dressy lavender shirt waists or perfectly good Norfolk jackets. Madeleine recalled there being three Fords and two Cadillacs." Brother Charles remembered "about" three Fords and a Buick.[29] They went first to Labelle and then to the headwaters of the Caloosahatchee and then turned south into the Big Cypress swamp. Charles remembered there were no roads beyond the "surroundings" of Fort Myers.[30]

Madeleine stated, "You'd get off into the pine woods and you'd see ruts, but you'd go bumping over these palmetto roots— they grow long and stick up. . . . Of course lots of times you'd hit

1914 version of Alligator Alley.
Courtesy of Edison-Ford Winter Estates.

this deep sand and you'd have an awful time getting out of it. You'd hit these ponds. You'd perhaps see a trail somewhere where somebody'd been through there before."[31] Madeleine said that you could get an accurate demonstration of the ride by going to Coney Island, spending 10 cents and riding the "Tickler." Charles remembered one pond that turned out to be a small lake and quite wide. The guide told him he would have to cross the pond and Charles asked how they would know where the high spot was. The guide replied, "Well, you just have to feel your way."[32] They managed to cross that pond, which Charles estimated was a distance of about a quarter of a mile. Some of the party thought the scenery monotonous, but Madeleine disagreed:

> Perhaps if one doesn't love these gnarled and twisted pine trees making Japanese designs against the blue sky (if one doesn't enjoy losing ones imagination in the purplish blue haze that stretches back on all sides as far as the eye can reach through the interminable lines of tree trunks—) if one doesn't delight in lovely groves of delicate gray cypress trees—little slender silvery things with just a touch of the most beautiful feathery green—in the midst of fantastic waving gray moss—above all if one has no fear of being suddenly dashed out into all this loveli-

ness over the back of the car, and not missed for several hours, until one has had plenty of time to absorb the scenery, then, well then it might be monotonous![33]

The safari continued to either Rock Lake or Deep Lake, depending on whose account you believe. *The Fort Myers Press*, which gave few details, said they went to Rocky Lake (thought to be Rock Lake). Charles Edison recalled it was Deep Lake. Whichever is correct, it was a place Madeleine described as "a hammock of palmettos and live oak trees by the side of a nice reedy little lake."[34] Charles recalled it as a pond, but that no one had ever found the bottom. The vegetation seemed very "jungly" around the lake. There Ford and Charles found an abandoned flat-bottom boat. Ford had his .22 target pistol and while the others put up the tents, Ford and Charles went out in the leaky old boat. They observed several snakes lying up on the grass in the hyacinths. Ford would position himself about 25 feet from the snakes and then pop those snakes in the eye. Charles said Ford was a crack shot and managed to shoot the heads off three of them. When they returned to camp and reported their activities to the ladies, one of them suggested they leave then and go home.[35]

One of the guides killed a wild turkey and fried it for supper.

Campsite in Big Cypress.
Courtesy of Edison-Ford Winter Estates.

Madeleine thought it very good indeed. The guides put up the tents and lined the ground with palmetto leaves so that blankets could be spread over them. A special tent was prepared for Thomas and Mina, "a dressy tent with mosquito netting and all the comforts of home."[36] With great pride, the guides then told Mrs. Edison her tent was ready. Realizing there were only two other tents, one large tent for the ladies and a smaller one for the men, Mrs. Edison graciously announced that the special tent set aside for the Edisons would be occupied by their guests, the Fords. As darkness approached, Mina Edison admonished the other campers to collect their things and choose their resting place. Madeleine recalled that no sooner had she "untangled her tooth brush" and entered the large tent than "there broke upon us one of those violent and unusual tropical storms that upon rare occasions make life miserable in this part of the country. Like rabbits before a hunting party the members of the expedition came hurtling one by one into the tent."[37] By the time the full fury of the storm arrived, the ladies' tent contained everybody but Theodore and the guides. Theodore was later found wrapped in mosquito netting in a pool of water in the Ford tent, while the guides were asleep in the men's tent. Madeleine stated that, "Conditions in the ladies tent could hardly have been improved upon at any tenement 'housing problem' show."[38] Men and women:

> huddled together in wildest confusion. This was enhanced when the ridge pole gave way and the side of the tent nearest the rain came loose from its moorings. Mother and Father sat on the sides to keep them down and Charles held up the ridge pole until something more permanent could be devised for it. Of course the tide was rising steadily outside and the blankets near the loose wing of the tent were soaked—but we were all very merry and whiled away the hours quoting epitaphs to each other—and singing songs of sunshine and green fields.[39]

When a lull in the storm occurred, Mina urged the Fords to make a break for their tent. Madeleine thought her mother had

Edisons and Fords with Burroughs at camp table. Bottle on table is
Poland Water, always on Ford's table.

Courtesy of Edison-Ford Winter Estates.

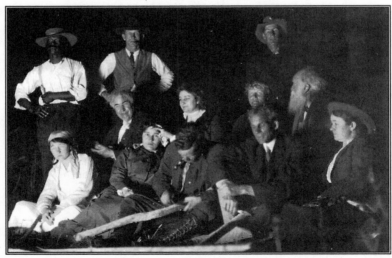

Night scene of the the campers.
Front row: Bessie (last name unknown), Madeleine, Charles, Ford,
Clara; second row: Edison, Mina, Lucy Bogue, Burroughs;
third row: Sam Thompson, Frank Carson and Len Hibble.

Courtesy of Edison-Ford Winter Estates.

not realized that the tent deluxe had no sides and no cots, but rather bedding right on the ground.[40] One wonders what the guides had in mind when they first served up the grander tent to Mina and her husband. Meanwhile back in the tent first intended to be the ladies' tent, Burroughs rolled into a blanket in one corner and Edison in the other. Mina and "Bogey" (Lucy Bogue) lay in a row next to Edison, and Bessie "came tumbling after," recalled Madeleine.[41] "That left Charles and Edsel and me still swimmin. . . . Edsel brought in one of the automobile cushions to act as a raft and after taking soundings all over the tent lay down where the water was shallowest."[42] Madeleine found an island in the middle of the tent while Charles jokingly persuaded Edsel to switch positions with him since Edsel was taller, and should the water rise, it would not be over his head. As the night progressed, Madeleine thought she felt the water coming up again and so sent out flood warnings. The wind was howling. Father awoke and remarked that "he'd caught cold from the cold cream he used on his face," a rather odd remark given the circumstances, but nevertheless a part of Madeleine's recollection.[43] About the same time, Madeleine heard a rattling of paper under Charles' raft and a "thrashing about and squirming hither and yon was taking place at his anchorage."[44] Although strangely curious, she was too exhausted to investigate. In the morning she learned that something on the tent above Charles' head had given way and let down a pattering stream of water on the leather cushion and he had thought it was a rattlesnake. She remembered making fervent prayers for daylight but had finally gone to sleep from pure exhaustion. When daylight did arrive, she found a "vague and dripping world entirely surrounded by a howling gale."[45] The intrepid explorers began to emerge from their soggy beds, Burroughs in a wet "red blanket still clinging to him like a piece of sea weed," the Michigan guests from the tent deluxe clad in similar array.[46] Bessie would not exit the tent until her clothes dried. Mr. Ford obliged by stretching a makeshift clothes line between two cabbage palms where Bessie's clothes and all the red blankets could be hung to dry.

As Madeleine described it, the guides started breakfast and somehow managed to build a fire. Everyone "remarked how well they had slept and what a lovely thing it is to live in the open. Mr. Burroughs suggested spending the summer. Mrs. Ford said she felt so selfish being entirely under water in the deluxe tent while we were only half covered. She said that "after a night of such liquid refreshment there was nothing she did not feel strong enough to bear, and demanded to be taken to see a snake forthwith."[47]

After breakfast, one of the guides killed a deer "and all the rest of us had our work cut out for us trying to keep the news from Theodore."[48] Theodore was a lifelong environmentalist and animal lover not likely to appreciate the death of one of God's creatures.

The trip began on Saturday and finished on the following Monday, providing for two nights out. Whether the stormy night at Deep Lake fell on Saturday or Sunday is not clear. Madeleine's account seems to suggest it happened on the first night. She states, "By and by—along about next Monday, we were asked to vote on whether we wanted to go home or stay another night. There are two expert swimmers among us it seems, for on a secret ballot there were two votes marked 'stay'—Majority ruled however, and we struck camp, lurching 54 miles back to our own clump of palm trees."[49] Charles recollection of the incident was similar:

> The next morning there was a council of war about whether to go on or whether to turn home. Everybody except Burroughs and my father and I had had enough. They all wanted to go home. This rain had drenched the bed that they'd been in, and they just couldn't see much of this camping life and these snakes. Father put up kind of a weak battle, and so it ended up with Burroughs and I being the only ones who wanted to go on. We couldn't go on if the rest of them went back, so we finally had to give the thing up. But we did get quite a ways down in the big cypress, and it was wild country—wild turkey and deer and all sorts of animals all through there. It was down toward Immokalee.[50]

Madeleine gave attribution to Charles as one of several poetic guns who blazed forth to lighten the darkness of the wilderness.

Camping

A Perfect Day

O this the end of a perfect day
And the end of a journey too
And if you are as wet as I think you are
Then I am as wet as you
For my clothes are soaked
And my blanket's damp
And the rain is leaking through
And if this is the end of a perfect day
Let us hope those days are few![51]

Charles wrote another untitled poem:

Consumption, pneumonia and grip
Will be the result of this trip
We'll all die together
From the inclement weather
On the door-mat of Heaven we'll drip.[52]

In his biography of Charles Edison, John Venable recounts a story that took place in or near Fort Myers and possibly as a side trip in one of the Fords while on the camping expedition. It seems that Charles and Edsel Ford ventured on an outing in the woods in a Model T when the car overheated and refused to run. They emptied the contents of a coffee jug into the thirsty radiator but the Tin Lizzie ran for only a short time before stalling again. Desperate, the boys did what seemed obvious, they urinated into the radiator, which was sufficient to get them back to safety.[53]

Although a week-long cruise around Lake Okeechobee had been planned for the Edison guests, it appears they canceled when the Fords and Burroughs decided to return to their homes on the afternoon train of March 10.[54] Before leaving the group did make a trip upriver aboard the *Ada May*, and went fishing around Four Mile Island.[55]

The Edisons invited local school children to visit them at Seminole Lodge to greet Mr. Burroughs on March 10.[56] When Ford and Burrough's early departure interfered with those plans,

The *Ada May* at the Edison dock.
Courtesy of Southwest Florida Historical Society.

the two men arranged to visit the children at the Andrew D. Gwynne Institute, the local public grammar school, just before their departure. There they went into each room, greeting the children, and Burroughs gave a short talk on his book, *Afoot and Afloat,* about his adventures in Yellowstone Park with former President Theodore Roosevelt. [57]

While still at Seminole Lodge, Madeleine wrote Edsel Ford to thank him for "her share of that 'jim—glorious' box of candy—which is disappearing rapidly under our careful supervision."[58] She told Edsel that they had supper at the end of the dock so her letter was being written there because Theodore insisted they spend the evening over water. Someone built a fire in the brick oven near the dock and she said jokingly that because of that the letter might never reach him. She told Edsel they had had some excitement that day because the resident bees had swarmed, but that the caretaker Zeeman and others had managed to chase them off. She spoke of the delicious orange blossom honey they had all enjoyed; she would love to send some to him but that it would probably ooze out all over the U. S. Postal Service. She told him not to forget that he was to come to her wedding in June.

W. G. Bee, sales manager for Edison Storage Battery Company, wrote Edison in Fort Myers to say that he was just back from Detroit and that Ford sent his regards.[59] He related that Ford had told him, "Billy, I had the best time of my life" while in Fort Myers. Bee said Ford wanted to know if Edison wished to dispose of the steam engine, which had been replaced by a gas engine at Fort Myers. Ford wanted to buy it partly due to sentiment and partly because he needed just such an engine at his farm. Edison scribbled a note to Bee on the margin, "Billy, This engine is absolutely no use to me & has a sentimental value to Ford. I will ship it to him, but as a present. If he was here now he would be delighted. We catch from 2 to 4 shark a day off dock & tarpon are running in the River."[60]

Three weeks after the Fords' departure, Ford wrote Edison thanking him on behalf of himself and Mrs. Ford and Edsel, for a very pleasant vacation, "in fact the most enjoyable one we have ever had. . . ."[61] He reported steady progress in the factory with 1,000 cars being produced each day and sent an article describing a new kind of worm gear and asking Edison for an opinion on its merits.[62]

The same letter recalled a subject discussed in Fort Myers concerning smoking. Edison had opined to Ford on the harmful effect of cigarettes. He asked Edison to advise him what injurious effect was produced and to what extent it was damaging. He continued in a postscript with a question about the chemical produced by cigarette smoke or by the burning of the paper. "I should like a special letter from you in your own writing explaining the above, and with your permission will use it expecting to do considerable good among our employees and others addicted to the habit."[63] Edison obliged with the following:

April 26, 1914
Friend Ford,

> The injurious agent in cigarettes comes principally from the burning paper wrapper. The substance thereby formed is called "Acrolein."
>
> It has a violent action on the nerve centers, producing degeneration of the cells of the brain, which is quite rapid among boys.
>
> Unlike most narcotics this degeneration is permanent and uncontrollable.

I employ no person who smokes cigarettes.
Yours
Thos. A. Edison[64]

The press criticized Edison for his statement about acrolein, with the charge that his information was obtained second-hand. Edison wrote the editor explaining that he, Edison, had almost lost his life as a result of breaking a glass tube filled with acrolein. On another occasion, one of his assistants almost died while experimenting with that substance. For more than two years, "I experimented continuously on the burning, carbonizing and distilling of all kinds of paper in the attempt to make suitable filaments therefrom for incandescent lamps. I believe that I can justly claim that some of my information is not second hand."[65]

1915

A disastrous fire on December 9, 1914, in West Orange prevented the Edisons from returning to Fort Myers in 1915. The fire originated in a shed filled with inflammable motion-picture film. The original phonograph building, a wooden structure, burned to the ground, followed by thirteen other buildings. Edison lost the capacity to manufacture phonograph records, but the laboratory and outbuildings containing the research and development area, and the library and office were saved. Edison vowed to rebuild and he did, with structures of reinforced concrete. Three months after the first fire, a second fire broke out, destroying a room where phonograph records were stored.[66]

Although it first appeared that Edison might still come to Florida in 1915, he did not. Harvie Heitman received word Edison would arrive on March 15.[67] The letter from Edison had apparently been written before the second fire broke out, and that fire may have been the deciding factor.

In July 1915, Mina Edison wrote to Clara Ford, thanking her for the hospitality shown her son, Theodore, on a recent visit Theodore had made to the Ford home in Dearborn, Michigan.[68] She invited the Fords to visit them again at Seminole Lodge and recalled the happy times during their visit to Fort Myers in the previous year. "The red blankets were carefully packed away, ready for our next camping trip. You really liked it after all, didn't you?"[69] She also mentioned Burroughs, who was not well at the time of the letter, and added, "He did seem to enjoy his time there so much."[70] Finally, she mentioned the new house into which she assumed the Fords were now well settled. This was a reference to Fair Lane, located on the River Rouge in the woods near Dearborn. Actually, the Fords did not move into their new home until January 1916.[71]

Though Fort Myers was not to be visited in 1915, the Edisons and son Charles traveled to San Francisco for the Panama-Pacific Exposition in October.[72] There they were joined by Ford, who had a small assembly line on exhibit at the Exposition where eighteen to twenty-five cars were produced in a period of three hours.[73] Edison had arrived for a special celebration of Edison Day on October 21, the anniversary of the invention of the first practical incandescent light bulb. There Edison and Ford rode in an open car in a huge parade honoring Edison.[74]

14

The Mangoes

*Where else in the world have two of the greatest
men of the century lived side by side?*
—James Newton

1915

While disastrous fires raged in the Edison compound in New
Jersey in late 1914 and early 1915, war was raging in Europe. The
heir to the throne of Austria-Hungary had ventured over to
Sarajevo, the capital of the Austrian province of Bosnia, in June
1914. While in an open touring car, he and his wife were shot
and killed by a student who, it was suspected, had carried out the
deed under the sponsorship of neighboring Serbia. The war was
on in Europe, although the United States would not join the
Allies until 1917.

Ford, a committed pacifist, held a strong desire to avoid the
rush to armed preparedness and the stockpiling of arms. Late in
1915, he began to talk to Madame Rosika Schwimmer, a
Hungarian touring the United States touting world peace and
her ideas for accomplishing it.[1] Ford became a convert and
impulsively agreed to send delegates to peace conventions in

The Mangoes.
Courtesy of Edison-Ford Winter Estates.

some of the remaining neutral countries of Europe. He arranged passage for himself and other delegates on a "Peace Ship," the *Oscar II*, and less than a month later, the ship left New York for Oslo, Norway. The mission proved a colossal failure and a blow to Ford's ego. Dissention reigned among the delegates. The skeptic press, which began the voyage with preconceived notions of Ford's naiveté, changed their opinion during the trip.[2] They became mightily impressed with Ford's sincerity, although they felt he had been grossly misled by the egotistical Madame Schwimmer and by the absence of a strategy by the others. Ford became sick as he disembarked the ship in Oslo and remained in bed for about five days before abandoning the mission and returning to New York. When he arrived, America seemed to forgive him for his naiveté in judgment and loved him for having risked his life and a considerable amount of money in the pursuit of peace. In his home state of Michigan, Ford won the Republican presidential primary in 1916—further evidence of his popularity.[3]

1916

Though the United States remained neutral for the first three years of the war, the defense budget and the Army grew dramatically. The country felt the terrible effect of the German blockade and the deadly capabilities of German submarines on its merchant marine and passenger vessels. The *Lusitania* had been sunk off the coast of Ireland on May 7, 1915—six months before the Peace Ship sailed—with 1,198 lives lost.

President Wilson created a Naval Consulting Board and despite Ford's concerns over the slippery slope of armed preparedness, his friend and mentor Edison agreed to head it.[4] The inspiration for the Naval Consulting Board came from a *New York Times* interview with Edison in 1915 in which Edison recommended the establishment of a department where the ideas of Americans, both military and civilian, could be developed to meet the conditions of warfare then being pursued in Europe. The board consisted of scientists who would bring the latest technology to the nation's wartime defense. Special emphasis would be given to the submarine, the dreaded naval armament of the Germans. Edison left the helm of Thomas Alva Edison, Inc. to become president of the Naval Consulting Board. His son Charles, then twenty-six, took his father's place at the company.[5]

Edison's duties on the board do not appear to have interfered with a four-week stay in Fort Myers in 1916.[6] While in Fort Myers, the local Fort Myers Ford dealership received a telegram from E. G. Liebold, Ford's strong-willed and influential personal secretary, directing it to present a touring car to Edison, with Ford's compliments.[7] The dealer then wrote Ford that a touring car had been delivered and that Edison had paid for the car with his check for $482.75, and that when the dealer realized it was to be complimentary, he refunded the amount and obtained a receipt from Edison.[8]

While in Fort Myers, Edison told his friend E. L. Evans, a noted local tarpon fishing enthusiast, that he was not happy with fishing that season.[9] Edison reportedly blamed the disappearance of the tarpon from the waters adjacent to his home on the netters—the commercial fisherman—who were depriving the mullet and other smaller fish of their natural feeding grounds. Edison

Edison stands by 1916 Model T given him by Ford.
Courtesy of Edioson-Ford Winter Estates.

said fishing remained Fort Myers' big attraction. He compared fishing to golf, but said golf was available everywhere while few places were blessed with fishing as rewarding as in the Caloosahatchee and its adjacent waters.

In mid-April, Edison invited the entire Captiva Island Huron School for Boys for a half-day visit at Seminole Lodge.[10] The inventor entertained the boys, showed them through the laboratory and grounds of the estate, and provided refreshments on the veranda of his home.

On April 23, the Edisons departed for New Jersey.[11]

Before the Edisons left Fort Myers, Ford, who was then in Michigan, received a letter from Robert W. Smith of New York City.[12] Smith related he had just placed his winter home, The Mangoes, adjacent to Edison's winter home, on the market. Since Ford had visited Edison in Fort Myers and had no doubt noticed the adjoining property, Smith thought he might be interested in acquiring it. The property was described as having 177 feet of frontage on McGregor and a depth of 450 feet to the Caloosahatchee River. The property contained about a hundred bearing grapefruit trees and fifty orange trees. In addition there were mango trees, paw-paws, lemons, limes, guavas, tangerines, coconuts, bananas and a vegetable plot. Smith recounted to Ford that it was the best-built structure in Fort Myers, as a result of Smith's taking his superintendent to Fort Myers to build the house about five years earlier. When Smith and his superintendent arrived, a tornado touched down in the community, tearing things up pretty generally, and as a result the superintendent doubled all the framing timbers of the house so that it was of very heavy construction. The four-bedroom house was equipped with electric lights, Venetian windows on the first floor, hardwood floors, tapestry wall coverings, beamed ceilings, and furnishings. Two photographs were enclosed with the request that they be returned if Ford was not interested.

Within a week, Ford replied that he was not interested, since he did not visit Florida enough to warrant a purchase there.[13] A month later, Ford had his secretary write to Smith, asking the price of the property.[14] Smith replied promptly, advising that his agent would contact Ford shortly.[15] The agent mentioned that negotiations for a sale had begun with other parties and he was not sure how far the matter had proceeded.

A few days later Ford received the price of $25,000, but he

Interior view of The Mangoes in 1916.
Courtesy of Edison-Ford Winter Estates.

was also advised that another party was considering the property and would be calling Smith in a month with his decision.[16] The agent mentioned that he personally preferred that Ford buy the property and that this sentiment was also that of the people of Fort Myers. He told Ford a company had been organized to build a first-class 18-hole golf course and that a fine new hotel in Fort Myers was in the offing.[17]

Ten days later, Ford wrote for more photographs and news about the other individual looking at the property.[18] Smith responded that the property remained for sale pending the arrival of the other individual interested in the property.[19] More photographs arrived and on May 26, Ford telegraphed Smith's agent with an offer of $20,000.[20] Two days later the agent notified Ford that Smith had agreed to split the difference at $22,500.[21] Ford wired back he would not meet the counteroffer.[22] Two days later, on May 31, the agent wired Ford that he had persuaded Smith to accept $20,000 and asked for instructions where to send the deed with draft attached.[23] The telegram ended with "three cheers" and a statement that Fort Myers was proud to have him become a winter resident. He said that if Smith had refused the lower price, the agent had been prepared to take up a public subscription among the local residents for the difference.

1917

In 1917 the war in Europe raged on and Edison found himself immersed in research for the Naval Consulting Board. Hence there was no time for a winter retreat to Fort Myers.[24] The United States finally entered the war on April 6 after Germany commenced unrestricted submarine attacks on all vessels on the high seas. Germany's unbridled aggression signaled to the American public the coming of war. These disturbing events no doubt had a chilling effect on any plans by the Edisons for making the trip south.

As Germany announced its sink-all-ships policy, Ford acquired a beautiful yacht, the *Sialia*, a sleek 202-foot vessel built in 1913, from James K. Stewart, one of the partners in Stewart-

Warner Speedometer Company. It was an ocean-going, twin-screw steel schooner with clipper-style bow and overhung stern powered by triple expansion oil-fired steam turbines of 1250 horse power and a fuel capacity of 150 tons, equipped with a one-kilowatt Telefunken wireless communication system.[25]

Ford wanted to personally investigate Cuba as a source of coal and iron ore.[26] He avoided public transportation, and a yacht allowed him to make the trip in privacy. The name *Sialia* was the ornithological name for the Eastern Bluebird of the United States, the "Bluebird of Happiness." A month after the purchase Ford, joined by his wife, his sister-in-law, her husband and their two daughters, and by John Burroughs, embarked on a cruise from Charleston, South Carolina. Ford took the party on the family railway car, the Fair Lane, from Dearborn to Charleston by way of Roxbury, New York, where Burroughs boarded. After two days at sea, the vessel reached Miami and the party stopped briefly for a visit with Harvey Firestone at his winter residence.[27] From there they proceeded around the tip of Florida and up the west coast to Punta Rassa.[28] The Caloosahatchee channel was not sufficient for the *Sialia*, hence the party made its way by motor launch up the river, where the Fords and their guests spent the day at The Mangoes, Ford's newly acquired winter home.[29] From there they returned to the *Sialia* and sailed for Cuba.

No coal or iron ore transactions with Cuba resulted from the trip. On the return from Cuba, a violent storm arose and none of the passengers was able to remain on his or her feet. To make matters worse, the ship received notice on its wireless that it had been enrolled for Naval Coast Guard Defense.[30] Ford had originally paid $250,000 for the yacht and the United States Navy Special Board for Patrol Vessels appraised it at $220,000. Ford graciously accepted the lower appraisal, adding he was glad to be of service. After the war Ford repurchased the *Sialia* from the government for $168,500. Refurbishing added an additional $150,000 to its cost.[31]

Ford had never been satisfied with the speed of the steam-powered *Sialia*. It had a cruising speed of 14 knots and a top speed of 16 knots. His giant cargo ships on the Great Lakes had

Ford's yacht *Sialia* made two trips to the Fort Myers area, anchoring off the Sanibel Lighthouse.

Courtesy of Henry Ford Museum and Greenfield Village.

opposed piston diesel engines and he decided he would like his yacht powered by diesels of similar design. To accomplish this, it was necessary to cut the vessel in two, add a 21-foot section amidships, and install the twin diesels. The yacht then measured 223 feet in length and the cost of the renovation was $1,600,000. The result was disheartening, since the *Sialia* was slightly slower after the transformation than before.[32]

1918

J. B. Parker, who operated Parker's Book Store in Fort Myers, ran an advertisement in *The Fort Myers Press* asking all patriotic Fort Myers citizens to "give $1.00 to secure music aboard one of our Government's Transports."[33] Smaller print explained that Parker's had been asked by the Transport Service to have Fort Myers place an Edison Army and Navy Model Phonograph and eighteen assorted Re-Creations (records) aboard one of the troopships. The ad made it clear that the vendor, a licensed Edison Dealer, was handling the matter at cost.

A telegram dated January 5, 1918, announced the plans of

Fort Myers' most esteemed citizen to arrive in Fort Myers in the middle of January.[34] The telegram implored Heitman to arrange for chickens, to have the house, bedding and rugs thoroughly aired, and to make sure the dock was in good condition but at the least possible cost. A letter asked that the bathing pool be cleaned and put in useable shape.[35] Heitman apparently communicated some significant expense concerning the maintenance of the dock, for letters from Edison's secretary followed asking him to spend as little on the dock as possible, since Edison wanted to rebuild the dock soon and did not want expensive repairs to the existing structure.[36]

Notice of a pending arrival ran in the paper prompting the Board of Trade to plan a rally at which representatives of each state would contribute their sentiments toward the venerated Wizard.[37] Although elaborate plans were made, the honoree never arrived, nor was a ceremony held. The *Press* reported the preparations for the event, but then failed to mention in subsequent editions why it never occurred.

In fact Edison was in the Florida Keys doing work for the Naval Consulting Board.[38] His son Theodore was also working for the Navy but on a separate project involving Theodore's own inventions. Beginning early in 1917, Edison occupied a specially converted yacht in Long Island Sound and also in the Florida Keys conducting experiments for the Navy.[39] His work resulted in forty-five inventions and plans for detecting submarines, torpedoes, and airplanes, the location of guns, the blinding of submarines and periscopes and the camouflaging of ships, the development of a sea anchor for quickly turning ships to avoid submarines, and a plan for night shipping to avoid submarines.[40] None of the plans were adopted by the Navy.

Mina Edison spent time in Key West with her husband and she also accompanied him on the working yacht in Long Island Sound.[41] She wrote to Charles from the Key West Naval Station, describing a passenger boat that ran from Key West to Fort Myers.[42] No doubt she had plans to leave Edison in the Keys and visit Fort Myers for part of the winter. "When I do go father dear wont seem so far away." She added that she hoped he would go with her to Fort Myers for a little while, but "I suppose that I

Edison at Key West while working with Naval Consulting Board.
Courtesy of Florida State Archives.

am doomed to disappointment," and she was. She also told of a recent fishing trip in the Keys when "Papa caught 30 Kingfish in 3 hours." She complained of the sea swells, which she referred to as ground swells, and said that the "Little Caloosahatchee is my fishing ground."

Mina Edison did get to Fort Myers during the 1918 season, presumably aboard the boat from Key West she had mentioned to Charles. Charles wrote his mother while she was in Fort Myers to tell her he was about to take his first vacation at Seminole Lodge since beginning work at Edison Industries.[43] He had been rejected from military service because of his poor hearing and was then suffering from asthma, neuralgia and an exhausting job.[44] Charles persuaded his mother to invite Carolyn Hawkins, the woman he had been courting since 1912, to join her in Florida as a guest.[45] Miss Hawkins was coordinator for the 2,200-bed Harvard Medical Unit, which had been sent overseas to handle the wounded and sick on the front. She managed to keep a cadre of doctors and supplies moving out and overseas. She too was close to burnout.

On arrival with Carolyn Hawkins in Fort Myers, Charles

decided it was time to pop the question. While strolling on the dock at Seminole Lodge on a moonlit night, Charles asked her, "Do you want a large wedding?" Her answer was no, so they decided to be married then and there.[46] His father was in the Keys on a ship somewhere and Theodore was also in the Keys but on a remote island. Madeleine was in Washington awaiting delivery of her second child.[47]

Carolyn's family was also scattered. When the two walked in from the dock, they told Charles' mother of their decision. She inquired when the event would take place and Charles said they weren't doing anything for the next two or three days, so telegrams announcing the nuptials went out to family members post haste.[48] Edison wired back oddly, "If it's going to be, then the sooner the better. Anyway, it won't be worse than life in the front line trenches. You have my blessings."[49] The couple settled on a small wedding, with only Charles' mother, the butler and long-time family friend and governess in attendance.[50] They didn't want the local residents to hear of the plan, which would have alerted the press and made things difficult for them. When the couple went downtown to purchase a ring, two reporters pursued them and they had to engage in diversionary tactics. The reporters "spotted us uptown when we were trying to buy a ring, and kept following us. We chose somewhere else and tried to shake them off, but they kept pursuing us."[51] They were also looking for a license, but the office which they supposed was the marriage license office turned out to be the telephone office. Of all places in a small town to inquire about a marriage license, the telephone exchange was the worst. Next they had to find a minister. In his recorded interview, Charles said they wanted a minister from Arcadia. Charles did not reveal the name of the minister, but *The Fort Myers Press* reported that the Reverend F. A. Shore, rector of St. Luke's Episcopal Church in Fort Myers, conducted the service.[52] Records at St. Luke's confirm that F. A. Shore, the rector at the time, performed the wedding.[53] There is no explanation for the reference to an Arcadia minister; Father Shore was the rector in Fort Myers, not Arcadia.

The bride found a white dress and a wedding bouquet in the forty-eight hours or so before the wedding, and Charles recalled he had never seen anything lovelier than his bride's bouquet. Oddly, he singled out the bouquet, saying nothing of the dress or for that matter, his bride, in the interview. Charles told his interviewer that after the engagement but before the marriage, the couple had gone to the Royal Palm Hotel to a dance. At the dance was a young man who took "quite a shine to my future bride and had given her quite a rush."[54] When the couple went for the marriage license, the judge turned out to be the young man who had paid so much attention to the bride-to-be.

Charles recalled the wedding location in the yard at Seminole Lodge. "As you came out of the house, there was a little short brick walk, and at the end of that little walk was a big camphor tree and a cinnamon tree. Up near the house was this large Japanese umbrella tree, and so it made a very nice setting, we thought, to have the ceremony back up the cinnamon and the camphor tree. We got a little carpet and rolled it out, and a little altar with two candles burning. It was a very lovely setting."[55] The date was March 27. The couple decided to honeymoon with a drive to the Gulf in the Model T, where Charles hoped to catch a couple of fish, cook them on the beach and return to Seminole Lodge. Regrettably, the mosquitoes forced

Seminole Lodge. A view of the Edison residence from the river side. A duplicate structure to the right (south) of the one shown was known as the Guest House. The Guest House was originally the home of Edison friend, Ezra Gilliland.

Courtesy of Florida State Archives.

them off the beach, so "we gradually mosied on back through the sand roads and got back to town. I then took my wife to Hunter's Drugstore and bought her an ice cream soda—that was the honeymoon."[56]

While Charles honeymooned in Fort Myers, Theodore, still on an island in the Florida Keys, worked on a promising invention of his own.[57] It was a "close range operation which was a way of getting large quantities of explosives carried short distances with a very light apparatus."[58] Though his father's accommodations were quite comfortable, Theodore was based on Man Key, an otherwise uninhabited island, from March 4 until about May 22.[59] The camp had five sleeping tents, a mess tent, a 14-by-32 foot work shop, electric lights (provided by a generator) and board sidewalks.[60] Mr. Werner, a friend named George, two sailors and a cook composed the experimenting crew.[61] Nature furnished birds, several scorpions, an octopus, a tarantula, violent storms and abundant sand fleas at dusk. The crew had a wonderful cook whose pies were noteworthy.[62]

Theodore wrote to his mother frequently from the island. Mother Edison had sent him a box of grapefruit from Seminole Lodge, which arrived on his third day on the island. He thanked her by letter and told of the sand fleas, which came out for about an hour at sunset and "bite like ."[63] He said he'd try to get up to Fort Myers to see her but had his doubts. Sunday was observed by working half a day. The crew played poker and craps in free moments. Theodore told his mother of his wins but nothing of his losses, if any.

He also bet on successful shots with the weapon the crew was testing.[64] He told his mother of successes in experimenting with two small machines. They also made test shots with a device he described only as a big engine and wheels. "Our biggest wheel went 500 feet when shot at 1,000 revolutions per minute. This shows us that at 3,000 R. P. M. we could shoot about 1,500 feet in sand."[65] Charles gave a better description of the device as related to him by his brother:

> It was sort of a fly wheel effect. He had a little
> gasoline motor on the frame, and then this shaft
> on which this wheel revolved. The wheel was

maybe four inches wide, and filled with TNT.
They would get it up just this side of a point in
speed where it would fly apart, and get it up to a
terrific velocity over a short period of time by
this little engine—a motor cycle type of
engine—and then they would pull the shaft out.
The wheel would drop and start spinning ahead,
much the same as a tire when it comes off your
car at high speed; it will keep rolling for a long
distance. This thing did that, and it would go
several hundred yards. On account of the speed
it was going, it had a gyroscopic action and you
couldn't divert it. It would hit a shell hole, for
instance, and dig its way out of the shell hole
and go right on in a straight line.[66]

Madeleine, writing from her home in New Jersey and in typical tongue-in-cheek fashion, related to her mother that as she
had seen no fragments in the air, she concluded, "that Theodore
hasn't blown himself up as yet."[67]

Theodore inherited his mother's fondness for bird life, and
in one of his letters he described an Oven Bird or Myrtle Warbler
that came into the tent.[68] His friend Fitzpatrick caught a fly and
the little bird sat on his hand and ate it. Theodore told how he
attracted island birds by leaving a dead fish out in the sun until
it attracted flies, attracting the birds as well.

Two weeks after Charles' wedding, Theodore told his mother
that "father came clear out to the island" on the *Sachem* but the
launch had broken down and they could not bring him ashore.[69]
On April 23, father arrived again and this time came ashore.[70]
Theodore sent one of his biggest shells through extra strong barbed
wire to a distance of 1,010 feet, but the next shot did not do so well.
The one "shot seemed to satisfy father and he outlined some tests
which may take us some time to finish."[71]

On April 1, 1918, Mina Edison, son Charles, and his bride
left Fort Myers aboard the steamer *City of Philadelphia* for Key
West en route to their homes in West Orange, New Jersey.[72]
Presumably they managed to rendezvous with Edison in Key
West, though probably not with Theodore. Although they could

have gone by steamer to New York City, they probably went by train since Flagler had extended rail service along Florida's east coast all the way to Key West. Carolyn returned to Boston, where she wound up her work with the Harvard Medical Unit, and Charles returned to the plant in West Orange to fill orders for batteries, bomb sites, dictating machines, chemicals and special munitions.

The war, politics and the absence of his esteemed neighbor in Fort Myers kept Ford from visiting his new winter home during the first season after the purchase. Ford remained a pacifist after the war began, but with a big shift in his attitude toward defense. As his country's involvement in the war became more evident, his patriotism motivated him to accelerate the production of war machinery. His pacifist notions gave way to duty and country. Six thousand ambulances and 33,000 cars and trucks were sold to American and allied governments at a 15 percent discount.[73] Ford produced 3,940 Liberty airplane engines by war's end. He made a massive effort to produce Eagle submarine patrol boats at the River Rouge plant, but the war ended just as they were coming into production. Ford also furnished helmets, caissons, armor plate for tanks, submarine detectors and tanks. Because of his valiant war effort, coupled with the Five Dollar Day, Ford's popularity in the nation increased significantly.

Meantime, Ford made a run for the U. S. Senate seat from Michigan as an independent. President Wilson encouraged him to run. He saw Ford as the only Wilson and League of Nations man capable of winning in Michigan. In the race, Ford maintained the position, "if they want to elect me let them do so, but I won't make a penny's investment."[74] He didn't and they didn't, but he lost by fewer than 2,200 votes to a Republican, Truman H. Newberry.[75]

15

Peacetime

The arrival of Mr. and Mrs. Thomas A. Edison in Fort Myers
for the winter season is always an occasion of
felicitation for the people of the city and county,
particularly is it true this year, when it is
known that Mr. Edison is to have a well earned
rest from his two years of labor for the
government in valuable war work.
—The Fort Myers Press

1919

With the war over, the country yearned for normalcy. The war effort had heated the economy, boosting post-war sales of the Edison phonograph, which had been on a decline during the war.[1] Some special phonographs had been made for entertaining troops on the transport vessels, but the phonograph works had for the most part been involved in the production of other war materials.

Exhausted from nearly two years devoted exclusively to war preparedness for the Navy, the seventy-two-year-old Edison fervently anticipated the 1919 winter season. During the year, Mr. and Mrs. B. E. Tinstman had taken over the management position from Heitman. Mrs. Tinstman had the sole charge for a time due to the absence of her husband. Corresponding with Edison's secretary, she advised that there was no veterinarian in Fort

Myers and thus no way to give the tubercular test to the cow that would supply the milk during the upcoming visit.[2] She stated that her personal physician had consented to give the test, but that he had made clear to her that this was not in his regular line of duty. A handwritten postscript on the typed letter said that everything was being rushed to completion in anticipation of the arrival of the Edisons.

When finally able to leave New Jersey, Edison told the press, "I am feeling great. I have always taken pretty good care of myself, and judged by my ancestors I am really only a middle-aged man now. My great grandfather lived to be 104, my grand-father was 102 when he died and my father reached 94."[3] The paper reported that Mr. Edison made a rapid calculation and commented that their three ages totaled 300 and that he hoped to maintain the century average.

When asked about his business interests he answered:

We are behind on our orders in most lines and doing our best to catch up. I should not be going away to Florida if my industries were not in ship shape condition. My son, Charles, managed the business during the two years I was engaged in war work, and when I got back I was very much pleased to see how well he had handled things. I have gradually developed an organization which relieves me from the details of business but, of course, I keep in general touch with conditions. . . . I also have a good bunch of men in the experimental laboratories, who are wide awake to the needs of our various industries. I feel that I am now going to be free to devote most of my time to special research work, and when I get back from Florida I intend to take up some work which I have long desired to do. My ambition is to lay out a line of work that will keep my labo-ratories busy for the next hundred years.[4]

With the Edisons for the 1919 season were Madeleine, Theodore, Mina's younger sister Mary, her husband, William Wallace Nichols, and a nurse. Madeleine's baby boy, born just after the wedding of Charles and Carolyn, was also present, along with his older brother. Charles and his bride were busy with the Edison business interests in New Jersey and remained there. Charles had been ill during this time and Mina's letters implored him to take care of himself, get stronger and come to Fort Myers where he could fully recover.[5] She added that, "Father says to come, so don't hesitate." Charles did not oblige.

Life in Fort Myers was "laid back" with only occasional excitement. Mina wrote to Charles and Carolyn that after a fine swim in the pool, they had a bad fright when two "aeroplanes" came flying over the house, one emitting smoke and its engine missing.[6] Just then, Lena, the maid, came running from the house shouting that the aeroplane had fallen and was burning up. Mina said that she ran into the bedroom, picked up the medicine chest, thermos bottle, glass, and whiskey flask and started up the street. Madeleine had also headed for the scene ahead of her mother and had encountered a man in an auto with three hunting dogs. She told the man of the accident, and he said he was a surgeon and would gladly go and help but Madeleine would have to keep his dogs. Madeleine had quite a time trying to hold the dogs. Aunt Mary, Mina's younger sister, had taken the baby from the nurse as she had feared for his life. As it turned out, when Mina reached the scene of the fire, she found it to be a bonfire, not an aeroplane crash, and she was told that the pilot had landed safely in a clearing just ahead.

Mina's letters to Charles and Carolyn were filled with minuscule facts. She told of Uncle Will and Theodore playing chess and cutting wood, and of Aunt Mary swallowing a fish bone at supper.[7] Immediately, Mina wrote, Uncle Will started in to scold her for doing such a silly thing but during the scolding he was administering to her with great affection. "What is that in human nature that causes one to love and scold at the same time," she asked.[8] She told of Madeleine dining and dancing at the Royal Palm Hotel with Uncle Will and Aunt Mary. Theodore, Papa and Mina remained home—Mina relating to Charles, "too much society for us."[9]

The Edisons did receive guests at Seminole Lodge from time to time, among them the Garveys and Mr. and Mrs. Pittman.[10]

They received an invitation from their good friends the Rays for dinner and to observe the dancing at the Royal Palm Hotel.[11] The men did not want to heed the Ray invitation, forcing Mrs. Edison to make excuses for them, but she and Madeleine accepted. Theodore acted as chauffeur and promised to pick them up at 10 P.M. On the stroke of ten Mr. Ray promptly escorted Mina and Madeleine outside to meet Theodore, but Theodore was nowhere to be found. The three walked up First Street to town, then back. Mina was embarrassed. Mr. Ray insisted they go back in and wait. In the meantime, Madeleine telephoned Seminole Lodge and learned that all three men, Papa, Theodore and Will, had gone to the movies and had not returned. Mina was fit to be tied. Finally at 11 P.M., Theodore rolled up, explaining that the movie ended later than expected.[12]

Edison's usage of the laboratory in Fort Myers changed from time to time according to the changing demands of the projects in which he was engaged. Activity in the laboratory in 1919 seemed to be on the wane so Edison decided to eliminate some of the raw material and equipment on hand. Fred Ott, Edison's assistant, was instructed to be on the lookout for materials that could be shipped back to West Orange.[13] On inspection, Ott selected certain material, laboratory equipment and chemicals to be shipped, including the two dynamos that had been shipped south in 1886.[14] Other equipment was sold locally to William H. Ross, a Fort Myers blacksmith located on Hendry Street.[15]

The Edisons left Fort Myers on the Thursday afternoon train on April 10.[16] Following their departure, the Fort Myers crew completed a number of maintenance and improvement projects. A leader was connected to the rainwater tank behind the kitchen so that the contents of that tank would go exclusively for drinking water.[17] To avoid shortages of rainwater used for drinking, a new twenty-five-foot by fifty-foot by six-foot concrete cistern was built next to the pool.[18] Rainwater collected in the pool could then be transferred for storage in the cistern and replaced by well water used for swimming. A rat hole in the dining room was sealed.[19] Repairs were made to the dock which included encasing the pilings in tile to better preserve them. Work was done on the irrigation system and repairs made to the porch roof.[20] The laboratory was altered so that the space formerly occupied by the boiler became an automobile garage with a new concrete floor.[21]

Pyrene fire extinguishers were ordered for Mrs. Edison's bedroom, the dining room, the sitting room, the kitchen and the garage, and chemical extinguishers were ordered for the caretaker's cottage, the laboratory, the guest house, the residence and the kitchen porch.[22] The fire extinguishers did not arrive when expected, however, Mrs. Tinstman did receive a mysterious box labeled "137 pounds of coffee," which she failed to understand. Before sending the coffee on to the Edisons in New Jersey, it was observed that the box did not have the feel of a load of coffee, so it was opened and lo and behold the fire extinguishers were found and no coffee.[23]

A big September storm threatened the trees, the buildings and the dock. The dock was particularly vulnerable as it was about to have a new deck installed.[24] Fortunately, the carpenter heeded Mrs. Tinstman's urgent request and made repairs to the porch roof, the garage and dock, and secured the lumber on the dock. The storm caused the surface of the water to crest nearly over the dock.

In 1919, Morton Milford acquired *The Fort Myers Press*.[25] Within weeks, an editorial appeared criticizing the length of the Edison dock as a hazard to navigation.[26] According to the paper: "It is passing strange that the peerless inventor of things electrical, a genius whom everyone honors, admires and respects should fail to devise some means of affixing, to his elongated dock, a light that might serve as a warning signal to unsuspecting navigators of small craft particularly that they may steer clear of the obstruction."[27] Mrs. Tinstman blamed the new owner of the paper for the unfavorable editorial, which she thought would never have happened under the previous ownership. Edison had lanterns posted on the end of the dock.[28]

At the request of Mrs. Edison, Mrs. Tinstman ordered bees for the hives at Seminole Lodge, but the beekeeper was unsuccessful in persuading any of the bees to remain on duty. Mrs. Tinstman stated that she would have the beekeeper try again and "if any of the bees would consent to stay," honey would be available when Mrs. Edison returned.[29] That winter Mrs. Edison again requested that guava jelly be made.[30] Mrs. Edison seemed to confirm the opinion of all true Florida "Crackers" that guava jelly is indeed the creme de la creme of the jelly world. Mrs. Tinstman promised to send a crate of mangos as soon as "the nice ones are ready. . . ." A letter from H. D. Silverfriend on Koreshan Unity letterhead promised Mrs. Edison a sample of their Mango Sauce made from green mangos grown on trees from the Edisons' estate.[31]

The original riverfront property purchased in 1885 had been acquired in the name of Thomas A. Edison, but the Gilliland house purchased in 1906 was acquired in Mina's name. In an effort to tidy up his holdings, Edison retitled his remaining Seminole Lodge property in Mina Edison's name.[32]

1920

The Edisons arrived for their annual visit on February 27, 1920. Mrs. Edison's sister, Mary Nichols, Mr. Nichols, and a niece, Rachel Miller, accompanied them.[33] Before they arrived, Tinstman had the rainwater in the pool transferred to the huge new concrete cistern on the north side of the pool, and in preparation for the arrival of the occupants, the pool was filled with well water for swimming. The rainwater in the cistern then became reserve drinking water.

Charles was finishing up his second year of marriage while managing the Edison interests in New Jersey. He wrote to his father in Florida with the details of the business and to express three concerns he had in the management at the disc record operation: first, the elimination of reckless experimentation in the method of production in favor of tried and true methods, second, the introduction of a higher grade of managers and foremen, and finally, the gradual elimination of the variables that upset the manufacturing plan. Charles took six single-spaced typewritten pages to explain the foregoing. The letter ended with an apology for worrying "Father" "in the last few days in 'Paradise'" and with the admonition that "fishing is very much more important than business anyway. . . ." [34] The Edisons were in Fort Myers until late April, although there is little record of their activity.

The cost of maintenance on the premises always seemed excessive and a bitter pill for the Edisons.[35] Nevertheless, the frame houses were thirty-four years old and set in a harsh climate. In 1920, they needed painting. The buildup had to be burned off before new paint could be applied. While burning off the exterior buildup, a corner of the kitchen caught fire, though the flames were quickly extinguished. The torch had sent flames through some rotten wood and ignited the wall.[36]

Once back in New Jersey and throughout the citrus season, Mrs. Edison received over fifty boxes of fruit, sent either to her or to her friends from Seminole Lodge.[37]

1921

The *Fort Myers Tropical News* announced that Thomas A. Edison and family would not be coming to Fort Myers in 1921.[38] Their absence was likely explained by the end of the postwar boom with the phonograph business on hard times with sales lagging and competition increasing.[39] Edison had begun a downsizing of the Edison industries. He and son Charles had some differences in strategy, and in the end, the old man prevailed. Over the next two years, employment in the Edison plants decreased from a 1920 high of 10,000 workers to a 1922 low of 3,000.

Although the Edisons failed to visit Florida in 1921, they took another camping trip with veterans of the 1914 Big Cypress excursion in Florida. In July, they traveled through Maryland for twelve days. The campers were saddened by the absense of John Burroughs, who had died in March. He had been a participant in the 1914 trip in Florida, the 1916 trip to the Adirondacks and Green Mountains of New England, the 1918 trip to the Smoky Mountains and the Shenandoah Valley, the 1919 trip through New England and the 1920 trip to the Catskills in New York. Harvey Firestone and his wife and two sons joined the Maryland adventure, as did President Warren G. Harding. The president's wife intended to participate, but a last-minute illness prevented her from going and cut the president's stay to just overnight. The Fords traveled on board their private yacht, the *Sialia*, from Detroit to Cleveland, where they joined the Firestones and motored from there to Maryland. Maryland was selected because of its proximity to the White House and for the president's convenience. Camping conditions were much less primitive on this and other post–Big Cypress campouts.

Mrs. Edison continued in her frugal mode, inspired by the ever-deepening Florida money pit into which so much of Edison's resources seemed destined. Cryptic annotations written by Mrs. Edison on the margins of letters from Edison's secretary, R. W. Kellow, questioned why Tinstman had gone ahead with the brick walk after he had been told to start no new projects and why had he bought wood when there was a "raft" of it on the place.[40] Kellow patiently answered her questions as best he could, stating that Tinstman had laid off all help except for the caretaker.[41] The wood expense, he wrote, was not for the purchase of wood but for labor in cutting up the wood which was part of the "raft" located on the premises.

In October, Tinstman sent the following telegram:

HIGHEST TIDE IN YEARS ALL DWELLINGS INTACT
FLOORING AND STRINGERS OF DOCK GONE BESIDES
TWO REST HOUSES SALVAGING WHAT TIMBER WE
CAN IMPOSSIBLE TO MAKE INSPECTION OF PAVVIL-
ION [SIC] BUT APPEARS ALL RIGHT FROM SHORE
WILL ARRANGE TO REPLACE FLOORING ON DOCK[42]

A letter gave more detail, reporting a number of trees down but no damage to the houses. It remained too rough to go out to the pavilion to check for damage.[43] The two rest houses were located toward the end of the dock near the pavilion. The electric launch *Reliance* had been torn loose and set adrift. Mr. Capling, "at the risk of his life," went after it and prevented its destruction against the railroad dock downtown. Tinstman suggested that Edison reconsider his decision not to carry tornado insurance.

Mina's brother, J. V. Miller, a Yale graduate and by then an assistant financial executive with Thomas Alva Edison, Inc.,

The 1,500-foot Edison dock.
Courtesy of Edison-Ford Winter Estates.

responded on behalf of the Edisons. Mr. Edison only wanted the docks rebuilt as far as the boat-house, which was 900 feet from the end of the dock where the pavilion was located.[44] "Mr. Edison feels that this year he cannot spend more than to rebuild only to the boat-house and they will use the little launch to go out to the pavilion." Tinstman reported in another letter that the piling had not been damaged and that about three-fifths of the stringers would have to be replaced and all of the floor boards on the dock. He stated the dock stretched 1,500 feet into the river.[45] It is easy to account for the first 1,051 feet of the dock but the record of the remaining 449 feet is more obscure.[46] Extensive dock construction with new piling was done in 1919 and could have been the time when the final addition of 449 feet was made.[47] Tinstman's recollection of a full 1,500 feet in length is validated by other evidence.[48]

Theft of fruit by locals prompted Mrs. Edison to ask why there was no police protection, why only the Edison fruit was stolen, and why so many incorrigible fruit bandits lived in Fort Myers.[49] Tinstman replied there were no more fruit thieves exploiting the Edison grove than anywhere else.[50] He explained that fruit thievery had always been present and that the lateness of the season encouraged "pilfering."

153

Tinstman sent Edison the calling card of John Wanamaker, the department store magnate from Philadelphia.[51] The card included the date when he and several others whose names were scribbled on the card, called at Seminole Lodge. Wanamaker had been one of the individuals invited by Henry Ford to go on the Peace Ship to Norway, but who, like Edison and Burroughs, had politely declined.[52]

16

Fishing

On fishing in the North: *One seldom catches enough*
to form the fundamental basis for a lie.
—Thomas Edison

1922

Edison's 1922 birthday, his seventy-fifth, was noticed around the globe. In the Soviet Union, Edison was hailed "as one of the great benefactors of mankind, whose electrical experiments are bout [sic] to play an important role in the Soviet scheme for the electrification of Russian industry."[1] Fort Myers remembered his birthday with congratulatory telegrams from his local friends and by *The Fort Myers Press.*[2] As to the Fort Myers well wishers, Edison wrote: "It is very pleasant to be so kindly remembered on my birthday, and I want to thank you for your message of congratulations and good wishes."[3]

The *Press* announced the intended visits of both the Edisons and the Fords in the latter part of March.[4] Fishing was high on the agenda for both. The paper borrowed a favorite expression of a well-known pioneer, merchant and fishing enthusiast, E. L. Evans, when it reported that both Edison and Ford "can handle rods and reels as well as any amateurs that ever wet a line."[5] Freddy Ott, Edison's trusted assistant and Fort Myers advance man, and Mrs. Doyle, an employee of the Edison household, arrived to make Seminole Lodge fit.[6] Both the Edisons and the Fords made it known that they would be in Fort Myers for a complete rest and would not be available for social affairs.[7]

The Fort Myers Press proclaimed the arrival with a banner headline, "THOMAS A. EDISON ARRIVES." He was accompanied by his wife, Mina, and his cousin, Mrs. Frank Potter. The party arrived on the early afternoon train and were met by Mr. Tinstman and Fred Ott.[8] Mrs. Doyle had dinner ready when the Edison party pulled into the grounds at Seminole Lodge. At 11:20 that night, the Fords arrived aboard their private railroad car, the Fair Lane.[9] They were sleeping when the train arrived and remained in their private car until the following morning, when Mr. Ford arose, walked around the vicinity of the train and then proceeded to walk from the station to his home next to Seminole Lodge. The Fords brought with them a cook and a butler.[10]

Promptly the Fords paid a visit to their neighbors, and while the women talked, the men drove downtown in the Model T given to Edison in 1916. They stopped at the Ford agency to talk with Mr. Hill, the proprietor, and shook hands with all the employees.[11] They both had in mind fishing, interrupted by a moderate amount of sleep and sustenance. The *Press* reported they seemed as happy as two boys out of school. While exploring the town, the two discovered there was in progress an evangelical crusade then in its third week in Fort Myers. The old time revival was located in a place referred in the *Press* as the "tabernacle." Ford led his friend into the tabernacle where it was reported the two participated in "song."[12] It was an unlikely place to find Edison. Later in the day when it was time for Mrs. Edison and Mrs. Ford to go shopping, Ford took a drive alone to the nearby woods to "drink in" the beauty of the tropical region. Later that night the Edisons, with Edith Potter, saw the film play, "Forever," at the Arcade Theater.[13] The first full day in town was then complete.

Mina Edison's younger sister, Mary Emily, and her husband, William Wallace Nichols, arrived a few days after the Edisons and settled in at Seminole Lodge.[14] On the same day, Edison went fishing and returned with a nice string of fish. Ford was not feeling very well and remained at home for a day or two to rest.[15] He recovered from his slump in a few days, and Nichols joined

The Fair Lane, the private railroad car of Henry Ford,
which made many trips to Fort Myers.
Reprinted by permission of Henry Ford Museum and Greenfield Village.

both Edison and Ford in a search for the elusive tarpon, but they
had to settle instead for another string of fish caught near Four
Mile Cove. Nichols had been fishing with a winter guest from
the Bradford Hotel on the previous day, and the guest had landed a seventy-five-pound tarpon in the river in front of the Edison
and Ford winter homes. Nichols was so enthusiastic he persuaded Edison and Ford to go on the following day with the same
guide.[16]

One of the places regularly visited by the Edisons was Ella
Jones Piper's Beauty Shop on Hendry Street.[17] Somehow, it is
hard to imagine that a womens' beauty parlor would be high on
the list of the rugged inventor who made his name as a down-in-
the-trenches, dirt-under-the-fingernails tinkerer and wizard, and
one who possessed no outward signs of vanity. Although a story
that appeared in the *Press* on April 1 sounds as though it could
have been an April Fool joke, it did not suggest that Mr. Edison
had his hair cut or nails manicured, but that Mrs. Edison did and
that he was present in the shop while drawing his pleasure from
ordering refreshing soft drinks. Edison did have his hair cut while
in Fort Myers but not in a barber shop.[18] Mike Pavese would
pack his barber's satchel and head for Seminole Lodge where he
would cut Edison's hair and shave him. Edison gave Pavese a sil-

Ella Piper, a close friend of the Edisons, operated a beauty parlor on Hendry Street.
Courtesy of Fort Myers Historical Museum.

ver dollar and some toy soldiers to give his young son, Frank. Frank still has the silver dollar but complains his sister lost his toy soldiers.

After almost two weeks, the Fords took their leave on April 4, 1922, boarding their private car parked on the tracks at the foot of First Street.[19] Since the train left early in the morning, they boarded the night before and slept aboard the Fair Lane. As the car pulled out at 7:10 A.M., they were "at breakfast."[20] E. G. Liebold, Ford's liaison with the press, lingered for a few days after the boss left. Liebold said Ford was delighted with Fort Myers and would arrange to spend more time there in future years. He also confided that Ford found the people of Fort Myers courteous in allowing the family the rest and recuperation they sought.[21]

In a note to Mrs. Ford following their departure, Mrs. Edison, who was still in Fort Myers, mentioned the "sparkling atmosphere and birds filling the air with music," the glorious weather they continued to have and how much the Edisons missed them.[22] A second letter from Seminole Lodge sought to enlist Mrs. Ford's support for a crippled children campaign being conducted in New York City. She apologized for taking advantage of the friendship, which she would not otherwise do, but decided to make an exception in that case.[23]

The Edisons remained in Fort Myers for another two weeks

after the Fords left. In that time Mrs. Edison shopped in the "up-to-date stores" in Fort Myers. Her husband drove to Alva, fished with C. A. Stadler, a New York state senator and local developer, and was quoted as saying his mind was in "cold storage" while in Fort Myers.[24] His mind had not always been in "cold storage" while in his "jungle." Before the war he had spent much productive time in the laboratory and in another year his mind would again be active while in pursuit of a domestic source for rubber.

When the Edisons departed Seminole Lodge, Charles Edison and his wife, Carolyn, arrived for a short vacation.[25] Like his father, Charles wasted no time before testing his piscatorial skills. After an uneventful half hour at the entrance to Yellow Fever Creek, Charles spotted a large fish under the boat, the *Press* reporting that he quickly grabbed a "harpoon" and threw it in one "dexterious" cast following which "it seemed as though an underwater cyclone had broken loose." [26] The "displeasure" of the fish was obvious in the ensuing "maelstrom" in the river. The fish charged the boat but careful seamanship prevented its overturn. The fish charged the boat again and again while the launch was brought alongside and the fisherman transferred to the larger boat. The fish continued to charge even the larger boat and to drag it in all directions for "two solid hours." When drawn to shore, it proved to be a saw fish—over fifteen feet long, with a four-foot saw.

But that was the *Press* version. Charles told a significantly different story—a much tamer version—to his mother.[27] After reporting that he had fished in vain each day for tarpon, "the curse was taken off enough to let me get a 600# 16-foot saw fish. That was some consolation—we harpooned it at the entrance to Yellow Fever Creek. It had been fighting another fish and was quite scared up and more or less all in, so it didn't put up much of a fight." He sent his mother a copy of the write-up in the *Press* saying, "Believe me, it was some story the way it was written up."[28]

The Edisons all had pet names for one another. Charles called his wife "Pony." He wrote his mother that other than Captain Menge and the Tinstmans, he and Pony had "neither sought company nor did it seek us—just a glorious two weeks by ourselves doing just what we blankety blank pleased."[29] He ended the letter with an admonishment to his mother, "Get joy out of what you are doing & what you are going to make possible for others to enjoy & then come home to us. . . ."[30]

In June, 1922, Ford acquired an additional 135 feet from C. W. Stribley, the property owner immediately south of The Mangoes. The acquisition expanded Ford's waterfront and his McGregor Boulevard frontage to 300 feet.[31] Stribley then acquired an additional 150 feet on his south side so that the action merely moved the neighbor south.

1923

Early in 1923 E. G. Liebold checked into the Royal Palm Hotel, a sure sign the Fords would soon be arriving.[32] Mrs. Doyle, the Edison's housekeeper, and Fred Ott arrived about ten days before the Edisons.[33] Mrs. Doyle had remarried and upon arrival was known as Mrs. Phillips. Madeleine's two young sons arrived a week in advance of their grandparents, as did a niece.[34] In New Jersey, Madeleine delivered her third child, another son, about the time her parents went south. Her husband, John, wrote to "Mother Edison" on March 12 advising that the baby still did not have a name and that Madeleine remained in the hospital, where the food was terrible.[35] The baby was eventually named Peter.

The Edisons pulled into Fort Myers on the afternoon train on March 14.[36] Two hundred friends and admirers greeted them at the station. B. E. Tinstman drove the Edisons in a big new Lincoln touring car to Seminole Lodge, where Mrs. Phillips had a hot meal waiting. The Fords followed in their private railroad car, the Fair Lane, on March 28.[37] The Lincoln, which belonged to Ford, also greeted Henry and Clara and took them to The Mangoes.

On the day following his arrival, Ford walked up one side of First Street and down the other.[38] While out, he got a shave at Pavese's Barber Shop, where he no doubt became privy to some of the best conversation in town. A likely topic was the propos-

Pavese Barber Shop. Henry Ford had his hair cut here. Mike Pavese
would cut Edison's hair at Seminole Lodge.

Courtesy of Southwest Florida Historical Society.

al to carve out a large tract of land in south Lee County to create a new county, three-fourths of which was owned by Barron
Collier. Edison and Ford would both voice their opposition to
this subdivision of Lee County.[39] Ultimately the legislature saw
things differently and carved out not one but two counties,
Collier in the southern part of the county and Hendry to the
east. Collier County was named for Barron Collier, and Hendry
County for Francis Asbury Hendry, who at one time had owned
the old Fort Thompson property in Labelle. Fort Thompson was
located in what was originally Lee County but which then
became Hendry County. Naples was in Collier County.

The Fort Myers Press carried a whimsical story concerning
the activities of the Edisons:

- Thomas A. Edison, sojourning with his family at
  their winter home here made a new acquaintance here yesterday. He met Spoeyto
  Cunicularia Floridian and wife, otherwise
  known as Mr. and Mrs. Burrowing Owl.

161

- In company with Mrs. Edison and their grand-children and another relative, the . . . wizard piloted by Capt. Fred Menge and Conrad Menge visited the home of Mr. and Mrs. B. Owl at their subterranean home not far from the golf links.
- Mr. Edison . . . is a lover of birds and all manner of wild life. . . . His friend Captain Menge knows a lot about birds . . . and he led the great inven-tor and his party direct to the small door of the earthen passageway leading to the inner shrine of Mr. and Mrs. B. Owl yesterday afternoon.
- . . . . After saying "Howdy" to Mrs. Owl who was at home looking after her household duties and paying their respects to Mrs. Owl's husband . . . Capt. Menge . . . arranged things so that Mr. and Mrs. Owl wouldn't be inconvenienced further and could go on uninterrupted with their domestic cares.[40]

In addition to visiting the Burrowing Owls, the famous fam-ily frequented the movies at the Arcade Theater.[41] They went on an all-day outing to Estero and Bonita Springs. Mrs. Edison served as guest of honor at a meeting of the Elizabeth Benevolent Society, a local charity named for Mrs. Elizabeth Miles, the wife of the founder of Miles Laboratories who was also a Fort Myers land developer.[42] Harvey Firestone visited the Edisons and Fords in March and in subsequent years he became a regular visitor on Edison's birthday and at other times when Ford was also in town.[43]

Edison's health, which had been lagging upon his arrival, began to improve. Charles wrote his mother saying he hoped and prayed that "father can have a little time down there when he feels like himself and can enjoy the comforts and beauties of that heavenly spot."[44] Charles also expressed concern over his moth-er's well-being, since she had not only the care of an ailing hus-band with which to contend but also the two older Sloane boys to tame.

The residents of Fort Myers wanted a hard road into the city from the North and launched a campaign to raise private funds to subsidize the State Road Department's construction expense. Mr. Edison, who always participated in projects seeking the betterment of the area, contributed $500, raising the amount of private contributions to $17,425.[45]

After a six-week stay, the Edisons departed for the long trip north. B. E. Tinstman, their local business agent, who had driven them to Seminole Lodge on their arrival, died a few weeks after their return to the North.[46]

1924

The seventy-seven-year old inventor and his wife rolled into the Fort Myers train station on February 27.[47] With them for the 1924 season were a season regular, Edith Potter, and Mrs. Edison's niece, Miss Elizabeth Miller. A maid also accompanied them. As on previous visits, Mrs. Phillips had arrived a week or so earlier to prepare the house and to have a hot meal waiting. A sister of Mrs. Edison, Mary Miller Nichols, and her husband arrived several days in advance of the Edison party and stayed at the Royal Palm Hotel until their hosts arrived. Another sister, Grace Miller Hitchcock, and her husband, Halbert Kellogg Hitchcock, were also guests during the visit.[48]

On the trip down, Harvey Firestone had accompanied the Edisons aboard the Atlantic Coast Line "Florida Special."[49] At Jacksonville, Firestone went on to Palm Beach while the Fort Myers crowd took a different route via Lakeland. Morton M. Milford, the editor of *The Fort Myers Press*, was on the train, returning from New York. The editor said that en route several people knocked at Drawing Room "I," the compartment occupied by the Edisons, and that they were granted admittance and treated cordially. Along the route people turned out to see the famous inventor. In Jacksonville and again in Lakeland he was surrounded by well-wishers. South of Lakeland, people gathered at each stop to see him. A school teacher at Samville brought her entire class in hopes they would catch a glimpse of the inventor. They did, for he waved a cordial greeting to them from his drawing room window.

Milford was fortunate to speak to Edison in Drawing Room "I" on a number of subjects of local interest, including fishing, the progress of the Tamiami Trail project, the status of completion of the wooden bridge crossing the Caloosahatchee River, Barron Collier's development of Everglades City, and the prospect for rubber plantations in the area.[50] Edison bragged about his new balloon tires sent by Firestone for his Model T Ford.[51] He inquired about his old friend, E. L. Evans. With a twinkle in his eyes, he said, "You know Captain Ed and I are the oldest citizens of Fort Myers."[52] Evans was the proprietor of one of the general stores in Fort Myers in 1885, the year that Edison first set foot in the town. When asked about plans during his vacation, Edison said, "I'm just going to rest and I'm going to fish and take some motor rides."[53]

Although "motor rides" were a favorite activity, the lack of roads and bridges severely limited the options for local travel. The Tamiami Trail from Tampa to Miami was completed as far south as Punta Gorda in 1921. A wooden bridge across the Caloosahatchee was opened on March 12, 1924, while the Edisons were in Fort Myers, but a hard surface road from Punta Gorda to Fort Myers was not in place.[54] A local dispute between the advocates of the Tamiami Trail who wanted a bridge across the mile-and-one-half-wide Caloosahatchee at Fort Myers plus hard-surfaced roads to Punta Gorda versus the advocates of the Dixie Highway, who argued for use of an existing bridge across the narrow Caloosahatchee at Olga and then to Arcadia, greatly impeded the process. The Olga bridge had been in place since 1915; however, work on the road to Arcadia had languished. The Tamiami Trail was finally completed through the Everglades to Miami and officially opened in 1928.

When the train pulled into Fort Myers, the Edisons' Pullman car stopped in front of a new mission-style passenger station, which today serves as the Fort Myers Historical Museum.[55] A large crowd gathered at the station to greet them. Frank Stout, who became Edison's agent following Tinstman's death, drove the Edisons to Seminole Lodge. Edison commented on the changes in the town since the previous year, noticeably the new four-story Knights of Pythius building on Hendry Street, later known as the Richards Building, and the handsome new seven-floor annex to the Franklin Arms Hotel on First Street.[56]

The 1920s marked the transition of the Edisons, particularly Mrs. Edison, from a general aloofness to the local citizenry to a manifest desire to be part of the town and its townspeople. Mrs. Edison addressed the Board of Governors of the Chamber of Commerce upon the invitation of Miss Flossie Hill of the Womens' Division of the chamber.[57] She described the importance of city parks and urged the audience to see that the city acquired property for parks before the price rose too high. Mrs. Edison's remarks fell upon a sympathetic audience, and the chamber's president, R. Q. Richards, challenged it to do what it could to promote the concept. Mrs. Edison invited the entire senior class at Fort Myers High School to Seminole Lodge to have their pictures taken with the inventor.[58] Her role and influence as a civic activist in Fort Myers continued to grow and she gradually became the city's most influential citizen.

Edison intended to rest and recuperate, which included reading, motoring and fishing. He did ample amounts of each,

Edison reads on porch at Seminole Lodge.
Courtesy of Edison-Ford Winter Estates.

165

including an automobile ride over the new wooden bridge to areas previously inaccessible on the north side of the Caloosahatchee.[59]

Firestone, a vice president and two rubber experts from Liberia and Singapore came to town in March to investigate the growing of rubber trees in Florida.[60] Firestone introduced the men to Edison, with whom Firestone had had previous conversations about rubber. Thenceforth, rubber would dominate the great mind and interest of the Wizard for his remaining years.

17

Rubber

Of all critical and strategic material,
rubber is the one which presents the greatest
threat to the safety of our nation and the success
of the allied cause. . . . if we fail to secure quickly a
large new rubber supply, our war effort and our domestic
economy both will collapse.
—Baruch Committee, 1942

1923–1944

In 1923, Harvey Firestone had begun to speak to Edison about the impending threat of the British-Dutch rubber cartel that controlled world production of hevea rubber in the Far-Eastern countries of Malaya, Ceylon, and Java. The British Rubber Restriction Act, which became effective in late 1922, cut production and doubled the cost of rubber, which impacted Ford and Firestone as well as Edison, who used rubber in the manufacture of storage batteries.

The rubber plantations owned by the British and Dutch in the Far East grew the *Hevea brasiliensis* tree, which was indigenous to Brazil.[1] In 1876, the British brought back seeds from Brazil to Kew Gardens in London, where young trees were grown. From there the trees were taken to British-controlled lands in Malaya and Ceylon, where they were successfully grown. This was the inception of the vast rubber plantations that were concentrated in southeast Asia. Before Japanese control during World War II, the British and the Dutch controlled these plantations. In 1922, the United States used over 70 percent of world production, mostly in the form of tires and tubes. When balloon tires were introduced in 1925, demand went up because more rubber was required for the production of the balloon tire.[2]

Stimulated by the influence of his longtime camping friend, John Burroughs, his plant breeding friend, Luther Burbank, and the chaotic conditions brought on by the British Rubber Restriction Act, Edison developed an intense interest in finding a domestic plant source for rubber. His concern was never to develop a domestic plant source to compete with foreign rubber in normal times, but to have a source in time of war or other emergency.[3] He had experienced major shortages of chemicals from foreign sources during World War I and had himself begun the production of some of those chemicals for domestic use during that time. It was generally believed that, because of the difference in wages for labor, it would be impossible to compete economically with foreign sources of rubber in ordinary times when supply was available. Nor was Edison interested in synthetic rubber made from non-plant sources. Synthetic rubber had not yet been accomplished and Edison believed it was many years away. Edison wanted a crop that could be planted and harvested in a short time and produce sufficient rubber to take care of emergencies.

Ford, concerned about the necessity for rubber availability for automobile production, set his sights on Brazil as a locale where rubber could be grown commercially.[4] Beginning in 1927 he established two plantations along the Tapajos River in an effort that spanned eighteen years. Fungus and pests finally caused him to abandon the project.

It was Firestone who led the fight against foreign restrictions while at the same time establishing rubber sources of his own to meet his own demands. He looked at conditions in the Philippines, Liberia, Mexico and Panama but settled on Liberia.[5] There an abandoned British *Hevea* plantation with 1,100 acres was acquired and another 1,000,000 acres was leased in 1926. Although the project was initially successful, lower rubber prices due to the repeal of the British Restriction Act in 1928 and the economic depression of the 1930s caused it to make little head-way during those times.[6] During World War II, Liberia became the primary source of rubber for the United States. England was dependent on rubber from Ceylon. The Japanese controlled the remaining Far East sources, totaling 90 percent of the world's rubber growing area.[7]

In 1923, Firestone sent Edison a supply of guayule rubber plants indigenous to Mexico and the Southwestern United States.[8] At that time the Intercontinental Rubber Company had 1,800,000 acres of guayule under cultivation in Mexico and the Southwestern United States. Edison studied the guayule plants and determined they yielded seven and one half grams of good rubber per bush, or 680 pounds per acre. Edison wrote Ford that he had a good means of extraction and that a rubber source could be harvested by machine from guayule with little or no labor cost. He had retained some of the seeds, planting some in his New Jersey greenhouse and sending the others to be planted in Fort Myers.[9]

Firestone came to Fort Myers in 1924 with his vice president and two rubber experts from Liberia and Singapore, lodging at the Royal Palm Hotel.[10] The experts traveled all over Florida searching for a location for growing rubber trees in large commercial quantities and were in town to confer with Edison. Edison then believed that rubber trees could be grown in certain sections of Florida.

In May 1924 Ford accquired 7,000 acres in LaBelle—twenty miles east of Fort Myers on the Caloosahatchee River—from E. E. Goodno, fueling further speculation on the development of rubber production in Florida.[11] The *Press* speculated that the purchase presaged the early development of an immense rubber growing industry in Florida. Ford had made a loan of $166,986.46 to E. E. Goodno in 1922, securing the loan with a mortgage on Goodno's property.[12] Two years later he canceled the debt and mortgage, gave Goodno $63,000, and took a deed to the entire 7,000-acre tract from Goodno. Ford had first become acquainted with Goodno when the 1914 camping excursion to the Big Cypress paused briefly in Labelle. After the transaction closed, Goodno stayed on to manage the property including a ranch, which raised chiefly Poll Angus cattle with some Brahma cattle and Angora goats.[13] Goodno also managed the Everett Hotel and other enterprises on the premises. The purchase triggered intense development interest and speculation in the area around LaBelle, although it is doubtful that Ford acquired the Goodno property with the idea of using it in the search for a rubber plant source.[14]

In 1925, Edison's interest in guayule waned. Because guayule required four years after harvest to replenish itself, Edison's goal of having a rubber source available soon after harvest was thwarted. He shifted instead to *Cryptostegia grandiflora*, a Madagascar vine. Two years later his interest would again be diverted, this time to the collection of all manner of plants and analysis of their individual rubber content. In March, 1925, Firestone sent another world rubber expert, M. A. Cheek, to investigate conditions in Florida. Cheek, who had been involved in rubber in the Far East for two decades, told reporters that evidence suggested that "rubber trees seem to be 'at home' here."[15]

Henry Ford came to Fort Myers ahead of Edison in 1925, arriving on January 24 with a small group of friends, but without Mrs. Ford.[16] Frank Campsall, Mr. Ford's private secretary, traveled with the party.[17] Ford drove to LaBelle and Fort Thompson with Campsall on January 27 and again two days later.[18] Fort Thompson was the Seminole War fort located on the Goodno tract. At about the same time, E. G. Liebold, Ford's former secretary and by then Ford's press liaison, was meeting with Governor Martin in Tallahassee about planting rubber trees in the Everglades.[19] Ford was contemplating growing rubber trees on his holdings in Hendry County and wanted whatever assistance the state might render in draining the land. The governor promised to put the drainage issue to the legislature in its next session.

When Ford had left, Edison too visited Fort Thompson to see Ford's fledgling rubber plantation. With him was Mrs. Edison, his cousin Edith Potter, Harvey Firestone, Firestone's son, Russell, and Captain Menge in a three-car caravan. From there they went on to nearby Fisheating Creek for lunch, and finally to Moore Haven, all on the west side of Lake Okeechobee.[20] Mr. Edison enjoyed the bird life, no doubt with commentary and identification by the resident expert, Captain Menge. At Moore Haven, the Edisons turned back, while the Firestones, Captain Menge and the others proceeded toward West Palm Beach for the night, and on from there to Firestone's palatial home in Miami Beach. The *Press* reported that Captain Menge made the return trip in record time, seven-and-one-half hours.

At the time of the excursion to Fort Thompson, Ford's rubber plantation consisted of a small rubber tree nursery and one or two acres of seed-beds.[21] Liebold said it measured about one acre and contained waist-high "shrubs," not trees.[22] The frenetic real estate activity spawned by the Ford purchase created a genuine concern for Ford. Liebold, said, "There is nothing at all to the Ford rubber plantation except a nursery of about one acre, and there never has been." Nevertheless, real estate activity continued at an extraordinary level, all based on the notion that Ford was about to invest heavily in the area. Liebold explained that Ford had come into possession of the tract in settlement of a debt and that Ford "has been so incensed by this sort of advertising that he has obtained two fraud orders against real estate scoundrels, but still they continue to bob up."[23]

In 1926, Firestone and his family checked into the Royal Palm Hotel in early March for a visit with his old friends, Edison then in residence and Ford on the way.[24] When approached by a reporter about Edison's and Ford's respective Florida experiments, Firestone was less optimistic than in previous statements. The tire mogul said, "I'm afraid I am not very enthusiastic about them. I don't believe that rubber, at least the best grades, can be raised successfully here."[25] Firestone had by then acquired the abandoned British plantation in Liberia and was negotiating for another million acres in Liberia on which to plant the Brazilian *Hevea*.

Edison's research had gone from the guayule plant to a vine that grows naturally in Madagascar, from which the latex would be extracted after being mowed by machinery similar to a reaper.[26] Edison planted five acres of the exotic vine at his estate. It was perhaps the unorthodox means favored by Edison that produced the skepticism of Firestone, although he remained supportive of Edison's efforts and quite interested in them. Edison preferred the vines to the lower-grade rubber trees being planted by Ford at Fort Thompson because the vines had a smaller percentage of resin and would therefore produce a higher grade of rubber. In 1927 the Edisons drove with Fred Ott to LaBelle and found the rubber trees planted by Ford dead from high water. Edison said Ford had selected the wrong plant.[27]From LaBelle, they traveled on to Moore Haven near Lake Okeechobee to view the hurricane damage that had occurred the previous September, when 300 persons drowned there.

G. H. Carnahan, president of the Intercontinental Rubber Co., paid the inventor a visit in late March 1927.[28] The company, based in New York, at one time owned rubber plantations in Sumatra and Africa but had abandoned those sites in favor of a plantation in Mexico, where it had a large tract of guayule rubber under cultivation. The company sought other locations within the United States where guayule could be grown. The Southern cotton states were in contention, as was Florida. Although the rubber was of a good quality, Edison expressed his desire to continue his investigation of other plants. His was a quest for a plant with a shorter period of regeneration than guayule.

In New Jersey, Articles of Incorporation were filed for the Edison Botanic Research Corporation in 1927, a corporation composed of Edison, Ford, and Firestone, the three giants of science and industry.[29] Ford and Firestone invested $25,000 initially and Edison was to contribute time and effort.

Edison had a rubber laboratory in West Orange and his existing laboratory facilities in Fort Myers.[30] It does not appear there was much laboratory work going on in Fort Myers at this stage of the rubber project. Most activity involved the growing of vines and other plants, but as the next phase of the investigation began, much laboratory work would of necessity be involved. As the project continued, Edison had researchers collect plants from throughout the nation. In the summer of 1927, Edison sent letters to a number of botanists engaging their services.[31] They would work in the summer and cover the southern states all the way north to New Jersey. Careful instructions were sent as to the packing of the plants before sending them to New Jersey for analysis. The botanists were not the only field collectors used in the process; many volunteers joined in. In addition, the Union Pacific Railroad directed each section foreman to make collections of locally available plants along its many miles of right of way and to forward them to the Edison laboratories.[32] There were a total of 2,222 species collected and classified in 977 genera and 186 plant families.

At the Fort Myers laboratory, specimens were taken and preserved for botanical identification.[33] The plant was first dried in an oven and then ground. A test sample was weighed and placed in an extractor. The sample was first treated with an acetone to remove the non-rubber constituents of the plant that might be soluble in benzol. The acetone extract was designated as "resin" and discarded. The remaining sample was then extracted with benzol. When the benzol evaporated, the extract was weighed and designated "rubber."[34] All dried benzol extracts were placed on Edison's desk. He then made notes on the color, degree of tackiness, and whether the elasticity was good, fair, or poor.[35] Later tests, and particularly those in Fort Myers, involved a bromination method for determining rubber content.[36]

In 1928, Edison brought in a crew of ten chemists and laboratory workers to Fort Myers.[37] Two botanists, a linguist and a plant expert arrived shortly afterwards, followed by a chief chemist.[38] He sent more than a solid carload of equipment for his rubber experiments for the season.[39] The equipment was to be installed in the old laboratory. W. A. Benney, superintendent of the Edison Botanic Research Corporation, oversaw the installation of the shiny new equipment and electric motors in the old laboratory. Test tubes, electrical stoves, gallons of acid and other chemicals came in for the accelerated rubber research program. Edison later reported to Liebold that the old Fort Myers laboratory had been fitted up for working in a large way with his plant investigation for a suitable domestic supply of rubber.[40]

W. A. Benney, the supervising agent for Edison Botanic

Research Corporation, remained in Fort Myers for the summer months to continue rubber experiments.[41] Two plant expeditions were scheduled for June from Fort Myers, one to proceed toward New Jersey while gathering plants in Georgia, South Carolina, North Carolina and Virginia, and the other to venture to Tallahassee and the surrounding area. Field collectors were also dispatched to gather specimens in the vicinity of Fort Myers.

Bob Halgrim began collecting plants for Edison while babysitting his grandchildren in New Jersey.[42] After returning to Fort Myers, Halgrim collected plants from much of Southwest Florida, extending from LaBelle to Moore Haven and from Clewiston to Everglades City. The specimens were returned to a makeshift workroom in the Model T garage across the boulevard from Seminole Lodge. Halgrim brought cuttings from large plants and whole plants when they were small enough to scoop up the entire plant. The plants were dried and then ground in a mortar and pestle. The powder was placed in a container, a chemical added, and, according to Halgrim. they were then able to analyze the rubber properties of the plant.[43]

Edison told reporters in 1928, "Plain goldenrod that grows wild in nearly every state is one of the best sources of rubber that I have found among native wild plants."[44] In 1930, the Wizard held high hope for a particular strain known as *Solidago leavenworthil*, chosen from over seventy varieties of the common weed. He had a two-acre plot of *Solidago leavenworthil* adjacent to his new laboratory on the east side of McGregor Boulevard. A new machine was on hand to facilitate the separation of the rubber from the plant. There were several tanks, one for each of several chemical processes to be performed on the harvested goldenrod. In the process of distilling, each of several tanks would advance the extraction of certain chemical components. If the process was found to be successful, a larger version of the machine was envisioned. Unfortunately, the machine contained copper pipes which had an adverse chemical reaction with the goldenrod extract. It was necessary to replace the copper pipes, with cast iron and replacement parts were not available by the end of the 1930 visit.[45] The copper was replaced with cast iron and the machine rebuilt for the 1931 season.[46]

Equipment used to distill rubber from goldenrod.

Courtesy of Edison National Historic Site.

Although goldenrod appeared to have finally become the plant of choice, Edison did not rule out other plant sources. In 1930, the inventor, accompanied by his friend Ford, departed their McGregor Boulevard residences en route to Marco, an island fifteen miles south of Naples, in search of a weed that had been reported to Edison by one of his field men and which may have held some promise as a domestic plant source for rubber.[47] It is doubtful they found the weed for nothing was reported.

Although Edison continued to work on goldenrod from his Florida estate, by 1930 he looked to the Ford plantation in Georgia for major crop production. In an interview in March, he stated that large crops would be planted in Georgia as soon as he had developed new machinery for processing the rubber.[48] He expressed enthusiasm for goldenrod and grew some specimen plants at the small plot in Fort Myers. Later in March, in an interview held in Miami while visiting Firestone, he was asked what effect the discovery of rubber in goldenrod would have on the industrial development of south Florida. Edison disappointedly answered that goldenrod did not grow well in south Florida.[49]

In the interview, Edison gave more detail about the progress of his rubber experiments.[50] He hoped to obtain enough rubber from goldenrod processed in his distilling machine for Firestone to make a complete set of automobile tires within the next two years. He said he was experimenting with a new variety of goldenrod that grew to a height of twelve feet, but only had a rubber content of 3 percent. Other reports showed the new, large variety to be fourteen feet high and that after cross-pollination with a smaller variety having a greater rubber content produced a twelve and one half foot plant with 12.5 percent rubber content in the upper leaves.

Alvin Lampp was a senior in high school when he worked for the inventor-turned-botanist.[51] His job was to take specific instructions as to what plant stalks to cut for testing. He would then be given two identical brass clips with identical numbers attached. He was instructed to take the clips to the plant bearing the same number, insert both clips, and only after both were inserted was he to sever the stalk between the two clips. The severed stalk containing one of the two clips was then returned to the laboratory for testing as to rubber content. If it tested well, the plant bearing the other clip was allowed to remain. If it tested poorly, Lampp was instructed to remove and burn the plant bearing the matching number. Lampp said he recalled that the plant beds were located in the area adjoining the new laboratory on the east side of McGregor Boulevard. He remembered there were approximately twenty plants in each plot and about 500 plots, each appropriately numbered and identified. Not all the plots contained goldenrod. When Lampp graduated, Mrs. Edison called him aside and presented him with an autographed two-volume biography of her husband.[52]

In January, 1931, Edison's assistant Fred Ott preceded the family to Fort Myers as usual, as had a full complement of laboratory assistants, including Walter Archer, superintendent, J. F. Prince, chemist, Walter Hullman, goldenrod supervisor, and Charles Daily.[53] In addition, a young Fort Myers High School graduate came on the payroll. He was C. A. Prince, the son of J. F. Prince, the chemist for the Edison Botanic Research Corporation.[54] Young Prince's job was to type reports on the

Specimen goldenrod.
Courtesy of Edison-Ford
Winter Estates.

Edison inspecting goldenrod patch behind new Fort Myers laboratory.
Courtesy of Edison-Ford Winter Estates.

analysis of the rubber content of various plants and to serve as secretary to Edison while he was in Fort Myers. Prince sat at a desk next to Edison's in the laboratory office in Fort Myers and also in New Jersey. Communications to Edison were all in writing because of his deafness which had worsened with age. Edison followed a pattern of scribbling abbreviated instructions with a laboratory pencil for Prince to follow.[55]

Edison failed to show at the laboratory early on his first day in Fort Myers in 1931, preferring to rest and recuperate after an arduous train trip. Mrs. Edison sent word that neither she nor Mr. Edison would be available for several days.[56] Without "the old man," the laboratory assistants went about their duties, which included the assembly of a revamped distilling machine that had been introduced the previous year but was flawed due to the copper pipes.[57]

When Edison gained sufficient strength to return to the laboratory, his health was such that he had to be transported across McGregor Boulevard by wheelchair. Tourists eager for a glance would gather at the gate to see him cross or take his picture. Edison disliked being photographed or seen in such a diminished state of health. To avoid being photographed, he would cover his face with his arms when in camera sight.[58]

The work on rubber continued until 1934 with Mrs. Edison's brother, J. V. Miller, in charge following Edison's death. The Depression was in full swing in the early thirties and the price of rubber fell to its lowest depths. Firestone discontinued shipments from his Liberian plantations. Despite these conditions, rubber experiments in Fort Myers continued. Harry G. Ukkelberg, armed with a master's degree from the University of Minnesota, was hired to look after the rubber experiments in Fort Myers.[59] Work was limited to the chosen species of goldenrod, and analytical testing went to West Orange.

In 1933, a total of 6,664 samples were shipped to New Jersey for analysis. There were 288 experimental beds and 24,008 plants involved. In 1934, the Edison family determined to abandon the rubber project and arrangements were then made to turn over all planting material and records to the United States Department of Agriculture. Ford continued his interest in the

Mina Edison by the new laboratory in 1934. Left to right:
Russell Firestone, Henry Ford, Mina Edison, Harvcy Firestone,
J. V. Miller, H. G. Ukkelberg.
Courtesy of Edison-Ford Winter Estates.

rubber project, hiring Ukkelberg to pursue the goldenrod work.
The United States government continued with a modest program involving goldenrod.[60]

Edison's vision of the importance of rubber in time of war was confirmed during World War II when Japan captured Malaya, Singapore, and the Dutch East Indies. The only rubber left for the Allies grew in Ceylon and Liberia. Providentially, synthetic rubber arrived earlier than Edison had thought possible and lessened the gravity of the war-time shortage. Work on goldenrod was finally discontinued in 1944. It was not the failure of goldenrod but rather the success of synthetic rubber that caused the demise of the former. Should the chemical components of the synthetic process become limited, then the goldenrod process could very well be resurrected.[61]

18

Edison Park

All Things Come to Him Who Hustles While He Waits
—Thomas A. Edison

1925

The Edison party complete with cousin Edith Potter and twen-ty-seven-year-old son, Theodore, arrived on February 5.[1] Henry Ford was also in town. It marked the first year that Edison arrived in Fort Myers in time for his birthday. In the North he had established a tradition of news conferences on his birthday, and since he would be in Fort Myers for that occasion in 1925, the news conference was held there. When the news conference came he was queried about his early memories of Fort Myers. "It was a small cattle village consisting of not more than ten houses," was his reply.[2] He said he came to town "aboard a sloop in charge of Nick Armeda's father" and stayed at "a little hotel near where the wild fig tree in the Royal Palm Hotel grounds now stands."[3]

Ford, while in Fort Myers, bought back from the local black-smith, William H. Ross, the tools that once equipped the Fort Myers laboratory.[4] Edison had sold them to Ross several years before. The tools recovered from Ross included drill presses, lathes, engines and other machinery. Ford went to Ross's shop on February 18 to assist in crating the goods for the Henry Ford Museum and Greenfield Village in Dearborn. Ford had been busy planning a massive two-part museum of Americana with one

The Edisons with
friend, Jim Newton,
at the entrance to
Edison Park.

Courtesy of Uncommon
Friends, Inc.

part devoted to the artifacts of American culture, including
tools, machines, automobiles, trains, antiques, and appliances,
and the other an adjacent village known as Greenfield Village,
where the homes and workplaces of great Americans were collected and reassembled. The project served as a tribute to Ford's
friend and mentor, Edison, as the two museums were known col-
lectively as the Edison Institute.

Ford left on February 21 on the afternoon special after a
month-long sojourn.[5] Following his departure, the Edisons,
Theodore, Mrs. Potter, Fred Ott and J. Fred Menge drove to
Naples in a Lincoln with a chauffeur provided by the local Ford
dealer.[6] They stayed overnight in Naples and spent the day there
on Wednesday, leaving for Marco, Caxambas and Everglades
City on Thursday morning. Barron Collier's yacht *Volemia* met
the party at Caxambas and took them through the Ten
Thousand Islands to Everglades City, a real estate development
built by the wealthy New York advertising magnate.[7] Menge
identified all the birds that they observed in the abundant
wildlife of the region. They left the following morning by car
from Everglades City and on the trip home came upon a wound-

ed blue heron whose upper bill had been shot away. Two of the party captured the creature while Captain Menge performed emergency surgery on its bill. Theodore documented the adventure with photographs.[8]

Another outing included a two-car caravan that left for Immokalee.[9] Freddie Ott brought up the rear with the Model T while the remaining party rode in the Lincoln. The trip afforded the inventor the opportunity to consult with William Brown, an Indian trader, in that outpost village.[10] Arrangements had been made for Brown to introduce Edison to Seminoles and to have them sing Seminole songs, which Edison planned to record. On the trip down, four turkey gobblers broke cover on the right side of the road and in plain sight of the Edison party. As the party neared Immokalee, a torrential rain occurred preventing the group from traveling the four miles from town to the Indian camp. On the return trip, a dark moving object crossed the road in front of the car and Edison exclaimed, "It's nothing but a 'Gillette,'" Edison's term for a razorback.[11] When the rain stopped, the remaining trip was just as exciting, for nature arranged a fandango performed by two whooping cranes in company with a gobbler. The gobbler disappeared into the rough while the cranes bowed and scraped and danced, to the Wizard's utter amusement.

Both arrivals and departures seemed to confirm the lingering affection Edison had for his "jungle." When about to leave Seminole Lodge in mid-April, 1925, he told a reporter, "I hate to leave Fort Myers."[12] He also told how the world was finding out about the beauty of the town and of Southwest Florida, about the impact the opening of the Tamiami Trail would have on the area, and how impressed he was with the great roads built in Collier County. "The roads there are narrow and of marl, crushed rock, shells, etc. . . . This makes a wonderful surface and by dragging regularly to fill up the holes and smooth the surface, a highway of unusual stability is obtained."[13] When the interview was reported, the reporter noted that during the season Edison's car was frequently seen parked in front of the Arcade Theater while its owner, the inventor of the movies, was inside enjoying a picture.

Shortly after arriving in the North, the Edisons departed

again for Cambridge, where son Theodore was married to Anna Maria Osterhout on April 25.[14] Unlike the small wedding of Charles in Fort Myers, Theodore and Ann held a large wedding attended by both the Fords and the Firestones.

Greenfield Village was where Ford intended to move both the Fort Myers laboratory and the great Menlo Park Laboratory where the secrets of recorded sound and incandescent light were discovered. Communications concerning the removal of the Fort Myers laboratory began in 1925, but the move was not completed until 1928. The initial correspondence is somewhat confusing. First there is correspondence between Mrs. Edison and Ford's press liaison, E. G. Liebold which suggests that the laboratory has already been offered to Ford in return for a replacement laboratory to be built by Ford for Edison.[15] Liebold initiated the correspondence and told Mrs. Edison that Ford had asked him to procure a sketch of the proposed replacement. Since the letter was addressed to Mrs. Edison and followed Ford's return from a trip to Fort Myers, it is possible that Edison was not involved at that point. Mrs. Edison had Fred Ott send a sketch to Liebold, from which Liebold then sent a blueprint of a proposed new building to Ott.[16] Later, Ott sent Liebold a sketch showing where the machinery was located in the old laboratory.[17] Edison then got involved in the communications, directing his assistant to write Liebold that, "Mr. Ford can have the old Laboratory building at any time, as Mr. Edison can put up a smaller building for a motor generator for charging his batteries and also to serve as a garage for his automobile."[18] Edison's response speaks of a replacement garage rather than a replacement laboratory, but that changes as the ongoing discussions and delays over the removal of the laboratory play out.

A year later, in 1926, communications regarding the removal of the laboratory persisted, with Mrs. Edison again taking an active interest. She was concerned about the vines growing on the laboratory and made inquiries about the best time to transplant the vines in preparation for the removal.[19] She remained interested in the plans for the new structure, since she had some specific requests to include and Ford made it known he wanted to accommodate Mrs. Edison.[20]

When word of the removal of the laboratory to Dearborn first reached the Chamber of Commerce in Fort Myers, the president issued a letter to Edison protesting vehemently. The president's letter stated:

> This laboratory has a historical value that for many years has been pointed out to visitors with pride as meaning so much in the development of this age, I feel that this means so much to Fort Myers that the citizens of this community would feel deeply grieved to know that it was to be moved to any city disassociated from it's real history. We appreciate the real importance associated with the fact that your real work was done in this building located at Fort Myers.[21]

The chamber hinted at working out a plan by which Edison would leave the laboratory to the city and it would be preserved forever by means of an endowment fund to provide for its perpetual care. The Rotary Club adopted a resolution supporting the chamber's opposition to the move and a plan for the laboratory's preservation.[22]

Edison wrote the chamber that "a long time ago I promised Mr. Ford that he could remove my Fort Myers laboratory to Detroit, to be reerected [sic] in his historical collection. On his part he was to replace the laboratory at Fort Myers exactly as it stands at the present time. You will see therefore that I am bound by an actual promise, and that I cannot now take back this promise."[23]

The chamber didn't drop the matter, but set about securing from Ford a release of the promise made to Edison.[24] Ford responded that all arrangements had been completed for the "re-erection" of the Fort Myers Laboratory at Dearborn, and that a "great many of the tools, machines, necessary equipment, etc are already in our possession and merely awaiting the construction of the building." [25] He reminded the chamber that it had no completed plans for the preservation of the building and that he did.

In November 1926 Mrs. Edison wrote to Liebold from her home in New Jersey inquiring whether he would be coming East soon, as she would like to speak to him in regard to the new

Seminole Lodge "garage," as the replacement structure was initially thought to be.[26] She also wanted the laboratory removal to be delayed until after the 1927 winter visit.[27] Liebold took the matter to Ford and he agreed that a delay until after the visit was the "proper thing to do."

Edison's concept of his future laboratory needs in Fort Myers were modest when he sent his response. No doubt at age 78, Edison no longer thought of Fort Myers as a working vacation site. He had, in fact, reduced his work load in Fort Myers in the years following his war work. But the Florida relaxation and vacation mindset changed with Edison's fascination with finding a domestic supply of rubber. His concept of laboratory needs in Fort Myers also changed with his newfound interest.

In December, the city had nearly completed plans for the opening of an airport two-and-one-half miles south of Fort Myers on the Tamiami Trail. Scheduled service between Tampa and Miami with an intermediate stop in Fort Myers would be available four times each day.[28] The flight to Miami would take one-hour-and-a-half and cost $32.50. If one chose to go by bus, it would take thirteen hours by way of West Palm Beach and cost $20. By train via Lakeland, the same trip took twenty hours and cost $16.[29]

1926

Four Ford-Stout all metal airplanes made up the planned South Florida service fleet. The four left the Ford Airport at Dearborn en route to Florida with a stop in Nashville. There one of the four, *Miss Fort Myers*, taxied into *Miss Miami* and *Miss Tampa*, leaving *Miss St. Petersburg* unscathed.[30] The mishap caused a two-week delay, and although *Miss Miami* and *Miss Tampa* saw service in Florida, *Miss Fort Myers* was more severely damaged and was returned for repairs. It ultimately became a part of Ford Air Service in its Detroit to Chicago run.[31]

By 1926, radio was seen as a competitor to the phonograph and some were advocating that Edison produce a combination radio-phonograph product. Edison rejected radio as a fad and resisted entry into that market until later.[32] His plan was to concentrate on a quality phonograph and innovative phonograph products. Among the products introduced in 1926 was a new twelve-inch phonograph record. Parker's Book Store, the local Fort Myers Edison dealer, advertised the new product and featured demonstrations of the record which played for forty-two minutes.

A large crowd gathered in early February to welcome the seventy-eight-year-old inventor and his wife as they stepped off the train for the 1926 season in Fort Myers.[33] Newton Baker, who had served as secretary of war in the Wilson administration, happened to be in Fort Myers and uttered a few words of greeting at the station, recalling his twenty-year friendship with the inventor.

The Edisons brought Madeleine's two oldest boys, Ted and Jack Sloane, ages nine and seven.[34] The youngest Sloane, Peter, was only two. Michael Sloane, born in 1931, was not yet on the scene. The Sloane children were the only grandchildren produced by the six Edison children. In anticipation of the visit Mina Edison contacted the Scoutmaster of Troop 1 for the name of a young man she could hire to look after the boys.[35] The scoutmaster sent back the names of two worthy candidates, John Woolslair and Bob Halgrim. Both had distinguished themselves in the small Fort Myers community. Woolslair had been afflicted with polio as a child which left him crippled in one leg.[36] Halgrim had been a counselor at Camp Jungle Wild (later named Camp Ropaco) on the Caloosahatchee River near Alva. Halgrim thought Mrs. Edison chose him because she believed him better physically fit to deal with the challenge of two rambunctious boys.[37]

Halgrim, then a senior in high school, entertained and watched over the Sloane boys during their stay.[38] They fished from the dock behind the Edison home, sailed and canoed in the Caloosahatchee, and went exploring in Yellow Fever Creek (now known as Hancock Creek).[39] Halgrim also gave the boys swimming and life-saving lessons at the pool. Afterwards, he was hired to go to Fisher's Island, New Jersey, where the Sloanes had their home, to look after the boys during the summer. Neither Mrs. Edison nor Mrs. Sloane would discipline the boys, which

Ted Sloane, Jack Sloane and Bob Halgrim in the Edison pool.
Courtesy of Edison-Ford Winter Estates.

made Halgrim's job somewhat difficult. Once, while Halgrim was restraining Jack Sloane, who had misbehaved, Mrs. Edison, who had witnessed the restraint, told Halgrim she had implicit confidence in his disciplinary efforts with the boys.[40]

While at Fisher's Island with the Sloanes, Halgrim began another endeavor which prolonged his relationship with the family back in Fort Myers. Edison had begun an extensive investigation into the likely prospect of a domestic plant from which rubber could be harvested. Halgrim began collecting plants with the Sloane children for analysis at the Edison Laboratory in West Orange. He continued to collect plants and to be involved in other aspects of the rubber investigation when back in Fort Myers.

Edison had traditionally joined the Edison Pioneers, a group composed of his early associates, for his birthday celebration in New Jersey or New York. February 11, 1926, marked his 79th birthday and the celebration that year took place at the Hotel Astor in New York City.[41] For the second year in a row Edison was in Florida and unable to attend. Edison wired the Pioneers:

"Many thanks." Feeling fine, weather beautiful.
Cocoanuts [sic] dropping all over place. Wish
you all were here.[42]

Though the honoree was absent, Charles, Theodore, their wives, Madeleine, Thomas Edison Jr., and Marion "Dot" Oeser all served as guests of honor at the festivities at the Hotel Astor.[43]

The traditional birthday press conference occurred for the second time in Fort Myers, with Edison freely answering controversial questions.[44] On prohibition, he was decidedly in favor, saying "the children today are the important consideration, and the dry law will keep them from ever knowing whiskey."[45] Edison did not drink, but smoked four cigars daily and chewed tobacco incessantly. He didn't spare Henry Ford the wrath of his opinions. When asked what he thought of Ford's crusade to revive old-fashioned dances and do away with jazz and the foxtrot, he said, "I think it is foolish and won't succeed."[46] While not optimistic about Ford's struggle to restore decent dances to the American scene, Edison was even less enthusiastic about dancing in general, thinking it an expression of the barbarian remaining in the human race. "If a chimpanzee had a sense of rhythm, he would dance himself to death."[47]

By the mid-twenties the Edisons had become more involved in community functions. The two attended a sing-a-long with performer Glen Ellison in which an Edison phonograph provided by Parker's Book Store was the musical backdrop.[48] Ellison sang in what *The Fort Myers Press* called "a sort of contest" with the machine, which played a recorded voice of someone else singing. Such performances were encouraged as a form of advertising by the Edison company to show that the Edison phonograph was free of scratchy sounds common to disc phonographs of that era. The report in the *Press* suggested that when the machine worked, the audience could not tell when the voice was that of the recording and when it was that of Ellison. Through some quirk of fate, however, the machine didn't work—too little oil and perhaps a small amount of dirt, thought the *Press*. It was no accident that the Edisons had been invited to participate. Though Edison was not ruffled, Mrs. Edison was somewhat embarrassed. "Wind it tighter," she pleaded, but the winding did not supply the oil nor remove the dirt. A second machine was found. Same problem. Finally a third machine was brought on stage and voila, success!

Edison let it be known that he wanted to go to the fairgrounds to see the Philadelphia Athletics in spring training, and that he would like to meet owner-manager Connie Mack while there.[49] The Edisons' visit drew the following account in the local press:

> A recruit by the name of Tom Edison broke into big league company yesterday and finished his first try-out with a batting average of .500, a mark which Babe Ruth, Ty Cobb and the best sluggers of the land have never been able to reach after a whole season of endeavor.
>
> Edison is a local boy, coming here when comparatively young by way of East Orange, N. Y. [sic]. He lives out on McGregor Boulevard. Although known to his intimates as an expert electrician few of them suspected his talent for baseball.
>
> Yesterday morning, unannounced, he appeared at the Fair Grounds where the Philadelphia Athletics are in the throes of their spring training. As he stood around watching the ball players do their stuff he attracted the eye of Kid Gleason, one of Connie Mack's right hand men.
>
> "Think you could hit one?" asked the Kid.
>
> "Sure," replied Edison with the confidence that is music to the ear of a baseball coach.
>
> "Let's go," decided Gleason promptly. "Here, Connie," he added, "you be catcher and I'll pitch."
>
> The Kid seized a ball and trotted to the box. Mr. Mack donned Mickey Cochrane's big glove and was right at home, for backstopping was one of the things he did best during his playing days. Mr. Edison was armed with the big bludgeon with which Al Simmons knocks 'em fenceward

and the moving picture men gathered around.

Misses First One

To the busy clicking of cameras Gleason wound up and delivered one of his best twisters.

As it cut across the outside corner Mr. Edison swang—and missed.

"Strike one" yelled everybody, fans, ball-players, rough riders and fair attaches.

Mr. Edison looked a bit surprised but unperturbed. He motioned to Gleason to serve up another and the Kid took a wind-up that would shame the writhingest Charlestoner that ever squirmed a step. Out of the tangle shot a low curve with plenty of smoke on it.

Mr. Edison swang again and caught the ball on what Sam Gray described as the "very beagle." It soared out of the infield for a Texas leaguer over first base, a hit that even so agile a ball hawk as Joe Hauser would have failed to get.

"Sign up, Connie," advised the chorus as Mr. Edison handed back the bat to Simmons and shook hands with the crowd which surged around to congratulate him.[50]

After the Wizard completed his successful tryout, Mack accompanied Edison on a tour of the fairgrounds where the first day of the county fair was in progress.[51]

While Edison was trying out at the fairgrounds, Mina Edison attended a luncheon with friends at the Royal Palm Hotel. She received a call while there that her oldest grandson, Ted, had been run over by the family chauffeur as he was backing up the family car.[52] Mrs. Edison immediately left the luncheon for Seminole Lodge and the ailing grandson who, it seems, had run behind the vehicle. His injuries were pronounced minor, with only a cut on his head and some bruises.

Madeleine arrived on March 1 to join her children and parents at Seminole Lodge. With her was her youngest child, Peter.[53] The Sloanes remained until the Edison party returned to the North.

Unlike his friend Ford, Edison had a predilection for jazz music. When the Louisiana Troubadours, a nine-piece jazz band, appeared at the Arcade Theater, Edison invited the group to Seminole Lodge to play and the Troubadours obliged.[54] The press report concluded, "Hank can have his old fiddlers," a reference to Henry Ford and his preference for old-time music, particularly fiddlers.

Jazz was not the only entertainment for the Edisons. Mrs. Ashby Jones entertained the couple and their daughter at a tea at her riverfront home.[55] The paper listed a number of guests—all women—and one wonders how the inventor endured such events with no male companionship, no cigars, and no chewing tobacco.

The Fords arrived in Fort Myers on March 8, 1926, aboard their yacht, which they left anchored off Punta Rassa.[56] While no published reports mentioned the name of the yacht, it was probably the 223-foot *Sialia*, upon which they had traveled to Punta Rassa in 1917.[57] The previous year it had been refitted with diesel engines , replacing the steam turbines it had during the first visit. The Fords had gone ashore at St. Augustine and after rounding the southernmost reaches of the state had stopped again on the gulf side at Boca Grande, a deep-water port located a few miles north of Punta Rassa.[58] There the yacht was quarantined for two days.[59] It reached the Sanibel Lighthouse at 11 P.M. and anchored there a short distance from Punta Rassa. With the Fords were Mr. and Mrs. J. A. Ives. Ives was the treasurer of the Ford Motor Company. On the morning following their arrival at the Sanibel Light House, Mrs. Ford and Mrs. Ives came up the Caloosahatchee by "speed launch," landing at the Ireland dock in Fort Myers. Ford and Ives decided they would walk into town from Punta Rassa, but Mrs. Ford, upon her arrival in town, arranged a car to get them. They had walked about seven miles when the car reached them.[60]

As if in defiance of the recent *Fort Myers Press* article disparaging Ford's fiddlers, Harvey Firestone was on hand to greet his northern friends bringing with him two championship Florida fiddlers from West Palm Beach to entertain them.[61] The entertainment didn't last long for the Ford party returned to the yacht that evening to spend the night and to begin another journey to Pensacola on the following day.[62] Firestone also departed by boat en route to Miami Beach by way of the Caloosahatchee River and Lake Okeechobee.[63]

The manager of the Arcade Theater in Fort Myers invited the Edisons to attend a showing of a movie called, "Lights of Old Broadway," starring Marion Davies.[64] The movie featured Edison as a young inventor and included visual vignettes of the inventor's life.

Charles Edison wrote his mother on her wedding anniversary to tell her he was re-reading Dickson's "life of him and that without malice aforethought but entirely as a coincidence I put the book down last night just at the point where you and he were on your 1st honeymoon. Some gal & some fellah!," Charles opined.[65]

Newspaper accounts suggest that Edison did not spend much time working in his laboratory during his 1926 stay but read extensively on diverse subjects, spending time also in an attempt to isolate the perfect rubber plant.[66] He read *The Brains of Rats and Men*, a technical book written by a University of Chicago professor, now in the archives of the Fort Myers museum.[67] The book had countless annotations inscribed by Edison within its margins. Entering annotations within the margins of books of all types was a trademark of the Wizard.

Across the street from Seminole Lodge lay a fifty-five acre tract with frontage on McGregor Boulevard. Jim Newton, a young man barely twenty years old, was working with a crew in the early stages of this boom-time residential development. As Fred Ott drove Mr. Edison out of the driveway onto McGregor, they observed the young man digging a trench. His outward appearance did not suggest that he was one of the regular laborers. They stopped to stare for Edison had always been impressed with men willing to get in the trenches with their crews. He had himself been very comfortable in the midst of a dirty job. Proof of Edison's own work ethic is evidenced by the autographed picture that he later gave Newton, on which was written, "All things come to him who hustles while he waits." [68]

A Pennsylvanian, Jim Newton first arrived in Fort Myers in

1924. It wasn't long before he began to pursue opportunities in the Florida real estate boom. The same year, he had an opportunity to buy the acreage adjoining the Edison property, on the east side of McGregor Boulevard extending all the way to Cleveland Avenue.[69] Since he was only twenty and the law required him to be twenty-one to be the president of his corporation, Newton had to go through a legal procedure to have his disabilities of non-age removed.[70]

Without the environmental studies, permitting or other government obtrusiveness of modern times, Newton had only to arrange his finances, hire surveyors, crews and equipment and start work. The subdivision was called Edison Park. Its entrance opened onto McGregor directly across the street from the Edisons. Newton commissioned a sculptor, Helmut Von Zengen, to create a statue that would grace the imposing entrance to the subdivision.[71] As a work in progress the statue remained enclosed by canvas so that passers-by would not see the incomplete work.

One night, some of Mrs. Edison's friends, flashlights in hand, peeked behind the tarp and to their surprise and great consternation, discovered a half-naked Grecian maiden. When word reached Mrs. Edison, she grew incensed that land speculators would disgrace Seminole Lodge with such a sculpture. Eager to put a stop to it, she sent for the man in charge of the development. Promptly, an appropriately dressed twenty-year-old appeared at her door. She told him she did not wish to speak to him, but wished rather to speak to the man in charge. Jim Newton then handed Mrs. Edison his business card and told her he was the man in charge. Finally convinced of his authority, she told him what her friends had discovered behind the tarpaulin and of her great dissatisfaction with the state of the maiden's undress. Newton told her that if she did not like the way the maiden was dressed, he would instruct the sculptor to cloak her. Zengen used marble dust to create a veil for the half-naked statue. He did an extraordinary job, for the statue has stood the test of time with no part of the additional clothing having crumbled to date.

Some 500 citizens attended the dedication of the statue.

Pathe News, a nationwide news service, filmed the occasion for the newsreels.[72] The Elks interrupted their convention downtown to attend.[73] The Fort Myers Band played and Mayor O. M. Davison accepted the statue on behalf of the city. Edison had promised young Newton he would be present for the dedication, but when the time came, he was sick with a temperature of 101. Hearing of Mr. Edison's condition, Newton dropped in on the old man moments before the ceremony, only to find that he was already in the Model T with Freddie Ott and about to drive across the street, fever and all. Edison proved he was a man of his word. At the appropriate time, Mrs. Edison pulled the cord to reveal the aptly clothed maiden.

Edison Park included a handsome new $165,000 elementary school, Edison Park School. An air-tight copper box containing mementoes of the times, including a copy of the *Fort Myers Tropical News* and a picture of the school, had been embedded in the cornerstone. The box also included an enlarged picture of Mr. and Mrs. Edison and James D. Newton standing in front of the Grecian statue at the entrance to the subdivision on McGregor Boulevard. [74]

Newton soon became a regular guest of the Edisons at Sunday dinners at Seminole Lodge which occurred midday. On some of those Sundays other guests attended, but more times than not, it would be Newton alone with the Edisons. Newton also visited Edison in midmorning after the old man returned from his laboratory for a rest. He would find Edison, by then an octogenarian, in the living room with his four New York papers, which he received daily, or sometimes they would go in the yard where Edison, who did the talking, would tell the young man of life as he knew it.[75] Newton would also take Edison to the picture show at the Arcade theater, before "talkies" became available. Newton says Edison loved the silent Westerns, especially those with William S. Hart and Tom Mix.[76]

Newton's father, Robley Newton, became Edison's Florida physician. Newton recalled an occurrence that typified the Edison personna—a professional encounter with Dr. Newton, the father, who learned that his famous patient had a stomach ache. The doctor asked how long he had had it and was told by the patient, "Oh, about forty years."[77]

Although nothing appeared in the local paper, the Edisons and daughter Madeleine traveled to Palm Beach at some time during their stay in Florida in 1926. A letter from Charles Edison to his mother dated about a week before their departure for the North mentions Madeleine's account that the Palm Beach trip was difficult for Edison. The letter admonished his mother to avoid such tiring trips in the future.[78] On April 20, the Edisons and Mrs. Potter departed for home.[79]

19

Ford

*I can only say to you, that in the fullest
and richest meaning of the term—he is my friend.*
—Thomas Edison

1927

Although the annual birthday gathering of the Edison Pioneers
did not prevent Edison from going south in 1925 and 1926, 1927
marked the beginning of his years as an octogenarian—80 distinguished years. He stayed north for the gathering which took
place at the Robert Treat Hotel in Newark following his annual
interview by the press, which occurred at the West Orange laboratory.[1] Ford and Firestone were both on hand.[2]

Shortly after the birthday the Edisons left for their "bower
in the . . . Peninsular Eden."[3] Firestone accompanied them as far
as Jacksonville and then continued separately down the east
coast of Florida to Miami. The Edisons arrived by Pullman compartment on the Atlantic Coastline train at 11:30 A.M. on
February 19.[4] Edison, wearing a black derby, stepped first from
the train. Freddie Ott had the brass radiatored Ford flivver at the
station to greet him, but the *Press* reported that all it got was a
"love pat from the boss" as he and Mina headed for his local
agent's big Lincoln. Freddie Ott packed the bags into the Model
T and the two-car caravan headed off to Seminole Lodge. Once

there, the sage of Menlo Park and Seminole Lodge looked about his "jungle" and found that the September hurricane that caused such devastation around Lake Okeechobee had been much kinder to him. Lunch included strawberries from their own garden.

On February 24 Edison and his bride of 41 years celebrated their anniversary by going to the Arcade Theater in the Ford flivver to see Harold Lloyd in *The Freshman*.[5] The following day, Edison joined 150 orphans from Arcadia for a special vaudeville performance at the Johnny J. Jones County Fair at Terry Park in East Fort Myers.[6] The orphans had been transported from Arcadia to Fort Myers courtesy of the Seaboard Railroad. Edison met the train, along with the Fort Myers Band and delegations from local churches and civic associations. At Seminole Lodge, the Edisons also entertained the midgets from the Johnny Jones Show at the county fair.[7] The Wizard talked and joked with them, and Mrs. Edison served refreshments and took them swimming in the pool.

Edison entertaining midgets from Johnny Jones Shows at county fair.
Courtesy of Edison-Ford Winter Estates.

A week later, while the inventor took a mid-day nap, a grass fire on the north of the estate threatened the laboratory and caretaker's house.[8] About eighty gallons of chemicals were sprayed on the fire, but failed to extinguish it. Fire Chief Corley Bryant then formed a fire bucket line from the river and the blaze was finally extinguished.

A fanciful account of Edison's trip to the ball park appeared in the *Tropical News*.[9] The paper reported that after his successful try-out for the Philadelphia Athletics in the preceding season, the nimble 80-year old inventor-slugger was anxious to give out a few tips to Ty Cobb. He "flivvered" out to Terry Park to meet the 41-year-old "Georgia Peach." Ty Cobb had not been in the organization in the previous year when the agile octogenarian had an encounter with Connie Mack, Kid Gleason, and the Athletics. Cobb had signed on for a cool $75,000. Edison picked up a bat, sauntered over to the plate, planted his feet on the south side of the plate and motioned for a little action. The Wizard took a swing and let loose with a drive that sent the ball caroming off the seasoned "Georgia Peach's" shoulder while turning him over backwards, reported the local press. With that the Wizard of Terry Park ambled over to the Model T as Freddie Ott cranked it and took his leave. [10]

Later in March, Edison hosted a party for members of the Philadelphia baseball club at Seminole Lodge.[11] Mrs. Edison called it Edison's largest party, with Havana cigars, fruit punch and a large measure of good-natured banter. Edison took the baseball champions around the grounds and through the laboratory, explaining the "rubber situation," and telling them "alligator stories."[12] The paper didn't say what the stories were but did report that they were interrupted by Mrs. Edison who thought they might rather prefer punch to alligators. Mr. Edison's wit quickly rebuffed her suggestion, telling her playfully there was nothing in the punch, and continued to regale the players with alligator tales. Edison told them he hoped they would win the pennant and the players left saying they would expect to see him out at practice in the next season.[13]

Jim Newton, the Edison Park developer, began taking the Edisons for automobile rides—a favorite pastime for the inven-

Connie Mack catches as Edison bats.
Courtesy of Edison-Ford Winter Estates.

tor. Newton took them to Venice, about sixty miles north on the Tamiami Trail, in his Packard Roadster. Edison rode in the front seat and Mrs. Edison and cousin Edith in the rumble seat.[14] While in Venice they met a number of people, including the mayor of that city. Edison interrogated the mayor on the irrigation system being utilized in the town and then met a swarm of newspaper men. He answered their questions patiently even though he had covered the same ground at his birthday interview just a month earlier.[15] The Edison Park development had slowed because of the end of the boom and young Jim was trading all manner of things for lots. The Packard Roadster was the result of one of those bartered trades.[16]

Mixing St. Patrick's Day with barbeque sounds a bit awkward but that is what Mr. and Mrs. Henry Stevens did at their Fort Myers Beach home on that special day.[17] The Edisons were among the 200 guests at their St. Patrick's Day beach party. Festooned with a green stove pipe hat, the Wizard munched on barbeque and toasted marshmallows at what was said to be his first barbeque.

Charles wrote his mother telling her things looked good at the business.[18] The 1926 balance sheet showed "a ratio of current assets to current liabilities of 11 to 1 and a very liquid condition." He called the phonograph division of the business a "sick pup," as it continued to flounder after several difficult years.[19] He reported considerable success in the campaign to reduce expenses in the phonograph sector and thought "father will be pleased when he hears about it when he gets back—if not before."[20] With business good aside from the phonograph, Charles reported that the company was campaigning strenuously for new orders and that several new production items were all but completed. He promised he would not wreck the business without giving his father a day's notice.[21]

The Fords did not come to Fort Myers in 1927. In March, while the Edisons were in Fort Myers, Ford was in an auto accident in Dearborn. Contrary to the advice of all those around him, Ford drove his own car and ignored his own celebrity and the precautions that go with that status. He had left the driveway of the Ford laboratories about 8:30 P.M. and was traveling alone in a small Ford coupe on the south drive of Michigan Avenue. He had just crossed the Rouge River bridge when a larger car passed and sideswiped his coupe, causing it to plunge down a steep embankment and come to rest between two trees. The 64-year-old auto magnate was rendered unconcious, but he later revived and was able to make his way by foot to Fair Lane, his nearby estate.[22] He remained at Fair Lane for two days before being hospitalized at the Henry Ford Hospital for two days.[23]

Mrs. Edison maintained a close relationship with the Fords through frequent correspondence with Mrs. Ford. Writing from Fort Myers to inquire about the accident, she complained about the accuracy of the press reports and told Mrs. Ford she must have direct news from her. "We are constantly thinking of you both and wish that you were right down here with us."[24]

Before leaving for the North, the Edisons traveled up the state about 150 miles to Leesburg.[25] Ostensibly the purpose of the trip was to search for rubber plants. When a reporter caught

Ford

him in the hotel lobby in Leesburg and inquired about his party's departure time, he said they would be leaving in the morning at 8 o'clock "if Mrs. Edison can get ready by that time."[26] Nothing is reported of the success of the search for plants.

The Edisons delayed their departure for the North as long as possible, finally leaving on May 3.[27] Prior to departing, they invited the science class from Fort Myers High School to Seminole Lodge and, of course, the students were shown through the laboratory. Dressing for the long trek back to New Jersey, Mr. Edison traded the floppy straw hat he had worn while in Fort Myers for his black derby. About 200 persons were at the station to see him off. Special good-byes came from Carl Roberts, James D. Newton, and W. M. Harley. Miss Flossie Hill, another special friend and the owner of a local ladies' apparel shop, got a hearty hug from Edison.

After returning to New Jersey, Mrs. Edison again wrote Clara Ford relating her disappointment that the Fords did not get to Fort Myers for the winter season.[28] She told her of the wonderful weather in Florida and how awful it must have been in virtually all points north. She wrote that she was "afraid that you have deserted us for Georgia as I understand you have a large tract of land there."[29] This was a reference to Ford's purchase of an old estate in Ways, Georgia, where he would eventually locate his winter residence, forsaking Fort Myers. She thanked Mr. Ford for the new Lincoln limousine he sent as a gift for Mrs. Edison's use. She said it arrived on her birthday, "it runs beautifully and no noise."[30] She complained that all the new accoutrements found in the car "make us lazy. By the movement of my hand, I turn on or off the light—window closes by another movement of the hand and so on."[31] Since she was about to leave for Chautauqua for a few days, she told her how much she would like to have Mrs. Ford join her there, a suggestion that had been made many times before. She wondered "if Mr. Ford had fully recovered from his accident?"[32] Finally, she complained about the heat wave in New Jersey, which was much hotter that it had ever been in Florida.

Charles and Carolyn arrived for a short stay in Fort Myers after the senior Edisons had left Seminole Lodge. Charles wrote

201

his mother, "Not very hot and a fine breeze. Fished yesterday off the dock. Pony got a channel cat—the first fish—and I got not so much as a nibble."[33] They began fishing on the day they arrived, and on the next morning they fished from the dock in the morning and then went to Yellow Fever Creek in the afternoon. Pony caught a snook and a jack and "Little Willie here scored zero,"[34] Charles confessed to his father. He complained only of a six-hour detour in Georgia on the way down, the result of a freight train wreck; "However *this* place & the River makes up for most any inconvenience in getting to it."[35] Ever the poet, Charles ended his letter, "There is a siren sound in my ears. It is the gentle murmur of cat-fish crooning to their young. With love to you and mother I go!" in search of the elusive fish.[36]

Bob Halgrim, who was then working for Edison in the laboratory, set about preparing the laboratory for the summer absence. This entailed removing all the chemicals from the shelves and boxing them until the following year. During the season he had met Edison in the mornings and walked him across

Charles Edison and his wife, Carolyn, display their catch.
Courtesy of Edison-Ford Winter Estates.

the street to the laboratory. Halgrim recalled that Edison's age at that time was taking a physical toll, though his mental capacity remained at its peak.[37]

Halgrim, who had just graduated from high school, attended Cornell in the fall with help from the Edisons. Though he had a significant relationship with Edison himself, he became a favorite of Mrs. Edison. While attending Cornell, Halgrim made Glenmont his weekend and vacation retreat. He obliged Mrs. Edison's invitation with his presence and stayed in Theodore's room. Once while at Glenmont during the Christmas holidays, he went with the family into the den where the Christmas tree was located for the opening of the presents. After all the presents were opened, everyone left the room and as Halgrim walked out of the room, she smiled at him and gave him a motherly kiss under the mistletoe.[38]

In June Ford's press liaison Liebold wrote to his counterpart, Wm. H. Meadowcroft at West Orange, to again bring up the matter of the removal of the Fort Myers laboratory to Ford's Greenfield Village in Dearborn.[39] He wanted to give Mr. Edison's agent in Fort Myers plenty of time to take care of the trees and shrubs so that no damage would be done in the move. He again mentioned the type of building Mr. Edison wanted in its place. Was it to be only a garage as previously discussed? Edison sent Liebold a blueprint of the existing laboratory, including the garage, and a cover letter stating he wanted a replacement laboratory with dimensions the same as the old one.[40] The only change shown from the original was an expanded garage somewhat larger than in the old building. Everything else would remain the same. Liebold then wired Edison that Ford would make arrangements to remove the laboratory building immediately.[41]

In September, Edison inquired when the removal would occur. His letter hinted that he wanted something more than the mere garage discussed in detail over the last two years. The correspondence was confusing. Edison told Liebold that he was working on a November shipment of machinery and supplies to equip the new Florida laboratory.[42] Liebold was puzzled and wrote back asking if Edison wished to store the machinery and supplies in the new garage or in the existing laboratory before it was dismantled.[43] Edison replied that until the new building replaced the old one, he would have no place to store the machinery and chemicals. Since time was short, the project should be delayed until after the 1928 winter season, otherwise his whole rubber project in Fort Myers would be "demoralized."[44] Ford agreed to the delay.[45] It had finally become clear that Edison wanted a replacement laboratory.

1928

Freddie Ott again shined the brass radiator on the Model T given Edison by Ford. He drove it to the station to meet Edison but its purpose was merely to carry the luggage; a gray Lincoln driven by local agent Frank Stout took the famous visitors to their home.[46] The Chamber of Commerce arranged for the Fort Myers Concert Band to be on hand when the Wizard descended from the train. The band played "Home Sweet Home." [47] Over a thousand people appeared to greet them.[48] The Edison party included cousin and perennial guest Edith Potter, Mina's sister-in-law Florence, and her two children, five-year-old Nancy and two-year-old Stuart.[49] The trip from New Jersey to Fort Myers had taken thirty-four hours.[50] The party occupied two compartments and a drawing room on the last car on the train. Two servants, a veteran maid, and a cook traveled with them.[51] Mrs. Edison wore a black straw hat with feathers falling from the crown to the brim. She had a dark fur-trimmed coat worn over a black satin tailored dress. Her sister-in-law wore a tan checked velour coat trimmed with fox and a small cloth hat. On entering the Lincoln for the ride to Seminole Lodge, little Nancy Miller sat in her famous uncle's lap clutching a large doll, almost a replica of herself with short dark curls and a small blue bonnet.[52]

When reporters asked how he felt, Mrs. Edison broke in saying, "He's feeling fine . . . and thoroughly enjoyed the trip from West Orange. He's troubled a little bit with old-fashioned dyspepsia which the doctors call something else, and I have placed him on a milk diet."[53]

The next morning, Edison first inspected his original but

newly refurbished laboratory and then mobilized his staff, setting them to work gathering plant specimens.[54] In the afternoon, he toured his "jungle" and conferred with his gardener on the condition of his favorite plants and trees. He made brief trips to his front porch to sit and read while automobiles passed by on McGregor Boulevard hoping to get a glimpse of him.[55]

This season would serve as a working vacation, with a full contingent of laboratory professionals in place and working. Much of the work involved procuring native plants and others from along the Atlantic seaboard so they could be tested for rubber content in the laboratory. The Madagascar vine, on which much hope had been lodged, was finally abandoned. Realizing that moving the Fort Myers laboratory to Dearborn could not be further delayed, a new laboratory was under construction on the east side of McGregor Boulevard. It seemed impractical that the old laboratory would have to be moved to Michigan after having been completely refurbished in the previous year, the new and extensive equipment used to refurbish it to be moved again from the old laboratory into the new one.

Edison speaks to reporters.
Courtesy of Edison-Ford Winter Estates.

Two days after the arrival, a handful of newspaper reporters caught up with the inventor at his jungle and posed a number of written questions to him. America so admired Edison that reporters would ask all manner of questions, including many far removed from his area of expertise. During the informal session, Edison said he was opposed to capital punishment. On the presidential elections, he said the American people would be "a bunch of sapps" if they didn't elect Herbert Hoover. As for colleges, there is something "radically wrong" with them. He did not believe that airplanes would replace automobiles. He told the assembled crowd that Harvey Firestone had sent him a set of tires made from guayule rubber, grown in California, and that they were being installed on a 1924 Ford roadster that was in a garage downtown. That evening, Edison went out to the movies with Mrs. Edison, her sister-in-law, and Jimmie Newton.[56]

The city of Fort Myers, through its recreational director, conceived the idea of a city-sponsored birthday party for Edison to be held in the municipal auditorium.[57] The event would include a rather extensive list of activities. Mrs. Edison seemed to prod the Wizard into acceptance of the idea, although he expressed his opinion to friends that all the preparations were "a lot of poppycock."[58] An attempt was made to persuade the popular national hero Charles Lindberg to participate in the party. The famed aviator had completed the first trans-Atlantic flight in 1927 and was just then winding up a flight through Latin American and Caribbean countries.[59] Fort Myers, though not in a direct flight path from Havana to St. Louis, was not that far out of the way. Lindbergh was scheduled to arrive in Havana on February 8 and by the birthday on February 11, he would be just a two-hour flight away. Mrs. Edison agreed to cable the invitation to San Juan. A response arrived on February 3:

> GREATLY APPRECIATE INVITATION BUT MUST BE IN HAVANA UNTIL THIRTEENTH WOULD BE GLAD TO MAKE SPECIAL TRIP FT MYERS IF SCHEDULE ALLOWED STOP PLEASE CONVEY MY SINCEREST ADMIRATION AND BEST WISHES TO MR EDISON CHARLES LINDBERGH

Two days after the birthday festivities, Lindbergh left

Havana at 2:36 A.M., flying over Key West to the West Coast of Florida and from there to Cedar Key, where he took a compass course to St. Louis—a 1,200 mile non-stop flight. He should have been over Fort Myers Beach between 4:30 and 5:00 A.M. No one saw or heard him go over.

Nine motion picture camera men plus reporters and photographers awaited the Wizard at 10 A.M. for the annual birthday interview.[60] Firestone was in town for the occasion. A niece of the inventor, Nellie Edison Poyer, was also there.[61] The city gave Edison an official birthday present—a 45-foot cypress flagpole placed in the yard near the riverfront at Seminole Lodge.[62] Before the interview, the Jubilee Singers from a local black church entertained both Edisons in their front yard and presented Mrs. Edison with a pink carnation corsage. She removed one carnation and pinned it to the inventor's lapel.

The press had become rather unmanageable at these interviews and Mrs. Edison asked Jimmie Newton if he would take charge of the interview and make an orderly procedure out of a chaotic one.[63] Newton served as official greeter and made sure that guests were properly cared for. With Firestone by his side,

The Jubilee Singers were a popular singing group from a Baptist Church in the black community.
Courtesy of Edison-Ford Winter Estates.

Edison escorted to birthday interview. Firestone on right.
Jim Newton is behind Edison.
Courtesy of Edison-Ford Winter Estates.

the celebrated inventor withstood the bombardment of written questions, answering them with his stubby laboratory pencil. When asked about the hereafter, he answered that he would spend his afterlife experimenting with whatever facilities he found.[64] When the reporters finished, Firestone entered the fray and inquired about Edison's loss of flesh—his extreme diet had caused him to drop about 40 pounds. Edison retorted, "Well, you're no fatty yourself!"[65] The interview concluded, Edison and Firestone, accompanied by Jim Newton, left the estate and walked across the street to the "rubber patch."

The massive birthday party began at 3 P.M. complete with a cake six feet in diameter, ninety inches tall and filled with eighty-one electric candles.[66] A band performed and the Edisons were escorted in by Boy Scouts.[67] Some 4,000 Lee County school children took part, including Edison Park School's stu-

School children entertain Edison in 1928 at
birthday party at the Pleasure Pier.
Courtesy of Edison-Ford Winter Estates.

dents led by their principal, Miss Pearl Bullock.[68] The school
children filed by the guest of honor carrying placards naming
various events in his life and many of his inventions. After the
procession, the platform participants and others, including
Newton, left for Seminole Lodge and an informal reception. Mrs.
Edison allowed her husband the day off from his diet so that he
could enjoy fresh strawberries from his garden for lunch. Later in
the evening, in a sentimental return to his youthful occupation,
the former telegraph operator was driven to the Western Union
office where the telegraph keys were turned over to him and a
message sent by him to Bellingham, Washington. There, an
inaugural celebration of a new Edison lighting system was in
progress and Edison's telegraph stroke set the power in motion.

A new seven-seater Lincoln limousine and one of the newly
introduced Model A Fords waited at the Seaboard Station in
East Fort Myers on February 18 when the Fair Lane pulled in
with the Fords and their friends, Mr. and Mrs. E. R. Bryan.[69]
Several hundred people gathered at the Atlantic Coast Line

Municipal Pier (Pleasure Pier), scene of birthday celebration.
Courtesy of Pavese Haverfield Dalton Harrison & Jensen, LLP.

Station, a mile away, where he had been expected. As if to prank the public, Ford directed Frank Stout, his Fort Myers agent and the driver of the limo, to stop on First Street at the front gate of the Royal Palm Hotel. There he, Bryan and Frank Campsall, his secretary, exited the car. The three walked through the busy Saturday night crowd along the business section of First Street, crossed the Atlantic Coast Line tracks and continued on foot to Seminole Lodge and The Mangoes. Not a single person recognized Ford except for one reporter, who stayed with the three for a while, asking questions and getting brief responses. Finally Campsall told the reporter, "Be good and maybe we can fix up an interview with the boss next week."[70] The reporter let the three go on without him. Mrs. Ford and Mrs. Bryan drove directly to the Edison home, where Mrs. Edison had a buffet turkey dinner awaiting them. The paper said she prepared it herself.[71]

A couple of days after Ford's arrival, Ford, Edison and Edison's guest, the noted German biographer Emil Ludwig, traveled about sixty miles north to Venice, Florida, to inspect rubber plants growing at the Oneco nursery.[72] At one stop, Ford told reporters that pilot Harry Brooks, who was flying Ford's new flivver airplane on a non-stop flight from Detroit to Miami, would fly to Fort Myers after landing in Miami. That evening, after returning from Venice, Ford learned that Brooks had been forced to land on a sandy beach in Titusville, Florida, due to a leaky pet cock. From there Brooks drove to Miami, picked up a new propeller to replace the one that was cracked during the landing on the beach, and returned to Titusville.[73] He was soon airborne again and flew low over Melbourne and then out to sea where the plane went down and sank.[74] Brooks was not heard from again. At The Mangoes, Ford remained in constant touch with the news, hoping his pilot would be found safe.

It was in 1927 that Edison first visited the well-known and respected horticulturist, Dr. Henry Nehrling, of Naples, Florida. The following year, after the Fords had settled in next door, the Edisons invited Nehrling to spend two days with them in Fort Myers. Nehrling spent the first day roaming the Wizard's "rubber plantation," across McGregor Boulevard from his home. He was

Ford and the Edisons stand before original Fort Myers laboratory which Edison gave to Ford for Greenfield Village.
Courtesy of Edison-Ford Winter Estates.

then shown the laboratory, where rubber was extracted from various plants by "3 or 4 experts" while there were "7 men working among the plants" outside.[75] From the laboratory they went to the library to see the botanical books. Nehrling observed that Edison had little interest in plants unrelated to his rubber research, an observation tainted by the inventor's then current rubber obsession. In fact Edison had on many occasions shown his interest in all forms of plants, stemming from the early planning of his gardens in Fort Myers and the later influence of his friend, Luther Burbank. Dinner that evening at Seminole Lodge found Dr. Nehrling flanked by Henry Ford on his right, Clara Ford on his left, Edison directly across the table and Mina Edison across from Ford. He found Mrs. Ford to be a great lover of roses; she described to him planting over 10,000 rose plants in her two-acre rose garden in Dearborn. Nehrling described Mr. Edison as "so talkative, so cheerful, so full of all kinds of jokes, that the time passed rapidly." The dinner conversation lasted until 11 P.M.[76] The following day was devoted to Mrs. Edison and her garden. Before leaving, Edison made out a contract engaging Nehrling to take charge of the beautification of the Edison gardens adding "all the plants of beauty and interest that" he could "find room for."[77]

On February 24, 1928, the Edisons celebrated their forty-second wedding anniversary by going to the County Fair with the Fords and Mrs. Miller.[78] With them on the midway were the mayor and the police chief. The men were particularly interested in the agricultural display booths, pointing at beautiful strawberries and large green watermelons. "Look there, Henry, that's what we grow down here," blurted Edison. When they came to the Tropical Motors display booth, they inspected an early model Ford side by side with a new Model A.[79] They ran into Conrad Menge, the brother of Captain J. Fred Menge.[80] Ford had first met Conrad Menge in 1925 while visiting Edison. Ford asked Menge to join the others as they walked around the midway. Menge later recalled the flea circus which they all stopped in to see. "This man came out with a flea, hitched up to a little wagon just about as big as your finger nail. . . . That little flea was walking along pulling this wagon! . . . Did Mr. Ford get a kick out of that flea! Boy!"[81]

At another meeting, Ford ran into Menge at a Sunday School picnic held by Mrs. Edison in the pavilion at the end of her dock.[82] Ford had heard that Menge played the fiddle and, since he had had a long-time affair with the fiddle, particularly when played by "old time fiddlers," he wanted to hear Menge play. Ford owned a Stradivarius and had it with him at The Mangoes. He told Menge, "I'm coming up to see you tomorrow."[83] He did drop in on Menge the next day and he brought with him his Stradivarius. "I understand you play the violin," Ford said. [84] So Menge played a few tunes, one that Ford had never heard. Menge didn't know the name of the tune. Henry called it a Southern schottische (round dance). He asked Menge to put it down on paper and then asked him to play his Stradivarius. Menge wanted to know if Edsel played the violin and Ford answered no, after which Menge said jokingly, "Mr. Ford, I want you to will me this violin whenever you pass out."[85] He laughed.

Menge then asked Ford why he was coming around to see an old Florida cracker and Ford replied, "I think I met a man who's not after my money."[86] Menge played more tunes, then told Ford he wasn't playing with his regular fiddle because it was broken. Ford offered to have it fixed and according to Menge he did and returned it and "it was fixed up beautifully."[87] Ford observed that Conrad was the best old-time fiddler he had ever heard.[88] After that Ford dropped in on Menge regularly until the vacation ended.

On one of those visits Ford found that Menge had left the house a short time before he arrived causing Ford to go chasing after him. Menge had assumed that Ford would not come over that day so he left for the beach to get some oysters.[89] Before Menge arrived at his destination, Ford caught up, passed him and waved. When Menge arrived at the beach, Ford watched as Menge tried to start the engine on his boat. He never got it started and Ford finally got tired of watching and drove back to town. That evening Menge felt he owed Ford a visit for not having been home when he called. He walked from his home in town to The Mangoes. Though the Fords were having supper they graciously invited Menge in. Ford pulled out a record, put it on the

Edison phonograph, and said, "Now, I want to see you dance to that."[90] He had Clara roll up the carpet and Menge danced the Southern schottische. Ford seemed as intrigued with dancing to the music of old-time fiddlers as he was to listening to them. Menge didn't stay long, but when he left Ford walked with him all the way to the railroad tracks downtown.

Ford occasionally visited Menge at the boat ways near the mouth of the Orange River, which is a tributary of the Caloosahatchee River located about five miles upriver from Fort Myers.[91] Conrad Menge had gone into the boat-building business after the family steamship business ended. On one such visit, Ford told Menge he wanted him to build a replica of the *Suwanee*, the stern-wheeler that had carried Edison on ventures into Lake Okeechobee and on fishing trips in the Gulf.[92] The *Suwanee* had sunk in Lake Okeechobee a few years earlier. The hull was to be built in two halves, loaded on flat cars and shipped by train to Dearborn. In Dearborn it was to be completed and used to carry the public on a canal circling Greenfield Village. Ford wanted the engines and machinery salvaged and placed in service on the replicated hull destined for Greenfield Village. So Ford and Menge set out for Lake Okeechobee to inspect the wreckage with Ford at the wheel.[93] When there, Menge dug the engines out of the sand, but found there wasn't much left of them. Menge then took the wheel for the drive back to Fort Myers. He later salvaged what he could.

Early in March the Fords departed after spending two very busy weeks at The Mangoes.[94] They made a characteristic surprise farewell, planned so as to avoid the press. "Now take good care of yourself," Ford told his mentor, as his wife warmly embraced Mrs. Edison.[95] Captain J. Fred Menge, his agent Frank Stout and Jimmie Newton, the young friend of both Ford and Edison, were on hand to say goodbye.[96] The world's richest couple then left the Seaboard Station on their private car, the Fair Lane.

Menge undertook the *Suwanee* reproduction project, completing the hull in the summer of 1928. The hull was then loaded on flat cars in two separate sections for shipment from Fort Myers to Dearborn and Greenfield Village.[97] Ford then convinced

Menge he should move to Michigan to finish the job.[98] Menge, his wife and two sons did. When there he put the two hull sections together and fitted out the ship and all the while continued to be one of Ford's favorite fiddlers.[99]

Through his friendship with the Edisons, Jimmie Newton met Henry Ford and his wife, Clara. Mrs. Edison first introduced him to Ford. Newton remembered seeing Ford outside the laboratory bending over a barrel containing some of the early light bulbs which Edison had for some reason stored in Fort Myers for many years. The first practical light bulb had been invented in the Menlo Park laboratory in New Jersey.

Newton's relationship with the Fords became as close as his friendship with the Edisons. He liked to tell the story of a morning visit he paid to the Fords at The Mangoes.[100] When he arrived, he found Ford dictating jokes to his general secretary, Frank Campsall, who would type them on individual bits of paper for Ford to put in his pocket. Afterwards, Newton followed

Conrad Menge's crew building hull of reproduced *Suwanee* at boat ways on Orange River. Hull was then transported to Dearborn, Michigan, where it was fitted out to carry passengers around Greenfield Village.

Ford through the gate separating the Ford and Edison properties, and soon found him swapping stories with Edison, Ford's stories coming from his pocket in typewritten form. Newton was called to The Mangoes to learn square dancing from the Fords, who were accomplished folk dancers.[101] Such sessions took place in the living room with the carpet rolled up and the chairs set aside.

The Fords introduced Newton to another industrial mogul, Harvey Firestone. Though Firestone did not own a residence in Fort Myers nor did he spend his winters there, he did spend time in Fort Myers visiting his friends, the Edisons and the Fords.[102]

Newton's career in Florida real estate was interrupted by Firestone in the spring of 1928. He had just finished his organizational duties for Edison's birthday press conference in Fort Myers and was about to get in his car when Harvey Firestone called to him.[103] Firestone congratulated young Newton on the fine job at the press conference and then pointed across McGregor Boulevard to the stately entrance to Edison Park dominated by a Grecian maiden properly veiled. He asked how things were going with the downturn in the real estate market. Firestone then inquired whether Newton was interested in letting the development go until conditions improved and moving into something else. Newton said he couldn't abandon his development project because he had made commitments to the lot owners to finish the streets and sewers. Later, Newton sent a picture to Firestone to autograph. When the picture was returned, there was with it an application for employment with Firestone Rubber and a personal letter from Mr. Firestone himself.[104] By this time things were coming to a close in the development and what remained could be handled in his absence by his father. Newton showed the letter to Mrs. Edison. She told her husband. The Edison reaction was generally apprehensive although not dismissive. The letter didn't describe the position and Newton assumed it would be in real estate, based on his experience. When he arrived at Firestone's office, he discovered that Firestone wanted an assistant to the president, although the title was toned down to secretary to the president. The unofficial job description included traveling with Firestone, accompanying him to meetings, making arrangements of all kinds and following through on instructions from him.[105] Newton took the job.

Meanwhile, the Tamiami Trail was nearing completion and Barron Collier, chairman of the Tamiami Trail Celebration Committee, announced that Edison and Ford had both agreed to be honorary members of the committee.[106]

Making their first trip over the completed Tamiami Trail, the Edisons left on April 5 for Miami to visit Firestone.[107] The current state of rubber experiments must surely have been on the agenda for discussion. Before the month was out, Mrs. Edison, accompanied by Mrs. Clarence B. Chadwick, crossed the Everglades again by automobile en route to a state beautification meeting, where both spoke on the beautification of the newly constructed Tamiami Trail.[108] Meanwhile Edison was in Everglades City to congratulate Josie Billy, the recently named Seminole chief.[109] The chief was at the fairgrounds in Everglades City at an exhibit of a model Indian village.

The fair in Everglades City was held in conjunction with the official opening of the Tamiami Trail connecting Tampa to

Firestone and the Edisons take time out to rest on the running board.
Courtesy of Edison-Ford Winter Estates.

the north and Miami to the south via Fort Myers. The opening festivities in Fort Myers began on April 25, when cars from all over the state rolled across the wooden bridge over the Caloosahatchee River into Fort Myers.[110] That night a band played in the park, followed by vaudeville acts and speeches by political incumbents. Abraham Lincoln spoke—not President Abraham Lincoln, but an Indian guide who took the former president's name and who had led the Trailblazers through the Everglades in 1923 during the monumental Tamiami Trail construction project. Old Abe spoke in his native tongue, which was then interpreted by W. Stanley Hanson, a prominent citizen of Fort Myers and possibly the foremost authority in the country on the Seminole tribes. On the following day at 8:30 A.M., the long caravan pulled out for Miami with a three-hour lunch stop in Everglades City. By the time the caravan reached Miami, more than 500 cars were included.[111]

Workers disassembling the original Fort Myers Laboratory in preparation for shipment to Greenfield Village in Dearborn Michigan.
Courtesy of Edison-Ford Winter Estates.

The Edisons held an open house at Seminole Lodge during the opening celebration for the Tamiami Trail, marking the first time the estate had been open to the general public.[112] Mr. Edison could be seen at work with his plants, but no interviews were permitted.

Shortly after the opening celebrations, Barron Collier visited Edison in Fort Myers, and Edison received permission to plant a ten-acre experimental rubber plot on the wealthy advertiser's land in Collier County.[113] Whether that project was carried out is unknown.

The Edisons left Fort Myers on June 12, a later and longer stay than ever before.[114] By all accounts, it was one of their most enjoyable and active visits. At least 150 people came to the station to wish them well. The 81-year-old inventor told an old friend as he boarded the train, "I don't want to leave, but she makes me," pointing playfully toward his wife.[115]

Frank Campsall, Ford's secretary, arrived in town just before the Edisons left, to supervise the dismantling of the old laboratory for its journey to Dearborn.[116] The paper reported that much of the machinery and several pieces of old experimental apparatus were also being moved to Michigan. The dismantling commenced June 18.[117] The parts were loaded on flat cars for shipment to Dearborn. The little Fort Myers laboratory, which had seen forty-two years of service in the South, was going north to join the relocated Menlo Park laboratory at Greenfield Village.

While in Fort Myers, Campsall attended to renovations and refurbishing of The Mangoes to give it new life for the next season.[118] A servants' wing and downstairs guest bedroom were added. In December, Mrs. Ford came aboard the private car, Fair Lane, to inspect the finished improvements.[119] Mrs. Ford spent the night aboard the private car and then returned to Dearborn on the next day.

In October 1928, Edison visited Dearborn to participate in the groundbreaking of the Henry Ford Museum and turned the first spadeful of freshly poured concrete.[120] After turning the spade, he stepped out, leaving two footprints. The concrete pad and the two footprints are inside the front door of that museum today.

ROBB & STUCKY COMPANY

INCORPORATED

Furniture, Rugs and Victrolas

INTERIOR DECORATORS

FORT MYERS, FLORIDA

P. O. BOX 2225

2116-18 HENDRY STREET

Mrs. Henry Ford

Feb.	4	1 Refrigerator		130	00
	6	1 Porcelain Top Table		8	00
	8	1 Mirror		2	50
		Altering 5 Pr. Curtains		7	50
	9	1 #594 Peel Cane Chair		50	00
		1 Peel Cane Basket		7	00
		1 " " Stool		3	75
		1 #514 Peel Cane Chair		26	00
		1 #658 C Table		22	50
		1 Wedgwood Green Table)			
		4 " " Chairs)		58	00
		2 Shades for Living Room		4	30
		5 " for Maid's Room		10	75
		4 " " Mrs. Ford's Room		8	60
		1 Shade " " " Bath		1	90
		Hanging & Installing Drapes			
		J. Shoemaker , 6 Hours		12	00
		R. Silver 16½ "		16	50
		R. Cox 11½ "		11	50
	12	10 Shades Sage and White		20	00
		2 " " " "		4	30
	13	1 #658 Peel Cane Table		27	00
	15	Filling 5 Panel Screen, Labor & Material,		6	95
	20	3 Pr. Shade Brackets and Nails			20
		Refilling Screen		2	50
		Shortening Drapes & Joining Valance			
		2½ Hours Labor	2.50		
		3½ Dozen Hooks	.35		
		Decorator's Labor	1.50		
		2 Double Rods	2.00		
		8 Extensions	2.40	8	75
	21	Installing and Making Chair Ruffle		2	50
		1 Chair #5175		15	00
	23	3 Pair Drapes		15	00
		2 Pr. Brackets		2	00
		2 " Ends		1	50
		½ Doz. Rings			25
		Painting Fixtures		1	65
		Altering and Hanging 2 Pr. Drapes		3	00
				491	90

Invoice from Robb-Stucky Company to Mrs. Henry Ford
for furnishings to The Mangoes.

Courtesy of Greenfield Village in Dearborn, Michigan.

Ford

The wooden bridge completed only a few years earlier proved inadequate for the newly opened and much celebrated Tamiami Trail. The city had a concrete bridge on the drawing board and began discussion of a name for the mile-long structure. "How would Edison Bridge sound?" asked the editor of the *Fort Myers Tropical News*.[121] Edison-Ford Bridge was also suggested.[122] Still three years before its completion, the bridge received an official name from the State Road Department, the Edison Bridge.[123]

In October, the same month as the groundbreaking in Dearborn, Congress moved to award Edison the Congressional Medal of Honor. President Coolidge, in a brief radio address to the nation, paid honor to the "wizard of electricity."[124] The occasion marked the forty-ninth anniversary of the invention of the first practical incandescent lamp. The Congressional Medal was presented to Edison by Secretary Andrew Mellon, secretary of the treasury, at the inventor's West Orange laboratory.

20

Hail to the Chief

❧

Four titans of the age whose names are known
to the ends of the earth, all before our eyes in
the familiar setting of our palm lined streets; riding
among us where we work and play and live our lives.
—The Fort Myers Press

1929

Except for the "chief weed stalkers," the Fort Myers laboratory staff of seven men had arrived on January 16, 1929, ahead of the Edisons.[1] The weed stalkers were on their way, after scouring the landscape in New Mexico and Arizona for plant specimens.
The old Fort Myers laboratory had finally been transported to Dearborn in June 1928, and a new laboratory stood across McGregor from the residence. All of the equipment shipped down in the previous year and installed temporarily in the old laboratory had been moved into the new quarters.

Mrs. Edison planned a surprise for her husband and secretly had a small private office and chemical laboratory constructed on the site of the old laboratory.[2] A rear door opened onto a sunken garden where the original laboratory once stood. The private office was a gray building with a small front porch. It contained a desk and chair before an open fire place, books for the bookshelves and a set of chemical experimental equipment. On the wall hung a yellow banner that had been presented to Edison when he was inducted in the local Civitan Club as an honorary member. Edison used the small laboratory at night and on Saturday afternoons. The proximity to the house made it easier for the aging Edison, particularly since the main laboratory had been constructed across McGregor Boulevard. It was perfectly designed for the small armies of newsmen who descended on Seminole Lodge from time to time.

Scarlet bougainvillea surrounded the sunken garden, trained to a trellis and in full bloom when the Edisons arrived. Protecting those shrubs and vines from harm during the removal of the old lab had been one of the chief concerns of Mrs. Edison. The garden consisted of twenty-five small beds of plants and flowers, laid out in a geometric pattern designed by Mrs. Edison. Italian cypress grew inside the trellis at regular intervals.[3] Other improvements included two diving boards installed at the pool, and a green-flagged tile patio also at the pool.[4] Sea shells were spread in the walkways leading to the pool area and other walkways on the estate were carpeted with pine straw.

The train arrived as expected at 6:50 P.M. on January 16, 1929. About 200 persons waited to greet the welcome couple.[5]

Edison arrives for winter stay.
Courtesy of Edison-Ford Winter Estates.

The band played, "I'll Take You Home Again, Kathleen," the inventor's favorite song. Two movie cameramen and two news photographers recorded the events. The Civitans gathered en masse. Special friends Carl F. Roberts and J. Fred Menge were among the first to greet the couple. Frank Stout had his Lincoln Touring car ready to transport the Edisons to their home on McGregor Boulevard. As was the custom, Fred Ott had the Model T, to carry the baggage. Mr. Benney, who headed the Edison Botanic Research efforts in Fort Myers, also came. The inventor seemed to be in excellent health, a fact Mrs. Edison attributed to the extraction of his teeth, which had occurred since he was last in Fort Myers. He was carrying about twenty extra pounds which, in those days, was a sign of robust health. He wore his usual black suit, string tie, and brown slouch hat, and carried a coat over his arm. When asked if he would go to Miami to see his friend, President-Elect Hoover, he said he would be too busy to make the trip and that, "If Mr. Hoover wants to see me, he'll have to come to Fort Myers."[6]

On the following day he traded the dark clothes of the North for his Florida garb, a cream-colored suit and vest, a white shirt with a wing tip collar, and a white bow tie.[7] Instead of the usual Seminole Lodge floppy straw hat, he donned a new Leghorn. Properly uniformed for his jungle laboratory, he began work on the following day at 7 A.M. By 10 A.M., the press arrived and he posed for pictures outside his new main laboratory. When asked if he liked his new private office and the small lab his wife had built for him, he replied, "Oh, I like it fine, but I like this big laboratory better."[8] He worked until late in the afternoon and then drove to Fort Myers Beach with Mr. Benney and Mrs. Edison.

A few weeks later, the Fords arrived aboard the Fair Lane, and Henry Ford again eluded the press and other bystanders by disembarking at the Anderson Avenue crossing (Dr. Martin Luther King Jr. Boulevard) and walking from there to Edison's new laboratory on McGregor.[9] Mrs. Ford was driven in a new brown Lincoln limousine. Ford's secretary, Frank Campsall, and Captain J. Fred Menge, accompanied Ford on his walk to his home. They walked first into Edison's new laboratory as the

Edison works while Ford looks on in new Fort Myers laboratory.
Courtesy of Edison-Ford Winter Estates.

inventor sorted through notes on rubber plants. When he looked up and realized his friend was in his midst, he jumped to his feet, put his arm on Ford's shoulder and expressed delight at his presence. They then inspected the new laboratory, followed by a tour of the adjoining ten-acre rubber tract situated next to the laboratory.

Before the Edison arrival for the season, rumours had circulated concerning the possibility of a visit by President-Elect Herbert Hoover on the inventor's 82nd birthday. It was said he would come over the newly opened Tamiami Trail from his pre-inaugural site on Belle Isle in Miami.[10] In fact he did come not over the Tamiami Trail route but by yacht from Miami, with a landing at the Edison's dock on the Caloosahatchee River.[11]

The *Saunterer*, Hoover's yacht, anchored in the channel while its distinguished passenger made his way by tender to the pavilion at the end of the lengthy dock in front of Seminole

Hoover disembarking the tender from the *Saunterer*
shown anchored in the channel.
Courtesy of Edison-Ford Winter Estates.

The Edisons with President-Elect Hoover in Edison's jungle.
Courtesy of Edison-Ford Winter Estates.

Lodge. It was 10:35 A.M. when Edison greeted his guest from the dock with an affable "Hello Fisherman."[12] Hoover was an enthusiastic fisherman who had planned to remain in the Gulf waters for several days after the birthday visit. He had landed two sailfish while in Belle Isle and wanted to add a tarpon to his credits.[13]

An army of newspapermen and photographers swarmed the grounds of Seminole Lodge to witness the event, but after initial greetings, the press was banished from the estate. In less than an hour, a procession of six automobiles pulled out for a tour through the city. In the lead car were town officials.[14] The president-elect, Edison, Ford, and Firestone followed in the second car, along with a bevy of secret service men in a third car. A fourth car carried Mrs. Hoover, Mrs. Edison, and Herbert Hoover Jr.[15] The entourage entered Edison Park by the Grecian Maiden statue at its McGregor entrance. They drove past the new Edison Park School where the pupils lined the curb, and then proceeded to Cleveland Avenue. From Cleveland they proceeded to Anderson Avenue. From Anderson the procession moved to Second Street, passing Gwynne Institute and its pupils, who also lined the curb. They moved then to Evans Avenue, where many Negro residents and children stood, and from there to East First Street, where children from Edgewood and Tice assembled. Turning south on East First Street, the dignitaries had a magnificent view of the royal palms and the stately homes that lined both sides of that street. Mrs. Frank Alderman stood at curbside in front of her home with a bouquet of roses for Mrs. Hoover. The caravan then proceeded through the business district to Broadway, then to Main Street, and from there it traveled south along Main and McGregor back to Seminole Lodge.[16] The paper reported 20,000 onlookers lining the streets for the distinguished group. Two hundred additional law enforcement personnel from nearby counties kept the peace and protected the president-elect.

Thirty minutes after the procession began it ended and lunch was served at the Edison estate.[17] After lunch Edison found a chair in the yard where a short catnap could be had while the guests milled about the open verandas surrounding the guest house. Children arrived to see the future president and

Edison and Hoover exit Seminole Lodge onto McGregor
Boulevard to prepare for parade through town.
Courtesy of Edison-Ford Winter Estates.

birthday honoree, among them Kathryn Miller (Kathryn Palmer), who recalled they were escorted over to see the Wizard, who was fast asleep in a lawn chair. When Mrs. Edison attempted to arouse him, she told him there were children there. His semi-conscious and uncharacteristically grumpy reply, overheard by Kathryn Miller, "Well tell them to go away!"[18]

The Hoover party remained at Seminole Lodge through the afternoon and then boarded the *Saunterer* at 4:30 and headed for Punta Rassa for some fishing on the following day. They spent the night aboard the yacht in the river, but due to rough weather, Hoover left by automobile at 8:40 the next morning from Punta Rassa and proceeded back to Belle Isle. The *Saunterer*, with Mrs. Hoover and guests, proceeded out to sea to Miami.

Edison conducted his traditional interview with the press from his new private office. At 9 P.M. that evening, he again positioned himself in the little private office for a radio address to the nation. His son Charles, speaking from West Orange, introduced his father, who then gave the nation a 101-word address, acknowledging the very eventful day and expressing his heartfelt thanks for the many messages wishing him well. While Edison spoke from his McGregor office, a crowd of 250 gathered at the municipal auditorium for a birthday concert. After the radio address, the Edisons and Fords made an appearance at the concert.

The following day, the wives of the inventor, the motor car manufacturer, and tire manufacturer all attended a meeting of the Woman's Community Club.[19] After the meeting, the Firestones left for Miami.

In a few days normalcy was beginning to return and the Edisons and Fords were off to Clewiston to see the new sugar mills recently built by the Southern Sugar Company.[20] The party watched the entire process, from the dumping of the cane in the cane pit until it went through the crushers, rollers, boiling pans and evaporators to come out as raw, brown sugar. After leaving the mills, Edison commented, "It is high time that American Industries have protection against foreign competition."[21] Protectionism and high tariffs were popular political and economic themes of the day and of the Hoover presidency. Hoover too had visited Clewiston and the mills a few days before his visit to Fort Myers.

Ford was in a makeshift office at The Mangoes on February 19, when a rare interview with reporters took place.[22] He reiterated a recommendation made in the previous year that the City of Fort Myers should concentrate on making itself beautiful as a first step toward development. He said he spent several hours a day while in Florida trying to perfect an automatic machine for the manufacture of parts for his cars and that Edison assisted him in the effort. Ford said he had great confidence in Edison's ability to come up with a plant source for rubber production within the United States. "He has progressed so far that he may give this country a new and profitable industry . . . supplying our rubber."[23] Unlike Edison, who didn't have much going for physical exercise, Ford said, "My favorite form of exercise is running or brisk walking, but I always rest before meals."[24] At sixty-five he said he often ran several miles a day and exercised vigorously upon rising and retiring.

The annual county fair at Terry Park in East Fort Myers was in progress following Edison's birthday. The Edisons always attended the fair. At the 1929 fair, they strolled around the midway and, according to the *Press*, Mr. Edison expressed interest in "Snooky," the chimpanzee who wore clothes, smoked and generally conducted himself as if a human. Edsel Ford and his wife arrived on February 21 and attended the fair with his parents.[25]

Other diversions occurred as well as the fair. Mrs. Edison entertained Mrs. Ford at a tea at the Charlotte Harbor Hotel in Punta Gorda.[26] The Woman's Community Club held an old-fashioned dance at the Elks Club, with the Fords as the honored guests.[27] *The Fort Myers Press* described the Elk's Club as a place where jazz was king and "saxophones get hot and flaming youth makes whoopee."[28] Old-fashioned waltzes and the Virginia Reel made a stark contrast to the music normally heard in that jazz age hall. Mrs. Edison attended and wore an old-fashioned costume with a sunbonnet from which long brown curls fell to her shoulders. She danced the Virginia Reel with Mr. Ford, after which the Fords did an exhibition of the Varsuvians. Lancers, schottische and quadrille dances were all revived for the evening.[29]

After the dance, the Fords remained another day before returning to the North aboard their private car. The Edisons said their good-byes at Seminole Lodge while Ford's agent, Frank Stout, and his friends, Miss Flossie Hill and Captain J. Fred Menge were at the train.[30] A few days later, Charles Edison and his wife, Carolyn, arrived for a brief vacation with his parents.[31]

Edison got away from rubber long enough to go fishing with his old friend, Captain E. L. Evans.[32] He caught a good-sized tarpon, keeping it on for fifteen minutes, after which the fish jumped high in the air and dived beneath the boat, which succeeded in fouling Edison's line in the propeller. Mrs. Edison also achieved some success when she, while in the Gulf with some lady friends, landed a 100-pound stingeree. She was with Captain C. C. Trowbridge, a legendary fishing guide, whose home and boats were on Hendry Creek.

Though never enthusiastic about exercise, the inventor

Carolyn Edison and Mina Edison by reflecting pond
and the small office presented to Edison by Mina. The reflecting
pond is located where the original Fort Myers laboratory had
been before its removal to Dearborn, Michigan.
Courtesy of Edison-Ford Winter Estates.

would occasionally go for short walks around the neighborhood.
Gloria Shortlidge, then Gloria Durrance, lived with her parents
in a house that adjoined the Edison property on the East side of
McGregor Boulevard. She recalls seeing the elderly Edison walking in front of her home on Larchmont Street when she was
about five years old. When she confronted him on the sidewalk,
he gave her a pleasant greeting and a friendly and memorable pat
on the head.[33]

To their delight, the senior class of 1929 at Fort Myers High
School received their diplomas from the formally unschooled but
venerated inventor.[34] The name of each of the seventy-two seniors was called out by the superintendent, after which the diploma was presented by Mr. Edison. Mrs. Edison delivered the
address, telling the graduates,

231

Oh, could I but instill into your minds tonight
the desire to be the rare person with the deter-
mination to achieve. I would feel that I had
redeemed myself in a slight degree for all the
opportunities I neglected in my first half of life.
To awaken late in life to all the wonders and
possibilities of this life is better than never to
have awakened, but to be awake in the early
years of life ready and keen to make life worth
while earns for one marvelous privileges.[35]

Among the seniors handed diplomas by Thomas Edison
were Barbara Balch, Sue Spears, Tommy Howard, Norwood
Strayhorn, Don Hawkins and Lynn Gerald.[36] Barbara Balch
remembered with greater pride another event shortly before
graduation, the senior play.[37] She and Tommy Howard had the
leading roles. After the curtain fell, Mrs. Edison presented her
with a bouquet of flowers, a custom observed on more sophisti-
cated stages but never before in the frontier town of Fort
Myers.[38]

On the eve of the Edisons' departure, the Fort Myers
Roundtable, whose meetings occurred at Seminole Lodge, had a
farewell party for both Edisons at the Arcade Theater.[39] The
Edisons and John V. Miller, Mrs. Edison's brother, attended. A
local dance group performed "Sweethearts on Parade" and a vio-
linist also played, accompanied by Barbara Balch on the piano.[40]
A message flashed on the movie screen bidding the honored
guest to "come back early next fall." The celebrated inventor
then found himself as the leading man in a movie produced by
Fox Movietone, entitled "A Day With Thomas A. Edison."[41]
The movie had been shot earlier in the season at Seminole
Lodge and portrayed its protagonist crossing McGregor to his
new laboratory early in the morning, and then going home for
dinner in the evening. The movie had its premiere a week earlier in Atlantic City, New Jersey, in connection with "Light's
Golden Jubilee" celebration—the fiftieth anniversary of the
invention of the first practical incandescent light bulb.[42]

Three days before the great stock market crash of October
24, 1929, the Edison Institute, the parent organization for the

Henry Ford Museum and Greenfield Village, held its dedication ceremonies in Dearborn for the completed Greenfield Village. The event also climaxed "Light's Golden Jubilee." The museum building itself, which was an expanded architectural version of Independence Hall located adjacent to Greenfield Village, was only partially complete. President Hoover and the first lady, the Fords, Madame Curie, John D. Rockefeller Jr., Charles Schwab, Adolph S. Ochs, Otto H. Kahn, George M. Reynolds, Julius Rosenwald, Orville Wright, Walter Chrysler, and George Eastman all attended.[43] Edison's old British secretary, Samuel Insull, came, as did his early laboratory assistant, Frances Jehl. Captain Conrad Menge, then residing in Dearborn, served as the unofficial Fort Myers representative at the celebration.[44] The children of the second Edison marriage attended with their families. The children of Edison's first marriage were conspicuous by their absence. They had declined Ford's invitation because of their view that Menlo Park, New Jersey, the site of the invention, should host the fifty-year anniversary of the incandescent light—not Dearborn.[45]

Following scheduled events at the Greenfield Village site, the Fords held a banquet in the unfinished Independence Hall museum building. President Hoover delivered the principal address. Edison, still recovering from pneumonia and sapped of strength, said:

> This crowning event of Light's Golden Jubilee
> fills me with gratitude. As to Henry Ford, words
> are inadequate to express my feelings. I can only
> say to you, that in the fullest and richest mean-
> ing of the term—he is my friend.[46]

The Menlo Park Laboratory, where the phonograph, light bulb and many of the early inventions were developed, had been moved lock, stock and clay—seven-car loads of New Jersey clay to undergird the structure—and reconstructed as the flagship of the many relocated historic buildings in the historic theme park. The Fort Myers laboratory was one of those moved and occupied a nearby site in the village.

It had been a year filled with seminal events, a personal visit in Fort Myers by the president-elect of the United States, a nationwide radio tribute, local tributes in both Fort Myers and West Orange, and a final tribute in Dearborn in celebration of incandescent light's golden jubilee attended by the sitting president and many of the great men and women from around the world.

21

Centerstage Mina

❦

*Thousands of smiling happy faces surrounding
Mrs. Edison and her flower guild ladies is a substantial
corroboration that the people believe and endorse
what she is doing to make Fort Myers the
most beautiful city in Florida.*
—The Fort Myers Press

1927–1931

In the early years, Mina Edison rationed her social activities in
Fort Myers and engaged in few if any civic activities. She was
there to relax with her precious "Dearie" and not to be socially
active. "Dearie" was content to be alone with "Billie" (his pet
name for Mina), his "jungle," and laboratory. Word would sometimes drift out that Mina would not accept calls in the upcoming
season so that her stay would afford both Mr. Edison and herself
the rest and relaxation they desperately needed. Other times she
displayed a dislike for the local people whom she believed were
taking advantage of her husband. In 1912 she wrote Charles, "I
feel like putting up a cement wall all about our place and letting
those thieves alone. I detest the people down here."[1] For many
years, her social relationships centered among the well-to-do seasonal visitors from the North, some of whom stayed at the Royal
Palm Hotel while others wintered in imposing homes. While

these social relationships continued throughout her visits, as time went on she included more and more of the townspeople in her social schedule, finally developing a genuine affection for the local residents. Much of this change in attitude came about in the late 1920s as she became a civic activist, which brought her in constant contact with local citizens. Her friends in and inter- action with the black community made her a pioneer in race relations in the town. In the end she was not only engaged in community affairs but a stalwart in all things social.

One of her first civic crusades involved a local political issue, the location of the new concrete bridge spanning the Caloosahatchee. The existing wooden bridge crossed the river from Fremont Street in East Fort Myers, about a mile upriver from the downtown business district. In a 1927 address to the Civic League, Mina Edison spoke against a proposed downtown location, arguing the new bridge should be located at the exist- ing wooden span east of town.[2] The expansive beauty of the river in the downtown area was the underlying reason for her concern, for she hoped to preserve a clear unobstructed view from the town center. A *Fort Myers Press* editorial followed with a hardy accord for the position advanced by Mrs. Edison, but did so not only for the aesthetic reasons offered by Mrs. Edison, but to ensure the retention of a commercial exposure to bridge traffic from East Fort Myers to and through the existing downtown business area.[3]

In 1928 Mina Edison founded the organization known as the Roundtable, composed of members of the combined civic clubs of the town. She became its first president.[4] The first meet- ing occurred at Seminole Lodge and members agreed on a pro- gram of work. The Rotary Club would concentrate on cleaning up vacant lots, the Chamber of Commerce on beautification of highways, and the Woman's Community Club would work on its plan of block gardening. She spoke to local clubs touting the pur- pose of the Roundtable, which was to avoid duplication of effort among the groups. She urged concentration on specific beautifi- cation projects and urged a coordinated effort through the Roundtable.[5] Representatives of the City Commission and County Commission attended its early meetings. As a result, replacement palms were soon set out on First Street and along McGregor.[6] A tax levy for beautification, which had been discontinued two years before, was restored. In 1929, the only Christmas that she and her husband spent in Fort Myers, Mina Edison herself participated in the delivery of baskets to the needy, a Christmas project of the Roundtable.[7] Of particular interest to her was the hearty cooperation from the black community, which had beautified the school grounds and other areas in the Dunbar area. She commended that section for its splendid cooperation and spirit.[8] Hailing her as a "social engineer of the finest ability," Florida environmental author and Presidential Medal of Freedom recipient, Marjorie Stoneman Douglas of Miami, wrote for McCall's magazine that Mina Edison's founding and nurturing of the Roundtable ought to be recognized as one of the most outstanding civic achievements, "since it is an achievement, not just in the material improvements of the city, but in the building up of a most amazing and creative community spirit."[9]

She served two days as a salesperson for the benefit of The Woman's Community Club at M. Flossie Hill's Womens' Apparel, where she was not only a salesperson but also general

Mina meets with Roundtable.
Courtesy of Edison-Ford Winter Estates.

manager of the benefit. Club members took over operation of the store for two days and in return received a percentage of the sales.[10] The project went so well that the group repeated the project the next month at Robb & Stucky Furniture. At Robb & Stucky, Mrs. Edison decorated one of the sidewalk show windows with a walnut Berkey and Gay dining table she selected from company stock.[11] She used her own linens, china and table accessories and again served as salesperson.

Decrying wives and mothers in the business world, Mina Edison addressed the Fort Myers Woman's Club. "Modern women are denying themselves the great happiness which comes of service to those near and dear to them." She continued, " . . . the spirit of the day seems to be that we must get into business, politics and offices to be recognized, but my plea is that we dignify the home and make men and women honor and respect us in our own field." She observed that many women saw the work of the home as real drudgery when, "I feel that one can create real art in handling linen and dishes. A linen closet properly kept is a joy forever."[12] Despite these opinions, she would later establish a relationship with the Business and Professional Womens' Club, becoming a member as a "home executive."

While the Roundtable and the Woman's Community Club were favorites of Mina Edison, nothing was closer to her in Fort Myers than the garden clubs. In all, she attended twenty-seven reported garden club and plant guild meetings during the 1930 season.[13] The plant guild and its member garden clubs held an event called the "Illuminated Fleet," which was held on the waterfront at Dean Park. It was a water festival and began in the late afternoon and continued after dark with illuminated boats passing in review from the Caloosahatchee waterfront adjacent to Dean Park on East First Street.[14] Two thousand people gathered for the passing of the illuminated fleet at 8 P.M., despite a drenching rain. Mrs. Edison served as general chairman and worked throughout the day to get the Plant Guild booths ready. The water festival occurred just a few months after the stock market crash of 1929, in the midst of a gloomy and pessimistic period of American history. To her credit, on the day following the festival, *The Fort Myers Press* ran a letter to the editor extending the sincerest congratulations to:

> our First Lady of Fort Myers upon the drawing together of so many thousands of people. Mrs. Thomas A. Edison and her flower Guild have done more this winter to banish gloomy pessimism than any one factor. Last night the thousands of smiling happy faces surrounding Mrs. Edison and her flower Guild ladies is a substantial corroboration that the people believe and endorse what she is doing to make Fort Myers the most beautiful city in Florida.[15]

Representing the National Plant, flower and Fruit Guild, Mina Edison in 1931 selected a site on the south side of the courthouse and ceremonially shoveled a spadeful of earth on the roots of a live oak planted by the guild as a living monument to George Washington.[16] The Plant Guild, which also met at Seminole Lodge, sought to divide the city into different guild zones, with each responsible for cleanup and beautification of its assigned area.[17] She met with the various zones and was guest of honor at the Seminole Park zone meeting, at which she congratulated the members for their neighborhood accomplishments and conveyed a message from her husband that everyone should plant vines, mentioning specifically the red bougainvillea, the trumpet vine and the bell-like begonia, so that a continuous colorful bloom would enhance the green background of existing palms and pines within the town.[18] She also addressed the guild in the Valencia Terrace zone, where she stressed the necessity of having every woman in every neighborhood cooperating with all agencies so that "the city would be fragrant with flowers from every home . . . and adequate care for birds so that they too would be loath to leave."[19]

Birdlife was yet another passion for Mina Edison. She attended a meeting of Girl Scouts and told them that she and Mr. Edison would rise in the morning, finish their breakfast and set about their daily routine of feeding the birds who happened by.[20] A few days later, she took the scouts on an all-day trip to the pelican rookery on Hendry Creek with Captain Trowbridge.[21] She spoke to a group of fifty persons in the clubhouse in Valencia Park on birds, praising the mockingbird and the blue bird but showing less respect for the sparrow, which along with cats she considered a "fellow-destroyer of bird life."[22]

Mina Edison had a special interest in the Dunbar community. She was not only the president of the Plant Guild itself, but also chairman of District No. Seven, the Safety Hill Garden Club, one of the several zones within the guild.[23] Dunbar was commonly known as Safety Hill and encompassed what was generally regarded as the black community. She was very complimentary of the contribution made by the Safety Hill Garden group and the significant improvements made by them to their neighborhood.[24] On her initial visit to the area, she drove nearly hub-deep in sand to inspect the school houses, but after the group was formed, the men of the neighborhood spent their free time hauling shell for the streets and planting trees, shrubs, and flowers to add a pleasing appearance to the schools and churches.[25] While there, she attended a program of music featuring one hundred voices singing songs and spirituals.

Early in the 1930 season, the chairmen of the respective garden clubs within the city were feted at a garden tea at Seminole Lodge in appreciation for their efforts.[26] The sunset tea was held outdoors under the live oaks on the river. Mrs. Effie Henderson sang love songs from a gondola which passed along the river's edge, with Bob Halgrim (the Sloane childrens' babysitter) as the gondolier.[27] In the next year Mina Edison entertained a group of sixty garden club members at a theater party at the Arcade Theater.[28] "New Moon," starring Lawrence Tibbett and Grace Moore, was playing. Also in 1931 she and Clara Ford were hostesses with the Edison Park Garden Group at an outdoor tea. Edison, Ford and Firestone, who happened to be on hand, were invited across the street to the tea, but they declined. Edison was resting and Ford and Firestone were "in conference."[29]

Mina Edison was also on the giving and receiving end of other teas, dinners, and parties. She attended a silver tea held by the Daughters of the American Revolution and also teas at the homes of friends.[30] She entertained at the Royal Palm Hotel with the Robley Newtons and Sidney Davis present, and with

Garden tea for garden clubs held at Seminole Lodge along seawall.
Courtesy of Edison-Ford Winter Estates.

others at the Hotel Charlotte Harbor in Punta Gorda. In 1928 she entertained seventy-five persons at a theater party featuring the American Legion's "Buddies," a war comedy then on tour.[31]

Mina Jane Geddes was Jimmie Newton's niece and the granddaughter of Dr. and Mrs. Robley Newton, all being exceptional friends of the Edisons. Mina Jane became the godchild of Mrs. Edison and on her first birthday in 1931, Mrs. Edison held a birthday party at Seminole Lodge.[32] In addition to ice cream and cake and presents for the birthday child, there were dolls, blocks, rattles and mechanical toys given as favors. Nat Cornwell was one of those at the party and still has the party favor, a set of wooden animals on wheels.[33]

Mrs. Clarence B. Chadwick was one of Mina Edison's companions in the Plant Guild. When she became ill and unable to attend guild meetings, Mina Edison recruited a group of twenty friends. After a sumptuous pompano dinner at the Gondola Inn, a popular eating spot built on piling over the river, the jovial and well fortified group went to the Chadwick home on East First Street and serenaded Mrs. Chadwick from her patio.[34]

At the age of 67, Mina Edison with her sister Grace

Hitchcock, were the guests of Mrs. Robley Newton at the Fort Myers Country Club, where she took up the game of golf for the first time, playing four holes.[35] She made each hole with lucky elevens. On the first tee, she missed the ball altogether, but redeemed herself on the next try, sending the ball on a ninety-yard straight drive. On the third hole, a water hazard, she made the green in five and lack of putting experience forced her to hole out in 11. She enjoyed the experience enough to become a member and order a full set of "sticks." Charles congratulated his mother on her new-found game. "I suppose that this time you are a regular bug & have father out on the links every day."[36] He asked his mother to ask Uncle Hal (Hitchcock) "if he remembers teaching me how to hold a club and then how mad he got when I made the first hole in three."[37]

Another literary group drawing Mina Edison's attention was the Valinda Society, named for Mina Edison's mother.[38] The group offered courses to its members through the New York-based Chautauqua Institution her father had helped found. Meetings were held at Seminole Lodge and, in late May, Mina Edison presented those who had successfully completed courses with Chautauqua diplomas.[39]

Underlying much of her civic interests was the enhancement of the natural beauty of the area. To her, beauty was manifest in nature itself, the gardens made by man, and the orderliness of one's surroundings. Music, another of her passions, was to the ear what beauty was to the eye. She spoke to the Fort Myers Music Club making a plea for music in the home, which she called home orchestras.[40] "The home orchestra seems to me an ideal way to foster a united family companionship. If there were more family groups who found recreation in music it would bring about a community spirit of happiness," she said.[41] The Music Club presented her an honorary life membership.[42] In May 1928 both Mr. and Mrs. Edison hosted a concert by the Fort Myers Music Club.[43]

Mina Edison became a very visible public speaker—greatly in demand in 1930. She was the featured speaker at the Chamber of Commerce, Girl Scout Troup 2, the Junior High School PTA, and the Rotary Club.[44] She also gave the commencement address at the junior high school graduation and taught the 100-member Young Mens' Wesley Bible Class.[45] She addressed a local cooking school sponsored by the *Tropical News* with helpful hints on food preparation, including an exhortation to say grace before each meal.[46]

Mrs. Edison had established a relationship with the Young Men's Wesley Bible Class at the First Methodist Church. Sidney Davis, the class teacher, frequently invited Mrs. Edison to be its guest teacher.[47] In 1930 she managed to bring her husband to a barbeque hosted by the class at Fort Myers Beach.[48] In the following year, Harvey Firestone was in town on his second visit for the year, most likely to trade reports on the status of a new plant source for rubber.[49] At the invitation of Mrs. Edison he attended the class, joining the singing of old and familiar hymns. When Mothers' Day arrived, a Sunday radio broadcast from a large Bible class in Miami was dedicated to Mrs. Edison and the Young Mens' Wesley Bible Class at First Methodist Church in Fort Myers.[50] Sidney Davis arranged to have a radio installed in the classroom so that the Fort Myers class could hear the broadcast. Mrs. Edison took on her traditional Mother's Day role of passing out red and white carnations to the members. Red carnations were given to those whose mothers were living, while white ones were reserved for those whose mothers had died. Mrs. Edison, who had established a special relationship with the class and would eventually become the class "Mother," held a movie theater party for members at the Arcade Theater, where "Trader Horn" was playing.[51]

Mrs. Edison's friendship with Sidney Davis continued and in 1931, when the Edisons began to show silent movies at Seminole Lodge, they invited Davis to a "picture" and supper at Seminole Lodge.[52] She corresponded with him frequently in a manner reminiscent of a mother or grandmother corresponding with a child or grandchild. In January, word reached Mrs. Edison in New Jersey that Davis had been ill but recovering and she wrote to him as she was about to leave for Fort Myers. The letter expressed her concern and hope that the roses she had sent expressed "our joy; at your recovery."[53] Davis himself had established a practice of sending flowers to Mrs. Edison on special occasions. He did so again when the Edisons arrived in Fort Myers in 1931. Mrs. Edison obliged with a hand-delivered note to Davis, "Thanks for carnations. Can't you come up and take supper with us this evening? 7 o:clock."[54] On Easter Sunday, Davis taught the Wesley Class with Mrs. Edison in attendance, after which she wrote to thank him for the message, "What a blessed day you gave me yesterday!" She also thanked him for the Easter lilies which had greeted her at Seminole Lodge upon returning from church.[55]

On Mothers Day in 1930, Mina Edison rode with her husband to Collier City about 60 miles south of Fort Myers. It was another of Barron Collier's developments and was located at Marco.[56] Collier had big plans for Collier City, which had a superior elevation and water access. Florida's boom had come to an end in 1926 and it was unusual to see land development as late as 1930, particularly after the stock market crash of 1929, but Collier was one of the last to feel the pinch, since his advertising business in New York had not yet felt the grip of the depression. The local press reported that several houses had already been built on some of the highest peaks on the island and the "natural scenic beauty of verdant hills and undulating valleys, outstretched arms of water reaching far into the valleys and the unsurpassed beauty of the Ten Thousand Islands seen in the distance beggar [sic] description."[57] The development was reached by turning off the Tamiami Trail a few miles south of Naples where "one travels about five miles over fairly good dirt roads to the ferry."[58] On the return trip through Naples, the party stopped at Tolbey's Coffee Shop for a glass of milk for Mr. Edison.[59] Mrs. Edison noted that Mrs. Tolbey was not wearing a Mother's Day flower in honor of her mother. In a gesture of spontaneity that typified the gracious lady, she unpinned her own white carnation and pinned it on Mrs. Tolbey.

Of all the groups where one would least expect to find her, it would be at the Business and Professional Womens' Club. It was Mina Edison herself who told another woman's club she deplored wives and mothers in the business field. Her popularity was such that even the professional women's group desired her company. Mina Edison entertained the professional women group at a luncheon at the Gondola Inn.[60] In 1931 she was honored as a Fort Myers pioneer by the Junior Woman's Club (it had been forty-five years since she first arrived in Fort Myers on her honeymoon and thus she easily qualified as a pioneer).[61] Adding to her long list of Fort Myers civic associations she was inducted into the Spanish American War Veterans auxiliary, her qualification coming from the death of her brother, Theodore Miller, killed while with the Rough Riders in the battle of San Juan.[62] Finally she became a regent of the Fort Myers chapter of the Daughters of the American Revolution.[63]

In 1931, the last visit in which her husband was with her in Fort Myers, Mina Edison caused the local Red Cross chapter to reverse an earlier decision not to participate in a $10,000,000 national drive to aid the victims of the Dust Bowl and the incredible drought in the Southwestern United States. As a result she became the honorary chairman of the local drive.[64] She lobbied local groups for support of the Red Cross in that mission.[65]

Both of the Edisons made charitable contributions to their adopted community. Since 1916, Fort Myers had its own hospital—Lee Memorial—and the Edisons were ardent supporters. On April 11, 1930, Mina Edison presented the private non-profit hospital with a $100 gift earmarked for its sustaining fund.[66]

To round out her many contributions to the community, Mina Edison presented it with her very own recipe for the removal of green pond scum, presumably for use in cleaning swimming pools (of which there were few) and fish ponds. The Fort Myers Press reported the formula on the society page with no explanation other than whose recipe it was:

> 1–8 oz. blue stone to 11,000 gallons of water.
> Place blue stone in cheese cloth and draw
> around pool several times. Small quantities will
> not kill fish. Potassium permanganate may also
> be used. Dilute the solution to a claret wine
> color and add to the water. It will kill the algae
> but not injure animal life.[67]

With the incredible devotion and energy unleashed by Mina Edison in the late twenties, she too became the object of veneration by the local community. In 1928 she appeared at a testimonial tea given by the Fort Myers Woman's Community Club in her honor and attended by 500 people plus 200 children from vacation Bible school.[68] The event was held in the Municipal Auditorium at the end of the pier located where the Caloosahatchee Bridge now commences its span across the river. "Dearie"himself made a brief appearance, no doubt ordered to be there, as he had been on so many other occasions by Mina. In 1931, the Plant Guild made a special gift of appreciation to Mrs. Edison of two large three-foot vases fashioned in blue-green pottery with wrought iron stands.[69] Also, in that year, a grateful town formally thanked Mina Edison for her continuous efforts in its behalf through a resolution of the Chamber of Commerce.[70] "Dearie," on his last visit to Fort Myers, must surely have been moved by the expressions of gratitude heaped on his beloved "Billie."

22

The Longest Stay

*Lately some microbes have spotted me and done some
experimenting with my internal machinery. . . .*
—Thomas Edison

1929

Reversing a tradition of Christmas with family at Glenmont, in
1929 "Dearie" and "Billie" boarded a train bound for Fort Myers
and his cherished "jungle," arriving at the station in Fort Myers
on December 5. This was his first and last Christmas in Fort
Myers. The couple remained at Seminole Lodge for their longest
stay ever, more than six months.

Although Edison had a bout with pneumonia during the
summer and a grueling schedule during the year, he looked fit as
he stepped off the train at 9:35 P.M. and greeted the usual crowd
of welcomers.[1] As had been the custom for several years, Mr.
Stout helped the Edisons into the Lincoln while Freddie Ott
loaded up the Model T with baggage. When they arrived at
Seminole Lodge they found the home filled with flowers, the
gifts of local friends. Edison took a short stroll about the starlit
grounds and returned to the veranda for a chair to "drink in the
delights of the tropical night."[2] The next morning, he was at the
laboratory thirty minutes before his crew.

The Atlantic Coastline porters who brought the celebrated
genius to Fort Myers rated his generosity on a much higher scale

The Edisons strolling through his jungle.
Courtesy of Edison-Ford Winter Estates.

than that of John D. Rockefeller. Rockefeller gave out dimes as tips while Edison passed out $5 gold pieces.[3]

Unlike the crowds that gathered at Glenmont for festive holiday meals, Christmas day at Seminole Lodge was relatively quiet with only a few guests coming for dinner.[4] Edison did not partake of the traditional fare but opted instead for his accustomed diet of milk. Presents came from friends as well as persons he had never met. Books came from publishers, hats and shoes from clothing makers, and a variety of gifts from a range of admirers. In the afternoon Edison ambled over to the goldenrod plantings behind the new laboratory on the other side of McGregor Boulevard.[5] Meanwhile, at Glenmont, the family remnant gathered for the sake of tradition. Charles Edison wrote his mother, "Glenmont could not have been any nicer—the tree and its fixings, the talk with you, n'everything was great. But— it wasn't like having you there. My what a difference!"[6]

After Christmas, Harvey Firestone surprised the Edisons with a one-day visit.[7] While in town he stated that though his automobile tires were made of imported rubber that year, it would not be long before they would be made of domestic rubber. "I haven't the slightest doubt that within the next decade thousands of acres of Florida land will be devoted to growing the plant which Mr. Edison finds is most suitable for the production of rubber on a commercial scale."[8] While Edison continued to view his rubber venture as an emergency measure and not one designed to produce rubber competitively for ordinary markets, both Firestone and Ford from time to time suggested otherwise.

1930

Mina Edison granted an interview to a journalist from *American Magazine* in which she gave an intimate description of her husband.[9] She said he had always taken a philosophical and stoic view of his deafness, but that recently he had voiced the wish that he could hear his favorite song again, "I'll Take You Home Again, Kathleen."[10] At that point in the interview, "Dearie" interrupted to give his view of the "talkies." He said:

> The talkies have spoiled everything for me. There isn't any more good acting on the screen. My, my how I should like to see Mary Pickford or Clara Bow in one of those good, old fashioned silent pictures. They concentrate on the voice now; they've forgotten how to act.[11]

"Billie" continued with her description:

> Mr. Edison is a man of strong likes and dislikes but it is upon the customs of people, rather than people themselves, that he turns a critical mind. He loves humanity. I have never heard him say he dislikes any particular person. Happiness, gayety, and cheerfulness are the things he craves in his everyday life. He detests confusion and disorder.
>
> He is sentimental and romantic, yet you couldn't induce him to read a novel which has nothing to recommend it other than a love story. Such books as Les Miserables and Toilers of the Sea are sources of the keenest pleasure to him.

Victor Hugo stands out in his mind as one of the greatest writers the world has ever known. Though he has little use for poetry, Longfellow's Evangeline and Tennyson's Enoch Arden rank close to the top of the list of favorite works.[12]

Early in January pilots from the Naval Air Station at Pensacola staged a private air circus directly over the Edison's home on McGregor.[13] In addition to Navy pilots, "Daredevil Burns" flew over the city doing his famous knee hang and other stunts.[14] The Navy pilots were dinner guests of the Edisons the night before the event.

The Fords, accompanied by his secretary, Frank Campsall, arrived in Fort Myers on the morning of February 7.[15] Announcement of Ford's visit raised speculation about whether he would arrive aboard the Atlantic Coast Line or the Seaboard Railway, which would in turn determine which train depot would host the arrival. This year the Fair Lane was connected to a Seaboard locomotive and stopped at the Seaboard Station in East Fort Myers.[16] True to his nature and his established Fort Myers tradition, Ford slipped off the train and made his way on foot into town and to The Mangoes, his home on McGregor Boulevard. Before reaching his home, he stopped at Edison's new laboratory and had a private reunion with his friend and mentor. The two then crossed the street and were joined by their spouses.[17]

During the afternoon, Ford, dressed in a gray tweed suit, a brown top coat and a derby hat, took another walk, this time through Edison Park Subdivision to Cleveland Avenue (Tamiami Trail).[18] From there he walked south a half mile to Linhart Avenue, then back to McGregor, where he walked north along that boulevard back to The Mangoes. Linhart Avenue lacked both pavement and sidewalks, so the walk was down the middle of the well-worn path. A few cars, some Fords, unceremoniously honked, forcing off the road the man who, many thought the richest in the world.

With Ford present, all that was needed to bring the famous three together for the annual Edison birthday party was Harvey Firestone; he arrived a day early.[19] The birthday started with the traditional 9:30 A.M. interview, which for the second time was

Ford, Edison and Firestone sitting on steps of new laboratory.
Courtesy of Edison-Ford Winter Estates.

held in the new little office constructed by Mina on the site of the old laboratory.[20] About twenty-five reporters and photographers came. Mina Edison had presented her husband with a yellow wheel chair, but for the birthday interview, he walked from the house to the new little office, using a cane, which he slyly told reporters was ornamental only. Once in the office, he parked his cane and sat at the desk and began to review the written questions that had been propounded. "How old do you feel?" was one of the questions. "Generally 50 years," Edison answered in writing with his sharpened laboratory pencil, "but lately some microbes have spotted me and done some experimenting with my internal machinery so I feel about 85 years."[21]

Questions were asked on a variety of subjects:

Q.: "In your opinion will television be practical for home entertainment?"

A.: "Some day."

Q.: "Do you think that absolute prohibition will ever be accomplished in the United States?"

A.: "Yes."

Q.: "What will become of common labor when the full automatic machine eliminates hand work?"

A.: "He will own a home and a lot of new things pro-

251

viding alcohol don't intervene."

Q.: "In your opinion do developments in electrical and poisonous gas and destructive implements make impossible or highly improbable another world war?"

A.: "No."[22]

Following the interview, Edison attended the dedication of a memorial plaque in Evans Park honoring both the Edisons.[23] Although the placque inscription indicates Light's Golden Jubilee as its focus, the likeness of Thomas Edison appeared on one side and of Mina Edison on the other. Also inscribed were the words, "Erected by the Citizens of Fort Myers." The affection of the town's people for both Mr. and Mrs. Edison was clearly apparent. Dr. Hamilton Holt, President of Rollins College in Winter Park, Florida, again gave the keynote address, having served in that capacity in the previous year. Two thousand people reportedly attended, including the Fords and the Firestones.[24] Edison wore a dark suit, a new pearl gray fedora, wing tip collar, and dark tie while Mina Edison wore a loose white gown, a white silk scarf, a wide-brimmed white straw hat and a long strand of pearls. She carried a large bouquet of red roses presented by the women of the dedication committee. Movietone, Pathe and Paramount recorded the event on newsreel.[25]

The plaque was placed in the public park on the property formerly occupied by Edison's old friend and crony, E. L. Evans.[26] Perhaps no one in Fort Myers had a closer, more enduring friendship with Edison than Evans, the association having begun within hours after Edison first set foot off the boat at the Keystone Hotel wharf in Fort Myers.[27] Their relationship had been one of man-to-man talk peppered with good-natured and salty banter. A month after the birthday, Edison was in the Heitman-Evans Store demanding to know, "Where is he?"[28] Captain Evans appeared and the two engaged in their usual ribbing and jesting. Edison wanted to know how his friend stayed so young and Evans answered, "By living in Florida all year around and not galavanting up North to catch my death of cold in that climate."[29]

The day after the birthday bash, the inventor, his wife, her sister Grace, and the Firestones attended the county fair.[30] They toured the local agricultural exhibits, prompting Edison to exclaim to Firestone, "Nothing like Fort Myers and the Lee County Fair. Wonderful exhibits this year."[31] The party then proceeded to the first midway attraction, a booth where dolls, lamps, and stuffed animals were won on the turn of a wheel. Mrs. Firestone won a baby doll and Mrs. Edison a stuffed rabbit. Mrs. Edison was asked what color rabbit she wanted, and she had to turn to her husband for help. "Yellow," he replied, and for the rest of the midway tour, Mr. Edison lugged the yellow rabbit for his lucky wife. The Wizard tried the game, but after seven tries with a nickel on number 11, he gave up. Before leaving, the group visited a German Police dog act in which a dog named "Silver King" shook hands with the inventor, presumably after the curtain fell. They passed the "Leaping Lena" ride and the "Whoopee" but remained comfortably on the ground. Edison was intrigued by the thirty-foot python, but Firestone refused to look at it. Before leaving, the women consulted Madame Zona about their respective fortunes.[32]

The Fords visited the fair on the following day, a Friday, with Mrs. Edison back for another round along with a group of forty-six persons from the Roundtable. [33] Edison had other plans that day but promised to attend the fair again before it closed. As the large group started its tour of the midway, Mina Edison admonished them to "just be boys and girls again."[34] Ford was reluctant to take his first ride on the merry-go-round, but with sufficient chiding mounted a white steed and was quite taken with the machinery propelling the carousel and with the music box. "Leaping Lena" was next and Mina Edison promptly took a seat in car number 5 next to Father Shore, the Episcopal minister. They moved on to the "Crystal Palace," Silver King, the German Shepherd "actor," the wax works, and the Filipino midgets.

The Fords entertained in their home on Sunday.[35] Guests included the Edisons and a few others. After dinner the party moved from The Mangoes to Seminole Lodge, where a fire burned in the fireplace. Later they were joined by Jimmie Newton and his parents, the Robley Newtons. Newton, the

developer of Edison Park, was visiting his parents in Fort Myers
after moving in 1928 from Fort Myers to Akron, Ohio, to be secretary to Harvey Firestone.

After almost a month in Fort Myers, the private railroad car
Fair Lane pulled out of the East Fort Myers Seaboard depot.[36]
Before leaving, Ford granted *The Fort Myers Press* an exclusive
interview conducted by Ronald Halgrim in the garage at The
Mangoes.[37] He told Halgrim he intended to prolong the useful
life of man through extensive experiments in the value and proper combination of foods consumed. He was not looking for a
"new-fangled" diet but rather the right combination of food coupled with proper exercise.

The most important thing is to group foods of one kind in a
single meal. . . . We find best results come from eating . . . fruits
for breakfast, proteins for lunch and starch at dinner. . . . The
biggest factor in causing sickness and in destroying the efficien-
cy of the body and mind, is over-eating and the lack of exercise.
Overeating puts older people out of business. I see no reason why
old people should cease to be useful if they eat properly, keep
working to some good end and keep their mind busy.[38]

Ford said he had a laboratory at Dearborn with trained people looking into the "food proposition." Their findings would be
released when completed. He told Halgrim his favorite forms of
exercise were walking, running, wood chopping and dancing. He
was not interested in competitive sports. Ford's views on diet and
the "food proposition" carried over to other forms of human consumption, including cigarettes and alcohol. Both Edison and
Ford had taken strong positions in favor of Prohibition. They
were recorded before the House Judiciary Committee as strongly
in favor of retaining the Eighteenth Amendment, Ford stating
his opinion that, "sane people of the nation" would not see it
repealed, and Edison claiming that "prohibition is the greatest
experiment yet made to benefit mankind."[39]

After Ford left, Firestone visited Seminole Lodge briefly
and made available to Mrs. Edison his big tri-motored, all-
metal airplane to take passengers for short flights for the benefit of the Plant Guild beautification program and their
Illuminated fleet Festival.[40] Fifty persons paid $2 each to take

the brief ride over the town.

Two weeks after the birthday festivities had occurred, the formally unlettered inventor led the academic procession at Rollins College in Winter Park, Florida, where he was awarded an honorary doctorate in science.[41] Edison had not always enjoyed the strong support of academia nor had he necessarily given it his. He did employ many college-educated assistants, including Ph.D.s. While in Fort Myers, Edison announced his second annual four-year scholarship to be awarded to a boy based on examinations conducted in West Orange.[42] Ford had strong views on education, supporting vocational and technical training. In a much publicized statement made while in Fort Myers, Ford vowed to spend the remainder of his life and $100,000,000 in support of his educational plans.[43]

The trip to visit Firestone in Miami became an annual event. For the 1930 trip, the Edisons were accompanied by their friends, Dr. and Mrs. Robley Newton.[44] During the two-day stay, the party visited the Firestone rubber gardens in Miami Beach, the Chapman Field experimental farm near Homestead, and the Miami Aquarium.

The Edisons made a trip into the Everglades on March 16. They traveled first to Immokalee and from there into the Everglades, then back to Fort Myers.[45] W. Stanley Hanson, local authority on Seminole Indians and on wildlife indigenous to the Everglades, went along. En route a flock of wild turkeys crossed their path, which provided the party with live entertainment.

Barron Collier, the namesake developer of Collier County, continued a friendship with the Edisons, inviting them to his Useppa Island tarpon retreat for lunch. For the outing, the Edisons were joined by houseguest Lucy Bogue, friends Sidney Davis, Mrs. Alexander Ray and others. The group drove first to Punta Gorda where they boarded one of Collier's yachts for a leisurely cruise to the island.[46]

Another house guest during the season was Edison's oldest child, Marion (Dot) Oeser.[47] Mrs. Oeser lived in Connecticut at the time, having returned to the United States from Germany after a failed eighteen-year marriage to a German military officer.

"Tree-Planting Day" was observed in Fort Myers with the

Edison and party visiting Seminoles near Immokalee.
Courtesy of Edison-Ford Winter Estates.

planting of two royal palms in Evans Park in honor of Mr. and Mrs. Edison.[48] In addition to the trees, the Woman's Community Club planted a petrie vine on one side of the Edison Jubilee plaque and a Crimson Lake bougainvillea on the other side. These were reported to be the favorite flowering vines of Thomas Edison and are, indeed, spectacular when in bloom.

Charles wrote his parents that he had decided to go to Arizona on vacation instead of Florida. "How I would love to come down to see you both. I know this tho [sic]. If I came to Fort Myers I would live in a boat, get plenty of sun and have a grand time but I wouldn't get any exercise whatsoever. I know it because that's what has always happened before. Not that I want *much* exercise but I know that *some* in high warm dry air would just put the finishing touches on me. So Arizona seems to be the best bet this time."[49] When summer arrived, his parents still in Florida, Charles wrote, "Glenmont looks its beautiful self. The flowering shrubs this year were exceptionally fine. But after the loveliness of Seminole Lodge that may not be such a thrill after all."[50]

The economic landscape was not nearly so beautiful, whether viewing the panorama in Florida or New Jersey. Charles, as head of Thomas Alva Edison, Inc. had quit the phonograph business a few days before the stock market crash of 1929, ostensibly to devote more money and energy to radio, a market that

Charles Edison entered very late because of the protestations of his father. Radio, too, would be phased out before the current year ended.[51] Cutting expenses in every conceivable way became the operative mode. Charles wrote: "The old expense guillotine is running red with gore and by the time you get back I think steps will have been all taken that will effect a balancing of receipts with disbursements after they become effective. All plans I am making are based on the theory that things are going to get steadily worse."[52]

Ending his longest visit in the forty-five-year Florida experience, the inventor was joined at the station by friends who had traditionally gathered at arrivals and departures:[53] Carl F. Roberts, Capt. J. Fred Menge, Capt. E. L. Evans, and Miss Flossie Hill. Leaders of the civic clubs and womens' organizations joined Mrs. Edison and presented her with bouquets of flowers. They left on June 11, 1930, aboard the Seaboard Air Line Railroad with Edison confiding that his chief regret was leaving his pet goldenrod patch, where the plants had not yet reached maturity. Showing his high spirits, he said he felt twenty years younger than when he arrived in December. With his cousin Edith Potter, he clamored aboard and made his way to the rear platform of the car, where he waived to the assembled crowd until the train was out of sight.[54]

23

A Light Extinguished

Years of incessant intensity have burned
out the machine which the world knows as
"the wizard of electricity."
—Fort Myers News-Press

1931

An imposing new $500,000 concrete bridge spanning the Caloosahatchee awaited the arrival of the famous inventor; it would bear his name. In the previous year, the Edisons had broken with tradition and come in early December but the stork prevented an early arrival in 1931. Madeleine's fourth child arrived January 8 and Mina's grandmotherly duties prevented their departure before January 20. From Newark the Edisons boarded the private car of the Firestones as far as Jacksonville.[1] With them were the Firestones, Mina's sister Mary Wallace, her husband, and Jimmie Newton. From Plant City they came by special Seaboard train, arriving at the East Fort Myers terminal while a welcoming party waited a mile away at the Atlantic Coast Line terminal.

The Tamiami Trail had three major bridges along its route, with the shortest at Bradenton, at just under a mile in length, another at Punta Gorda that was a mile and a quarter, and the new concrete bridge over the Caloosahatchee in Fort Myers that was a mile and a half. The Fort Myers bridge was to take the name of the great inventor and to be officially dedicated on February 11, his birthday. Like the presidential visit in 1929 and the dedication of the plaque in 1930, the dedication of the new Edison Bridge would be no paltry occasion. The head of the State Road Department would be present, as would Governor Doyle Carlton. Firestone came over from Miami with his son Roger and his secretary, Jimmie Newton. A new friend, Cyrus Curtis, publisher of the *Saturday Evening Post*, was on hand, but the inventor's friend and neighbor, Henry Ford, did not arrive until later in the season.

The event began at 2:30 P.M. when twenty high school girls clad in white dresses met the bridge's namesake at his Seminole Lodge gate and escorted him to the "Fountain," located at the intersection of McGregor and Cleveland, where the parade began.[2] Among the high school girls serving as special hostesses were Virginia Sheppard, Bernese Barfield, Lillian Tooke, and Dorothy Bishop. Later in 1938 an annual pageant was begun honoring Edison and Virginia Sheppard became the first Queen of Edisonia. Bernese Barfield became the second Queen of Edisonia in 1939. Lillian Tooke became the third Queen of Edisonia in 1940. Dorothy Bishop was later married to C. A. Prince, who as a young man sat by Edison and typed his reports for the Edison Botanic Research Corporation.

The governor, who delivered the dedicatory address for the new Edison Bridge, was introduced by Mayor Josiah Fitch. Said the governor:

> We honor ourselves in giving this bridge the name of Edison, he whose genius has enriched the hearts and homes of millions throughout the world, yes, brightened the paths of humanity in every land. Nothing that we do or say can add luster to his name; but by this token we may remind ourselves and generations yet to be of a great and noble life spent in a grand and noble service.
>
> We are happy to claim him as our own and treasure his name not merely in stone and bronze but in the tenderest sentiments of the human heart.[3]

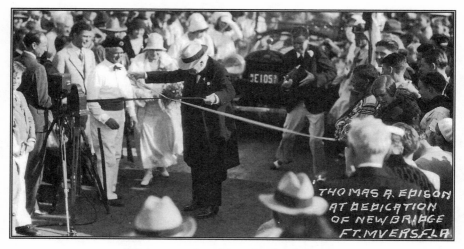

Edison cuts the ribbon for the dedication
of the Edison Bridge in 1931.
Courtesy of Edison-Ford Winter Estates.

Before the dedication, Edison conducted the annual press interview in the new small office located a short distance from his house.[4] He kept the press waiting for fifteen minutes after sleeping later than usual. When fortified with a breakfast of milk and invigorated with a shave by Mike Pavese, the aging inventor was ready to face the crowd of reporters and camera men. Accompanied by Harvey and Roger Firestone, he walked out of his residence without the aid of his wheelchair and made his way to the small office.[5]

One of the early questions was his outlook on the problem of unemployment. "This question is several sizes too large for me."[6] What was his opinion of Einstein's theory? "I don't understand it." What do you think of sound movies? "I never heard one." He predicted it would take three years to regain the level of business activity that prevailed before the Depression. "A gradual rise has now started." Perhaps the most controversial question was whether he thought Hoover's administration was a success or a failure, to which the Wizard answered, "a success." At the conclusion of the questioning, he gave more detail about the progress of his rubber experiments.

For the occasion, Queenie, the Edisons' cook, prepared a large and small-layer birthday cake with a white coconut icing, which she called a Sunshine Cake.[7] Edison declined to partake of his own cake; however, many of the visitors at *Seminole Lodge* did. At the suggestion of a friend, Mrs. Edison then gave the remaining cake to the Red Cross to be sold piece by piece downtown. Wearing a regulation Red Cross cap, Mrs. Edison presided over the cake sale booth.[8] The proceeds, $107, were earmarked for the drought-stricken Dust Bowl in the Southwestern United States.

In honor of the birthday, President Hoover sent a bouquet of eighty-four carnations picked from the White House garden— a flower for each of Edison's years.[9] Lucky visitors at Seminole Lodge received not only a slice of Queenie's Sunshine Cake but also a carnation from the president.

Although the famous couple had been in residence less than three weeks, two high school journalism students, eager for a scoop, had tried since Edison's arrival to gain an audience with him.[10] Failing at every turn, they confronted Mrs. Edison while she attended Sunday School and she promptly gave them an appointment. When face to face with the inventor, they inquired about his national scholarship and he told them that it was to be discontinued unless Henry Ford agreed to take it up. The boys reported the scoop to Ronald Halgrim, their school advisor, and he reported it out on the wire. Though the paper failed to indicate a reason given the young journalists, it was no doubt because of the Depression and budget tightening.

Children were important to both Edisons. Mrs. Edison invited the Tice fifth grade class to Seminole Lodge, where she showed them through the grounds and laboratory.[11] Mr. Edison made an appearance while they were in the laboratory. C. A. Prince, the son of Edison's chemist in the rubber investigation, observed the "old man" engaged in some "Tom Foolery" with the students.[12] According to Prince, Mrs. Edison was speaking at great length to the children while her back was turned on her husband. He proceeded to gesture behind her with his hand and arm as though he was cranking a phonograph or a Model T and winding her up to keep her talking. Prince recalled the children having a good laugh.

Henry and Clara Ford, together with secretary Campsall, slipped into town without any notice on February 20, more than a week after the birthday.[13] On the following day, the Fords and a local friend drove to Punta Rassa where they boarded the ferry, *Best,* bound for Sanibel and the annual Sanibel fair.[14] On the way over, Ford spent time in the engine room inspecting the diesel engine powering the ferry. He spoke to H. E. Whidden, one of the crew, concerning the engine and Whidden didn't realize with whom he was speaking until the end of the trip. At the fair, Ford and the ladies had pork sandwiches for lunch, which prompted Ford to inquire where he could get a drink of water. He was told there was no water but maybe he could get a drink of liquor if he wanted one. Ford's retort: "I'd dig a well first."[15]

The forty-fifth anniversary of Seminole Lodge coincided with the forty-fifth anniversary of the couple who had been its seasonal inhabitants. "Billie" and "Dearie" spent a quiet anniversary on February 24 among the botanical accoutrements of the lodge, the connecting arbor and trellis covered with the blue trumpets of the Thumburgia and lined with fern and sansevieria. Live oaks, palms, pines and a single acacia tree surrounded the lodge. Beds of pansies, phlox, sweet alyssum, nasturtiums and verbena were scattered about the lawn. In honor of the occasion, the Edison children sent a sheaf of deep red tulips with bridal wreath, jewel blossoms, and fern.[16]

"Sammy" Insull, Edison's secretary in the 1880s, had continued his career with the assembly of a large group of public utilities under his guidance. In honor of Insull, the public utility companies over which he presided gave him a banquet at the Palmer House in Chicago, fifty years after Edison had given him his first job. Edison was asked to participate. Armed with two microphones in his new small office at Seminole Lodge, he delivered his congratulations over a private wire directly to the banquet hall.[17] Insull had been the recipient, but more often the sender, of letters and telegrams to Edison, both on his first visit to Fort Myers and on the honeymoon there.[18] Moreover, he had been the person Edison wired during his courtship with Mina, "Come to Boston, at Gill's house there is lots of pretty girls."[19]

When it was time for the annual trip over the Everglades to

see the Firestones, the Edisons arrived at the Firestone home in Miami as Ford was departing the Firestone home for a return trip to Fort Myers before dark.[20] A week later, it was Firestone's turn to visit Fort Myers. While in Fort Myers, Ford challenged Firestone to chin himself on a eucalyptus tree outside the new laboratory.[21] Ford, then age sixty-seven, chinned himself six times. Firestone was able to pull his chin up to the branch but once. C. A. Prince recalled that Firestone's son Roger was able to chin himself only three times.[22]

Prince also recalled an outing in which he and his parents had gone for a drive on the Tamiami Trail and upon their return had car trouble in Bonita Springs.[23] Who should have come along but the Edisons and Scarth, the chauffeur, in the Edison's Lincoln. Edison recognized Prince, stopped and had Scarth tie two ropes together and tow Prince into the service station at the intersection of McGregor Boulevard and the Tamiami Trail. Scarth was then instructed to take the Edisons home and then return to the station to pick up the Prince party and deliver them to their home.[24]

While still in Fort Myers, Ford granted an interview with

Front row: Ford, Edison and Firestone sitting; backrow: unknown, unknown, Roger Firestone and Jim Newton.
Courtesy of Edison-Ford Winter Estates.

some newsmen at The Mangoes.[25] He praised President Hoover and his efforts to guide the country out of the Depression and to enforce prohibition. He was especially critical of the dishonest speculators who had inflated the price of stocks at the expense of the gullible. He said that wage adjustments (cuts) presented a difficult problem for American industry but that he had had no problem in his own plants for there had been no wage cuts. On education, he advocated that private industry take up the responsibility for technical education after the elements of reading and writing were completed. In Dearborn, male students twelve and older received pay for their technical work. Work done by the students was sold to the factories, which in turn supported the running of the technical schools. What about the girls, he was asked. "That is hard to answer. But if education can be converted to finding a way to eliminate the drudgery of housework, you've gone a long way."[26]

The Fords climbed aboard the Fair Lane on March 17 for their trip back to Dearborn by way of Savannah and their holdings there.[27]

After the Ford's departure, the *Press* learned of a fleet of a half dozen Ford automobiles that had been in Fort Myers while the Fords were in residence. Two were eight-cylinder vehicles, which the *Press* reported were new low-priced vehicles to be called Edsel Eights.[28] The vehicles had been driven to Fort Myers non-stop from Detroit on an extensive but secretive road test. Regular Model As with four-cylinder engines made up the remaining cars in the fleet. The paper reported that the racket from the Model As was sufficient to conceal the distinctive sound of the eight-cylinder engines.[29] While the press referred to the two engines as "eights" and not V-8s, they were in fact the latter.

The initial development of the V-8 had more than one brush with Fort Myers, both in Florida and in Michigan. Ford himself tested the new engine while in Fort Myers.[30] Carl Schultz, one of those working on the design phase of the new engine, was in Florida working with Ford. He brought with him an experimental V-8 engine and test stand so that he and Ford could work on it in the small garage at The Mangoes.[31] If Ford needed new parts in his testing, collaborators in Michigan rushed them to him in Florida. Of course, the development work for the radical new engine was top secret. In Michigan, it was the relocated Fort Myers laboratory at Greenfield Village where the initial work on the V-8 took place. Schultz along with fellow V-8 designer Ray Laird, worked in the Fort Myers laboratory on the design drawings. The first V-8 vehicles were built there, chassis design was done there, the final test work was done there, in fact the initial work was all centralized around the Fort Myers laboratory in Michigan.[32]

A week after the Fords left, Edison set out for Terry Park where the "Mackmen" were in the third inning of the final game of spring training against the Boston Braves.[33] When the "old man" walked in, the fans rose and cheered and the players paused for a moment to pay tribute. Connie Mack's Philadelphia Athletics won 3 to 2. The day had been billed as "Connie Mack Day," with the mayor commencing the event with a speech in tribute to Mack and his team, and a gift to Mack of a Panama hat.[34]

With the advent of the "talkies," visiting the local movie theaters had become far less interesting for the inventor of the moving picture, who for reasons of his deafness preferred the silent movies. Not to be deprived, he obtained home projection equipment and showed movies in the living room at Seminole Lodge.[35] On one evening, the Edisons invited the twenty high school girls who served as escorts in the bridge dedication to be their guests at a private movie showing.[36]

While his deafness altered his appreciation for the talkies, it did not seem to affect his love of music, particularly live music from bands. When the Clearwater High School Band won first place at a band contest in Miami, the band stopped by the Edisons' estate for a brief concert on their return trip.[37] The band members received a warm and appreciative welcome from their hosts.

Hamilton Holt, the president of Rollins College, was the first person to contribute a stone for the famed Friendship Walk which wound its way from the Friendship Gate on the common border of the Edison and Ford properties to Seminole Lodge.[38]

Former employee Samuel Insull sent a stone, as did Henry Ford, Harvey Firestone, and a host of national, international and local friends.[39] Barbara Brown, another Fort Myers godchild of Mrs. Edison's, received a stone from her godmother in commemoration of her christening.[40] Friendship Gate was moved several times to accommodate the gigantic root system of a specimen Morton Bay fig tree planted on the line. The famous gate no longer exists on the premises, nor does the tree which ultimately had to be removed in the mid-1990s because its size and condition posed a danger to the lodge and visitors.

The "Trail Blazers," who struck out across the Everglades in 1923 to blaze the path for the Tamiami Trail, earned a local respect and status equivalent to that of war heroes. If Southwest Florida had had its own Medal of Honor to bestow it would have been upon those brave men who pioneered the route through the swamps, the hammocks, and the river of grass from the terminus of the existing grade to Miami. Long after

The Morton Bay fig tree on the boundary between Edison and Ford homes. Ford home is in background. Sadly, the tree was removed when it became diseased and posed a threat to the house and visitors.

Courtesy of Edison-Ford Winter Estates.

the feat, the group maintained an organization of its original partipants and in 1931 sponsored a beautification project along the completed trail.[41] The project involved the planting of trees along the roadside at Estero, about fifteen miles south of Fort Myers. The chosen tree to grace the roadway was the cajeput—then loved, but now derided and scorned by all. An exotic from New South Wales, the cajeput was brought to Southwest Florida in 1912 as an aid to draining the swamps and is now pervasive in the Southwest Florida landscape, having displaced palm, pine, cypress and other indigenous trees. Its most distinguishing feature is its white paper bark which peels off in sheets. The first cajeput to be set out in the Trail Blazer ceremony at Estero was by Mina Edison. The dedicatory address by Russell Kay at the Art Hall on the Koreshan Unity grounds petitioned the almighty, "Reverently . . . we are moved with a faith that . . . the Tamiami Trail . . . will become the most beautiful . . . and the most intensively used highway in all this great nation of ours."[42] If it did not become the most beautiful, then perhaps it became the most intensively used, as

Mrs. Edison plants cajeput tree in beautification project in Estero.
Courtesy of Southwest Florida Historical Society.

motorists along the Estero route in any given February will attest.

On June 9, Charles and Carolyn Edison rolled into Fort Myers for a brief vacation and to be on hand to accompany his parents back to West Orange.[43] Edison was at the Atlantic Coast Line station to greet his son, who was then the president of Thomas Alva Edison Inc. Charles carried an overcoat on his arm, causing his father to inquire why he had brought that unnecessary article of clothing. Charles, who loved Fort Myers (and fishing) almost as much as his illustrious father, hoped to get in some tarpon fishing before he left. A few days later, Charles caught a forty-pound tarpon.[44] Charles had his own boat and guide while his father, mother and wife fished from another boat. Charles continued to fish, catching a sixty-pounder on one day and three on the final day of fishing—forty, seventy and eighty pounds respectively.[45] Ending his final day with three tarpon prompted him to tell a reporter the next day, "I had the finest time of my life yesterday."

While the National Electric Light Association met in Atlantic City, Edison was at Seminole Lodge. The father of incandescent light was introduced to the convention by amplified telephone and from there broadcast to the nation.[46] An NBC announcer in Fort Myers introduced the inventor, giving a detailed and vivid "word picture" of the beautiful grounds at Seminole Lodge where the broadcast originated. He said:

> I am speaking from Mr. Edison's private laboratory set in the paradise-like grounds at Fort Myers, Florida, where Edison has spent his winters for the last forty-five years. The grounds are absolutely beautiful. It is a perfect day. It is quiet except for the singing of many birds and the rustle of the cool breeze in the palm fronds. The calm Caloosahatchee River flows close by.
>
> Mrs. Edison, the charming and serene wife of the inventor, is sitting near-by and listening to the broadcast. Mr. and Mrs. Charles Edison also are here. From the window we can see a tropical paradise of rare palms, flowers and beautiful trees. There are bananas in bright green bunch-

es outside the windows. Golden grapefruit lay on the ground like croquet balls. It is too beautiful to describe, the rich soil and Florida sunshine making all vegetation luxuriant and bright colored.[47]

W. Alton Jones, the president of the Electric Light Association, sent greetings over the nation's air waves from all those assembled, calling the day "Edison Day." "Down in Fort Myers, Florida, sits the man who is responsible for the creation of the great electrical industry."[48] Mr. Edison's remarks were brief:

> I appreciate your greetings. My message to you is to be courageous. I have lived a long time. I have seen history repeat itself again and again. I have seen many depressions in business. Always America has come back stronger and more prosperous. Be as brave as your fathers before you. Have faith. Go forward.[49]

On June 15, 1931, Thomas Edison departed his beloved Fort Myers for the last time.[50] His health had improved since his arrival and there were no major setbacks during his stay. There was no indication of the onset of his final illness except for one observation made by C. A. Prince. Prince had been sent to the veranda where Edison was sitting in a chair. He inquired what laboratory items he wished to have sent back to New Jersey.[51] The old man's scribbled reply was, "Just take everything."[52] Prince interpreted the reply as a prognostication of the coming deterioration in his health and that he would never return.

The trip back followed tradition, with the Edisons standing on the back platform of the train waving to the assembled crowd until out of sight. They would be on the train for thirty-six gruelling hours.

After Edison returned to Glenmont, he received a coin bearing his likeness from the Chamber of Commerce. Elligibility for receipt of the coin was catching a 100-pound tarpon by a non-resident.[53] There was a special exception for Edison. Seventy-five persons were eligible for the coin when minted. The Chamber wrote this explanation:

269

Searching for a new industry to compare with
your rubber experiments in Fort Myers, the
Chamber of Commerce decided to mint a few
coins. Enclosed you will find the first coin struck
from original dies.

We trust that you will carry this coin and that
it will bring you added health and happiness. We
also hope that it will bring you back to Fort
Myers in the fall.[54]

On July 6 Mina Edison received a birthday gift of roses from
Sidney Davis, prompting her to write a thank you note and sadly
apprise him that "Dearie" was in a sanitarium in Morristown for
tests. She told Davis she had brought the roses to his bed to cheer
him up.[55] A few weeks later, Edison's personal physician, Dr.
Hubert S. Howe, who had been enjoying a brief vacation at
Sands Points, Long Island, received an urgent call from West
Orange. Hurriedly, he was able to charter an amphibian airplane
to take him from Manhasset Isle to Newark. Howe was a neurol-
ogist with offices in New York City. His patients included not
only the foremost inventor of the time but also the foremost con-
ductor, Arturo Toscanini.[56] Upon landing in Newark, Dr. Howe
drove with a police escort to Glenmont, where he joined two
other physicians who were with the aged inventor.[57] That night
the physicians issued a joint statement:

Mr. Edison has been failing in health since his
return from Florida six weeks ago. He is suffering
from chronic nephritis and diabetes. The diabet-
ic condition is now under control and the kid-
ney trouble seems improved as compared with a
week ago.

This afternoon he suffered from a sudden collapse, but at present he has recovered from this
and is resting quietly.[58]

Two of the doctors left Glenmont for home late that
evening, but Howe remained for the night. When shortly after
midnight Howe reported that Edison was sleeping normally,
Charles left Glenmont for his home just a few doors down in
Llewellyn Park. Madeleine, who also lived in Llewellyn Park, did

likewise, as did Theodore and Thomas Jr. [59] William lived in Delaware and did not arrive until the next day. Marion lived in Connecticut and was not yet present.

Ford had visited Edison at Glenmont in the previous week. Firestone spoke to John Sloane, Madeline's husband, and was told about the "nasty collapse" and that he was resting quietly but that his condition was not satisfactory.[60]

On August 2, the day following the collapse, Fort Myers churches offered prayers for Edison's speedy recovery.[61] On that Sunday morning, Charles stated his father was 100 percent better than the previous day.[62] Day three brought more improvement and day four even more optimism. The patient was by then going for automobile rides, preferring the open touring car to the closed sedan.[63]

The Fort Myers News Press printed Associated Press bulletins each day on the patient's progress. Building on a diagnosis of the cause by Dr. Howe—"the wear and tear of time"—*The Fort Myers News Press* editorialized, "Years of incessant intensity have burned out the machine which the world knows as 'the wizard of electricity.'"[64] Nevertheless, the machine was showing some improvement.

By day six, Edison took a four-hour automobile ride through the mountains of Orange, New Jersey, and even smoked a cigar. The old man was quoted as saying he would live another ten years.[65] By mid-month, Mina Edison wrote to Davis in Fort Myers that Mr. Edison was much better allowing her to finally get back to her writing.[66]

The old man continued to improve, enjoying long automobile rides in the open touring car, sometimes in the morning and again in the afternoon. But a month after the collapse, things began to deteriorate again. Dr. Howe issued a bulletin saying he was "slowly and definitely failing."[67] He was suffering from four ailments: uremic poisoning, which had settled in his kidneys; diabetes; ulcers of the stomach; and Bright's disease. Of these, the uremic poisoning was the worst of the maladies. By September 9, Charles said his father was not "as well as he was a week or two ago."[68] His doctor had convinced him that he must augment his milk diet with certain other foods, believing that a part of his weakened condition was the result of the milk diet, which he had stubbornly followed for several years. Despite the steadily weakening condition, the automobile rides continued.

By the end of September the automobile rides were declined by the patient.[69] The old man simply wasn't up to the exertion.

On October 4 in Fort Myers, the Chamber of Commerce and the Ministerial Association sponsored a city-wide day of prayer for its beloved winter visitor.[70] Ronald Halgrim said he hoped the day of prayer would be observed not only in the churches of the city but also in all of the homes. Daily bulletins indicated in early October that virtually every night was restless.[71] Day nurses and night nurses were on constant duty, along with Mrs. Edison. Charles Edison was quick to tell anyone who would listen that his mother was as much an aide to his father's medical condition as were the physicians.[72] His mother had kept a constant bedside vigil throughout the illness. In the darkest hours following the weekend of the collapse, he would ask for her whenever she left his sight even for a moment. Charles Edison was almost as attentive as his mother was. Two cables were received in one day from Pope Pius asking for the latest information on the inventor's medical condition and expressing to the family the Holy Father's deep interest.[73] Edison had sent the Pope a special dictating machine in the previous year and had received in return a gold medal from the Pope. President Hoover requested that the three medical bulletins being issued each day be relayed directly to the White House.[74] Ford and Firestone telephoned frequently, in addition to receiving special bulletins. Bulletins were sent to Fort Myers, where his many southern friends lived, and also to Cardinal Hayes in response to the request of the Pope.[75] Firestone visited Edison on October 6 but was not able to converse with him.[76] Ford was due in a few days.

Edison found it increasingly difficult to take fluids, which were necessary to remove the uremic poisoning from the body. Dr. Howe attributed his survival to a very strong heart that was able to withstand the weaknesses posed by other conditions.[77]

In the garage on the Glenmont Estate, a makeshift pressroom was established where telephone and telegraph lines connected the world with the latest medical information.[78]

By October 15, Edison, who had been in a "stupor" for several days, lapsed into a coma.[79] On the following day, Charles Edison was quoted as saying, "I am afraid the end is near."[80] Marion "Dot" Oeser, who before the marriage to Mina had been inseparable from her father, arrived at Glenmont from her home in Connecticut.[81] Son William and his wife also arrived from their home in Delaware. Among the callers at Glenmont that day was Fred Ott, the assistant who had each year preceded the Edisons to Fort Myers in order to ready the equipment, supervise the opening of Seminole Lodge, and shine up the radiator on the Model T. [82]

Before dawn on October 18, Arthur L. Walsh, the vice president of Thomas A. Edison Industries, Inc., made his way from the house at Glenmont to the garage where the press were gathered. He read a bulletin: "Thomas Alva Edison quietly passed away at 24 minutes after 3 A.M., October 18, 1931. (signed) Dr. Hubert S. Howe."[83]

Tributes to the fallen wizard came from far and wide. Pope Pius sent a message of condolence to the family. President Hoover and New York Governor Franklin Roosevelt sent their condolences. Ford was deeply moved by his mentor's death and said he "changed the face of the world in his lifetime" and his work "will influence all the future."[84] In Fort Myers, Mayor Fitch, Captain E. L. Evans, and a few other personal friends received telegrams from Mrs. Edison notifying them of the death of her husband. Mayor Josiah Fitch quickly dispatched a telegram to the widow:

> The City of Fort Myers, Florida, acting through its mayor and council sends to you the deepest and sincerest sympathy of all its people in this, your hour of bereavement.
>
> We feel that your loss is also ours. We have lost not only a great man but a wonderful personality whose beautiful nature made sweet all he touched.
>
> We shall always feel honored by the recollection that he made this city his home for many, many winters.

His loss to us is a personal one. We do him
honor for his great gifts to humanity but we feel
more keenly the loss of an old friend. May God
bring to you comfort at this time through the
realization of your unceasing love and care for
him during all of your lives together. Few have as
many thoughts to bring them comfort in the loss
of a loved one as have you. The honor the whole
world pays him is part of your great reward.

When this time of stress is over and you are
able to settle down to the carrying on of your life
guided by his memory, we hope that you will
then realize that you hold as deep a spot in our
hearts as did he and we will welcome you among
us again as eagerly as though you brought him
with you. Your services to Fort Myers have been
many, and valuable, and we hope to have your
help and presence for many years.

Yours very sincerely,
Josiah H. Fitch, Mayor
Martin E. Shultz,
F. E. Forehand,
Dan P. Morrison,
R. G. Truebger,
Councilmen[85]

The local press singled out the sadness of one of the four
Pavese brothers, who together operated a barber shop on First
Street. For years, Mike Pavese had shaved Edison twice each
week while he was in residence. The inventor's old friend, E. L.
Evans, said, "He was congenial. He always loved to meet people
and to talk with them. He was contrary to the general practice,
a big man who placed himself on the plane of ordinary persons.
He never tried to impress others with his knowledge, and to hear
him speak of an achievement other than in a depreciating [sic]
or joking manner was unknown."[86]

In response to a nationwide presidential request, Fort
Myers, in the company of cities and towns throughout the
nation, turned off its lights for one minute at precisely 10 P.M.

Florida Power and Light turned the switch for the Fort Myers community and plunged the city into total darkness, not only out of respect for the president's supplication but in memory of and respect for an old friend.

During the funeral in West Orange, Fort Myers businesses closed from 2:30 to 3 P.M. and a citywide service was held at the municipal pier. The Reverend Kent Pendleton, pastor of the First Christian Church, gave the prayer followed by an address by the Reverend O. T. Anderson, pastor of the Edison Park Congregational Church. Anderson acknowledged that Edison's faith was not orthodox, "But neither was Jesus' faith orthodox in the religious circles of his day. With his scientific mind, Mr. Edison was slow to assert as fact that which could not be proved by scientific method. . . . Mr. Edison spoke of God as the 'Supreme Intelligence.' He spoke of Christianity that it is 'the most beautiful of all human conceptions.' Of prayer, Mr. Edison said, 'Somehow I cannot be impressed by the idea that merely spoken prayers are likely to be answered, but I am absolutely sure that lived prayers are certain to be answered.' Concerning immortality, Mr. Edison said, 'Today the preponderance of probability very greatly favors belief in the immortality of the soul of Man.'"[87]

24

The Widow

❧

*We are attached to those in Fort Myers in
a different way from others.*
—Mina Miller Edison

1931–1947

The winter season in Fort Myers was much different following
the death of Edison. The rubber investigation was still on but in
a diminished way. The one constant was the continued presence
and special relationship of Mina Edison with Fort Myers and its
people. She was present each year of her remaining life, with the
exception of the peak war years in 1943 and 1944. Perhaps a letter to her friend Sidney Davis following the painful first year's
visit expressed the Fort Myers relationship best:

> Dear Sidney,
>
> It was extremely difficult to pull out of Fort
> Myers, one of the hardest things, if not the hard-
> est since Dearie has left me. Some way he
> seemed very near to me there different from any
> other place. We are attached to those in Fort
> Myers in a different way from others.[1]

The first year in Fort Myers following her widowhood had
indeed been memorable. On the first birthday following Edison's
death over 600 persons participated in an outdoor memorial
service in Evans Park in Fort Myers.[2] A chorus composed of

members of the town choirs sang and Dr. Ludd M. Spivey, president of Florida Southern College, delivered the address. High school girls were on hand to lay a floral wreath at the Edison memorial plaque in Evans Park.[3] One of those girls was Bernice Barfield, who later became Mrs. Sidney Davis after which she and her husband both enjoyed the personal friendship of Mina Edison. Mrs. Edison did not arrive in time for the service, due to the annual Edison Pioneers celebration in New Jersey. Though unable to be present, her thoughts were with the people of Fort Myers, for she sent each patient at Lee Memorial Hospital a bouquet of flowers with a note saying, "This token of cheer is sent with my sincere wish that your recovery may be speedy and in memory of Mr. Edison."[4] Within days of the birthday she was in Fort Myers for her first visit without "Dearie."[5]

Mina Edison continued her interest in the Roundtable, the Woman's Community Club, the Music Club, the Girl Scouts, and the Plant Guild.[6] In terms of personal interest and involvement, her passion seemed to be with the local Fruit, Flower and Plant Guild and its many affiliated garden clubs. She served as its president until 1934, when she retired as president and held elections for a new slate of officers at Seminole Lodge.[7] She received the title of honorary president of the guild in 1936. Berne Davis recalled that if a morning guild meeting at Seminole Lodge went overtime, Mrs. Edison would order lunch from her kitchen for all those present. She participated in the annual flower shows, winning six ribbons in 1940.[8] She remained as chairman of the Safety Hill District Garden Club, a club representing the black community in Fort Myers. The Safety Hill Club, under Mrs. Edison's leadership, sponsored the Jubilee Singers at a garden club benefit concert at the Municipal Pier.[9] The singing group was a black Baptist Church choir, known for their singing of spirituals in the old-fashioned way. In other years, garden club musicale benefits with the Jubilee Singers were held at Dunbar High School.[10] Mrs. Edison continued to have a hand in these performances.

While planning the 1933 year's activities of the Plant Guild at Seminole Lodge, the guild voted to beautify the Tamiami Trail with oleanders planted on both sides of U.S. 41 between Fort

Myers and Punta Gorda. As president, Mrs. Edison submitted the plan to the State Road Department and telegraphed both the chairman of the road board and the governor.[11] Governor Dave Sholtz directed the road department to extend its cooperation. Meanwhile, James Hendry accumulated 4,000 cuttings to be used in the project. Each district garden club planned to have its members in a team, with one New Deal worker assigned to each team. Unfortunately there were bureaucratic delays and Mrs. Edison left for New Jersey before the project could be started.[12] It is not clear whether the project went forward in her absence.

Mina Edison brought a noted naturalist from the American Museum of Natural History to Fort Myers for a free lecture under the auspices of the Plant Guild.[13] She continued to arrange lectures for the Plant Guild and she instituted monthly plant education courses for the garden clubs, which were held at Seminole Lodge.[14]

Despite the pall cast by the Great Depression in 1933, Mrs. Edison agreed to participate in the annual flower show, commenting on how fine it was to see "the same old spirit and good cheer" at the plant show "in spite of the times."[15] She brought her mounted birds and some arrangements of shells, along with plants for sale, including one or two orchids in bloom. She remained active in the annual flower show, entering seventeen species of Hibiscus in the 1936 show and winning eleven ribbons in the 1937 show.[16]

Mrs. Edison loved nature and had a special reverence for plants and birds. She made the grounds at Seminole Lodge available to the Plant Guild for summer classes for boys and girls in the study of plant and bird life.[17] Birdlife too was a passion for her and when she was given a beautiful pet peacock she gave it the free run of the gardens at Seminole Lodge. The bird was very lonely and tried to escape several times. Mrs. Edison attempted to find it a mate, but before she could do so it died, so she had it stuffed.[18]

Although she had always been a strong Methodist, in the 1930s Mina Edison had a shared allegiance to both the First Methodist Church and its Young Mens' Wesley Bible Class and the Edison Park Congregational Church, the latter located just a stone's throw from Seminole Lodge. The Womens' Society of the Edison Park Church began to sponsor a garden tour in 1935, and the Edison and Ford homes were consistently included. The tour traditionally ended at the Burroughs home on First Street, with refreshments offered at that site.[19]

Mrs. Edison remained active in the Wesley Bible Class at the First Methodist Church, where she was known as the class "Mother."[20] During the Christmas season following the death of Edison, Mina Edison remembered the young men in her class in Fort Myers. She wrote its teacher, Sidney Davis, thanking him for Christmas roses he had sent on behalf of the class, telling him how often she thought of the class and how happy she was to be "a part of it."[21]

While in Fort Myers, she invited the young mens' class along with their girl friends to a moonlight garden party at Seminole Lodge.[22] She arranged guest lecturers for the class.[23] In the year following Edison's death, Harvey Firestone paid a visit to Seminole Lodge, and Mrs. Edison invited him to the class, which he had already visited once the year before Edison died.[24] Mrs. Edison attended a Wesley Class party at the Red Coconut at Fort Myers Beach in 1933.[25] In 1934, she was in charge of decorations for the Easter service by the class.[26] In 1937, she sent white and red carnations to "her boys" in the class for observance of Mothers' Day.[27] In 1941, she hosted a special joint meeting of the Wesley class and the Pan American League with a speaker on Pan American affairs.[28]

A rather extraordinary event took place in 1933 when she was invited to Sebring, Florida, to witness the naming of an Indian maiden who was to take the name Mina Miller Edison. Mrs. Edison attended the ritual which was spoken entirely in the language of the Seminoles and interpreted to her by W. Stanley Hanson of Fort Myers.[29]

Mina traveled about Southwest Florida enjoying all the many amenities of the area.[30] One of her favorite dining spots was at the Rustic Tea Garden operated by the Koreshan Unity within its grounds in Estero. There, at various times, she took her son Theodore, her sister Grace, her step-son Thomas Edison, Jr., and a dinner group of twenty which she hosted following a scenic cruise on the Imperial River.[31]

Mina Edison, the widow, continued to entertain at Seminole Lodge. She held teas for the Jubilee Singers and for other friends, including Miss Jettie Burroughs. She also hosted the literary Valinda Society, named for Mary Valinda Miller, Mina's mother, and took guests on river cruises and theater parties preceded by dinner at the Gondola Inn.[32]

The Gondola Inn had been another favorite dinner spot for the Edisons. It was built out over the river on piling just a few blocks north of Seminole Lodge and afforded beautiful river vistas at its window seats. The restaurant was opened in 1930 by Frank Pellegrin, and in 1936 it was enlarged, prompting the local press to devote two pages to its formal reopening.[33] Pellegrin told of visits by both the Edisons and the Fords. At one party, the Fords participated in an old-fashioned dance while Pellegrin, dressed as a gondolier, played his accordion. Ford had donned a chef's cap and apron before whirling about the dance floor with Mrs. Ford. Mrs. Edison wore a red wig. On the menu for the occasion were buckwheat cakes, onion soup, steak, blueberry pie and stick candy. Pellegrin said that buckwheat cakes were Ford's favorite food. Broiled pompano, he said, was Edison's favorite. Since the restaurant had been open only during the last two years of Edison's life when he was on a strict milk diet, the accuracy of Pellegrin's description of Edison's favorite dish is called into question.

In 1934, Mrs. Edison entertained at her Fort Myers home with a performance by a popular musical trio.[34] Guests sat in the living room, on the wrap-around porches and on the veranda. Among them were son Theodore, daughter-in-law Ann, cousin Lewis Miller Alexander, sister Grace Hitchcock, young friend Sidney Davis, and friend and popular musician Effie Winkler Henderson.[35] "Miss Effie," as the latter was affectionately known, had a granddaughter, Barbara Norris, now Barbara Brown, who became a godchild of Mrs. Edison. Barbara received a child's toy piano from her godmother on one of her early birthdays and she keeps it among her valued possessions today.[36]

Mrs. Edison, the widow, continued to make speeches—for the continuation of prohibition, to the local Girl Scouts and to the Women's Club.[37] She was given the title "honorary president" of the Chamber of Commerce.[38] The Rotary Club heaped praise on her.[39] The Dunbar High School, which in the days of segregation served the black community, honored her and invited her to speak at the dedication of its new building.[40] Ella Piper, a legendary member of the black community, lauded her efforts in behalf of that community.

Although seldom seen in self-serving battles, Mrs. Edison's ire was raised when a neighbor tried to have his property across the street from Seminole Lodge rezoned for a filling station. The action occurred when she was in West Orange. She sent a telegram calling it a "catastrophe." The Reverend O. T. Anderson and members of the Edison Park Community Church were also opposed, and the measure failed.[41]

Automobile drives had been a favorite pastime for the Edisons when Dearie was living and continued to be for Mina, the widow. Scarth, the chauffeur took her on drives occasionally. Once while headed toward Fort Myers Beach, she came upon an accident on McGregor Boulevard when a car headed for Fort Myers Beach overturned and Mrs. Edison and her chauffeur, Scarth, were first on the scene. She and the chauffeur pulled the occupants from the car and stretched them on the ground where Mrs. Edison, with her first aid kit in hand, treated their cuts and bruises.[42] She then helped them into her own car and had Scarth drive them to their home. Those occupants included Florence Larimer, later Florence Black, one of the longest serving and most devoted members of the Edison Winter Home Board.[43]

In 1934, patriotism overcame her family's past loyalties to former President Hoover when she became the patroness at a Fort Myers Birthday Ball honoring his victorious opponent, Franklin Delano Roosevelt.[44]

An old time friend of Mina Edison was often seen in her company in 1934. Edward Hughes had been Mina's friend since childhood. They had both been from prominent families who spent summers at Chautauqua. Hughes, a lawyer and widower, was also the retired chief executive of the Franklin Steel Works.[45] During the 1935 season, Hughes was a frequent visitor at Seminole Lodge. In October 1935, Mina Edison became Mina

Hughes at a wedding in the Founder's cottage at Chautauqua in New York.[46]

Hughes was not a newcomer to Florida, for he had spent several winters in DeLand. He was quick to adapt to Fort Myers, saying its cool breezes kept the temperature at a comfortable level. He also liked the fishing around Fort Myers, telling a reporter he was a member of the Florida Liar's Club, that "all the big ones had got away" and "that a delegation asked me to quit so there would be some left."[47] The *News Press* reported that he had favored the filling of the Tamiami Trail canals with alligators to give the tourist something to look at.

Hughes' bride, a bit more serious than he, also had some thoughts reported in the *Press*. Hers were about Fort Myers:

> My love for Fort Myers has grown for many, many years. It has from the first been one of the quaint, alluring places of the South with its beautiful Caloosahatchee river winding through luxuriant and tropical shores. Its citizens always of the highest type, with the desire to always preserve its attractions. It is gratifying to think that the dreams of many are being realized, that Fort Myers is true to its traditions and will ever increase in beauty.[48]

According to Janett Perry, her Fort Myers secretary, Mrs. Hughes said the principal reason for the marriage was so the two could travel together.[49] When Mrs. Perry mistakenly called Mrs. Hughes by her former married name, she told her that she would always be Mrs. Edison. The Hugheses traveled frequently, including a trip to Europe.[50] While in Fort Myers, they made excursions to Miami with friends, to the East coast of Florida, and to Boca Grande.[51]

It is a popular myth that Ford did not return to Fort Myers after his mentor's death in 1931. In fact, the Fords were at The Mangoes in 1934 for three weeks. On that visit, Ford busied himself working in a little machine shop in his garage. When a reporter dropped in on him, he was at a small electric lathe with innumerable attachments, working on some new idea for the diesel engine. This machine shop was in the same tiny automobile garage from which he had worked on the V-8 in a prior year. "The diesel has got to come," said Ford. "I do not know or care in just what shape, but it is our business to find out."[52] In 1936, Mrs. Ford, with her sister, returned to Fort Myers for one day aboard their private railroad car. She left her husband in Ways, Georgia, where he was overseeing the reconstruction of an old sawmill. Ford had an interest in "old" sawmills as he did in other "old" objects of Americana. Before leaving Fort Myers, Mrs. Ford ordered a "mess" of Spanish mackerel from Kelley's Fish Market. She had some of them prepared for dinner on the train with enough left over and packed in ice for another repast in Georgia.[53] Both Fords came in 1940, but did not stay at The Mangoes, since the Fort Myers estate had been rented to Lewis Conant, Ford's agent in Fort Myers. The Fords stayed instead at the Royal Palm Hotel.[54]

Charles and Carolyn Edison visited his mother at Seminole Lodge in 1933 and 1934.[55] While in Fort Myers Carolyn landed a 102-pound tarpon and received an Edison Tarpon Medal from the Chamber of Commerce, as did all others who landed 100-pound tarpon.[56] Several years later, in 1939, Peter Sloane, the Edisons' grandson, visited Seminole Lodge during his Easter vacation from Phillips Exeter Academy. While fishing with Capt. E. E. Damkohler, Peter landed a 100-pound tarpon and received a Tarpon Medal.[57]

Charles was not to be outdone by his wife, so he returned without her in 1934 in search of the elusive tarpon, this time staying in Boca Grande with a party of five business friends. His group landed six tarpon.[58] Charles had run Thomas A. Edison, Inc. since 1917, with intermittent interruptions by his father. He, like his father, had been an enthusiastic Hoover supporter, but when Roosevelt came along he embraced the New Deal. For that he was rewarded with an appointment as assistant secretary of the Navy in 1936, a not inconsiderable position that had been formerly held by both Presidents Theodore and Franklin Roosevelt.[59] From the inception of his tenure as assistant secretary, Charles Edison was essentially the secretary of the Navy in all but name due to an elderly and ailing incumbent secretary, Claude Augustus Swanson. When Swanson died in 1939,

Roosevelt named Edison secretary of the Navy, and he was confirmed by the Senate in January 1940.[60] Later in 1940, he ran for governor of New Jersey as a Democrat and was elected to a three-year term.[61] He became less enamored of Roosevelt in time and did not support him in his final and successful bid for a fourth term.[62]

The Edison Bridge, dedicated with much fanfare in 1931, was not lighted until 1937. When the bridge lights were finally turned on, the switch was turned in Washington, D.C., by Assistant Secretary of the Navy Charles Edison.[63]

Late 1936 witnessed the death of Fred Ott, who had been at the inventor's side as early as 1874.[64] Ott had always arrived in Fort Myers a few days ahead of the Edisons to get things in order. A few months later, Queenie Adams, the Edisons' cook, both in Fort Myers and in New Jersey, was nearing the end of a terminal illness and returned to her home town in Fort Myers to die among family and friends.[65] Finally, death claimed Captain Fred Menge, who had been one of the close friends of the Edisons in

Governor Edison at his desk.
Courtesy of Edison National Historic Site.

Fort Myers and had captained the steamboat *Suwanee* when the family went on excursions up and down the river, including two memorable trips to Lake Okeechobee.[66]

The Edison Pageant of Light, a community tradition celebrating the inventor's birthday, was the brainchild of Ronald Halgrim and Joe Ansley, both members of the Fort Myers Jaycees.[67] They sold their idea to the Jaycees and the first Edison Pageant celebration was held in 1938. There was a coronation of a king and queen, King James Hendry III and Queen Virginia Sheppard, a parade, memorial service, and three days of events. The king and queen were crowned by Mrs. Hughes in the first year and in most successive years up to her death.[68] The celebration continued in 1939, 1940, and 1941, becoming more elaborate each year.

The first "illuminated" Edison Pageant night parade occurred in 1940.[69] After that time, the grand parade was always at night. Following Pearl Harbor, there was a four-year hiatus in the annual event. Postwar celebrations became even more elab-

James Hendry III and Virginia Sheppard, the first king and queen of the Edison Pageant of Light.
Courtesy of Fort Myers Historical Museum.

orate. In 1942, President Roosevelt ordered that February 11 be called Thomas Alva Edison Day and Governor Spessard Holland ordered that flags be displayed at public buildings throughout the state in honor of that day.[70] The postwar pageant in Fort Myers was a full week with a tennis match, golf exhibition, boat carnival, speed boat regatta, street dance, baby parade, grand parade and two dances, including the Coronation Ball at which the new king and queen were crowned by Mrs. Edison.[71] The last event of the week was the traditional memorial service. When the celebration resumed in 1946, Mrs. Edison entertained a large group associated with the pageant. [72]

Mina Edison was a prolific correspondent. Her letters were not only to her children and considerable family members but to friends as well. Letters to her Fort Myers friend Sidney Davis were signed simply, Mina Miller Edison, until 1932, after which they were signed, "Your adopted mother," and beginning in 1934, "Mother Ga."[73] Mother Ga was the name she penned in letters to her grandchildren. "Mother Ga" wrote Davis in June 1938 that she had heard through the grapevine of his special girl friend. When that girl friend became his wife, she wrote, "I am claiming her now as well."[74] The newlyweds Sidney and Berne Davis lived at the Seville Apartments, one block north of Seminole Lodge. Berne Davis recalled that one of her first official duties as Mrs. Sidney Davis was preparing and hosting a dinner party for Mrs. Edison, her sister Grace Hitchcock, her brother John Miller, Jettie Burroughs and her sister Mona Fisher.[75] She received bouquets of flowers from each of the guests during the day, and that evening, each of the guests climbed two flights of stairs to the tiny apartment on the third floor. The guests were all eager to see the apartment and the wedding gifts and the dinner was a success. Berne Davis also recalled dinners at Seminole Lodge. Guests parked on McGregor Boulevard and proceeded to the main gate where they were greeted by Scarth, the chauffeur, and escorted to the guesthouse, the old Gilliland residence, where the dining room and a living room were located. Sidney would then leave the party and walk across the connecting trellis and veranda to the main house, greet Mrs. Edison and escort her back to the guesthouse. If there were any talented musicians among the guests, they would be asked to perform after dinner.[76]

The necessity of promoting political unison among the various nations of the Western hemisphere caught Mrs. Hughes's attention in 1939, and she issued invitations to eighty local residents to attend a meeting at Seminole Lodge to establish a chapter of the Pan American League. The founder of the movement, Mrs. Clark Stearns of Miami, attended the organizational meeting. The group worked with the student Pan American Club already organized in the Fort Myers High School.[77] In the following month Mrs. Hughes crowned the first Pan American queen at the Pan American Ball held at the Legion Coliseum.[78]

The Hugheses had planned to be in Fort Myers for the entire 1940 winter season. Their plans went awry when Mr. Hughes, the seventy-seven-year-old childhood friend and second husband of Mina Miller Hughes, died at Glenmont on January 19, 1940.[79] Mrs. Hughes did manage to come in late March to be a part of the flower show, the plant guild meeting and the crowning of the new Pan American queen.[80] She left Fort Myers early in order to participate in the premier showing of *Edison The Man*, with Spencer Tracy. Both Mickey Rooney, who starred in *Young Tom Edison*, and Spencer Tracy were to be guests of Mrs. Hughes at Glenmont.[81] When she left Fort Myers, she urged the city to be even more vigilant in its quest for city beautification. To achieve this, she insisted, required organization, through clubs and groups dedicated to that goal. "Where such groups are organized and take pride in their neighborhoods, the result is . . . where other people want to come and live. Keep Fort Myers clean and beautiful, neat and happy and you will grow and attract the best types of citizens."[82]

In 1941 Mrs. Hughes reverted to her former married name of Mina Miller Edison.[83] When she arrived in Fort Myers that year, she was greeted by her sisters, Mary Nichols and Grace Hitchcock, who were already in town.[84] During that last pre-war season, she praised the city for its beauty but admonished it to rid itself of the ugly billboards that ruined the city at its entrances.[85]

When Mina Edison came in 1942, it was just a few months after Pearl Harbor. She was accompanied by a house guest, Mrs.

Mina Edison sits next to Mickey Rooney, who
starred in the movie, *Young Tom Edison*.
Courtesy of Rusty Brown.

Russell Colgate, a neighbor from Lewellyn Park in West Orange.
She was absent in 1943 and 1944. Writing to Sidney Davis in
1943, she advised she would not be coming that year because
transportation was difficult and she would not be able to visit
friends due to gas rationing.[86]

Jimmie Newton had met yet another twentieth-century
celebrity, Charles Lindbergh, and the two had become close
friends. In March 1941, the Lindberghs were at Fort Myers
Beach to embark on a three-week sail with Newton aboard his
32-foot ketch. The group sailed down the coast to the Ten
Thousand Islands and Shark River and from there across Florida
Bay to the Dry Tortugas.[87] In the previous year, the Lindberghs
had visited Newton and cruised with him on a ten-day fishing
trip in the Ten Thousand Islands with guide Charlie Green.[88]
The Lindberghs also became dinner guests at Seminole Lodge
each year. Janett Perry, Mrs. Edison's Fort Myers secretary,
recalled that when they came for dinner, there were no other
guests but them. Mrs. Perry would not even tell her husband of

their presence at Seminole Lodge. Fort Myers, said Mrs. Perry, came to respect the privacy of the noted aviator and his wife while the Lindberghs remained aloof and cautious.[89]

With World War II came two large air bases at Fort Myers. Page Field was not known by that name when it was first activated. In the early stages, it was called Palmetto Field, a less-than-affectionate reference to the palmetto stumps removed by the early soldiers stationed there.[90] It was finally named for a World War I Air Ace from Fort Myers. Mrs. Edison visited what was still called Palmetto Field and was given a thorough tour, including the runways and the tents where the soldiers were housed. The tour ended at the officers' mess, where she had lunch.[91]

Mrs. Edison entertained soldiers at Seminole Lodge with pool parties. She arranged to have a section set aside at the Edison Theater on Hendry Street for soldiers as her guests.[92] She hosted a birthday party at Seminole Lodge for one of the soldiers.[93] Showing a genuine affection for the young men in uniform, she also displayed appreciation for those who were veterans. When a black veterans' home was opened on Anderson Avenue, now Dr. Martin Luther King Jr. Boulevard, she had high praise for the "colored" soldiers.[94] Once, arriving in Fort Myers, she had Scarth, her chauffeur, drive her to Walgreens, a recently opened art deco building on First Street. While there she was spotted by a soldier who told her he had just made a bet with other soldiers that she was Mrs. Edison. She replied, "Soldier, you have just won the bet." She engaged the soldier in conversation, invited him to Seminole Lodge, and wrote his mother to tell her what a nice young man he was.[95]

Gunners on World War II bombers were trained at Buckingham Gunnery School, located in East Lee County. In 1945, Mina Edison spent just two weeks in Fort Myers but managed to visit the Buckingham Gunnery School accompanied by her friend, Sidney Davis, her niece Elizabeth Miller, and her New Jersey attorney, Albert R. Jube.[96] A week later she returned to the Buckingham gunnery air base with Chesley Perry, who was then her local agent and the husband of her local secretary, Janett Perry.[97] While there she was shown men shooting 50-millimeter machine guns. When the fearless lady told the commanding officer she would like to shoot the guns, he quickly made arrangements and she fired off a deafening burst at a moving target. She was then invited to lunch at the Officers' Club but declined, telling her host she would rather have lunch with the G.I.s. With that she was whisked to the mess hall where she had lunch with the soldiers. Afterwards, she told the colonel that she wanted to invite twenty-five G.I.s to Seminole Lodge on Sunday for lunch and entertainment. The men were to bring swimming trunks for a pool party. Mrs. Perry had the duty of arranging for twenty-five young ladies to attend the party and obtaining movie tickets for each of the guests.[98]

During the brief stay in 1945 Mrs. Edison also became the guest of honor at a soldiers' dance at the servicemen's center (now the Hall of 50 States) across from the downtown Yacht Basin. A base orchestra provided the music and county commissioner and perennial frier of fish, Al Gorton, prepared the fish. She stayed late and thoroughly enjoyed herself.[99] Before leaving for New Jersey, she entertained a number of friends at Seminole Lodge, including Sidney and Berne Davis and Chesley and Janett Perry.[100]

The Edison Pioneers, who faithfully met on Edison's birthday each year and frequently caused Mrs. Edison to miss the memorial service held in Fort Myers, met at the Hotel Astor in New York City on February 11, 1946. A delegation from Fort Myers chartered a twin-engine Cessna to take Walter S. Turner, president of the Chamber of Commerce, Graydon Jones, general chairman of the Edison Pageant, Nancy Powell, former Gladiolus Queen and her successor, Jean Elizabeth Powell, reigning Gladiolus Queen, and a specially crafted gladiolus wreath to the Pioneers' service. Because the plane was delayed the group missed the first half of the program, but arrived in time for the last half. When finally in the hall, the delegation received an ovation from the Pioneers.[101] Later the group drove to Rosedale Cemetery, near West Orange, and placed the wreath on Edison's tomb.[102]

Mina Edison arrived in Fort Myers for the last time on February 13, 1947. She was accompanied by her son, Governor Charles Edison, his wife, Carolyn, chairman of the National

Edison Centennial Committee E. O. Siebert, and executive secretary of the Edison Pioneers, John Coakley.[103] The Edison Pageant of Light was in full swing. As tradition required, Mrs. Edison crowned the newly elected royalty, Ted Evans and Esther Ann Reynolds.[104] Ted Evans was the grandson of Edison's friend and contemporary, Captain E. L. Evans.

In April 1947 came the sad news that Henry Ford was dead at the age of 83. The *News Press* ran an editorial entitled, "Three Cronies Reunited," a reference to the three friends, Edison, Firestone, who died in 1938, and now Ford, who had enjoyed so many pleasant experiences in Fort Myers.[105]

Sixty-one years after her honeymoon visit to Fort Myers, Mina Miller Edison departed her beloved Seminole Lodge and Fort Myers, a town whose cultural and civic life was greatly enhanced by her presence. In August 1947, she too would be reunited with her own "Dearie," with whom she had shared not only a deep and abiding love, but also an uncommon affection for Fort Myers and its people.

25

The Shrine

*Those who visit the Edison Shrine will not come
to marvel at the works of those who have outlived him but
to pay homage to the paths he walked, the home
in which he was comforted, the palms
he planted and the dock
from which he fished.*
—Fort Myers News-Press

1939–1941

In March 1939, Mrs. Edison, then known as Mrs. Hughes, informed Mayor Dave Shapard that she intended to build a public library and museum of art and natural science in honor of Thomas A. Edison. She wanted the library and museum to be located on the Edison property on the east side of McGregor, near the new laboratory. The announcement was made following a conference among Mrs. Hughes, the mayor, and Sidney Davis. The *News-Press* said Mrs. Hughes had considered the concept of a suitable memorial in Fort Myers and "decided that what Fort Myers needed most was a library—a place for grown-ups and children to read and study and learn about arts and sciences. . . . Mr. Edison was a student all his life. . . . I am sure that a library in Fort Myers would be gratifying to him. . . ."[1] Mina Hughes had plans drawn by her architect that called for a 20,000-volume library and separate wings for an art gallery and museum of natural history. Plans included a separate room for valuable Edisonia and an open-air quiet room for reading or "just plain meditation." The location would be on eight acres across McGregor from her home, five of which were planned to be a tropical park and botanical garden.[2] Mrs. Hughes barely mentioned the library project during her abbreviated Fort Myers visit in 1940, which came shortly after the death of her second husband. When she left, she did admit that plans were still being made and that construction of the library would definitely take place.[3]

Having once again assumed the name Edison, she arrived in 1941 with a renewed interest in establishing the memorial library and museum in Fort Myers. She brought plans for the structure and arranged for her architect to come south.[4] "The work will be started in June or July unless we get into war," she said.[5] In the meantime she set about meeting with library and other officials in Fort Myers to work out permanent arrangements.[6] When war came, she told the *News-Press* that plans for the library were on hold because of the greater priorities of the times.[7]

Architectural rendering of proposed library. The library was put on hold during the war years and never revisited.
Courtesy of Edison-Ford Winter Estates.

1945

As the war drew to a close, the idea of a suitable Edison Memorial was revisited. No longer was there discussion of a library but instead a university—Edison University—with a seventeen-page prospectus describing it. This time in 1945, the concept came not from Mina Edison but from an ad hoc committee. Ed Smith was chairman of the committee, working with Mayor Fitzsimmons, Sidney Davis, Frank Bail, Lewis Conant, and others.[8] The prospectus called for a large technical university to be established on a 270-acre campus, which would include much of the undeveloped area of Edison Park Subdivision. The main office was to be in the area of the Edison estate lying east of McGregor Boulevard, where they had previously thought of locating the library. The Edison residential structures were to remain intact. Plans called for Mrs. Edison to donate Seminole Lodge to a foundation, for a $50,000,000 capital campaign, of which $30,000,000 would be used for acquisition of additional lands, structures and equipment and $20,000,000 put safely away in a permanent endowment to provide operational funds. The major gifts to the capital campaign were expected to be provided by power and utility companies in memory of Thomas A. Edison and "in perpetuation of his contributions to the advancement of civilization and free enterprise."[9] The prospectus was reviewed by Mrs. Edison and by her son, Charles. Dr. Hamilton Holt, president of Rollins College in Winter Park and a friend of the Edison family, was also brought in. Mrs. Edison gave tentative and later final approval to the concept. The plan seemed at first to be on track, but like the library, the concept lacked wings and did not fly.

1947

Two years later, in 1947, the *News-Press* reported that the Edison estate would be a "Shrine for Inventor."[10] Mrs. Edison, who had been in town only a week, signed a deed conveying Seminole Lodge and the laboratory and grounds across McGregor

Boulevard to the City of Fort Myers.[11] When the deed was signed, Mrs. Edison, Mayor David Shapard, Governor Charles Edison, and Graydon Jones were present. Delivery of the signed deed occurred later at a public ceremony at the Civic Center in Fort Myers on March 7.[12] The gift was not connected to either of the previous concepts for a memorial. Behind the negotiations that culminated in the deed were representatives of the Fort Myers Junior Chamber of Commerce and in particular, its president, Graydon Jones, and two members, Frank Carson and William Dowling. Mayor David Shapard and City Attorney Ralph Kurtz were also involved, as was Mrs. Edison's attorney, Albert. Jube.[13]

The property continued to be called the Edison "shrine," with the *News-Press* editorializing, "Fort Myers will be proud to maintain the place reverently as a shrine."[14] Mrs. Edison was reported to have dedicated the property to be maintained perpetually as a "shrine" honoring Mr. Edison.[15] At the public ceremony where delivery of the deed took place, family friend Sidney Davis was master of ceremonies. Davis introduced Mrs. Edison, who said that she had decided to give the property to the city not only because it was a suitable memorial but out of appreciation for the love and esteem in which she and her husband had been held by the citizens of Fort Myers. She recalled that her husband had been one of the city's foremost boosters and that he had a conviction that the city would have a great future. "I believe he would heartily approve of this dedication," she added. [16] Mayor Shapard then accepted the deed on behalf of the city, stating it was the city's proudest possession and pledging the full and perpetual support and maintenance of the property. The mayor then complimented the Junior Chamber of Commerce for its role in bringing the dedication to fruition. Mrs. Edison was invited to return to Seminole Lodge at any time and to enjoy in full the property, the gates to be closed while she was present.[17]

Seminole Lodge alone was insufficient as a suitable memorial to the Edison Fort Myers experience. Ford was also present during many of those years. His international stature and presence as a next-door neighbor and the great fondness which each had for the other, made his winter home, The Mangoes, an

Fort Myers Junior Chamber of Commerce members Frank Carson, Graydon Jones and Sidney Davis look on as Mayor Dave Shapard thanks Mrs. Edison for the gift of Seminole Lodge.

Courtesy of Edison-Ford Winter Estates.

important component of the shrine.

The Mangoes remained in private ownership from 1947 to 1988, when the City of Fort Myers purchased it from Mrs. Thomas Biggar, who, with her husband, had purchased the property from Ford in 1947. They had been prominent citizens of the city and had always considered themselves as custodians of an historic structure, doing very little in the way of alteration or modernization. Mr. Biggar died many years before the city acquired it. Although Mrs. Biggar had on many occasions said she wanted The Mangoes to be opened to the public as an historic site, nothing had ever been finalized.

In the early 1980s, an ad hoc committee was formed to work with Mrs. Biggar in the hope that a way could be found for the city to acquire The Mangoes and preserve it for posterity along with Seminole Lodge. That committee included Carl Roberts, L. D. Bochette, George Mann, Jim Newton, Mayor Art Hamel and the writer. Carl Roberts' father had been a special friend of the

Edisons and Carl himself was an old-time friend of Mrs. Biggar, as was Jim Newton, the same Jimmie Newton who had developed Edison Park across from The Mangoes. By then he had retired with his wife, Ellie, at their home on Fort Myers Beach. L. D. Bochette was a neighbor who lived across McGregor Boulevard from the Ford-Biggar home. George Mann was also an old friend of Mrs. Biggar and coincidentally, the husband of Barbara B. Mann.[18] The writer was then chairman of the Edison Winter Home Board and had the additional benefit of having grown up with Mrs. Biggar's sons, spending many youthful summer days in her back yard or in her sons' boats on the river behind her home. Mayor Hamel, Carl Roberts, and Jim Newton each made contact with Mrs. Biggar to see under what conditions she might agree to sell and for what price. In each attempt, both the price and the conditions were unmanageable and the committee gradually considered the matter unattainable and went out of existence.

1987

Because the writer was a contemporary of the Biggar sons, it seemed awkward and inappropriate to personally contact the mother of his friends; however, when the committee gave up, it was not easy to simply let the matter go. One day after work in 1987, as if by some unexplained force, the writer's car turned off McGregor into Mrs. Biggar's driveway and pulled around the shell grade to her back door. As luck would have it, Mrs. Biggar was home and her son Gordon was visiting her. In a conversation in the dining room, the subject of a sale to the city was again raised and Mrs. Biggar seemed relieved that the matter was again up for discussion. It was abundantly clear that her dream was to see The Mangoes preserved for future generations, although the method for accomplishing that feat was not clear. As the conversation continued, Mrs. Biggar seemed receptive to the idea of selling the home, although the price was again more than the city could afford. A discussion with Mayor Hamel followed resulting in an offer prepared by the writer for the purchase of the home by the city for $1,500,000, a price less than her initial offering price but thought by the writer and Mayor Hamel to be fair to both Mrs. Biggar and the city. The contract was made contingent on approval by the Edison Winter Home Advisory Board and the City Council. Mayor Hamel signed the offer on behalf of the city subject to such approvals and the contract was then sent to Mrs. Biggar.[19] After several weeks, Mrs. Biggar signed the contract and returned it to the writer. The Edison Winter Home Advisory Board then approved, as did the City Council, and all that remained was the completion and closing of the contract.

The city got what it needed—the remaining historic site for a fair price—and Mrs. Biggar, who had always wanted her home to take its place as a part of the legacy of the two American giants, received a fair price. The shrine was complete.

Acknowledgments

A substantial amount of the credit for this book must go to my friend Les Marietta, who as historian for the Edison-Ford Winter Estates, gathered copies of a vast amount of relevant correspondence and documents relating to Edison. Les spent much time researching the rich resources at the Edison National Historic Site in West Orange, New Jersey, and the archives at the Henry Ford Museum and Greenfield Village in Dearborn, Michigan. Les came to know the archivists at both institutions. He became acquainted also with individuals involved in the monumental Edison Papers Project, which is a joint effort of the Smithsonian Institution, Rutgers University, the New Jersey Historical Commission and the National Park Service. I am deeply indebted to Les for his research efforts and for his friendship both before and during this project. His death in 2001 left a void among all those persons associated with the Edison-Ford Winter Estates in Fort Myers.

I must thank my longtime friend, Edith Pendleton, Ph.D., dean of instruction at Edison Community College in Fort Myers, for her editorial contributions. Deedee, as my family knows Dr. Pendleton, did what she could to untangle my legal jargon and to advise me when there was no transition between subjects. A new friend, Judy Serrin, made additional editorial suggestions for which I am grateful.

I deeply appreciate the several interviews I had with Bob Halgrim, who had a special relationship with the Edisons. I did not interview my friend, Jim Newton, although I had an opportunity in the early part of 1998 to tell him of my project and how I planned to proceed. He encouraged me to go forward. Jim died in 1999, or as Jim would say, he "graduated." Before graduation, I did manage to send a list of questions to his close friends, Merle and Vern Erikkson, who were with him daily. My thanks to Merle and Vern for presenting my questions and obtaining answers when possible.

I didn't know C. A. Prince until I viewed a recent video history of him conducted by the Edison Winter Home staff. I then had an opportunity to interview him, and found him knowledgeable and cooperative. Late in this project my daughter introduced me to Alvin Lampp, a former employee of Edison's who worked in the goldenrod plots in Fort Myers. Janett and Chet Perry welcomed me into their home while I recorded two hours of their involvement with Mrs. Edison. My good friend Berne Davis did likewise.

Nancy Arnn, Mrs. Edison's niece and my fellow trustee at the Charles Edison Fund, has been particularly helpful in unraveling family relationships and in identifying family friends. As a small child, Nancy spent a winter with the Edisons at Seminole Lodge, the Edison's Fort Myers enclave, and spent much time with them at Glenmont, the family home in West Orange, New Jersey.

I have also interviewed Barbara B. Mann, Sue Bennett, Lucille McInnis, Barbara Brown, Katie Palmer, Gloria Durrance Shortlidge and Nat Cornwell, all of whom had personal experiences with the Edisons. Among those who had knowledge through family or otherwise, I spoke locally to Frank Pavese, Nick Armeda, and Mary Frances Howard. Tom Whitney of Boise, Idaho, telephoned me out of the blue and sent me valuable information about his grandfather, who had been an employee of Edison in St. Augustine. I was able to reciprocate with other information he didn't have.

Charles A. Tingley, librarian at the St. Augustine Historical Society, showed me around the society's library and put me in touch with Tom Whitney. Stan Mulford, of the Fort Myers Historical Museum, has critiqued my references to early Fort Myers and I made several corrections as a result. Katherine

Wilburn, Pete and Genevieve Bowen, and Doug Bartleson, of the Southwest Florida Historical Society have spent hours helping me to locate and scan early photographs. Father Jim English, the assistant rector at St. Luke's Episcopal Church in Fort Myers, located the original church marriage records evidencing the marriage of Charles Edison at Seminole Lodge. My friend Rusty Brown sent me an original photograph of Mrs. Edison and Mickey Rooney.

All of the staff at the Charles Edison Fund office welcomed me in New Jersey as I pored over original family correspondence in their custody. Particularly, I would thank Alberta Ench, her daughter Christina D'Amico, Lorraina Lalicata, and Patrick Warren. Sharon Disotell, Denise White, Karen Wojnar, and Esther Childs from my law office have been helpful with advice on word processing and in binding interim manuscripts. Also from my law office was Claudia Maggard, talented both as a legal assistant and an artist. Claudia is responsible for the beautiful etching of the original Edison winter home which is this book's frontispiece.

Evelyn Horne, who worked for the Koreshan Unity for 57 years, provided me with the recipe for the Koreshan mango sauce of which Mrs. Edison was fond. David Driapsa, a respected landscape architect from Naples, Florida, provided me with information relating to the horticulturist, Dr. Henry Nehrling, and his relationship with the Edisons.

Ford Bryan is the author of a number of books on the Ford family and has generously sent materials to me and corresponded with me on several occasions. He has also read certain chapters and commented on them. Donn Werling, who is director of Fair Lane, the Henry Ford Estate in Dearborn, and the author of *Henry Ford, A Hearthside Perspective*, has read and commented on selected chapters relating to Ford.

I appreciate the special interest of my friend, Neil Baldwin, the author of *Edison, Inventing the Century*, and the executive director of the National Book Awards. I first met Neil when he was interviewing Fort Myers people as he was writing his book.

Paul Israel, the author of *Edison, A Life of Invention* and the director of the Thomas A. Edison Papers project, honored me by critiquing my manuscript. Both Paul's book and Neil's book have been used extensively in that part of my research relating to Edison outside of Florida. Doug Tarr, former archivist at the National Historic Site, took time to have lunch with me in West Orange and has retrieved a number of documents for me.

At the Edison-Ford Winter Estates in Fort Myers, James Gassman, the Estates' former educator, has been very supportive, as has Judy Surprise, its former director. Staff members Mary Anna Carrol, Lori Van Wagner and Barbara Turner have all assisted me in the local archives. James Hagler, the Estates' former curator, not only assisted me in the archives but also has helped me to locate photographs from local sources. Pam Minor, the present curator has also provided great help in locating and scanning photographs from the estate archives. David Marshall brought me photographs from a private source.

My friends Ann Campbell, Mel Brinson, Mary Hanson, David Robinson, and Paul Flynn have read several chapters and made constructive comments. Nanette Smith and Robin Brown read the entire manuscript and are deserving of medals.

My engineer friend, Robin Dean, has assisted me in understanding certain technical aspects of my research. Stuart and Cotten Brown spent many hours cleaning up old photographic images.

Finally, my friend and fellow trustee of the Charles Edison Fund, John Keegan, who serves also as president of that organization and of the Edison Preservation Foundation as well, read this manuscript, and to prove he had read every word did a very generous foreword in which he very succinctly mentioned practically everything described in this book.

Notes

Abbreviations used for archival sources in these endnotes include the following:

ENHS–Edison National Historic Site in West Orange, New Jersey;
HFM&GV–Henry Ford Museum and Greenfield Village in Dearborn, Michigan;
CEF–Charles Edison Fund in Newark, New Jersey; and
EFWH–Edison-Ford Winter Homes in Fort Myers, Florida.

Chapter One: A New Beginning

1. Samuel Insull to Edison, February 24, 1885, ENHS.
2. Paul Israel, *Edison: A Life of Invention* (New York: John Wiley and Sons, 1998), 234.
3. Marion Edison Oeser, "The Wizard of Menlo Park," ENHS.
4. *The Fort Myers Press*, November 22, 1884.
5. Israel, *Edison*, 237; Neil Baldwin, *Edison: Inventing the Century* (New York: Hyperion, 1995), 147.
6. Ibid.

Chapter Two: In Search of Eden

1. Thomas Edison to Samuel Insull, February 28, 1885, ENHS.
2. Gilliland to Samuel Insull, March 5, 1885, ENHS; Edison to Samuel Insull, March 5, 1885, ENHS.
3. Insull to Charles Batchelor, March 7, 1882, March 24, 1882, ENHS; Hoyt and Dickson to Edison, April 8, 1882, ENHS; Insull to Benjamin Hardwick, April 3, 1882, ENHS; Edison to Insull, 13 and 15 February 13, 1883, February 15, 1883, ENHS; Mary Edison to Insull, February 27, 1884, ENHS; Insull to Clarendon Hotel, February 6, 1884, ENHS.

4. Charles A. Tingley, Research Librarian, St. Augustine Historical Society, St. Augustine, Florida, interview with author on October 15, 1998.
5. Matthew Josephson, *Edison, A Biography* (New York: McGraw-Hill Book Company, 1959), 289.
6. Ibid.
7. Lillian Gilliland to Edison, February 12, 1929, ENHS.
8. *Fort Myers Tropical News*, April 25, 1928.
9. Samuel Insull to Theodore Whitney, February 27, 1885, ENHS.
10. Edison to Theodore Whitney, March 14, 1885, Tom Whitney private collection.
11. Ibid.
12. Theodore Whitney to Edison, 6 April 1885, ENHS.
13. Theodore Whitney to Edison, March 31, 1884, April 25, 1884, Thomas A. Whitney private collection.
14. *The Fort Myers Press*, March 28 1885. Edison recalled in an interview with the *Fort Myers Tropical News*, April 25, 1928, that the yacht was a fishing sloop—not an elegant yacht as was reported at the time in *The Fort Myers Press*. He also remembered that the sloop was owned by a man named Armeda and that his party hired Armeda and his son, Nick, to take them further south along the coast to Punta Rassa.
15. Karl H. Grismer, *The Story of Fort Myers* (St. Petersburg: St. Petersburg Printing Company, 1949), 114. Nick Armeda's grandson, also Nick Armeda, resides in Fort Myers today. Armeda's grandson told the author he knows of no connection his grandfather had with the Edison party's charter to Punta Rassa. Nick Armeda, interview with author in Fort Myers on August 10, 2000.
16. Ibid.
17. Joe A. Akerman, Jr. *Florida Cowman: A History of Florida Cattle Raising* (Kissimmee, Florida: Florida Cattlemen's Association, 1976), 55, 107.
18. Thomas A. Gonzalez, *The Caloosahatchee* (Fort Myers Beach: The Island Press Publishers, 1982), 6.
19. Ibid., 8.
20. Grismer, *Fort Myers*, 82.
21. Ibid.
22. Akerman, *Cowman*, 55.
23. Gonzalez, *The Caloosahatchee*, 16.
24. Canter Brown, Jr., *Florida's Peace River Frontier* (Orlando: University of Central Florida Press, 1991), 217.
25. Gonzalez, *The Caloosahatchee*, 9.
26. Akerman, *Cowman*, 108.
27. Akerman, *Cowman*, 107.
28. Akerman, *Cowman*, 112.
29. Gonzalez, *The Caloosahatchee*, 15.
30. Ibid., 108.
31. Ibid.

32. Akerman, *Cowman*, 159.
33. A model of the Summerlin House was recreated to scale in miniature and built from wood salvaged from the original structure. It is on display at the Fort Myers Historical Museum.
34. Grismer, *Fort Myers*, 137.

Chapter Three: Bamboo

1. Edison to Theodore Whitney, March 14, 1885, Theodore Whitney private collection.
2.. Karl H. Grismer, *The Story of Fort Myers* (St. Petersburg: St. Petersburg Printing Company, 1949), 114.
3. *The Fort Myers Press*, December 1, 1884; Florence Fritz, *Bamboo and Sailing Ships* (n.p. 1949); *Garden and Forest*, March 6, 1889, vol. 2, 120.
4. George R. Adams, "The Caloosahatchee Massacre: Its significance in the Second Seminole War," *Florida History Quarterly* XLVIII (April 1970), 377.
5. John K. Mahon, *History of the Second Seminole War, 1835–1842 Revised Edition* (Gainesville: University of Florida Press, 1985), 255. General Alexander Macomb was the American general and Chief Chitto-Tustenuggee was believed to be the principal chief of the Seminoles. Colonel Harney had been sent to relieve General Zachary Taylor, but General Taylor retained responsibility for military operations while General Macomb negotiated with the Indians.
6. Adams, "The Caloosahatchee Massacre," 371.
7. James W. Covington, *The Seminoles of Florida* (Gainesville: University Press of Florida, 1993), 98.
8. Adams, "The Caloosahatchee Massacre," 378.
9. Thomas A. Gonzalez, *The Caloosahatchee* (Fort Myers Beach: The Island Press Publishers, 1982), 17.
10. James W. Covington, *The Billy Bowlegs War* (Chuluota, Florida: The Mickle House Publishers, 1982), 80.
11. W. W. Mackall, A. A. General "Order No. 14," Headquarters, Western Division, Tampa Bay, Florida, February 14, 1850, *Journal of the Council of American Military Posts*, vol. 12, no. 3: 48.
12. Walter E. Burke, Jr., *Quartermaster: A Brief Account of the Life of Colonel Abraham Charles Myers Quartermaster General C.S.A.* (n.p. 1976), 21.
13. Covington, *Billy Bowlegs War*, 1.
14. Ibid.
15. Ibid., 79.
16. Ibid.
17. Walter E. Burke, Jr., *Quartermaster: A Brief Account of the Life of Colonel Abraham Charles Myers Quartermaster General C.S.A.* (n.p. 1976), 23, 27.
18. Ibid, 31.

19. Rodney E. Dillon, Jr., "The Battle of Fort Myers," *Tampa Bay History*, (Fall Winter 1983): 28.

20. Joe A. Akerman, Jr., *Florida Cowman, A History of Florida Cattle Raising* (Kissimmee, Florida: Florida Cattlemen's Association, 1976), 90.

21. An organization of local men, mostly stockmen and farmers who knew the South Florida area and whose mission was to protect the herds from capture by Union forces, procure beef for the Confederate armies, and combat the deserter problem.

22. Canter Brown, Jr., *Florida's Peace River Frontier* (Orlando: University of Central Florida Press, 1991), 173.

23. Dillon, "The Battle of Fort Myers," 30.

24. Francis C. M. Boggess, *Veteran of Four Wars* (Arcadia, Florida: Champion Job Rooms, 1900), 69.

25. Brown, *Peace River*, 173.

26. Ibid., 159, 166.

27. *The Fort Myers Press*, August 8, 1926.

28. Ibid.

29. *The Fort Myers Press*, April 2, 1908.

30. E. G. Wilder, "Escapade in Southern Florida," *Confederate Veteran* 19 (1911): 75.

31. *The Fort Myers Press*, August 8, 1926.

32. *New York Times*, March 18, 1865.

33. Dillon, "The Battle of Fort Myers," 31,32.

34. Boggess, *Veteran of Four Wars*, 69.

35. Wilder, "Escapade," *Confederate Veteran*, 75.

36. *The Fort Myers Press*, advertisements, January 3, 1885.

37. Ibid., June 13, 1885. Towles later became a difficult link in the long and affectionate relationship between Edison and Fort Myers when he failed to complete to Edison's satisfaction the collection and planting of royal palm trees along McGregor Boulevard.

38. Ibid., January 3, 1885.

39. Gonzalez, *The Caloosahatchee*, 68.

40. An article in *The Fort Myers Press* on Saturday, June 6, 1885 noted its second arrival in Fort Myers on Friday "of last week" (which would have been either June 5 or May 29). From that inference is drawn that the first landing in Fort Myers was on either May 22 or May 29.

41. Conrad Menge, *Early Dredging in the Lake Okeechobee Region* (Fort Myers: Southwest Florida Historical Society, 1950).

42. Karl H. Grismer, *Tampa* (St. Petersburg: The St. Petersburg Printing Company, 1950), 133.

43. *The Fort Myers Press*, January 3, 1885.

Chapter Four: Myers Discovered

1. *The Fort Myers Press*, March 28, 1885.

2. Ibid., March 14, 1885.

3. Ibid., April 25, 1928.

4. Ibid., March 28, 1885.

5. Receipt for property from Huelsenkamp and Cranford, March 21, 1885, ENHS.

6. The small house was probably built by Summerlin and could have been used by him while in Fort Myers. It is known now as the Caretaker's Cottage. A garage and second story over the garage was added later by Edison as chauffeur's quarters.

7. Edison-Summerlin deposit receipt contract, March 21, 1885, EFWH.

8. *The Fort Myers Press*, March 28, 1885.

9. Ibid.

10. Karl H. Grismer, *Tampa* (St. Petersburg: The St. Petersburg Printing Company, 1950), 174.

11. *The Fort Myers Press*, March 28, 1885.

12. Peter T. Knight to Edison, July 25, 1885, ENHS.

13. Abstract of Title certified by Peter T. Knight as Clerk of the Circuit Court of Monroe County on July 25, 1885, ENHS.

14. The Gilliland seashore cottage outside of Boston.

15. Dagobert D. Runes, ed., *The Diary and Sundry Observations of Thomas Alva Edison* (Westport, CT: 1968, reprint of 1948 Philosophical Library Edition, 20.

16. Ibid., 30.

17. *The Fort Myers Press*, August 1, 1885.

18. Alden Frank Architect invoice, September 23, 1885, ENHS.

19. Ezra Gilliland to TAE, September 17, 1885, ENHS.

20. *The Fort Myers Press*, December 26, 1885.

21. Ezra Gilliland to TAE, September 17, 1885, ENHS. .

22. Huelsenkamp to Edison, September 18, 1885, ENHS.

23. Huelsenkamp to Edison, September 21, 1885, ENHS.

24. Edison per Gilliland to Samuel Insull, October 23, 1885, ENHS. The laboratory in New York City where Edison spent most of his time was located on the top floor of the building occupied by Bergmann and Company at the corner of 17th Street and Avenue B while the Edison corporate headquarters was located at No. 65 Fifth Avenue. Insull joined Edison as a young man in 1881. He was at first the private secretary handling a large component of correspondence and later in 1883 began to accept additional financial responsibilities and became a member of the board of directors of some of Edison's light companies. Paul Israel, *Edison: A Life of Invention* (New York: John Wiley and Sons, 1998), 220.

25. John Tomlinson to Peter T. Knight, November 2, 1885, ENHS. Tomlinson, later fell out of favor with Edison.

26. *The Fort Myers Press*, October 17, 1885.

27. Ibid.

28. Ibid., October 31, 1885.
29. Ibid., November 7, 1885.
30. Ibid., November 21, 1885.
31. Edison and Gilliland to Joseph Vivas, December 5, 1885, ENHS; *The Fort Myers Press*, December 5, 1885. Vivas had been one of the first four settlers to arrive in Fort Myers from Key West in 1866.
32. Kennebec Framing Company of Fairfield, Maine invoices, November 25, 1885, November 27, 1885, and December 3, 1885, ENHS.
33. *The Fort Myers Press*, January 9, 1886.
34. Metropolitan Steamship Co. invoice, November 21, 1885, ENHS.
35. Edison by Gilliland to A. K. Keller, December 29, 1885, ENHS.
36. *The Fort Myers Press*, January 9, 1886.
37. Memorandum to Thos. A. Edison, no date, ENHS.
38. *The Fort Myers Press*, January 16, 1886.
39. Payroll memorandum, no date, ENHS.
40. *The Fort Myers Press*, January 16, 1886, January 23, 1886. A.G. Zipperer to Eli Thompson, no date, ENHS. The memorandum from Zipperer to Thompson requested payment for "maintenance" of men at Punta Rassa from January 18 to January 25.
41. N.A. Benner and Co., Shipping and Commission Merchants invoice, January 11, 1886, ENHS. Memorandum re distribution of goods lost on *F.A. Milliken*, no date, ENHS.
42. Bergmann and Co. invoice, December 18, 1885, ENHS.
43. Catalogue and Price List of Edison Light Fixtures manufactured by Messrs. Bergmann and Co., New York City, no date, ENHS. Bergmann and Co. was one of the Edison companies.
44. Hallett V. Cumston invoice, October 10, 1885, ENHS. Although this invoice appears in the Invoices for Fort Myers scrapbook, there appears to be no evidence that it arrived in Fort Myers. Since it was bought in October, it would logically have come on one of the shipments in either January or February. Gilliland wrote to Insull in March, about the time Edison and his bride arrived, that there was no music to be heard, not even a Jews Harp. He ordered an organ and there is evidence the organ was shipped.
45. Wm. McShane and Co. invoice, February 12, 1886, ENHS.
46. Lewis and Longer invoice, December 2, 1885, ENHS.
47. Sprague Electric Railway and Motor Co. invoice, November 28, 1885, ENHS.
48. Edison Lamp Co. invoice, December 2, 1885, ENHS.
49. Babcock and Wilcox Co. invoice, December 19, 1885 ENHS.
50. Dynamo was an early name for generators. It was frequently used for generators using direct current—not alternating current. Edison was a persistent advocate of direct current for reasons of safety. Ultimately, alternating current became the medium of choice.
51. Bauman Brothers invoice, January 6, 1886, ENHS.

52. Park and Tilford statement, February 1, 1886, ENHS.

53 James McCutcheon and Co. invoice, February 13, 1886, ENHS.

54. Edison Machine Works invoice, February 12, 1886, ENHS.

55. Bauman Brothers invoice, February 15, 1886, ENHS.

56. Lewis and Conger invoice, February 1886, ENHS.

57. M. Gally, inventor and manufacturer or musical instruments, invoice, March 4, 1886, ENHS.

58. F.W. Toppan invoice, March 10, 1886, ENHS.

59. Patterson Brothers to Edison invoice, December 19, 1885, ENHS.

60. John Simmons to Edison invoice, December 19, 1885, ENHS.

61. Babcock and Wilcox to Edison invoice, December 19, 1885, ENHS; Babcock and Wilcox is in existence at this writing.

62. Edison Machine Works to TAE invoice, December 18, 1885, ENHS; Edison's lighting system comprised the larger central system such as was used in the Pearl Street Power Station in New York City and the smaller isolated system as would be used at Seminole Lodge. As an inventor and entrepreneur, Edison's passion was with the central system.

63. *The Fort Myers Press*, February 13, 1886.

64. Ibid., January 23, 1886.

65. Ibid., February 20, 1886.

Chapter Five: Enter Mina

1. *Akron Times*, March 4, 1886.

2. Paul Israel, *Edison: A Life of Invention* (New York: John Wiley and Sons, 1998), 237; Neil Baldwin, *Edison: Inventing the Century* (New York: Hyperion, 1995), 146.

3. Matthew Josephson, *Edison, A Biography* (New York: McGraw-Hill Book Company, Inc. 1959), 302.

4. Israel, *Edison*, 233.

5. Marion Edison Oeser, "The Wizard of Menlo Park," 6, ENHS.

6. Ibid.

7. Kathleen L. McGuirk, *The Diary of Thomas A. Edison* (Old Greenwich, CT: The Chatham Press, 1971), Introduction 10.

8. Ibid.

9. Dagobert D. Runes, editor, *The Diary and Sundry Observations of Thomas Alva Edison* (Westport, CT: 1968, reprint of 1948 Philosophical Library Edition), 14.

10. Ellwood Hendrick, *Lewis Miller* (Princess Anne, MD: Yestermorrow, 1925), 86.

11. Baldwin, *Edison*, 153.

12. Edison to Samuel Insull, June 5, 1885.

13. Runes, *Diary*, 3.

14. Ibid., 22.

15. Ibid., 5.
16. Israel, *Edison*, 246. The tasimeter employed a carbon button similar to the one used in his telephone transmitter, but its function was to measure heat, and was so sensitive that it was able to measure the heat rays of distant stars.
17. Baldwin, *Edison*, 150; Hendrick, *Lewis Miller*, 45.
18. Lewis Miller to Mina Edison, April 26, 1887.
19. Hendrick, *Lewis Miller*, v.
20. Israel, *Edison* 247.
21. Oeser, "The Wizard of Menlo Park," 6.
22. Edison to Lewis Miller, September 30, 1885.
23. Baldwin, *Edison*, 162.
24. Israel, *Edison* 248.
25. Baldwin, *Edison*, 162.
26. Israel, *Edison* 249.
27. Ibid., 250.
28. Ibid., 250.
29. Ibid.; Baldwin, *Edison*, 171.
30. *Daily News*, March14, 1886. The paper reported that the couple left Palatka aboard the Florida Southern Railway which ran from Palatka to Gainesville. Gainesville would have been a junction with the old Florida Railway traveling from Fernandina to Cedar Key from which the couple could have traveled to Fort Myers.
31. A. Solary, Carriages and Buggies of Jacksonville, invoice, May 20, 1886, ENHS.
32. *The Fort Myers Press*, February 27, 1886.
33. *The Fort Myers Press*, March 20, 1886. The March 20, 1886, edition of the *The Fort Myers Press* was on a Saturday. The article states that Edison and his wife arrived on the *Manatee* on Monday morning. A story in the *The Fort Myers Press* many years later in the April 25, 1928 issue, stated that the honeymooners proceeded down the Saint Johns visiting different points of interest and finally to Plant City, Florida, where they took a horse and buggy a distance of over 100 miles to Olga, which is situated on the Caloosahatchee River about 10 miles up river from Fort Myers. They could have traveled by steamer on the St. Johns River from Palatka to Sanford and from there they could have traveled by Plant System railway to Plant City, Florida near Tampa. While the foregoing is possible, it is not likely because *The Fort Myers Press* announced their arrival on the scheduled steamboat, the *Manatee*. More likely, the couple would have come from Palatka to Sanford, Florida and from there by rail through Plant City to Tampa and from there on a steamer to the town of Manatee and from there on board the steamboat, *Manatee*, as suggested by the *The Fort Myers Press* article. Of course, they could also have come from Cedar Key to Tampa and Manatee and then aboard the *Manatee* to Fort Myers.
34. *The Fort Myers Press*, May 23, 1885.

Notes

35. *The Fort Myers Press*, March 20, 1886. Keystone Hotel invoice, undated, ENHS. Frierson House invoice, February 28, 1886, ENHS. The handwritten invoice from the Keystone Hotel showed three days charges for Edison, his wife and maid, and three weeks charges for Misses Edison and Johnson. The Frierson House invoice billed Edison for board for four persons, most likely Eli Thompson, the superintendent, A. K. Keller, in charge of the steam launch, L. G. Perris and J. S. Knowles, all of whom were involved in the construction of the dwellings, the laboratory and machine shop.
36. *The Fort Myers Press*, April 3, 1886.
37. Ezra Gilliland to Samuel Insull, March 7, 1886, ENHS; Gilliland invoice for boxing organ to go to Florida, March 17, 1886, ENHS.
38. Edison to Samuel Insull, March 11, 1886, ENHS.
39. Israel, *Edison* 250.
40. Ibid.
41. Edison Notebook entitled Fort Myers Florida, April 17, 1886, ENHS.
42. Edison Memo Book, N-86–04–05, ENHS. Also mentioned were Poinciana trees, a lemon hedge, pecan trees, soft shell almonds, Brazil nuts, date palms, English walnuts, Filberts, figs, peaches, grapes, strawberries (specified a patch 20 by 100), red and black raspberries, castor beans, olives, Jamaica apple, egg fruit, mangos, alligator pears (avocados), sapodillas, Spanish gooseberry, paw paw, pomegranates, mulberry tree, orange trees, guavas, peanuts, tobacco (20 feet square), persimmons, tamarind and a double row of sugar cane (50 feet long).
43. Ibid.
44. M. Ewing Fox, invoice, September 22, 1886, ENHS.
45. *The Fort Myers Press*, May 1, 1886, April 17, 1886.
46. E. T. Gilliland to Eli Thompson, June 5, 1886, ENHS; Edison payment voucher for Nick Armeda, July 6, 1886, ENHS.
47. E. T. Gilliland to Eli Thompson, June 5, 1886, ENHS.
48. Israel, *Edison* 257.
49. *The Fort Myers Press*, June 16, 1887. The *Press* reported his departure on May 2, 1887.
50. Ibid., February 19, 1887.
51. Lewis Miller to Mina Edison, April 26, 1887. ENHS. The letter is from father to daughter and suggests that Mina returned to New Jersey earlier than her husband.
52. A letter from William to Mina Edison suggests the boys were in school in New Jersey. William Edison to Mina Edison, March 27, 1987, ENHS.
53. A group photograph on the porch of the Edison home shows a woman who is very likely Mina and clearly shows Charles Batchelor. Gilliland is standing by the mule. The photo is marked 1886, however it shows Edison with a bandaged ear which suggests it should have been 1887 when the abessed ear actually occurred. The photo is part of the Edison Winter Home collection.

54. *The Fort Myers Press*, February 12, 1887.

55. Lewis Miller to Mina Edison, April 26, 1887.

56. Elmer and Amend, Importers and Manufacturers of Chemicals invoice, January 15, 1886, ENHS; Elmer and Amend, Importers and Manufacturers of Chemicals invoice, February 2, 1887, ENHS; Elmer and Amend, Importers and Manufacturers of Chemicals invoice, April 5, 1887, ENHS.

57. Andrew J. Corcoran, Windmills, invoice, May 19, 1887, ENHS. cliv. E. and H. T. Anthony and Co., Photographic Equipment and Supplies invoice, January 31, 1887, ENHS. Hartley and Graham, Firearms invoice, January 22, 1887, ENHS; Henry A. Davidson Boats and Oars invoice, January 22, 1887, ENHS (for one 15' boat and one 13' boat); N. A. Benner, Shipping Merchant invoice, February 18, 1887, ENHS. Also ordered were tarpon line, Spanish Mackerel squids, sheep head hooks, spiral and egg sinkers, dual-forged tarpon hooks, and a cast net. Abbey and Imbrie, Fine Fishing Tackle of New York invoice, January 22, 1887, ENHS. He brought enhancements for the house and grounds including two cisterns, a windmill and a pump. N. A. Benner and Company, Shipping and Commission Merchants, January 15, 1887 (for shipping aboard the schooner, Dora Matthews), ENHS. Andrew J. Corcoran, Windmills, invoice, May 19, 1887, ENHS.

58. D. Van Nostrand, Bookseller, invoice, April 8, 1887, ENHS.

59. *The Fort Myers Press*, March 10, 1887.

60. Combination Gas Machine Company invoice, January 24, 1887, ENHS; Grismer, *Fort Myers*, 115.

61. *The Fort Myers Press*, March 10, 1887.

62. Bergmann and Company, invoice, February 7, 1887, ENHS.

63. *The Fort Myers Press*, April 21, 1887.

64. Browning, King and Company, Uniform Dept. invoice, January 22, 1887 and January 24, 1887, ENHS.

65. *The Fort Myers Press*, April 7, 1887.

66. Crystal Ice Works, Bartow, Florida, invoice, March 31, 1887, ENHS; Steamer *Alice Howard* invoices, February 10, 15, 17, 19, 22, 24, 26, March 3, 5, 8, 10, 11, 12, 15, 19, 22, 24, 29, 31, April 2, 5, 7, 9, 12, 14, 18, 19, 21, 23, 1887, ENHS.

67. P. Barnett of English, Florida to Edison, May 2, 1887, ENHS; Steamer *Alice Howard* freight invoices, April 7, 9, 12, 14, 1887, ENHS.

68. It is not clear whether this excursion took place in 1886 or 1887. Bathhouses, cottages and a small hotel were in place by the summer of 1887 which seems to point to 1887.

69. Canter Brown, Jr., *Florida's Peace River Frontier* (Orlando: University of Central Florida Press, 1991), 283.

70. Hendrick, *Lewis Miller*, 117. Although this autobiography suggests that both Edisons were present, it is likely that it was just Edison and not Mina. A letter written by Lewis Miller to Mina from Fort Myers refers to

the earlier departure of Mina Edison. Lewis Miller to Mina Edison, April 26, 1887. ENHS.

71 Ibid.

72. Ibid.

73. Ibid.

74. Israel, *Edison* 257.

Chapter Six: Exit Damon

1. Damon and Pythias were lifelong friends in a foreign land, one condemned to death for speaking against the excessive power of the King, and the other having committed no such offense. They stood in the court of Dionysius, the ruler of the Greek colony of Syracuse. Pythias, the condemned friend, had requested permission of Dionysius to return to his home to say good-bye to his wife and children and put his affairs in order. Damon, the innocent friend, offered to remain in prison as security for the return of Pythias and to face execution if the latter failed to return. When Pythias voluntarily returned, the King was so overwhelmed by the loyalty of Damon in acting as a stand-in, and the loyalty of Pythias in returning to face certain death and to save his friend from the same fate, that he freed both and asked if he could become a part of their friendship.

2. Dagobert D. Runes, editor, *The Diary and Sundry Observations of Thomas Alva Edison* (Westport, CT: 1968, reprint of 1948 Philosophical Library Edition), 38.

3. Ibid., 30.

4. Paul Israel, *Edison: A Life of Invention* (New York: John Wiley and Sons, 1998), 234.

5. Ibid., 237.

6. Thomas A. Edison v. Ezra T. Gilliland and John C. Tomlinson, Equity Case No. 4652, U. S. Circuit Court, Southern District of New York (1889), National Archives, Northeast Region, New York, N.Y. See Bill of Complaint. The foregoing case did not go to trial, hence it was never proven by testimony although the facts alleged were sworn to by Edison.

7. Ibid.

8. Ibid.; *New York Herald*, January 19, 1889.

9. Matthew Josephson, *Edison, A Biography* (New York: McGraw-Hill Book Company, 1959), 317.

10. Edison v. Gilliland and Tomlinson, supra. See Bill of Complaint.

11. Ibid.

12. Ibid., See Affidavit of Thomas A. Edison filed in case.

13. Ibid.

14. Edison v. Gilliland and Tomlinson, supra. See Bill of Complaint. Exhibit B.

15. Ezra T. Gilliland to Jesse H. Lippincott, undated letter except for annotation "Served September 15th 1888, CPB" (Charles P. Bruch, attorney for

Gilliland), ENHS. The letter calls for $50,000 cash to be exchanged for 1/5 of sender's stock in North American Phonograph Company; Ezra T. Gilliland to Jesse H. Lippincott, August 20, 1888 with annotation "Handed to Jesse H. Lippincott in person at 11:45 A.M. Tues Aug 21 88, CPB (Charles P. Bruch, attorney for Gilliland), ENHS. Letter calls for $50,000 cash to be exchanged for 1/5 of sender's stock in North American Phonograph Company.

16. Ibid. See Affidavit of Thomas A. Edison filed in case.
17. Edison to Gilliland, cable, September 11, 1888, ENHS.
18. *The Fort Myers Press,* January 17, 1889.
19. Edison to Wm. E. Hibble, January 31, 1889, ENHS.
20. Edison to Wm. E. Hibble, March 5, 1889, ENHS.
21. Thomas A. Edison v. Ezra T. Gilliland and John C. Tomlinson, supra.
22. Alfred O. Tate to Wm. E. Hibble, December 20, 1889, ENHS.
23. Alfred O. Tate to Wm. E. Hibble, January 3, 1890, ENHS.
24. Edison to Major Evans, September 21, 1891, ENHS.
25. *The Fort Myers Press,* April 28, 1892.
26. Tootie McGregor Terry, offered to construct a fifty-foot boulevard from Whiskey Creek to Punta Rassa if the county would construct a road from Monroe Street (in downtown Fort Myers) to Whiskey Creek.
27. See Chapter Twenty.
28. Lillian Gilliland to Edison, February 12, 1929, ENHS. The letter refers to Winthrop Beach, which was the name of the town where Woodside Villa was located and the location where Edison visited the Gillilands when courting Mina. The occasion for the letter was the birthday of Edison which traditionaly was celebrated in Fort Myers with a press conference and the great man responding to reporter's questions. Mrs. Gilliland tells of listening to him which no doubt referred to a radio news program carrying the interview. Hoover was president elect.

Chapter Seven: The Absence

1. Dagobert D. Runes, ed., *The Diary and Sundry Observations of Thomas Alva Edison* (Westport, CT: 1968, reprint of 1948 Philosophical Library Edition, 20.
2. William E. Hibble to Alfred O. Tate, November 22, 1890, ENHS.
3. William E. Hibble to Alfred O. Tate, December 6, 1890, ENHS. .
4. William E. Hibble to Alfred O. Tate, November 22, 1890, ENHS.
5. M. M. Edison to Alfred O. Tate, February 24, 1890, ENHS.
6. Alfred O. Tate to William E. Hibble, March 5, 1890, ENHS.
7. William E. Hibble to Alfred O. Tate, March 14, 1890. ENHS.
8. Ibid.
9. Ibid.
10. William E. Hibble to Alfred O. Tate, December 6, 1890, ENHS.

11. When Edison's mother died in 1871, Samuel Edison began a liaison with a 17-year-old girl and the affair produced three children.
12. Edison to William E. Hibble, January 20, 1891, ENHS.
13. William E. Hibble to Edison, January 27, 1891, ENHS. Symington later in 1901 wrote to Edison from Port Huron, Michigan for a handout of twenty dollars because the winter was coming and he was then age 84 and could not get by without it. Edison sent $10.
14. William E. Hibble to Alfred O. Tate, May 12, 1891, ENHS.
15. Ibid.
16. H. A. Parker to Edison, May 13, 1891, ENHS; Alfred O. Tate to H. A. Parker, May 28, 1891, ENHS; Alfred O. Tate to William E. Hibble, May 28, 1891, ENHS; H. A. Parker to Alfred O. Tate, June 3, 1891), ENHS.
17. James Evans to Edison, June 22, 1891, ENHS.
18. Evans had platted the James Evans Homestead in 1876, which included most of downtown Fort Myers. It was generally the area occupied by Fort Harvie (later Fort Myers). Evans was first in Fort Myers in 1859 on a survey crew and permanently in 1873 after acquiring the homestead.
19. Edison to W. C. Battey, December 26, 1896, December 29, 1896, January 14, 1897, ENHS.
20. Edison to Eugene H. Lewis, November 12, 1897, ENHS; Edison to James Evans, November 12, 1897, ENHS.
21. Edison to J. L. Hickson, January 31, 1898, ENHS.
22. Edison to John Thomas, January 31, 1898, ENHS.
23. Edison to James Evans, February 21, 1899, ENHS.
24. Edison to James Evans, March 21, 1899, ENHS.
25. Edison to James Evans, July 26, 1899, ENHS.
26. *Tampa Tribune*, March 4, 1900; *The Fort Myers Press*, March 8, 1900.
27. The Tampa Bay Hotel is now the home of the University of Tampa.
28. *Tampa Tribune*, March 4, 1900; *The Fort Myers Press*, March 8, 1900.
29. Ibid.

Chapter Eight: Return to Eden

1. *The Fort Myers Press*, February 28, 1901.
2. Ibid.; The Fort Myers Hotel was built in 1898 by Hugh O'Neil and later became the Royal Palm Hotel. It was reportedly the site of the first royal palms in the town. The stately old hotel with its lush grounds, pool, annex and recreation room was demolished in the late 1940s.
3. Ibid., February 28, 1901.
4. Ibid.
5. Charles Edison, interview by Wendell Link in New York City on April 14, 1953, tape recorded, typewritten, 72, CEF.
6. There was no news account of their departure. However, statements exist with dated purchase entries for groceries and carriage teams through

April 6. Lybass and Mann, Proprietors of Fort Myers Livery, Feed and Sale Stables, March 30, 1901 and May 1, 1901, ENHS; H. E. Heitman, Groceries, April 30, 1901, ENHS; Evans and Co. Hardware and Furniture, April 1, 1901, ENHS; Fort Myers Meat Market, March 30, 1901, ENHS.

7. Ewald Stulpner to Edison, May 31, 1901, ENHS.

8. John Randolph replaced Alfred O. Tate as secretary to Edison in 1893.

9. Ewald Stulpner to Edison, September 30, 1901, ENHS; Ewald Stulpner Statement, October 31, 1901, ENHS.

10. Lybass and Mann Livery Stable invoice to Edison, March 30, 1901, ENHS.

11. Ewald Stulpner to Edison, May 31, 1901, ENHS.

12. Fort Myers Livery and Transfer Co. Invoice, May 26, 1902, ENHS.

13. Ewald Stulpner to Edison, June 1, 1902, ENHS.

14. E.L. Evans to Edison, June 5, 1901, ENHS.

15. E. L. Evans to Edison, October 20, 1903, ENHS.

16. Ibid., Marginal notation on letter directing his secretary to send $50.

17. *The Fort Myers Press*, February 6, 1902.

18. Ibid., February 13, 1902.

19. Ibid., February 20, 1902; Harvie Heitman to Edison, May 8, 1906, ENHS; Deed from R. Ingram O. Travers, et ux to Mina O. Edison, June 18, 1906, recorded in Deed Book 21 Page 158, Public Records of Lee County. Title was taken in the name of Mina Edison.

20. *Harper's Weekly*, December 31, 1901, as quoted in *Fort Myers Press*, January 30, 1902.

21. *The Fort Myers Press*, February 6, 1902.

22. Ibid., March 6, 1902.

23. Fort Myers Livery and Transfer Co. Invoice, March 31, 1902, ENHS; Evans and Co. Invoice, March 31, 1902, ENHS; Fort Myers Meat Market Invoice, April 1, 1902, ENHS; H. E. Heitman Invoice, Undated Invoice but entries range from February 28 to March 1, ENHS.

24. Lee County Telephone Co. Statement, April, 1902, ENHS; the statement recites that the company serves Naples, Estero, Buckingham and Alva.

25. It is not clear who Mr. Colgate was. It is not likely that it was Henry Colgate, the soap maker and Edison's neighbor from Llewelyn Park in New Jersey, but it could have been his son. Colgate's son was a friend of Charles Edison, the inventor's son. Charles would have been twelve at the time and could have brought along a friend.

26. Ibid., March 3, 1904; Plant System of Railways Invoice, March 1, 1902, ENHS. Naptha was one of the by products of the refining of crude oil and was used in early internal combustion engines, primarily in the hit and miss engines popular in 1902.

27. Frederick Ott Expenses to and from Fort Myers, April 5, 1902, ENHS.

28. *The Fort Myers Press*, March 3, 1902.

29. Ibid., March 13, 1902.

30. Ibid., January 23, 1902.

31. Ibid., March 20, 1902. Other guests included Mr. and Mrs. Earnest Norton, Mr. and Mrs. Saunders Jones, Mr. and Mrs. F. H. Abbott, Mr. and Mrs. John Murphy and Mr. and Mrs. Floweree.
32. Ibid. His party included A. D. Hermance and Thomas James.
33. Ibid., April 3, 1902.
34. T. B. Campbell to Edison, May 1, 1902, ENHS; *Fort Myers Press*, April 1, 1902.
35. Henley and Berger Invoice, June 19, 1902, ENHS.
36. Ewald Stulpner to Edison, June 1, 1902, June 19, 1902, ENHS.
37. Ewald Stulpner to Edison, June 1, 1901, ENHS. Summerlin House is the name used to describe the Edison Winter residence. Later it became known as Seminole Lodge.
38. Ewald Stulpner to Edison, November 10, 1902, ENHS.
39. Ewald Stulpner to Edison, July 9, 1902, ENHS.
40. Evans and Co. to Edison, September 5, 1902, ENHS.
41. *The Fort Myers Press*, February 19, 1903, February 26, 1903.
42. Ibid., February 19, 1903.
43. Ibid. G. F. Ireland was responsible for the plumbing and A. A. Maywald the painting.
44. Ibid.
45. Ibid., March 5, 1903.
46. Ibid., March 26, 1903. Floweree was a wealthy cattleman from Montana. He ventured to Fort Myers with his friend and fellow cattleman John T. Murphy. They bought adjoining riverfront lots, Murphy building Immokalee Anchorage (owned today by the City of Fort Myers and known as the Murphy-Burroughs House) located at the corner of First Street and Fowler at the Edison Bridge, and Floweree building Hunter's Rest on the adjoining riverfront lot.
47. Ibid., April 2, 1903.
48. Ibid.
49. Paul Israel, *Edison: A Life of Invention* (New York: John Wiley and Sons, 1998), 414.
50. *The Fort Myers Press*, February 26, 1903.
51. Israel, *Edison*, 410.
52. *The Fort Myers Press*, March 19, 1903.
53. Ibid., March 26, 1903.
54. Ibid., March 19, 1903.
55. Israel, *Edison*, 407.
56. *The Fort Myers Press*, April 2, 1903.

Chapter Nine: *The Reliance*

1. *New York Home Journal*, February 9, 1904.
2. Ewald Stulpner to Edison, November 1, 1903, ENHS.

3. Ewald Stulpner to Edison, February 3, 1904, ENHS; Glen Saint Mary Nurseries invoice, December 15, 1903, ENHS.
4. *The Fort Myers Press*, March 3, 1904.
5. Ibid.
6. Ibid., March 3, 1904; The Electric Launch Company Order Form January 26, 1904 ENHS.
7. Atlantic Coast Line Freight Bills, February 17, 1904, February 22, 1904, February 23, 1904, March 3, 1904, ENHS.
8. The Electric Launch Company to Edison, January 26, 1904, ENHS.
9. *The Fort Myers Press*, March 31, 1904.
10. Charles Edison, interview by Wendell Link in New York City on April 14, 1953, tape recorded, typewritten, 76, CEF.
11. Ibid.
12. Ibid.
13. *The Fort Myers Press*, March 3, 1904
14. Ibid., April 14, 1904.
15. Clarence I. Peck to Edison, Warranty Deed, July 29, 1904, Deed Book 18, Page 149 Public Records of Lee County, Florida.
16. Ewald Stulpner itemized expenses, March 2, 1905, July 1, 1905, ENHS.
17. *The Fort Myers Press*, February 16, 1905.
18. Ewald Stulpner to Edison, no date; J. L. Young Statement, January 28, 1906, ENHS.
19. *The Fort Myers Press*, March 1, 1906.
20. Ibid., March 29, 1906. Misses G. C. Waymouth, Elizabeh Robinson, Elsie Wilcox, Margaret Gregory and Coburn Musser were the classmates
21. Ibid., April 5, 1906.
22. Charles E. Harner, *Florida's Promoters* (Tampa: Trend Publications, 1973).
23. *The Fort Myers Press*, March 29, 1906.
24. Ibid., April 12, 1906.
25. Ibid.
26. Ibid., April 6, 1906.
27. Edison and Evans and Company Contract, handwritten, no date, pages 3 and 4 only, ENHS.
28. Ewald Stulpner to Edison, May 1, 1906, ENHS.
29. Fred Ott to Edison, April 26, 1906, ENHS.
30. Ibid. Handwritten annotation to secretary, Randolph, to reimburse Ott.
31. H. M. Holleman to Edison, June 22, 1906, ENHS.
32. Ewald Stulpner to Edison, October 4, 1906, ENHS.
33. Later drawings and references to the dock cite its length as 1,500 feet. It is difficult to reconcile the construction of 357 feet by Vivas in 1885, the 562 feet by Campbell in 1902 and the 132 feet by Campbell in 1906 which totals 1,051 feet with the 1,500 feet. At some point an additional 449 feet were constructed.
34. Since the part of the fence paralleling the shore would have been approximately 660 feet, the two components connecting to the shore would have

been approximately 370 feet each, hence the fence would have been about 370 feet from shore. The fence was to have three two-by-six heart pine members with one bolted just below low tide, another just above, and the third in the middle. The contract required that the job be completed no later than March 1, 1907. That "drop dead" date was not met and another contractor ultimately finished the dock a year later. Ewald Stulpner to Edison, September 18, 1907, ENHS.

35. Ewald Stulpner to Edison, October 4, 1906, ENHS.

36. Ewald Stulpner to Edison, November 3, 1906, ENHS.

37. Ewald Stulpner to Edison, January 3, 1907, ENHS.

38. *The Fort Myers Press*, February 28, 1907. For the last leg of the train trip from Jacksonville to Fort Myers the Edisons rode the Atlantic Coast Line train #83 with accommodations in a drawing room and sections 8, 9 and 10 in car "PG." Colin Studds, Eastern Passenger Agent for The Pennsylvania Railroad Company, January 26, 1907. ENHS

39. Ewald Stulpner to Edison, June 1, 1907, ENHS.

40. E. F. Bonaventure Art Galeries Statement, March 1, 1907, ENHS.

41. *The Fort Myers Press*, March 7, 1907.

42. Ibid.

43. Ibid., March 14, 1907, and March 21, 1907.

44. Ibid., March 28, 1907.

45. Executive Office, Tallahassee, Florida, April 2, 1907; Reprinted in *The Fort Myers Press*, April 4, 1907.

46. *The Fort Myers Press*, April 18, 1907.

47. Ibid.

48. Ibid., April 25, 1907.

49. Proctor and Company to Mrs. Thomas A. Edison, October 7, 1907, ENHS.

50. Proctor and Company to Mrs. Thomas A. Edison, November 8, 1907, ENHS.

51. Proctor and Company to H. E. Heitman, November 27, 1907, ENHS.

52. Proctor and Company Invoice, January 1, 1908, ENHS.

53. Ewald Stulpner to Mrs. Thos. A. Edison, December 7, 1907, ENHS.

54. See Chapter Ten.

55. Edison to *Fort Myers Press*, December 2, 1907, ENHS.

56. Phosphate mining in the 1890s in nearby Desoto County spawned a great interest in that industry. Edison apparently thought phosphate might also have a presence in Lee County.

57. Lee County Well Works to Edison, December 27, 1907, ENHS; See annotated response from Edison.

Chapter Ten: A Royal Avenue

1. *The Fort Myers Press*, April 4, 1907.

2. Ibid., April 18, 1907.

3. Ibid.
4. Ibid.
5. Ibid.; Minutes of Town Council of the City of Fort Myers, May 13, 1907.
6. Caxambus was a small fishing settlement lying east of Marco.
7. Ewald Stulpner to Edison, April 28, 1907, ENHS.
8. Ewald Stulpner to Edison, May 10, 1907, ENHS.
9. Edison to Ewald Stulpner, May 13, 1907, ENHS.
10. *The Fort Myers Press*, May 23, 1907.
11. Ibid.
12. Ibid., June 27, 1907.
13. Ewald Stulpner to Edison, June 14, 1907, ENHS.
14. Edison to Ewald Stulpner, June 12, 1907, ENHS.
15. Ewald Stulpner to Edison, June 14, 1907, ENHS.
16. Ewald Stulpner to Edison, July 6, 1907, ENHS.
17. W. H. Towles to Edison, July 5, 1907, ENHS.
18. Ibid. Edison annotated Towles' July 5 letter with directions to his secretary to extend the contract and send the advance.
19. Ewald Stulpner to Edison, August 6, 1907, ENHS.
20. Ibid.
21. Oneco is located near Tampa.
22. Edison to Ewald Stulpner, August 19, 1907, ENHS.
23. Ewald Stulpner to Edison, October 3, 1907, ENHS; Tampa Floral Co. Receipt, October 3, 1907, ENHS; Reasoner Brothers Royal Palm Nurseries Receipt, October 8, 1907, ENHS.
24. Reasoner Brothers Royal Palm Nurseries Receipt, October 8, 1907, ENHS.
25. Edison to Ewald Stulpner, December 9, 1907, ENHS; Ewald Stulpner to Edison, December 16, 1907, ENHS.
26. Ewald Stulpner to Edison, January 19, 1908, ENHS.
27. *The Fort Myers Press*, September 7, 1911.
28. Ibid.
29. H. E. Heitman to Edison, June 6, 1908, ENHS.
30. Edison to H. E. Heitman, June 9, 1908, ENHS.
31. W. H. Towles to Edison, October 20, 1908, ENHS.
32. Ibid.
33. H. E. Heitman to Edison, November 24, 1909, ENHS.
34. H. E. Heitman to Edison, November 24, 1909, ENHS.
35. *The Fort Myers Press*, September 7, 1911.
36. H. E. Heitman to Edison, May 20, 1910, ENHS.
37. *The Fort Myers Press*, September 7, 1909.
38. Ibid., October 27, 1914.
39. Ibid.
40. *Fort Myers Weekly Press*, September 7, 1911.

Chapter Eleven: Rejuvenation

1. Manhattan Eye, Ear and Throat Hospital Statement, March 10, 1908, ENHS; *Fort Myers Press*, February 27, 1908.

Notes

2. J. T. Rogers to Colin Studds, March 11, 1908, March 13, 1908, ENHS; Colin Studds to J. T. Rogers, March 12, 1908, ENHS.
3. John Randolph to Edison Phonograph Monthly, March 17, 1908, ENHS; Dr. Arthur B. Duel Statement, April 1, 1908, ENHS.
4. J. T. Rogers to Colin Studds, March 11, 1908, ENHS; Colin Studds to J. T. Rogers, March 12, 1908, ENHS.
5. Colin Studds to J. T. Rogers, March 12, 1908, ENHS.
6. Mina Edison to Charles Edison, March 17, 1908, CEF.
7. Ibid.
8. Ibid.
9. Ibid.
10. *The Fort Myers Press*, April 2, 1908.
11. Ibid.
12. General Terry married Tootie McGregor, the widow of Ambrose McGregor. The McGregors purchased the Gilliland house next door to the Edisons and resided there for several years.
13. *The Fort Myers Press*, April 2, 1908.
14. Ibid.
15. Brentano's Statement, April 1, 1908, ENHS.
16. Miss M. Flossie Hill Statement, April 18, 1908, ENHS.
17. Mina Edison to Charles Edison, March 28, 1908, CEF; *Fort Myers Press*, April 2, 1908.
18. Ibid.
19. Ibid.
20. Ibid. Yellow Fever Creek, now known as Hancock Creek, is located opposite Seminole Lodge on the north side of the river. Charles Edison to Mina Edison, undated, CEF.
21. Mina Edison to Charles Edison, March 28, 1908.
22. Ibid.
23. Ibid.
24. Mina Edison to Charles Edison, April 14, 1908, CEF.
25. Ibid.
26. Mina Edison to Charles Edison, April 15, 1908, CEF.
27. Mina Edison to Charles Edison, April 20, 1908, CEF; *The Fort Myers Press* (April 30, 1908) reported their departure on April 28, not April 21.
28. G. R. Shultz to Edison, June 5, 1908, ENHS.
29. *The Fort Myers Press*, January 30, 1908.
30. G. R. Shultz to Edison, August 3, 1907, ENHS.
31. Fred Ott to P. Brady, January 30, 1909, ENHS.
32. *The Fort Myers Press*, February 18, 1909.
33. Ibid.
34. Ibid., July 2, 1908.
35. Mina Edison to Charles Edison, March 20, 1909, CEF; A tea house was

constructed by the pool, however the pool had not been constructed as yet in 1909. It is not clear where the tea house referred to in the letter was located.

36. Ibid.
37. Robert Conot, *Thomas A. Edison, A Streak of Luck* (New York: Da Capo Press, 1979), 318.
38. Mina Edison to Charles Edison, March 20, 1909, CEF.
39. Theodore went on to obtain an engineering degree from Massachussetts Institute of Technology and became an inventor in his own right.
40. Fort Myers Wagon Works Invoice, March 15, 1909, ENHS.
41. George T. Brown to Edison, March 10, 1909, ENHS.
42. A. A. Gardner to Mrs. Thomas A. Edison, undated, ENHS.
43. *The Fort Myers Press,* March 25, 1909.
44. Ibid.
45. F. P. Holland to Edison, June 21, 1909, ENHS.
46. Ibid. See marginal annotation by Edison. See also acknowledgment of fish story in response from F. P. Holland to Edison, July 3, 1909. ENHS.
47. Proctor and Co. to H. E. Heitman, November 23, 1909, ENHS.
48. Proctor and Co. to H. E. Heitman, November 27, 1909, ENHS.
49. Proctor and Co. to H. E. Heitman, November 19, 1909, ENHS.
50. Proctor and Co. to H. E. Heitman, November 27, 1909, ENHS.
51. T. A. Edison Pay Roll, December 18, 1909, December 23, 1909, ENHS.
52. Edison to H. E. Heitman, January 4, 1910, ENHS.
53. *The Fort Myers Press,* February 3, 1910.
54. Ibid., February 24, 1910.
55. Ibid., March 3, 1910, March 10, 1910, March 17, 1910.
56. Ibid.
57. Ibid., March 24, 1910.
58. Ibid., March 31, 1910.
59. Ibid., March31, 1910.
60. Ibid., December 19, 1907, January 2, 1908.
61. Edison to H. E. Heitman, May 3, 1910, ENHS.
62. *The Fort Myers Press,* November 10, 1910.
63. Charles Edison, recorded interview conducted by Wendell Link in New York City on April 14, 1953, tape recorded, typewritten, 55, CEF.
64. A descendant of Oscar Oeser by his second marriage has become a great friend of the Edison Winter Home Museum in Fort Myers. In 1992, Madame Mylene Favre of Paris, presented the museum with a gift of an Edison Phonograph given by Edison to his daughter Marion on the occasion of her marriage to Madame Favre's grandfather, Oscar Oeser. That instrument is on display at the museum. Marion Edison Oeser was the first wife of Oscar Oeser and Madame Favre is a descendant of the second marriage. The gift was brought from her home in Paris.
65. See this Chapter, 1908.
66. See Chapter Nine.

67. H. E. Heitman to Edison, May 19, 1911, ENHS.
68. George Shultz to Edison, February 11, 1911, ENHS.
69. Edison to Heitman, May 10, 1911, annotation on letter from G. R. Shultz to Edison, May 1, 1911, ENHS.
70. G. R. Shultz to Edison, September 20, 1912, ENHS.
71. Ibid.
72. H. E. Heitman to Edison, April 29, 1911, ENHS.
73. See discussion of differences between these two men in Chapter Ten.
74. H. E. Heitman to Edison, July 8, 1911, ENHS.
75. *Fort Myers Weekly Press*, January 11, 1912, February 8, 1912.
76. H. E. Heitman to Edison, July 7, 1911, ENHS.
77. H. E. Heitman to Edison, July 12, 1911, ENHS.
78. H. E. Heitman to Edison, August 8, 1911, ENHS.

Chapter Twelve: Epistles From Mina

79. *Fort Myers Weekly Press*, March 14, 1912. Mina Edison to Charles Edison, March 14, 1912, ENHS. Madeleine's friends were Peggy James, Rosalind Bonyer and Julie Thompson.
80. Ibid.
81. *Fort Myers Weekly Press*, January 18, 1912, January 25, 1912.
82. Ibid., February 15, 1912, February 22, 1912.
83. Ibid.
84. Mina Edison to Charles Edison, February 4, 1912, CEF. Mina Edison to Charles Edison, March 14, 1912, CEF.
85. Mina Edison to Charles Edison, March 18, 1912, CEF.
86. Mina Edison to Charles Edison, March 20, 1912, CEF.
87. Mina Edison to Charles Edison, April 1, 1912, CEF.
88. Mina Edison to Charles Edison, March 20, 1912, CEF.
89. Mina Edison to Charles Edison, April 4, 1912, CEF.
90. Mina Edison to Charles Edison, April 1, 1912, CEF.
91. Mina Edison to Charles Edison, March 14, 1912, CEF.
92. Ibid.
93. Ibid.
94. Mina Edison to Charles Edison, March 20, 1912, CEF.
95. Ibid.
96. Charles Edison to Mina Edison, June something or other (undated), CEF.
97. Mina Edison to Charles Edison, March 20, 1912, CEF.
98. Ibid.
99. Ibid.
100. Madeleine Edison, "Rules for Guests at Seminole Lodge," Undated, Unsigned. CEF.
101. *Fort Myers Weekly Press*, March 27, 1912, April 11, 1912.
102. Mina Edison to Charles Edison, March 18, 1912, ENHS.

103. Mina Edison to Charles Edison, March 27, 1912, CEF.
104. Madeleine Edison, Attachment to "Rules for Guests at Seminole Lodge,"
    Undated, Unsigned, CEF.
105. *Fort Myers Weekly Press*, April 4, 1912, April 11, 1912.
106. Mina Edison to Charles Edison, March 20, 1912, CEF.
107. Mina Edison to Charles Edison, April 1, 1912, CEF.
108. Ibid.
109. Ibid.
110. Mina Edison to Charles Edison, April 7, 1912, CEF.
111. Ibid.
112. Mina Edison to Charles Edison, April 9, 1912, CEF.
113. *Fort Myers Weekly Press*, April 18, 1912.
114. Ibid., April 25, 1912.
115. Ibid.

Chapter Thirteen: Camping

1. *Fort Myers Daily Press*, February16, 1914.
2. Ibid., February 17, 1914.
3. Ibid., February 19, 1914.
4. Ibid., February 21, 1914.
5. Ibid., February 23, 1914.
6. Ibid.
7. Ibid.
8. Ibid.
9. Ibid.
10. Allan Nevins, *Ford: The Times, The Man, The Company* (New York:
    Charles Scribner's Sons, 1954), 512; Robert Lacey, *Ford The Men and the
    Machine* (Boston: Little, Brown and Company, 1986), 117; David L.
    Lewis, *The Public Image of Henry Ford* (Detroit: Wayne State University
    Press, 1976), 69.
11. Lacey, *Ford*, 5.
12. Ibid., 150.
13. Henry Ford to Mrs. Thomas A. Edison, February 24, 1913, ENHS.
14. *Fort Myers Daily Press*, February 28, 1914.
15. Ibid.
16. Lacey, *Ford*, 111.
17. Nevins, *Ford*, 497.
18. Matthew Josephson, *Edison, A Biography* (New York: McGraw-Hill Book
    Company, 1959), 458; Neil Baldwin, *Edison: Inventing the Century* (New
    York: Hyperion, 1995), 327.
19. *Fort Myers Daily Press*, February 25, 1914.
20. Ibid., February 25, 1914.
21. Ibid., February 20, 1914.

22. Ellwood Hendrick, *Lewis Miller* (Princess Anne, MD: A Berrybook Yestermorrow, 1925), 69.
23. *Fort Myers Daily Press*, February 25, 1914.
24. *The World Book Encyclopedia*, s.v. "Frederick Albert Cook."
25. *Fort Myers Daily Press*, March 5, 1914.
26. Ibid.
27. Madeleine Edison Sloane, handwritten, undated, and unsigned account, CEF.
28. Ibid.
29. Charles Edison, interview by Wendell Link in New York City on April 14, 1953, tape recorded, typewritten, 78, CEF.
30. Ibid.
31. Madeleine Sloane account.
32. Charles Edison interview, 78.
33. Madeleine Sloane account.
34. Ibid.
35. Charles Edison interview, 79.
36. Madeleine Sloane account.
37. Ibid.
38. Ibid.
39. Ibid.
40. Ibid.
41. Ibid.
42. Ibid.
43. Ibid.
44. Ibid.
45. Ibid.
46. Ibid.
47. Ibid.
48. Ibid.
49. Ibid.
50. Ibid.
51. Charles Edison interview, 79.
52. Madeleine Sloane account.
53. Ibid.
54. John Venable, *Out of the Shadow* (Philadelphia: Dorrance and Company, 1978), 255; Venable states that the foregoing took place around 1909. The Fords did not come to Fort Myers until 1914, and because both Edsel and Charles were in Fort Myers in 1914, it is believed that this was the year the outing took place.
55. *Fort Myers Daily Press*, March 5, 1914, March 10, 1914.
56. Ibid., March 10, 1914.
57. Ibid.
58. Ibid.
59. Madeleine Edison to Edsel Ford, March 29, 1914, HFMandGV.

60. W. G. Bee to Edison, April 1, 1914, HFMandGV. Through the storage battery company, Edison had been trying to develop a storage battery capable of starting the Ford Model T.
61. Ibid.
62. Henry Ford to Edison, March 31, 1914, HFMandGV.
63. Ibid.
64. Ibid.
65. Edison to Henry Ford, April 26, 1914, HFMandGV.
66. Edison to Editor, *Brooklyn Eagle*, May 20, 1914, HFMandGV.
67. *The Fort Myers Press*, March 10, 1915.
68. Ibid., March 11, 1915.
69. Mina Edison to Clara Ford, July 14, 1915, HFMandGV.
70. Ibid.
71. Ibid.
72. Lacey, *Ford*, 151.
73. Josephson, *Edison*, 449.
74. Lewis, *Public Image*, 118.
75. Ibid.

Chapter Fourteen: The Mangoes

1. David L. Lewis, *The Public Image of Henry Ford* (Detroit: Wayne State University Press, 1976), 9; Robert Lacey, *Ford The Men and the Machine* (Boston: Little, Brown and Company, 1986), 135.
2. Lacey, *Ford*, 143.
3. Lewis, *Public Image*, 97.
4. Paul Israel, *Edison: A Life of Invention* (New York: John Wiley and Sons, 1998), 446.
5. Ibid., 453.
6. *The Fort Myers Press*, April 24, 1916.
7. E. G. Liebold to Hill and Co., March 25, 1916, HFMandGV.
8. J. W. Hill to Henry Ford, April 1, 1916, HFMandGV.
9. *The Fort Myers Press*, April 11, 1916.
10. Ibid., April 19, 1916.
11. Ibid., April 24, 1916.
12. Robert W. Smith to Henry Ford, March 7, 1916, HFMandGV.
13. G. C. Anderson, Assistant Secretary to Henry Ford, to Robert W. Smith, March 13, 1916, HFMandGV.
14. E. G. Liebold, Secretary to Henry Ford, to Robert W. Smith, April 13, 1915 (letter mistakenly dated 1915 rather than 1916), HFMandGV.
15. Robert W. Smith to Henry Ford, April 17, 1916, HFMandGV.
16. James Hutton to Henry Ford, April 20, 1916, HFMandGV.
17. The first Fort Myers golf course was in East Fort Myers but it was short lived. The golf course referred to in this letter is the present-day Fort Myers

Notes

Country Club, a city-owned facility located about one mile south of the Edison and Ford homes on McGregor Boulevard. It is not clear what hotel is referred to here. It very likely was the Franklin Arms Hotel completed in 1924, eight years after the letter. The war could have put it on hold for a couple of years. Another two or three years could have been involved in the planning and construction.

18. G. S. Anderson, Assistant Secretary to Henry Ford, to James Hutton, May 1, 1916, HFMandGV.

19. Robert W. Smith to Henry Ford, May 5, 1916, HFMandGV.

20. G. S. Anderson to James Hutton, May 26, 1916, HFMandGV.

21. James Hutton to G. S. Anderson, May 29, 1916, HFMandGV.

22. G. S. Anderson, Secretary to Henry Ford, to James Hutton, May 29, 1916, HFMandGV.

23. James Hutton to Henry Ford, May 31, 1916, HFMandGV.

24. Israel, *Edison*, 450.

25. Ford R. Bryan "*Sialia*—Henry Ford's Yacht,"(n.p.), HFMandGV.

26. Ibid.

27. Ibid.

28. *The Fort Myers Press*, March 13, 1917, March 17, 1917.

29. Ibid.

30. Bryan, "*Sialia*."

31. Ibid.

32. Ibid.; A model of the *Sialia*, presented by author and Ford historian, Ford Bryan, is on display at the Edison Ford Winter Home Museum in Fort Myers. The model depicts the yacht before the additional twenty-one feet were added.

33. *The Fort Myers Press*, January 24, 1918.

34. R. W. Kellow to H. E. Heitman, January 5, 1918, ENHS.

35. R. W. Kellow to H. E. Heitman, January 15, 1918, ENHS.

36. R. W. Kellow to H. E. Heitman, January 31, 1918, ENHS.

37. *The Fort Myers Press*, January 29, 1918.

38. Mina Edison to Charles Edison, Undated, CEF.

39. Israel, *Edison*, 451.

40. Ibid., 450.

41. Mina Edison to Charles Edison, Undated, CEF. Israel, *Edison*, 451; Neil Baldwin, *Edison: Inventing the Century* (New York: Hyperion, 1995), 346.

42. Mina Edison to Charles Edison, undated, CEF.

43. Charles Edison to Mina Edison, February 12, 1918, CEF.

44. Charles Edison, interview by Wendell Link in New York City on April 14, 1953, tape recorded, typewritten, 147 CEF.

45. Charles Edison interview, 147–48.

46. Ibid.

47. Israel, *Edison*, 397; Baldwin, *Edison*, 353.

48. Charles Edison interview, 149.

49. Ibid., 150.

50. Lucy Bogue is the person identified as the baby nurse in the recorded interview with Charles Edison. John Scarth is the individual referred to as Scarth in the recorded interview with Charles Edison.
51. Charles Edison interview, 150.
52. *The Fort Myers Press*, March 27, 1918.
53. Church and Clergyman's Record Book, St. Lukes Episcopal Church, Fort Myers, Florida.
54. Charles Edison interview, 150.
55. Ibid., 151.
56. Charles Edison interview, 151.
57. Ibid.
58. Ibid., 148.
59. Theodore Edison to Mina Edison, March 23, 1918, CEF. Theodore Edison to Mina Edison, March 6, 1918, CEF. Theodore Edison to Mina Edison, May 21, 1918, CEF. In the last mentioned letter, Theodore states that the tests were completed that day and that they would be packing to leave the next day.
60. Theodore Edison to Mina Edison, March 11, 1918, CEF.
61. Theodore Edison to Mina Edison, March 12, 1918, CEF.
62. Theodore Edison to Mina Edison, March 13, 1918, CEF.
63. Theodore Edison to Mina Edison, March 6, 1918, CEF.
64. Theodore Edison to Mina Edison, March 12, 1918, CEF.
65. Theodore Edison to Mina Edison, March 20, 1918, CEF.
66. Charles Edison interview, 148.
67. Madeleine Edison Sloane to Mina Edison, March 6, 1918, CEF.
68. Theodore Edison to Mina Edison, May 11, 1918, CEF.
69. Theodore Edison to Mina Edison, April 20, 1918, CEF. The *Sachem* was a larger vessel mentioned several times by Theodore in his correspondence to his mother. It brought the equipment and ferried Thomas Edison and other visitors to the island. It could not come closer than approximately one mile, according to Theodore, who told his mother that the motor launches had to be used for that purpose.
70. Theodore Edison to Mina Edison, April 24, 1918, CEF.
71. Ibid.
72. *The Fort Myers Press*, April 2, 1918.
73. Lewis, *Public Image*, 94.
74. Ibid., 98.
75. Ibid. It is interesting to note that Henry Ford bought another yacht after selling the *Sialia*, this one from old political rival, Truman Newberry.

Chapter Fifteen: Peacetime

1. Paul Israel, *Edison: A Life of Invention* (New York: John Wiley and Sons, 1998), 454.

Notes

2. Mrs. B. E. Tinstman to R. W. Kellow, February 5, 1919, ENHS.
3. *The Fort Myers Press,* February 14, 1919.
4. Ibid.
5. Mina Edison to Charles Edison and Carolyn Edison, February 21, 1919, CEF.
6. Ibid.
7. Mina Edison to Charles Edison and Carolyn Edison, undated, CEF.
8. Ibid.
9. Ibid.
10. Ibid.
11. Ibid.
12. Ibid.
13. R. W. Kellow to Fred Ott, January 24, 1919, ENHS.
14. Fred Ott to R. W. Kellow, March 23, 1919, March 31, 1919, ENHS; R. W. Kellow to Fred Ott, April 4, 1919, ENHS; R. W. Kellow to John P. Constable, May 19, 1919, ENHS; Inventory of materials attached to letter to Constable.
15. *The Fort Myers Press,* April 9, 1919.
16. Ibid., April 11, 1919.
17. R.W. Kellow to Mrs. B. E. Tinstman, May 22, 1919, ENHS.
18. Mrs. B. E. Tinstman to R. W. Kellow, June 24, 1919, ENHS; R. W. Wallace and Company specifications for 50,000 gallon water reservoir, June 24, 1919, ENHS; Certification of completion as specified by J. A. Davidson and Son, Civil and Consulting Engineer, November 8, 1919, ENHS.
19. Ibid.
20. Albert S. Herman to R. W. Kellow, June 14, 1919, ENHS; Mrs. B. E. Tinstman to R.W. Kellow, June 24, 1919, ENHS.
21. R. W. Kellow to Mrs. B. E. Tinstman, June 25, 1919, ENHS; Mrs. B. E. Tinstman to R. W. Kellow, July 1, 1919, ENHS.
22. Fred Ott to R. W. Kellow, May 22, 1919, ENHS; R. W. Kellow to Mrs. Edison, May 23, 1919, ENHS; R. W. Kellow to Mrs. B. E. Tinstman, June 28, 1919, ENHS.
23. Mrs. B. E. Tinstman to R. W. Kellow, July 8, 1919 (two letters same date), August 16, 1919, ENHS; R. W. Kellow to Mrs. B. E. Tinstman, July 14, 1919, July 18, 1919, ENHS.
24. Mrs. B. E. Tinstman to R. W. Kellow, September 15, 1919, ENHS.
25. Karl H. Grismer, *The Story of Fort Myers* (St. Petersburg: St. Petersburg Printing Company, 1949), 261.
26. *The Fort Myers Press,* probably on December 1, 1919, or within a few days before or after. Microfilm copies of the *The Fort Myers Press* for December are missing from all available sources; however, a letter from B. E. Tinstman to R. W. Kellow, December 5, 1919, encloses a copy of the editorial with no indication as to its date. The letter and enclosure are at the Edison National Historic Site. That letter indicates the editorial appeared a few days before the letter.
27. Ibid.

28. R. W. Kellow to Mrs. B. E. Tinstman, December 12, 1919, ENHS.
29. R. W. Kellow to Mrs. B. E. Tinstman, October 7, 1919, ENHS; Mrs. B. E. Tinstman to R. W. Kellow, October 10, 1919, ENHS; R. W. Kellow to Mrs. Edison, October 14, 1919, ENHS.
30. Mrs. B. E. Tinstman to R. W. Kellow, July 15, 1919, ENHS.
31. H. D. Silverfriend to Mrs. Thomas A. Edison, August 12, 1919, ENHS; R. W. Kellow to H. D. Silverfriend, September 4, 1919, ENHS; The Koreshan Unity recipe for Mango Sauce was obtained from Evelyn Horne, a retired 57 year employee of the Koreshan Unity: 10 green apple mangos or 5 cups, sliced; Cover with water; 4 cups sugar; Cook until tender; simmer 20 minutes; add 1/4 teaspoon ginger and one teaspoon cinnamon; Seal in jars.
32. Thomas A. Edison to Mina Edison, Deed dated July 29, 1919, and recorded in Deed Book 54 Page 102 of the Public Records of Lee County.
33. *The Fort Myers Press*, February 28, 1920.
34. Charles Edison to Father, April 14, 1920, CEF.
35. Edison to R. W. Kellow; annotations on letter from R. W. Kellow to Mrs. Edison, November 2, 1920, ENHS.
36. B. E. Tinstman to R. W. Kellow, November 9, 1920, ENHS
37. B. E. Tinstman to R. W. Kellow, October 15, 1920, ENHS.
38. *Fort Myers Tropical News*, February 22, 1921; The *Tropical News* was a competing paper to *The Fort Myers Press*. It was a morning paper and the *Press* was an evening paper.
39. Israel, *Edison*, 454.
40. R. W. Kellow to Mrs. Mina Edison, February 16, 1921, ENHS.
41. R. W. Kellow to Mrs. Mina Edison, February 21, 1921, ENHS.
42. B. E. Tinstman to J. V. Miller, October 26, 1921, ENHS.
43. Ibid.
44. J. V. Miller to B. E. Tinstman, November 9, 1921, ENHS.
45. B. E. Tinstman to J. V. Miller, November 10, 1921, ENHS.
46. In 1885, 119 yards or 357 feet were constructed. In 1902, 562 feet were added. 1906 saw a contract for another 100 feet together with a 32 foot pavillion that was completed in 1908.
47. Martin Jay Rosenblum, R.A. and Associates concluded in the "Edison Winter Estate Historic Structures Report, 1999" that the dock had reached 1490 feet by 1918.
48. Fire Insurance For Dock and Dock Buildings attachment to letter from R. W. Keller to A. C. Frost, September 6, 1918, ENHS; Sketch of Thomas A. Edison Property by J. A. Davison and Son, September, 1923.
49. R. W. Kellow to B. E. Tinstman, February 25, 1921, ENHS.
50. B. E. Tinstman to R. W. Kellow, February 28, 1921, ENHS.
51. B. E. Tinstman to R. W. Kellow, March 10, 1921, ENHS; Mr. John Wannamaker Calling Card, February 4, 1921, ENHS.
52. David L. Lewis, *The Public Image of Henry Ford* (Detroit: Wayne State University Press, 1976), 80, 88.

Notes

Chapter Sixteen: Fishing

1. *The Fort Myers Press*, March 12, 1922.
2. Ibid., February 11, 1922.
3. Ibid., February 24, 1922.
4. Ibid., March 8, 1922.
5. Ibid.
6. Ibid., March 18, 1922.
7. Ibid., March 23, 1922.
8. Ibid., March 22, 1922
9. Ibid., March 23, 1922.
10. Ibid.
11. Ibid.
12. Ibid., March 25, 1922.
13. Ibid., March 24, 1922.
14. Ibid., March 28, 1922.
15. Ibid., March 29, 1922.
16. Ibid., March 30, 1922.
17. Ibid., April 1, 1922.
18. Frank Pavese, interview with author in Fort Myers on January 6, 1999.
19. *The Fort Myers Press*, April 5, 1922.
20. Ibid.
21. Ibid.
22. Mina Edison to Clara Ford, April 11, 1922, ENHS.
23. Mina Edison to Clara Ford, April 17, 1922, ENHS.
24. *The Fort Myers Press*, April 14, 1922, April 17, 1922.
25. Ibid., May 2, 1922.
26. Ibid., May 16, 1922.
27. Charles Edison to Mina Edison, May 29, 1922, CEF.
28. Yellow Fever Creek is located on the north side of the Caloosahatchee River opposite the downtown of Fort Myers. It is now known as Hancock Creek.
29. Charles Edison to Mina Edison, May 29, 1922, CEF.
30. Ibid.
31. *The Fort Myers Press*, June 28, 1922.
32. Ibid., February 6, 1923.
33. Ibid., March 1, 1923.
34. Ibid., March 15, 1923.
35. John Sloane to Mina Edison, March 12, 1923, CEF.
36. *The Fort Myers Press*, March 15, 1923.
37. Ibid., March 29, 1923.
38. Ibid.
39. Ibid., May 1, 1923.
40. Ibid., March 29, 1923.
41. Ibid., March 29, 1923.
42. Ibid., May 2, 1923; The organization is charitable in nature and exists to

this day. Its main mission today is the sewing of baby clothes for poor families by its members. The author's wife is a member as was his mother.
43. *The Fort Myers Press*, March 29, 1923.
44. Charles Edison to Mina Edison, April 25, 1923, CEF.
45. *The Fort Myers Press*, May 3, 1923.
46. Ibid., May 29, 30, 1923.
47. Ibid., February 27, 1924.
48. Ibid., March 27, 1924.
49. Ibid.
50. Ibid.
51. Ibid., February 21, 1924. The tires were installed by Hill and Company, the local Ford dealer as well as the Firestone dealer.
52. Ibid.
53. Ibid.
54. *Fort Myers Tropical News*, March 12, 13, 1924.
55. *The Fort Myers Press*, February 27, 1924.
56. Ibid.
57. Ibid., April 10, 11 and 12, 1924.
58. Ibid.
59. Ibid.
60. Ibid., March 14, 1924.

Chapter Seventeen: Rubber

1. Byron M. Vanderbilt, *Thomas Edison, Chemist* (Washington, D.C.: American Chemical Society, 1971), 276.
2. Ibid., 279.
3. Ibid., 275.
4. Ibid., 281.
5. Ibid., 280; *The Fort Myers Press*, March 19, 1925.
6. Vanderbilt, *Chemist*, 280.
7. Ibid., 273.
8. Edison to Henry Ford, September 14, 1923, HFMandGV.
9. Ibid.
10. *The Fort Myers Press*, March 14, 1924.
11. Ibid., May 28, 1924.
12. The loan which occurred in 1922 was a year prior to serious rubber discussions. It is not clear what the loan was for, however. Goodno had written to Ford soon after his initial meeting with Ford on the 1914 camping trip and receiving no response wrote again a year later. E. E. Goodno to Henry Ford, March 20, 1914, April 2, 1915, HFMandGV. Those letters contained a request for a loan to enable Goodno to build a railroad from LaBelle to Fort Myers. The passage of time from the letters to the date of the 1922 loan—about seven years leaves unclear the final purpose of the

1922 mortgage loan.
13. Ford R. Bryan, "Henry's So-Called Rubber Plantation in Florida" (unpublished), HFMandGV.
14. *The Fort Myers Press*, June 6, 1924.
15. Ibid., March 19, 1925.
16. Ibid., January 24, 1925.
17. Frank Campsall was E. G. Liebold's successor as Ford's private secretary. Liebold became Ford's press liaison.
18. *The Fort Myers Press*, January 28, 1925, January 30, 1925.
19. Ibid., February 16, 1925.
20. Ibid., March 26, 1925.
21. Ibid., March 13, 1925.
22. Ibid., November 7, 1925.
23. Ibid.
24. *Fort Myers Tropical News*, March 6, 1926.
25. Ibid.
26. Ibid., September 17, 1926.
27. Ibid., March 18, 1927.
28. Ibid., March 29, 1927. .
29. Ibid., July 31, 1927.
30. Ibid., June 21, 1927.
31. Vanderbilt, *Chemist*, 287.
32. Ibid., 289.
33. Ibid., 290.
34. Ibid.
35. Ibid., 291.
36. Ibid., 292.
37. *Fort Myers Tropical News*, November 30, 1927.
38. Ibid., January 5, 1928, January 7, 1928.
39. Ibid., November 30, 1927.
40. Edison to E. G. Liebold, December 16, 1927, HFMandGV.
41. *Fort Myers Tropical News*, June 12, 1928.
42. Bob Halgrim, interview by author in Fort Myers, January 16, 1999.
43. Bob Halgrim later became the director of the Edison Winter Home and was responsible for the creation and development of the Edison Winter Home Museum in Fort Myers.
44. *Fort Myers Tropical News*, June 5, 1928.
45. *The Fort Myers Press*, April 11, 1930, June 10, 1930, January 23, 1931.
46. *Fort Myers Tropical News*, January 23, 1931.
47. Ibid., March 1, 1930.
48. Ibid., March 17, 1930.
49. *The Fort Myers Press*, March 12, 1930.
50. Ibid.
51. Alvin H. Lamp, interview with author in Orlando, Florida on November 8, 2001.

52. Frank Lewis Dyer and Thomas Commerford Martin, *Edison: His Life and Inventions* (New York: Harper and Brothers, 1910, 1931). During the interview and with deserved pride, Lampp displayed the autographed volumes to the author.

53. *The Fort Myers Press*, January 23, 1931.

54. Ibid., March 12, 1930.

55. C. A. Prince video interview, conducted by James H. Gassman, David Marshall, and Robert Beason in Fort Myers on June 25, 1999.

56. Ibid.

57. *The Fort Myers Press*, January 23, 1931.

58. Prince, video interview. Prince, employed by Edison in June 1930, states the laboratory staff referred to Edison affectionately as "the old man," but not so that he could either hear them or read their lips.

59. Prince video interview.

60. Vanderbilt, *Chemist*, 299.

61. Ibid., 303.

62. Ibid., 315.

Chapter Eighteen: Edison Park

1. *The Fort Myers Press*, February 6, 1925.

2. This is undoubtedly an understatement since there were reported to be 349 inhabitants in 1885.

3. Ibid., February 11, 1925. He didn't give the name of Armeda's father nor did he mention the presence of the son. The *Fort Myers Press* had stated in its March 28, 1885, edition that Edison came to the city on the yacht, *Jeannette*, with Captain Dan Paul and no mention of Armeda. Other accounts said that Armeda was the 16-year-old cabin boy aboard the yacht. Karl H. Grismer, *The Story of Fort Myers* (St. Petersburg: St Petersburg Printing Company, 1949), 114. The grandson and namesake of Nick Armeda states that Captain Dan Paul was no relation to his grandfather; nor was he aware of any family history connecting his grandfather with the yacht which brought the inventor to Fort Myers from Cedar Key. Nick Armeda, Interview by Author in Fort Myers on July 20, 2000. While Armeda's presence on the sloop is not confirmed, his path crossed that of Edison on several subsequent occasions.

4. *The Fort Myers Press*, February 19, 1925.

5. Ibid., February 21, 1925.

6. Ibid., February 21, 1925.

7. Ibid.

8. Ibid.

9. Ibid., April 7, 1925.

10. Ibid.

11. Ibid.

12. Ibid., April 16, 1925.
13. Ibid.
14. Ibid., April 25, 1925.
15. E. G. Liebold to Mrs. Thos. A. Edison, March 30, 1925, ENHS.
16. E. G. Liebold to Frederick P. Ott, April 29, 1925, ENHS.
17. Frederick P. Ott to E. G. Liebold, May 18, 1925, ENHS.
18. Wm. H. Meadowcroft to E. G. Liebold, July 15, 1925, ENHS.
19. Frank M. Stout to Mrs. Thomas A. Edison, July 13, 1926, HFMandGV.
20. E. G. Liebold to Mrs. Thos. A. Edison, June 17, 1926, June 29, 1926, HFMandGV.
21. S. O. Godman to Edison, July 24, 1926, HFMandGV; *Fort Myers News Press*, July 25, 1926.
22. *Fort Myers Tropical News*, July 25, 1926, July 28, 1926.
23. Edison to S. O. Godman, July 30, 1926, HFMandGV.
24. S. O. Godman to Ford, August 2, 1926, HFMandGV.
25. E. G. Liebold to S. O. Godman, August 12, 1926, HFMandGV; *Fort Myers News Press*, August 18, 1926.
26. Katherine Reghler to E. G. . Liebold, November 2, 1926, HFMandGV.
27. Katherine Reghler to E. G. Liebold, November 25, 1926, HFMandGV.
28. *The Fort Myers Press*, December 13, 1925.
29. Ibid.
30. Ibid., January 13, 1926.
31. Ibid., May 30, 1926.
32. Paul Israel, *Edison: A Life of Invention* (New York: John Wiley and Sons, 1998), 256; *The Fort Myers Press*, September 16, 1926.
33. *The Fort Myers Press*, February 5, 1926.
34. Ibid., February 5, 1926.
35. Bob Halgrim, interview on January 16, 1999.
36. Woolslair was very athletic despite his crippled leg. He went on to become a leading lawyer in Fort Myers. His daughter, Wisty Wooslair, became the 1957 Queen of the Edison Pageant of Light celebration in Fort Myers.
37. Bob Halgrim, interview on January 16, 1999.
38. *The Fort Myers Press*, February 18, 1926.
39. Bob Halgrim, interview on January 16, 1999.
40. Ibid.
41. *The Fort Myers Press*, February 12, 1926.
42. Ibid.
43. Ibid.
44. Ibid., February 12, 1926.
45. Ibid.
46. Ibid.
47. Ibid.
48. Ibid., March 2, 1926.
49. Ibid., February 24, 1926.
50. *Fort Myers Tropical News*, February 25, 1926.

51. *The Fort Myers Press*, February 24, 1926.

52. Ibid., February 25, 1926.

53. Ibid., March 2, 1926.

54. Ibid., March 5, 1926.

55. Ibid., March 6, 1926.

56. Ibid., March 9, 1926.

57. See Chapter Fourteen.

58. *The Fort Myers Press*, March 3, 1926.

59. Ibid., March 9, 1926.

60. Ibid.

61. Ibid.

62. Ibid., March 10, 1926, March 12, 1926.

63 Ibid.

64. Ibid., March 9, 1926.

65. Charles Edison to Mina Edison, February 22, 1926, CEF; W. K. L. Dickson and Antonia Dickson, *The Life and Inventions of Thomas Alva Edison* (London: Chatto and Windus, 1894).

66. *The Fort Myers Press*, April 20, 1926.

67. C. Judson Herrick, *Brains of Rats and Men: A Survey of the Origin and Biological Significance of the Cerebral Cortex* (Chicago: University of Chicago Press, 1926).

68. James D. Newton, *Uncommon Friends* (New York: Harcourt Brace Jovanovich, 1987), 5.

69. Named for Manuel Gonzalez, one of the original Fort Myers civilian settlers arriving in 1866.

70. A legal procedure by which a court of equity is asked to remove the legal disability of non-age so that a minor may be treated as an adult. Florida corporation law required that a corporation's officers have attained the age of majority. To have the disability of non-age removed, it was necessary to bring a witness or witnesses before the court to vouch for the minor's capacity and responsibility.

71. *The Fort Myers Press*, April. 7, 1926.

72. Ibid., April 8, 1926.

73. Ibid., April 7, 1926.

74. *Fort Myers Tropical News*, May 13, 1926.

75. Newton, *Uncommon Friends*, 7.

76. Ibid., 8.

77. Ibid., 20–21.

78. Charles Edison to Mina Edison, April 14, 1926, CEF.

79. *The Fort Myers Press*, April 21, 1926.

Chapter Nineteen: Ford

1. *The Fort Myers Press*, February 4, 1927.
2. Ibid.
3. Dagobert D. Runes, editor, *The Diary and Sundry Observations of Thomas Alva Edison* (Westport, CT: 1968, reprint of 1948 Philosophical Library Edition), 16.
4. *The Fort Myers Press*, February 19, 1927.
5. *Fort Myers Tropical News*, February 25, 1927.
6. *The Fort Myers Press*, February 25, 1927.
7. *Fort Myers Tropical News*, February 27, 1927.
8. *The Fort Myers Press*, March 6, 1927.
9. *Fort Myers Tropical News*, March 8, 1927.
10. Ibid.; Mrs. Edison was later critical of the press for the "made up" story of the inventor's baseball prowess.
11. *The Fort Myers Press*, March 26, 1927.
12. Ibid.
13. Ibid.
14. James D. Newton, *Uncommon Friends* (New York: Harcourt Brace Jovanovich, 1987), 14; *Fort Myers Press*, March 12, 1927.
15. *The Fort Myers Press*, March 12, 1927.
16. Ibid.
17. Ibid., March 15, 1927.
18. Ibid.
19. Ibid.
20. Ibid.
21. Ibid.
22. Ibid., March 31, 1927.
23. David L. Lewis, *The Public Image of Henry Ford* (Detroit: Wayne State University Press, 1976), 144.
24. Thos. and Mina Edison to Mrs. Ford, April 6, 1927, HFMandGV.
25. *The Fort Myers Press*, April 8, 1927.
26. Ibid.
27. Ibid., May 4, 1927.
28. Mina Edison to Clara Ford, July 16, 1927, HFMandGV.
29. Ibid.
30. Ibid.
31. Ibid.
32. Ibid.
33. Charles Edison to Edison, May 12, 1927, CEF.
34. Ibid.
35. Ibid.
36. Ibid.
37. Robert C. Halgrim, interview by author in Fort Myers on January 16, 1999.
38. Ibid.
39. E. G. Liebold to Wm. H. Meadowcroft, June 8, 1927, HFMandGV.

40. J. V. Miller to E. G. Liebold, July 25, 1927, HFMandGV.
41. E. G. Liebold to Edison, August 24, 1927, HFMandGV.
42. Wm. H. Meadowcroft to E. G. Liebold, September 19, 1927, HFMandGV.
43. E. G. Liebold to Wm. H. Meadowcroft, September 29, 1927, HFMandGV.
44. Edison to E. G. Liebold, October 1, 1927, HGMandGV.
45. E. G. Liebold to Edison, October 4, 1927, HFMandGV.
46. *The Fort Myers Press,* January 12, 1928; January 14, 1928.
47. Ibid., January 13, 1928.
48. Ibid., January 14, 1928.
49. Nancy Arnn, nee Nancy Miller, is a not infrequent visitor to Fort Myers. She is a trustee of the Charles Edison Fund and finds her way to Fort Myers on the business of that organization from time to time. She is the current entailed owner of the Miller Founder's Cottage in the center of the Chautauqua Institution campus in New York.
50. *Fort Myers Tropical News,* January 14, 1928.
51. Ibid.
52. Ibid.
53. Ibid.
54. Ibid., January 15, 1928.
55. Ibid.
56. Ibid., January 17, 1928.
57. Ibid., January 29, 1928.
58. Ibid., February 11, 1928.
59. Ibid., February 3, 1928.
60. *Fort Myers Tropical News,* February 10, 1928.
61. Ibid., January 17, 1928.
62. Ibid.
63. Newton, *Uncommon Friends,* 23.
64. *Fort Myers Tropical News,* February 12, 1928.
65. Ibid.
66. Ibid., February 10, 1928, February 12, 1928.
67. Harvey Firestone, Mayor Bolick, Dr. Hamilton Holt, the president of Rollins College and principal speaker, Mr. and Mrs. J. V. Miller, Mrs. Edison's brother and sister-in-law and others sat on the platform with the Edisons.
68. *Fort Myers Tropical News,* February 12, 1928. The writer and his wife are alumni of Edison Park Elementary School. Miss Bullock was principal during their matriculation.
69. Ibid., February 18, 1928, February 19, 1928. Two months earlier on December 14, 1927, the Fort Myers showroom of Tropical Motors showed the widely advertised successor to the Model T. Fifty orders with cash deposits were taken on that first day for the new Model A. *Fort Myers Tropical News,* December 13, 1927.
70. *Fort Myers Tropical News,* December 13, 1927.
71. Ibid. It is doubtful that Mrs. Edison prepared the meal though she may have

helped. She had a cook and two maids with her.

72. Ibid., February 22, 1928.

73. Ibid., February 23, 1928.

74. Ibid., February 26, 1928.

75. H. Nehrling to Arno and Irene Nehrling, March 1, 1928, reprinted in *American Eagle,* date illegible. The letter is signed by "Your old father." The American Eagle was the official organ of the Koreshan Unity located in Estero, Florida.

76. Ibid.

77. Ibid.

78. *Fort Myers Tropical News,* February 25, 1928.

79. The *Tropical News* described the old Ford as a 1903 model, however it would have been a very rare car if it were, since 1903 marked the beginning of the Ford Motor Company and the year of their first model. The family of the present Ford dealer in Fort Myers acquired the business in 1927 and with it a 1908 Ford, Model N. The old Ford was probably that 1908 Model N.

80. Conrad Menge, Sr., oral history, interview conducted on March 22, 1951, typewritten (Ford Motor Company Archives, Oral History Section, Dearborn, MI), HFMandGV; *Fort Myers Tropical News,* February 25, 1928.

81. Menge interview.

82. Ibid.

83. Ibid.

84. Ibid.

85. Ibid.

86. Ibid.

87. Ibid.

88. Ibid.

89. Ibid.

90. Ibid.

91. The Orange River is a tributary of the Caloosahatchee River.

92. Menge interview.

93. Ibid.

94. Ibid., March 4, 1928.

95. Ibid.

96. Ibid.

97. Ibid., July 20, 1928.

98. Menge interview.

99. *The Fort Myers Press,* May 10, 1929.

100. Ibid., 15.

101. The Mangoes was the name given to the Ford Winter Estate in Fort Myers. Henry Ford abhorred modern jazz and clung to square dancing and old time folk music.

102. Harvey Firestone's winter retreat was in Miami Beach, Florida.

103. Newton, *Uncommon Friends*, 35.
104. Ibid., 38.
105. Ibid.
106. *Fort Myers Tropical News*, February 12, 1928.
107. *The Fort Myers Press*, April 6, 1928.
108. Ibid., April 28, 1928.
109. Ibid.
110. *Fort Myers Tropical News*, April 26, 1928.
111. Ibid.
112. Ibid., April 26, 1928.
113. Ibid., May 1, 1928.
114. *The Fort Myers Press*, June 13, 1928.
115. Ibid.
116. Ibid., June 7, 1928.
117. Ibid., June 19, 1928.
118. Ibid., June 9, 1928.
119. Ibid., December 11, 1928.
120. Ibid., October 4, 1928.
121. *Fort Myers Tropical News*, August 12, 1928.
122. *The Fort Myers Press*, August 14, 1928.
123. Ibid., December 13, 1928.
124. Ibid., October 21, 1928.

Chapter Twenty: Hail to the Chief

1. *The Fort Myers Press*, January 16, 1929.
2. Ibid.
3. Ibid.
4. Ibid.
5. Ibid., January 17, 1929.
6. Ibid.
7. Ibid., January 18, 1929.
8. Ibid.
9. Ibid., February 8, 1929. Anderson Avenue is now known as Dr. Martin Luther King Jr. Boulevard.
10. Ibid., February 5, 1929.
11. Ibid., February 12, 1929.
12. Ibid.
13. Ibid.
14. Town officials were Mayor Elmer Hough, President J. S. Gillentine of the Chamber of Commerce, and Police Chief C. G. Enos.
15. The last car carried Mr. and Mrs. Ricard and Mr. and Mrs. Milbank, part of the president elect's yachting party.
16. *The Fort Myers Press*, February 12, 1929.

Notes

17. Ibid.
18. Kathryn Palmer, interview by author in Fort Myers on February 14, 2001. Kathryn Palmer is the former Kathryn Miller. She was the fourth Queen of Edisonia, crowned in 1941.
19. *The Fort Myers Press*, February 13, 1929.
20. Ibid., February 17, 1929. Clewiston is located near Lake Okeechobee about sixty miles east of Fort Myers.
21. Ibid.
22. Ibid., February 20, 1929.
23. Ibid.
24. Ibid.
25. Ibid., February 22, 1929.
26. Ibid., March 2, 1929.
27. Ibid., March 5, 1929.
28. Ibid.
29. Ibid., March 5, 1929. The fiddlers for the evening were Harold Moreland, Harry Manley and Earl Bobbitt. The square dances were called by J. W. Cole.
30. *The Fort Myers Press*, March 7, 1929.
31. Ibid., March 12, 1929.
32. Ibid., May 19, 1929.
33. Gloria Shortlidge, interview with author in Fort Myers, June 10, 2001.
34. Ibid., June 1, 1929.
35. Ibid.
36. The performing arts hall located on the Edison Community College campus in Fort Myers bears the married name of Barbara Balch—Barbara B. Mann Hall. Sue Spears became Mrs. Cecil Bennett; Tommy Howard became the President and Chairman of the Board of First Federal Savings and Loan Association of Fort Myers; Norwood Strayhorn became a member of the state legislature and a prominent lawyer; Don Hawkins became the owner of the Coca Cola Bottling Company in Fort Myers; and Lynn Gerald one of the most respected circuit judges in the state.
37. Barbara B. Mann, interview by author in Fort Myers, July 1, 2000.
38. Mary Frances Howard, interview by author in Fort Myers, September 21, 2000.
39. *The Fort Myers Press*, June 9, 2000.
40. Included in the dance were Helen Mickle, Olive Towles, Lillian Tooke, Winifred Wintle, Juanita Kay, Rebecca Barden, James Jackson, Ernest Kinzie, Thomas Howard, Bayard Chamberlin, Raymond Campbell and Jesse Jones.
41. *The Fort Myers Press*, June 9, 2000.
42. Ibid.
43. Neil Baldwin, *Edison: Inventing the Century* (New York: Hyperion, 1995), 396.
44. *The Fort Myers Press*, October 20, 1929.

45. Baldwin, *Edison:* 396.

46. Matthew Josephson, *Edison, A Biography* (New York: McGraw-Hill Book Company, 1959), 480–481.

Chapter Twenty-One: Centerstage Mina

1. Mina Edison to Charles Edison, March 18, 1912, CEF.
2. *The Fort Myers Press,* March 9, 1927.
3. Ibid., March 11, 1927.
4. Ibid., March 8, 1928, May 17, 1928.
5. Ibid., March 9, 1928.
6. Ibid., June 25, 1928.
7. Ibid.
8. Ibid., Mary 17, 1928.
9. Ibid., September 10, 1929. Marjory Stoneman Douglas was the author of the classic, *The Everglades: River of Grass* (New York: Rinehart, 1947). In recognition of her environmental activism, she was awarded the Presidential Medal of Freedom in 1993.
10. *The Fort Myers Press,* March 13, 14, 15, 1930.
11. *Fort Myers Tropical News,* April 1, 1930.
12. Ibid., April 19, 1928.
13. *The Fort Myers Press,* February 5, 18, 19, March 5, 6, 8, 10, 11, 18, 20 21, 24, 25, 29, April 7, 14, 18, 22, 24, 29, 30, May 6, 7, 12, 13, 14, 17, 28. 1930; *Fort Myers Tropical News,* January 5, 11, 15, 22, 25, 29, February 9, 19, 21, 1930. Included in the list of garden clubs were Safety Hill Garden Club, Dean Park Garden Club, Valencia Garden Club, Poinsettia Garden Club, Hibiscus Garden Club, Seminole Garden Club, Riverside Garden Club, Poinciana Garden Club, Edison Park Garden Club, Fountain Garden Club and West Virginia Garden Club.
14. Ibid., March 11, 1930.
15. Ibid., March 12, 1930.
16. Ibid., May 7, 1931.
17. Ibid., February 2, 1929.
18. Ibid., February 22, 1929. The meeting was held at the home of Mrs. Watt Lawler.
19. Ibid., March 27, 1929.
20. Ibid., June 5, 1929.
21. Ibid., June 5, 1929.
22. Ibid., May 20, 1931.
23. Ibid., April 30. 1930.
24. Ibid., May 13, 1930.
25. Ibid., March 7, 1929.
26. *Fort Myers Tropical News,* January 10, 1930; *The Fort Myers Press,* January 10, 1930.

Notes

27. Robert Halgrim had a long relationship with the Edison's beginning with the baby-sitting job for the Sloane boys in 1926 and continuing to Mrs. Edison's death in 1947. *Fort Myers Tropical News,* February 28, 1930, March 2, 1930.

28. *The Fort Myers Press,* February 26, 1931.

29. Ibid., March 14, 1931.

30. *Fort Myers Tropical News,* January 11, 1930, January 30, 1930; *The Fort Myers Press,* January 16, 1930, February 17, 1930. Teas at the homes of friends included Mrs. A. W. Kelley and with Mrs. Ford at Mrs. Rea's.

31. Ibid., June 5, 1928.

32. Ibid., April 29, 1931.

33. Nat Cornwell, interview by author in Fort Myers, June 5, 1931. Cornwell is a retired architect.

34. *The Fort Myers Press,* April 18, 1930.

35. Ibid., February 1, 1930.

36. Charles Edison to Thomas and Mina Edison, February 7, 1930, CEF.

37. Ibid.

38. Valinda was the maiden name of Mrs. Edison's mother.

39. *The Fort Myers Press,* April 2, 1930, May 29, 1930, May 30, 1930; *Fort Myers Tropical News,* April 3, 1930.

40. *The Fort Myers Press,* April 14, 1928.

41. Ibid.

42. Ibid., October 19, 1929.

43. Ibid., May 9, 1928.

44. *The Fort Myers Press,* March 8, 1930, May 24, 1930, April 16, 1930, April 18, 1930, April 29, 1930, April 30, 1930.

45. Ibid., May 11, 1929; May 29, 1930. Her strong Methodist background, though not in sharp evidence in Fort Myers outside the Wesley Bible Class, manifested itself in isolated instances. For example, she poured tea with Mrs. W. P. Franklin at a Methodist Missionary Conference held at the Elk's Club at which 400 attended in 1931.

46. Ibid., February 4, 1931.

47. Ibid., May 10, 1930.

48. *Fort Myers Tropical News,* April 18, 1930.

49. Ibid., April 12, 1931.

50. Ibid., May 8, 1931.

51. Ibid., May 8, 1931.

52. Mina Edison to Sidney Davis, May 23, 1931, EFWH.

53. Mina Edison to Sidney Davis, January 18, 1931, EFWH.

54. Mina Edison to Sidney Davis, February 16, 1931, EFWH.

55. Mina Edison to Sidney Davis, April 6, 1931, EFWH.

56. *Fort Myers Tropical News,* May 12, 1930.

57. Ibid.

58. Ibid.

59. Ibid., May 15, 1930.

60. *The Fort Myers Press and Tropical News*, June 5, 1931.
61. *The Fort Myers Press*, April 17, 1930, April 23, 1930.
62. Ibid., May 28, 1930.
63. Ibid., May 9, 1930.
64. Ibid., February 4, 1931. Local grower Thomas Biggar sent two carloads of tomatoes to aid in the relief effort. Mr. Biggar and his wife later purchased The Mangoes from Henry Ford in 1947 and Mrs. Biggar sold the home to the City of Fort Myers in 1988.
65. Ibid., February 15, 1931. Among the groups lobbied was the local chapter of the Daughters of the American Revolution. She had served as the National Chaplain of that organization in 1924.
66. Ibid., April 12, 1930.
67. Ibid., April 12, 1930.
68. Ibid., June 5, 1928.
69. Ibid., April 30, 1931.
70. *The Fort Myers Press and Tropical News*, June 4, 1931.

Chapter Twenty-Two: The Longest Stay

1. *The Fort Myers Press*, December 7, 1929.
2. Ibid.
3. Ibid., December 8, 1929.
4. Ibid., December 26, 1929.
5. Ibid.
6. Charles Edison to Mina Edison, January 6, 1930, CEF.
7. *The Fort Myers Press*, December 31, 1929.
8. Ibid.
9. Ibid., Jan 21, 1930. The interview was by James R. Crowell and was printed in the January edition of the magazine and reported generally in *The Fort Myers Press*.
10. Ibid.
11. Ibid.
12. Ibid.
13. Ibid., January 5, 1930.
14. Ibid.
15. Ibid., February 8, 1930; *Fort Myers Tropical News*, February 8, 1930.
16. *The Fort Myers Press*, February 8, 1930.
17. Ibid.
18. Ibid.
19. *The Fort Myers Press*, February 11, 1930. Firestone was accompanied by his wife and by his daughter and son, Elizabeth Firestone and Roger S. Firestone, all of whom were registered at the Royal Palm Hotel.
20. Ibid., February 12, 1930.
21. Ibid.

Notes

22. Ibid.
23. *Fort Myers Tropical News*, February 12, 1930.
24. *The Fort Myers Press*, February 12, 1930.
25. Ibid.
26. Evans Park is now the site of South Trust Bank and the down ramp from the Caloosahatchee Bridge. Ted Evans, the grandson of E. L. Evans, is the president of the bank.
27. *Fort Myers News-Press*, October 19, 1931.
28. *The Fort Myers Press*, April 25, 1928.
29. Ibid.
30. Ibid., February 13, 1930.
31. Ibid.
32. Ibid.
33. Ibid., February 14, 1930.
34. Ibid.
35. *The Fort Myers Press*, March 2, 1930.
36. *Fort Myers Tropical News*, March 5, 1930.
37. *The Fort Myers Press*, March 5, 1930; Ronald Halgrim was the Secretary of the Chamber of Commerce and a brother of Bob Halgrim who worked for the Edisons.
38. Ibid.
39. Ibid.; *Fort Myers Tropical News*, March 6, 1930.
40. *The Fort Myers Press*, March 12, 1930.
41. *Fort Myers Tropical News*, February 25, 1930.
42. Ibid., February 22, 1930; *Fort Myers Press*, April 9, 1930.
43. *Fort Myers Tropical News*, February 14, 1930, February 25, 1930, March 3, 1930. Edison Institute received $20,000,000; Berry College in Georgia received $3,000,000; Tuskeegee Institute considerable; 15 grade schools in Michigan were sponsored as were additional schools in Wayside, Massachusetts, and Richmond Hill, Georgia; Henry Ford Trade Schools in Dearborn, Michigan, and Dagenham, England, received large sums as did the Henry Ford Institute for Agricultural Engineering in England. Ford Bryan to author, November 23, 2001.
44. Ibid., March 29, 1930.
45. Ibid., March 18, 1930.
46. Ibid., April 13, 1930.
47. *The Fort Myers Press*, April 17, 1930.
48. Ibid., May 7, 1930, May 9, 1930.
49. Charles Edison to Thomas and Mina Edison, February 7, 1930, CEF.
50. Charles Edison to Mina Edison, June 1, 1930, CEF.
51. Paul Israel, *Edison: A Life of Invention* (New York: John Wiley and Sons, 1998), 456.
52. Charles Edison to Mina Edison, June 1, 1930, CEF.
53. *The Fort Myers Press*, June 12, 1930.
54. Ibid.

Chapter Twenty-Three: A Light Extinguished

1. *The Fort Myers Press*, January 22, 1931.
2. Ibid., February 12, 1931. The Fountain was located in the middle of the intersection and was later moved to a location on McGregor Boulevard at the entrance to the Fort Myers Golf and Country Club.
3. *The Fort Myers Press*, February 12, 1931.
4. Ibid.
5. Ibid.
6. Ibid.
7. Ibid., February 14, 1931.
8. Ibid., February 15, 1931.
9. Ibid., February 14, 1931.
10. Ibid.
11. Ibid., April 28, 1931.
12. C. A. Prince video history, interview conducted by James H. Gassman, David Marshall, and Robert Beason on June 25, 1999, EFWH.
13. *The Fort Myers Press*, February 21, 1931.
14. Ibid., February 22, 1931.
15. Ibid.
16. *Fort Myers Tropical News*, February 25, 1931.
17. Ibid., March 1, 1931.
18. See Chapters Two, Four and Five.
19. Edison to Samuel Insull, June 5, 1885, ENHS.
20. *The Fort Myers Press*, March 8, 1931.
21. Ibid., March 14, 1931.
22. Prince, video history.
23. Ibid.
24. Ibid.
25. *The Fort Myers Press*, March 15, 1931.
26. Ibid.
27. Ibid., March 18, 1931.
28. Ibid., March 31, 1931.
29. Ibid.
30. R. H. Laird, "I worked for Mr. Ford," *Dearborn Historian*, vol. 10, no. 1, 1970: 14.
31. Ford R. Bryan, "Industrial Archaeology in Greenfield Village," unpublished. HFMandGV.
32. Emil Zoerlien, interview on September 15, 1951, typewritten, no indication who conducted interview, 32, 42–44, HFMandGV.
33. *The Fort Myers Press*, March 24, 1931.
34. Ibid.
35. The movies were furnished him by his friend George Eastman of Kodak.
36. *The Fort Myers Press*, April 17, 1931, April 18, 1931.
37. Ibid., April 21, 1931.
38. Ibid., April 29, 1931.

39. The Friendship Walk consisted of stones given by the following: Hamilton Holt; Gillentines, Mrs. Alexander G. Rea; Alice C. Garvey; Katharine M. Roys; Lucius and Sarah; C. H. and Ora Weir; Harvey Firestone; F. Merck; W.M. Buswell; John K. Small; Burroughs; Samuel Insull; Col. J. G. Gilmore; Lucy, The Huffs, The Barnes; Moeder; Jimmie Newton; A. Young; C. Young; Tilden Homestead; "Porta" "Rico;" Edie Cleveland; Will and Mary Nichols; Perkins; Seminole Employees; Morehous and Billie Stevens; Gra-al Monhegan; Community Congregational Church; Bernese and Sidney Davis; Springfield College; Mrs. Edison's friends in National Recreation Association; Mr. and Mrs. Van Evrie Kilpatrick; H.N. and H.m. Davis; Elsa and Lewis Conant; Dot and James Hendry; Mary and Wade Bell and Charles Kline; "Miss Effie;" Cark S. Ell; Jean and David Shapard; Jonnie and R. A. Henderson, Jr.; Bertha and Fred Lowdermilk; and Mr. and Mrs. Graydon Jones.
40. Barbara Brown, interview by author in Fort Myers, September 25, 2000.
41. *The Fort Myers Press,* April 5, 1931.
42. Ibid. Local Boy Scouts participated in the occasion, among them Hugh Richards and Joe Pendleton.
43. *The Fort Myers Press and Tropical News,* June 9, 1931.
44. Ibid., June 12, 1931.
45. Ibid., June 15, 1931.
46. Ibid., June 11, 1931.
47. Ibid.
48. Ibid.
49. Ibid.
50. Ibid., June 15, 1931.
51. Prince video history.
52. Ibid.
53. *The Fort Myers Press and Tropical News,* July 2, 1931.
54. Ibid.
55. Mina Edison to Sidney Davis, July 8, 1931, EFWH.
56. Dr. Howe's nurse was Miss Alice Stevenson, who later served as secretary to Charles Edison. Miss Stevenson became a resident of Fort Myers following the death of Charles Edison in 1969. Miss Stevenson was well known to the author and to many others in the Fort Myers community. She told the writer that Toscanini, a patient of Dr. Howe, arranged for her to have an orchestra seat for all performances.
57. *Fort Myers News-Press,* August 2, 1931.
58. Ibid.
59. Ibid., August 2, 1931.
60. Ibid.
61. Ibid., August 3, 1931.
62. Ibid.
63. Ibid., August 5, 1931.
64. Ibid., August 4, 1931. There had been two competing newspapers in Fort

Myers since 1920, when the *Fort Myers Tropical News,* a morning paper, began publication. The *Fort Myers Press,* which had been around since a few months before Edison's first arrival in 1885, continued as an afternoon paper. On May 30, 1931, it was announced that the two would merge into one—The *Fort Myers News-Press.*

65. Ibid., August 7, 1931.
66. Mina Edison to Sidney Davis, August 14, 1931, EFWH.
67. *Fort Myers News-Press,* September 9, 1931.
68. Ibid.
69. Ibid., September 30, 1931.
70. Ibid., October 3, 1931, October 5, 1931.
71. Ibid., October 4, 1931, October 5, 1931.
72. Ibid., August 7, 1931.
73. Ibid., October 5, 1931.
74. Ibid., October 8, 1931.
75. Ibid., October 9, 1931.
76. Ibid., October 7, 1931.
77. Ibid., October 9, 1931.
78. Ibid., October 10, 1931.
79. Ibid., October 16, 1931.
80. Ibid., October 17, 1931.
81. Ibid.
82. Ibid., October 18, 1931.
83. Ibid., October 19, 1931.
84. Ibid., October 19, 1931.
85. Ibid.
86. Ibid.
87. Ibid., October 22, 1931. Reverend Pendleton was the grandfather of Edith Pendleton, Ph.D, to whom the writer is indebted for reading and critiquing this manuscript. Mrs. Edison attended the Edison Park Congregational Church, which was across the street from Seminole Lodge in Edison Park although that church had only recently been built and dedicated on February 14, 1932. Before and after her participation at the Edison Park Church, she was the class "mother" and very much a part of the Young Men's Wesley Bible Class at the First Methodist Church on First Street in Fort Myers.

Chapter Twenty-Four: The Widow

1. Mina Edison to Sidney Davis, May 2, 1932, EFWH.
2. *Fort Myers News-Press,* February 12, 1932.
3. Ibid., February 13, 1932.
4. Ibid., February 13, 1932.
5. Ibid., February 25, 1932.

6. *Fort Myers News-Press*, March 22, 1933, March 25, 1934, April 8, 1932, March 22, 1933, March 5, 1933, March 6, 1933, March 27, 1932, March 2, 1933, April 8, 1934, April 28, 1934, May 5, 1933, March 21, 1934, April 10, 1934, February 28, 1936, February 28, 1937, April 8, 1933, May 4, 1933, May 5, 1933, May 7, 1933, March 21, 1934, April 8, 1934, April 9, 1934, April 10, 1934, February 28, 1936, March 15, 1936, February 28, 1937, April 9, 1932, March 25, 1937.
7. Ibid., March 28, 1934.
8. Ibid., April 3, 1940.
9. Ibid., April. 1, 1932, April 3, 1932, April 4, 1932, April 5, 1932, April 10, 1932.
10. Ibid., May 3, 1933. The Safety Hill District Garden Club was composed largely of members of the African American community, then known as the colored community. Dunbar High School was the segregated colored high school.
11. *Fort Myers News-Press*, April 19, 1933.
12. Ibid., May 5, 1933, May 6, 1933, May 11, 1933.
13. Ibid., March 12, 1932. The naturalist was Dr. Clyde Fisher.
14. Ibid., March 9, 1933; May 3, 1933. The Patio de Leon was a beautiful patio surrounded by Mediterranean style buildings. It ran from First Street to Main Street in the business section of the city. It fell into disrepair for many years, but is currently undergoing a renaissance.
15. Ibid., March 9, 1933.
16. Ibid., March 7, 1934; March 28, 1934; April 10, 1935; March 13, 1936; April 11, 1936; March 13, 1937; February 23, 1939; April 14, 1942; March 31, 1945.
17. Ibid., March 31, 1932.
18. Ibid., April 12, 1933, August 26, 1933.
19. Ibid., March 11, 1936.
20. The Wesley Bible Class at the First Methodist Church continued in existence until the mid 1990's when its remaining membership began to die out. The writer taught the class on occasion during the 1970s and 1980s and many of its members at that time had been members in the days of Mrs. Edison, the class mother.
21. Mina Edison to Sidney Davis, December 14, 1931.
22. *Fort Myers News-Press*, March 13, 1933.
23. Ibid., April 12, 1932.
24. Ibid., March 20, 1931, March 21, 1932.
25. Ibid., April 19, 1933. The Red Coconut is yet an active recreational mobile home park at Fort Myers Beach.
26. Ibid., March 31, 1934.
27. Ibid., May 9, 1937.
28. Ibid., March 14, 1941.
29. Ibid., March 19, 1933.
30. Ibid., May 11, 1933, March 21, 1934, April 11, 1934, April 14, 1934, April

16, 1934, March 8, 1936, April 7, 1936, April 9, 1936, March 13, 1937. She "motored" to St. Petersburg, drove to Captiva to visit the Clarence B. Chadwicks, went on a yacht outing with son Charles and daughter-in-law Carolyn, traveled to Bokeelia on Pine Island, visited friends on Burgess Island near Bokeelia and visited H. D. Silverfriend at the Koreshan Unity in Estero. She fished with popular guide, Clarence Trowbridge, on Hendry Creek.

31. Ibid., October 19, 1931, April 25, 1933, March 9, 1934, March 18, 1934, March 21, 1934, April 21, 1934, April 10, 1934, April 16, 1935. Mr. Edison had patronized the Rustic Tea Garden also but would have only his glass of milk.

32. Ibid., April 12, 1932, March 17, 1933, March 24, 1933, March 28, 1933, April 18, 1933, April 10, 1934, April 12, 1934, April 14, 1937. The Gondola Inn was situated on West First Street across from Henley Circle where the present Chart House is located. It was built on piling and afforded excellent views of the river.

33. Ibid., September 24, 1936.

34. Harold Moreland on the violin, John Houston at the piano, and Floyd Moreland, flautist.

35. *Fort Myers News-Press*, April 20, 1934.

36. Barbara Norris Brown, interview by author in Fort Myers, August 15, 2000.

37. *Fort Myers News-Press*, April 9, 1932, April 12, 1932, March 25, 1937.

38. Ibid., April 20, 1934.

39. Ibid., March 22, 1933.

40. Ibid., April 11, 1937, April 12, 1937.

41. Ibid., July 7, 1934.

42. Ibid., April 10, 1934.

43. The Edison Winter Home Board, later known as the Edison-Ford Winter Estates Board, was an advisory board appointed by the mayor and City Council to oversee the operation of the winter estates and museum and to make recommendations to the mayor and Council regarding its governance. In 2003 it was disbanded and replaced by an independent non-profit corporation to which the homes and museum were leased.

44. *Fort Myers News-Press*, January 17, 1934.

45. Ibid., April 16, 1935.

46. *New York Times*, October 30, 1935, October 31, 1935; *Fort Myers News-Press*, October 30, 1935, October 31, 1935; The Founder's Cottage had belonged to Mina's father, the co-founder of Chautauqua. It then became the property of Mina Edison and is today the property of Nancy Arnn, Mina Edison's niece and the granddaughter of Lewis Miller, the founder of Chautauqua.

47. *Fort Myers News-Press*, June 7, 1936.

48. Ibid.

49. Chesley Perry and Janett Perry, interview by author in Fort Myers, November 22, 1998.

50. Mina Edison to Sidney Davis, July 30, 1937, EFWH.
51. *Fort Myers News-Press*, March 8, 1936, March 13, 1937 April 7, 1936.
52. Ibid., February 16, 1934, February 17, 1934, February 21, 1934, March 7, 1934.
53. Ibid., December 17, 1936.
54. Ibid., March 18, 1940, March 19, 1940.
55. Ibid., April 20, 1933, April 1, 1934.
56. Ibid., April 23, 1933.
57. Ibid., April 4, 1939.
58. Ibid., June 14, 1934.
59. John D. Venable, *Out of the Shadow, The Story of Charles Edison* (Philadelphia: Dorrance and Company, 1978), 121.
60. *Fort Myers News-Press*, January 4, 1940.
61. Venable, *Out of the Shadow*, 168.
62. Ibid., 210.
63. *Fort Myers News-Press*, November 7, 1937, November 26, 1937.
64. Ibid., October 31, 1936.
65. Ibid., January 18, 1937.
66. Ibid., January 29, 1937.
67. Ibid., May 12, 1937.
68. Ibid., February 3, 1946.
69. Ibid., February 10, 1940.
70. Ibid.
71. Ibid., February 9, 1946.
72. Ibid., February 21, 1946.
73. Mina Edison to Sidney Davis, August 20, 1934, June 10, 1938, July 15, 1938, May 11, 1939, June 25, 1939 EFWH.
74. Mina Edison to Sidney Davis, May 11, 1939, EFWH.
75. Jettie Burroughs and Mona Fisher were the daughters of Nelson Thomas Burroughs. Burroughs was the owner of the Murphy-Burroughs home located at the corner of First Street and Fowler Street in Fort Myers. That home is now owned by the City of Fort Myers and is open to the public. Jettie Burroughs was involved with garden club activity with Mrs. Edison and served as chairman of the annual garden tour which for several years included three homes, the Edison home, the Ford home and the Murphy-Burroughs home.
76. Berne Davis, interview by author in Fort Myers, September 28, 2000.
77. *Fort Myers News-Press*, March 21, 1939, March 23, 1939.
78. Ibid., April 14, 1939.
79. Ibid., January 20, 1940.
80. Ibid., March 21, 1940, April 3, 1940, April 10, 1940, April 12, 1940.
81. Ibid., March 2, 1940.
82. Ibid.
83. Ibid., February 20, 1941.
84. Ibid.

85. Ibid., April 27, 1941.
86. Ibid., April 14, 1943.
87. Ibid., March 7, 1941, March 9, 1941, March 27, 1941.
88. Ibid., February 7, 1940.
89. Chesley Perry and Janett Perry interview.
90. *Fort Myers News-Press*, April 12, 1942.
91. Ibid.
92. Ibid.
93. Ibid., April 20, 1942. Master Sergeant Ottis Stephenson was the honored soldier.
94. Ibid., April 15, 1942.
95. Chesley Perry and Janett Perry interview.
96. *Fort Myers News-Press*, March 18, 1945, March 22, 1945.
97. Ibid., March 27, 1945; Chesley Perry became Mrs. Edison's Fort Myers agent following Frank Stout. Perry was employed by the *Fort Myers News-Press* and later became its publisher.
98. Ibid.; Chesley Perry and Janett Perry interview.
99. *Fort Myers News-Press*, March 24, 1945.
100. Ibid., April 1, 1945. Other prominent citizens attending were Col. and Mrs. Othel Deering, the commanding officer at Buckingham Gunnery School, Mr. and Mrs. Carl Hanton, Mr. and Mrs. Virgil Robb (Robb and Stucky), Mr. and Mrs. Harry Fagan, Mr. and Mrs. Frank Alderman, Mrs. A. G. Rea, Mrs. C. B. Chadwick, Mrs. John K. Woolslair, Mrs. A. T. G. Parkinson, Mrs. James Hendry, Miss M. Floridaossie Hill and Miss Jettie Burroughs.
101. *Fort Myers News-Press*, February 11, 1946, February 12, 1946.
102. Edison's body was later re-interred on the grounds at Glenmont by the grave of Mina.
103. *Fort Myers News-Press*, February 13, 1947.
104. Ibid., February 15, 1947.
105. Ibid., April 9, 1947.

Chapter Twenty-Five: The Shrine

1. *Fort Myers News-Press*, March 8, 1939.
2. Ibid., May 3, 1939.
3. Ibid., May 2, 1940.
4. Ibid., February 20, 1941.
5. Ibid., April 20, 1941.
6. Ibid., April 21, 1941.
7. Ibid., March 8, 1942, March 9, 1942.
8. Ibid., February 23, 1945.
9. Ibid.
10. Ibid., February 20, 1947.

Notes

11. Ibid.
12. Ibid., March 7, 1947.
13. Ibid.
14. Ibid.
15. Ibid.
16. Ibid.
17. Ibid.
18. Barbara B. Mann was one of the seniors in the class of 1929 to whom Edison had presented a diploma. She is also the namesake of the Barbara B. Mann Performing Arts Hall located on the Edison Community College campus.
19. Contract between City and Mrs. Biggar, November 6, 1987 EFWH.

Selected Bibliography

Books

Akerman, Joe A. Jr. *Florida Cowman: A History of Florida Cattle Raising.* Kissimmee, Florida: Florida Cattlemen's Association, 1976.

Blackman, William Fremont. *History of Orange County, Florida.* Chuluota, Florida: The Mickler House Publishers, 1973.

Boggess, Francis C. M. *Veteran of Four Wars.* Arcadia, Florida: Champion Job Rooms, 1900.

Baldwin, Neil. *Edison: Inventing the Century.* New York: Hyperion, 1995.

Brown, Canter Jr. *Florida's Peace River Frontier.* Orlando: University of Central Florida Press, 1991.

Burke, Walter E. Jr. *Quartermaster: A Brief Account of the Life of Colonel Abraham Charles Myers Quartermaster General C.S.A.* n.p. 1976.

Conot, Robert. *Thomas A. Edison: A Streak of Luck.* New York: Da Capo Press, Inc., 1979.

Covington, James W. *The Billy Bowlegs War.* Chuluota: Florida: The Mickle House Publishers, 1982.

Covington, James W. *The Seminoles of Florida.* Gainesville: University Press of Florida, 1993. Dickson, W. K. L., and Dickson, Antonia. *The Life and Inventions of Thomas Alva Edison.* London: Chatto and Windus, 1894.

Friedel, Robert, and Israel, Paul. *Edison's Electric Light: Biography of an Invention.* New Brunswick: Rutgers University Press, 1986.

Fritz, Florence. *Bamboo and Sailing Ships.* n.p. 1949.

Fritz, Florence. *Unknown Florida.* Coral Gables: University of Miami Press, 1963.

Gannon, Michael. *The New History of Florida.* Gainesville: University Press of Florida, 1996.

Gonzalez, Thomas A. *The Caloosahatchee.* Fort Myers Beach: The Island Press Publishers, 1982.

Grismer, Karl H. *Tampa.* St. Petersburg: The St. Petersburg Printing Company, 1950.

Bibliography

Grismer, Karl H. *The Story of Fort Myers: The History of the Land of the Caloosahatchee and Southwest Florida*. St. Petersburg: St. Petersburg Printing Company, 1949.

Harner, Charles E. *Florida's Promoters*. Tampa: Trend Publications, 1973.

Hendrick, Ellwood. *Lewis Miller: A Biographical Essay*. Princess Anne, MD: Yestermorrow, 1925.

Hendry, F. A. *Early History of Lee County and Fort Myers*. Manuscript 1908, reprinted by the Captain F. A. Hendry Reunion Committee, April 12, 1985, Fort Myers Historical Museum, Fort Myers, Florida.

Herrick, C. Judson. *Brains of Rats and Men: A Survey of the Origin and Biological Significance of the Cerebral Cortex*. Chicago: University of Chicago Press, 1926.

Israel, Paul. *Edison: A Life of Invention*. New York: John Wiley and Sons, 1998.

Jenkins, Reese V.; Reich, Leonard S.; Israel, Paul B.; Appel, Toby; Butrica, Andrew J.; Rosenberg, Robert A.; Nier, Keith A.; Andrews, Melodie; Jeffrey, Thomas E.; eds. *The Papers of Thomas A. Edison*. Baltimore: The Johns Hopkins University Press, 1989. vol. 1. *The Making of an Inventor*.

Jehl, Francis. *Menlo Park Reminiscences*. 1937. Reprint, with an Introduction by William S. Pretzzer. New York: Dover Publications, 1990. 3 vols.

Josephson, Matthew. *Edison: A Biography*. New York: McGraw-Hill Book Company, 1959.

Lacey, Robert. *Ford: The Men and the Machine*. Boston: Little, Brown and Company, 1986.

Lewis, David L. *The Public Image of Henry Ford: An American Folk Hero and His Company*. Detroit: Wayne State University Press, 1976.

Mahon, John K. *History of the Second Seminole War, 1835–1842* Revised Edition. Gainesville: University of Florida Press, 1985.

McGuirk, Kathleen L., ed. *The Diary of Thomas A. Edison*. Old Greenwich, CT: The Chatham Press, 1971.

Nevins, Allan. *Ford: The Times, The Man, The Company*. New York: Charles Scribner's Sons, 1954.

Newton, James D. *Uncommon Friends: Life with Thomas Edison, Henry Ford, Harvey Firestone, Alexis Carrel, and Charles Lindbergh*. New York: Harcourt Brace Jovanovich, 1987.

Robinson, Ernest L. *History of Hillsborough County, Florida*. St. Augustine: The Record Company, 1928.

Rosenberg, Robert A.; Israel, Paul B.; Nier, Keith A.; Andrews, Melodie; eds. *The Papers of Thomas A. Edison*. Baltimore: The Johns Hopkins University Press, 1991. vol. 2 *From Workshop to Laboratory*.

Rosenberg, Robert A.; Israel, Paul B.; Nier, Keith A.; King, Martha J.; eds. *The Papers of Thomas A. Edison*. Baltimore: The Johns Hopkins University Press, 1994. vol. 3 *Menlo Park: The Early Years*.

Rosenberg, Robert A.; Israel, Paul B.; Nier, Keith A.; Carlat, Louis; eds. *The Papers of Thomas A. Edison*. Baltimore: The Johns Hopkins University Press, 1998. vol. 4 *The Wizard of Menlo Park*.

Runes, Dagobert D., ed. *The Diary and Sundry Observations of Thomas Alva Edison.* Westport, CT: Philosophical Library, 1948.
Tebeau, Charlton W. *A History of Florida.* Coral Gables, Florida: University of Miami Press, 1971.
Vanderbilt, Byron M. *Thomas Edison, Chemist.* Washington, D.C.: American Chemical Society, 1971.
Venable, John D. *Out of the Shadow: The Story of Charles Edison.* Philadelphia: Dorrance and Company, 1978.

Oral and Video Histories

Edison, Charles. Interview conducted by Wendell Link in New York City, April 14, 1953. Tape recorded and typewritten. Charles Edison Fund.
Menge, Conrad Sr. Interview conducted at the Ford Motor Company Archives, Oral History Section, at the Henry Ford Museum and Greenfield Village, Dearborn, MI, March 22, 1951. Tape recorded and typewritten. Henry Ford Museum and Greenfield Village.
Prince, C. A. Interview conducted by James H. Gassman, David Marshall, and Robert Beason at the Edison Winter Home in Fort Myers, June 25, 1999. Video taped. Edison Winter Home.
Zoerlien, Emil. Interview conducted at Ford Motor Company Archives, Oral History Section, at the Henry Ford Museum and Greenfield Village, Dearborn, MI, September 15, 1951. Typewritten, 32, 42–44. Henry Ford Museum and Greenfield Village.

Unpublished Sources

Bryan, Ford R. "Henry's So Called Rubber Plantation in Florida." Henry Ford Museum and Greenfield Village.
Bryan, Ford R. "Industrial Archaeology in Greenfield Village." Henry Ford Museum and Greenfield Village.
Bryan, Ford R. "*Sialia*—Henry Ford's Yacht." Henry Ford Museum and Greenfield Village.
Menge, Conrad Sr. "Early Dredging in the Lake Okeechobee Region." Southwest Florida Historical Society.
Oeser, Marion Edison. "The Wizard of Menlo Park." Edison National Historic Site
Rosenblum, Martin Jay, R.A. "Edison Winter Estate Historic Structures Report." Philadelphia, 1999. Edison Winter Home.

Bibliography

Author Interviews

Armeda, Nick. Interview by author, Fort Myers, Florida, August 10, 2000.

Bennett, Sue Spears. Interview by author, Fort Myers, Florida, July 11, 2000.

Brown, Barbara. Interview by author, Fort Myers, Florida, September 25, 2000.

Cornwell, Nat. Interview by author, Fort Myers, Florida, June 5, 2000.

Davis, Berne. Interview by author, Fort Myers, Florida, September 28, 2000.

Galloway, Sam Jr., Interview by author, Fort Myers, Florida, November 8, 2000.

Halgrim, Robert C. interview by author, Fort Myers, Florida, January 16, 1999.

Howard, Mary Frances. Interview by author, Fort Myers, Florida, September 21, 2000.

Lampp, Alvin H. Interview by author, Orlando, Florida, November 8, 2001.

Mann, Barbara B. Interview by author, Fort Myers, Florida, July 1, 2000.

McInnis, Lucille. Interview by author, Fort Myers, Florida, August 17, 2000.

Palmer, Kathryn. Interview by author, Fort Myers, Florida, February 14, 2001

Pavese, Frank. Interview by author, Fort Myers, Florida, January 6, 1999.

Perry, Chesley and Perry, Janett. Interview by author, Fort Myers, Florida, November 22, 1998.

Shortlidge, Gloria. Interview by author, Fort Myers, Florida, June 10, 2001.

Tingley, Charles A. Research Librarian, St. Augustine Historical Society. Interview by author, St. Augustine, Florida, October 15, 1998

Journals

Adams, George R. "The Caloosahatchee Massacre: Its Significance in the Second Seminole War." *Florida History Quarterly*, XLVIII, April 1970, 368.

Mackall, W. W. A. A. General "Order No. 14," Headquarters, Western Division, Tampa Bay, Florida, February 14, 1850, *Journal of the Council of American Military Posts*, vol. 12, no. 3, 48.

Dillon, Rodney E. Jr. "The Battle of Fort Myers," *Tampa Bay History*. Fall Winter 1983, 27.

Wilder, E. G. "Escapade in Southern Florida," *Confederate Veteran* 19 1911, 75.

Laird, R. H. "I worked for Mr. Ford." *Dearborn Historian*, vol. 10, no. 1, 1970, 14.

Index

Index

359

Index

Index

weed stalkers, 222
World War II, 179
Rustic Tea Garden, 279

Sachem, 143
Safety Hill, *see* Dunbar
Safety Hill Garden Club, *see under*
    garden club
Samville, 163
Sanford, Florida, 22
Sanibel, Florida, 262
Sanibel Lighthouse, 73, 191
Saturday Evening Post, 259
Saunterer, 225, 228
Scarth, John, 281, 286, 289
Schultz, Carl, 265
Schwab, Charles, 233
Schwimmer, Madame Rosika, 130
Seaboard Railway, 197, 258
    Fort Myers Station, 209, 214,
    250, 254
seawall, 77, 91
Sebring, Florida, 279
Seminole Indians, 9, 182, 256
    Chief Billy Bowlegs, 9, 14, 15
Seminole Lodge, 78, 89, 95, 98, 104,
    105, 114, 116, 125, 126, 128,
    133, 139, 140, *141*, 147, 149,
    150, 153, 155, 156, 158, 159,
    160, 164, 165, 173, 182, 190,
    192, 193, 194, 196, 197, 198,
    201, 206, 209, 210, 212, 219,
    223, 225, 226, 227, 228, 230,
    232, 236, 239, 240, 241, 242,
    244, 247, 248, 253, 254, 256,
    259, 260, 261, 262, 265, 268,
    273, 277, 278, 279, 280, 281,
    283, 286, 288, 289, 290, 291,
    294, 295, 296
    Rules for Guests, 107, 109
Seminole Park, 239
Sevigne, Madame de, 76
Seville Apartments, 286
Shapard, Mayor Dave, 292, 295
Shark River, 288

Sheppard, Virginia, 259, 285, *285*
Sholtz, Governor Dave, 278
Shore, Rev. F. A., 140, 253
Shortlidge, Gloria, *see* Durrance,
    Gloria
Shrine, 294–298
Shultz, George, 8, 10, 13, 75, 94
Shultz Hotel Company, 94, 100, 93
Shultz, Josephine, 10
Shultz, Martin E., 274
Sialia, 135–137, *137*, 152, 191
Siebert, E. O., 291
Silverfriend, H. D., 150
Simmons, Al, 189
Sloane, Jack, 186, *187*
Sloane, John, 160, 271
Sloane, Madeleine Edison, *see*
    Edison, Madeleine
Sloane, Peter, 160, 186, 190, 283
Sloane, Ted, 186, *187*, 190
Smith, Ed, 293
Smith, L. A., 6, 20
Smith, Robert W.
Smoot, Tom, Jr., 296, 297
Southern Sugar Company, 229
Spanish American War, 245
Spears, Sue, 232
Spivey, Dr. Ludd M., 277
Stadler, C. A., 159
St. Augustine, Florida, 7, 22, 191
    San Marco Hotel, 5
St. Johns River, 6, 22
St. Lucie, 63, 68
St. Luke's Episcopal Church, 140
steam engine, 127
Stearns, Mrs. Clark, 287
Stevens, Mr. and Mrs. Henry, 199
Stewart, James K., 135
Stewartsville, New Jersey, 66
Stewart-Warner Speedometer
    Company, 135, 136
Stillwell, Mary, *see* Edison, Mary
    Stillwell
storage battery, 112
Stout, Frank, 164, 204, 210, 214,

Index